My position requires constant interaction with top-level ~
from other major corporations. Using the principles in *The Men's
Clothing Guide* I'm confident my appearance is at or above the
level of those I'm meeting with. I can't wait to see this book in
print so my wife, Ellen, and I will no longer need to call Steve
before we go shopping.

—Luis Rodriguez, National Director of New Business
Development, GE Clinical Services, Jupiter, FL

Steve helped me find a great store near my home that carried a
couple of hard-to-find labels that are personal favorites. I highly
recommend Men's Specialty Retail Services.

—Peter Knell, undergraduate, Bradley University, Peoria, IL

Thanks, Steve for finally writing a book about men's fashions that I
can understand and use. For those looking to change their image,
either professionally or personally, buy this book—and send a copy
to those you know can use some help.

—Randal Walker, National Service Manager,
Shimadzu Medical, Torrance, CA

Best Wishes,
Steve Brinkman

The

MEN'S CLOTHING GUIDE

How and Where to Buy
the Best Men's Clothing
in America

The

MEN'S CLOTHING GUIDE

How and Where to Buy
the Best Men's Clothing
in America

Dapper Press, Inc.

Published by Dapper Press, Inc.
El Cerrito, CA 94530

Edited by Priscilla Stuckey
Cover design by Rebecca Sheldon and Kimberly Markison
Book layout by Kimberly Markison
Indexed by Julie Lauer

Printed in Canada.
10 9 8 7 6 5 4 3 2 1

Distributed by SCB Distributors Inc.
15608 South New Century Drive, Gardena, CA 90248
(310)532-9400
www.scbdistributors.com

Library of Congress Cataloging-in-Publication Data
Brinkman, Steve (1958–   ).
        The men's clothing guide: how and where to buy the best men's clothing in America.
        Includes index.
        ISBN 0-9724317-0-5
        1. Consumer Education. 2. Business. 3. Self-Help. I. Title.
        LOC# 2003092866

Dedication

To my daughters, Aurora Hope and Diana Grace—you are my teachers and my guiding lights, and the reason I am here now.

And to Bart McLean, my friend and adviser—the only person who believed in this project from the beginning.

Contents

Contents

PART ONE

A Customer's Perspective on Men's Fashion

A number of men's fashion books are on the market already—*Dress for Success, Gentleman's Guide to Grooming and Style,* and *Dressing the Man,* to name a few. So why should you read this book? Because here you will receive practical and irreverent advice from the customer's point of view about everything dealing with men's fashion. My opinion is based on twenty years of dressing up—and down—for business. In preparing this book, I traveled to cities across the United States, interviewing a host of people currently working in the menswear business. My mission was to learn as much as possible about this multibillion-dollar industry, including:

- How to choose clothing that best fits your needs and personality

- How to look your best in any situation

- How to buy high fashion for low prices

- How to achieve timeless style and avoid fads

- How to maintain your wardrobe and make the most of every clothing dollar

I'll share all these secrets and more. I firmly believe the average man likes to dress well and wants to develop his own sense of style rather than wear clothes someone else has selected for him. Great clothes you got for a good value only add to your sense of style and accomplishment. I'll show you where, when, and how to find them. If you don't feel you have enough clothes, or you feel so out of touch with fashion that you want to empty your closet and start over, this book will help! Here you will find tips on how to restock that closet, what colors will look good on you, and how to mix in your own favorite colors. There's no set standard for men's dress any longer; if it looks good and feels good, by all means wear it!

The Men's Clothing Guide is the most comprehensive guide to date on where to buy high-quality clothes at great prices. I'll cover online shopping, factory outlet malls, department stores, and independent menswear stores. You may find, like me, that the specialty stores become your favorite places to shop, because they stock more unique items and frequently offer better service than other kinds of stores. Unfortunately, many of these shops are vanishing from the marketplace as corporate America swallows up the little guy. I have a plan to help fix that, which I present at the end of the book.

The Men's Clothing Guide can change how you look at yourself and the clothing you wear every day. Most of all, it will help you find the best values in men's clothing today for yourself, your family, and your friends.

About the Author

I'm an average guy with an above-average interest in men's fashion. I've been that way since I was young. I couldn't buy fancy clothes then, but my mom took me shopping often and taught me to ferret out bargains our family could afford. She also has a great sense of color and showed me how to put an outfit together. This is an unusual skill for a male, and she deserves all the credit.

I confess I wore more than my share of polyester in the seventies, and even a few leisure suits. Then after college I wore a shirt and tie to work for ten years without having any idea what I was doing. I didn't know what a properly tailored suit should look like, and I didn't know what colors or styles flattered me. I bought quantity, not quality. The sleeves on my shirts shrank, and I'd have to wear them rolled up. My suits and slacks wore out prematurely because they were made of inferior fabric. Like many of you reading this book, I was a fashion disaster. Then about seven years ago, my wife bought me an Italian cotton shirt in New York. This shirt was more expensive, but it fit me properly and it didn't shrink after washing. It also looked better with a coat and tie and felt much better against my skin. I resolved to upgrade my wardrobe, and I started frequenting stores with better merchandise. In the ensuing seven years I have educated myself on quality and used the bargain-hunting skills I learned while growing up to fill my closet with better clothes.

About two years ago I left a lucrative sales position in the medical industry to research and write this book. Since then I've logged more than 150,000 miles visiting men's clothing stores around the country, to provide you with the valuable information contained in this book. And I'm starting a new business that will help you locate outstanding buys quickly and easily in real time. This business is described in more detail at the end of the book and on my website, www.MensSpecialtyRetail.com.

I hope you find *The Men's Clothing Guide* entertaining and educational. I'm confident it will help you dress with style and self-assurance and assist you in obtaining maximum value for your clothing dollar.

1

Dos and Don'ts of Dressing for Success

People *will* judge you by your appearance, usually within a few seconds of meeting you. The next two to three minutes will confirm or deny their initial impression. It is critically important that you put your best foot forward, particularly in business situations. This means wearing clothes in colors and styles that flatter you.

As you begin your sartorial journey, your aim is not to stand out from the crowd but to fit in crisply and professionally, whether the situation calls for business formal or business casual. As you gain confidence, you'll become comfortable wearing more distinctive clothing that better defines your personal style. It may be a particular designer or a certain accessory, but you will find something you especially like to wear. Those around you will notice the change for the better. You will radiate self-confidence, happiness, and charm. These feelings will extend beyond work settings to all of your interactions with others. Your wife or current love interest will notice and like the difference. Or if you're not attached, you'll have more action than you can handle. Your life will become more interesting and fun. This is because you'll feel better about yourself and more successful from the inside out.

In business, particularly in sales, there's an unwritten law called the "mirror rule." It states that your dress for each business day should mirror that of those you will interact with on that day. I think you should dress just a little better than the people you're going to meet that day. It's a sign of respect that they were worth the extra attention.

So I propose a new mirror rule: if you stand in front of the mirror before you go somewhere, and what you have on makes you feel better about yourself, keep it on. If it doesn't, take it off and pull something else out of the closet. All of us enjoy contact with happy, successful people, and we're more likely to deal with someone who dresses well.

If you don't have enough clothes, or you feel so out of touch with fashion that you want to empty your closet, follow that urge! In most cases, it's better to start over from scratch. Starting over allows you to consider each purchase carefully, evaluating how it works with other items in your closet. It also gives you a chance to treat yourself with nice clothes for goals you've accomplished personally and professionally. And the quicker your mind adapts to the new, happier, and more successful you, the better.

But how much is too much, particularly when you're trying to establish a clothing budget? Here are a few simple guidelines.

How Much to Spend

In 1900 Americans spent 15 percent of their income on clothing.[1] At that time most clothing was custom-made and tended to wear out more quickly than it does today. Many men, particularly those who lived in rural areas, wore the same thing for days, and methods of laundering were much harder on clothes than the ones we use today. The national average for clothing expenditures today, male and female, is about 5 percent of one's income.[2] That's just not enough for you to look your best, at least as you begin to build your wardrobe from scratch.

Americans often look to Europe for direction in fashion and assistance in developing personal style. One reason might be that Europeans spend significantly more on clothes. Opinions from people I interviewed in the retail industry varied, but some stated Europeans spend as much as 14 percent of their income for clothing compared to our 5 percent. They shop more deliberately and spend more on higher-quality items. Looking good at all times seems to be more important in Europe, and people who live there tend to dress better for all occasions.

Between 10 and 15 percent of your income is a reasonable budget for clothing, at least for the first six to twelve months you're refilling your closet. You might have to spend a little more initially to build a quality wardrobe. However, you will then have the basics you need and can spend a lot less on clothing later on. This goal can best be achieved when you emphasize *quality not quantity* in your wardrobe selections. Remember, I learned this lesson the hard way with shirts that shrank and suits that lost their shape. I can speak from personal experience: your clothing dollars will go a lot farther when you invest them in high-quality clothing that fits you and flatters you.

How to Spend It

Buy quality over quantity. This is my mantra; you will read it often in *The Men's Clothing Guide.* Purchase labels that stand for quality in fabric, appearance, and construction. Buy clothes that fit your coloring and body type. This is the only way to make your clothing dollars stretch to fit your budget. It is also the best way to ensure that your clothing budget buys you items that are comfortable and long lasting. Later we will get into more specifics of how and where to shop. But for now, the concept is quality not quantity.

Where to Spend It

Most people today shop at outlet malls. There are some drawbacks to service at these malls, and I cover this topic in later chapters. It has also been my experience that outlet mall prices are often no better than specialty store or department store prices, *if you know when their sales are.* Later I will describe how you can have a real-time awareness of all the best values in America.

You will often find better selections of designer merchandise at quality department stores. However, good service at these stores can be intermittent or nonexistent. Plus, turnover is high in the retail profession, and your favorite salesperson can leave suddenly. However, if you find a local specialty men's store that carries merchandise you like, please patronize them. They value your business and in fact can remain in business only by offering better service, or better merchandise, than their competitors. Moreover, if you shop with the proprietor, you needn't worry about your favorite salesperson leaving. He or she's not going anywhere unless the store itself does.

How Not to Go Broke Building Your Wardrobe

The key to building the right wardrobe for you without going broke is making a clothing budget. Once you have arrived at an acceptable amount to spend on clothing, stick to your limit. Building a quality wardrobe is important, but not at the expense of financial security. If you spend too much money on clothes trying to impress people, you'll never have any money and you won't be a success in anyone's mind, including your own. Think of the vicious circle that puts you in: you may have to continue working for people you may not especially like in order to support your clothing habit.

At all costs, avoid dangerous accumulations of credit card debt while building your wardrobe. Remember, credit card companies are borrowing their money at prime rate (currently around 4 percent) and charging you 13–22 percent, making 9–18 percent by doing nothing but sitting back and watching you buy things. In particular, avoid accumulating balances on the department stores' credit cards. The free gifts and additional discounts are great, but the interest they charge is over 20 percent. If you buy something discounted by 30 percent with a 22 percent card and you take a year to pay, it's only 8 percent off. You've then basically paid full price. If your debt goes beyond a year, you wind up paying more than full price. Use cash, or pay your credit card bills in full every month when due.

I hope this chapter of *The Men's Clothing Guide* has helped you set a reasonable clothing budget and given you some initial suggestions on how and where to purchase your clothes. Remember the mantra: buy quality not quantity. Stick to your budget, and pay cash whenever possible!

2

Color, Cut, Style: What's Right for You

Dress T-shirts add creative elements of layering and color to any man's closet.

You can buy great-quality clothes for a great price and still wind up looking ridiculous if you don't purchase items that fit you and flatter you. Take color, for instance. To look your best, dress in colors that complement your skin tone. Darker colors highlight pale skin, while lighter colors soften lighter skin tones. The reverse is true with a dark complexion: dark blends with dark, light highlights dark. If you want a look that allows you to blend with your surroundings, choose colors that will soften your skin tones. But you may want to own some items that highlight your complexion, for special occasions that call for you to make a bolder statement.

The same guidelines apply to your hair color. Lighter colors blend with lighter-colored hair, and darker colors mix well with darker hair.

Finally, your eyes are your most important feature. Wear things that highlight and draw attention to them. Green eyes look great with shades of green—emerald, hunter, apple, and sea foam. Hazel eyes go well with gold, bronze, tan, yellow, a wide array of pastels, and white. Brown eyes also look good with tan, gold, bronze, and peach, navy blue, deep purple, and black as well. Blue eyes go well with any shade of blue—powder, sky, French, aqua, midnight, or navy—and most shades of gray. If you have doubts about how a piece of clothing goes with your eyes, examine yourself in a mirror with your intended purchase across the bridge of your nose. If you don't notice an improved highlight to your eyes, try another garment.

The two tables below make better sense of all these guidelines. They're not etched in stone but are intended as a starting point in helping to develop a strategy to building your wardrobe. The ultimate deciding factor should be how it looks on you. Remember the new mirror rule: if you stand in front of that mirror and like what you see, buy it. Especially if it's a bargain.

Color Compatibility Chart/Fair Complexion

Hair Color

Tailored Clothing	Blonde	Red	Gray/White	Light Brown	Medium Brown	Dark Brown	Black
Navy							
Olive							
Gray							
Black							
Khaki							
Brown							
Taupe							

Eyes Key: Blue · Green · Hazel · Brown

Furnishings	Blonde	Red	Gray/White	Light Brown	Medium Brown	Dark Brown	Black
White							
Ecru							
Soft Blue							
Med. Blue							
Burgundy							
Red							
Green							
Gold							
Orange							
Yellow							
Pink							
Purple							

Color Compatibility Chart/Medium Complexion

Hair Color

Tailored Clothing	Blonde	Red	Gray/White	Light Brown	Medium Brown	Dark Brown	Black
Navy							
Olive							
Gray							
Black							
Khaki							
Brown							
Taupe							

Furnishings — Eyes Key: Blue, Green, Hazel, Brown

Furnishings	Blonde	Red	Gray/White	Light Brown	Medium Brown	Dark Brown	Black
White							
Ecru							
Soft Blue							
Med. Blue							
Burgundy							
Red							
Green							
Gold							
Orange							
Yellow							
Pink							
Purple							

Color Compatibility Chart/Dark Complexion

Hair Color

Tailored Clothing	Blonde	Red	Gray/White	Light Brown	Medium Brown	Dark Brown	Black
Navy							
Olive							
Gray							
Black							
Khaki							
Brown							
Taupe							

Eyes Key: Blue · Green · Hazel · Brown

Furnishings	Blonde	Red	Gray/White	Light Brown	Medium Brown	Dark Brown	Black
White							
Ecru							
Soft Blue							
Med. Blue							
Burgundy							
Red							
Green							
Gold							
Orange							
Yellow							
Pink							
Purple							

The following table is designed to give you a few commonsense guidelines for matching clothing color and fabrics with seasons of the year. It's more important to match fabric weights with weather conditions than to wear seasonally colored clothing. Darker colors bring sophistication to an outfit regardless of the temperature outside. Lighter and more distinctive colors add a touch of individuality to an ensemble and should be matched to your personal palette using the preceding Color Compatibility Chart. Wearing a favorite color that flatters you can brighten an already sunny day or lighten your mood in the dead of winter. And if you're fortunate enough to live where it's temperate year-round, wardrobe choices will be easier. You'll be able to buy everything in medium- and lightweight fabrics and wear them year-round. As you buy more clothes and become more self-confident, you'll take more color risks successfully. If you're unsure about a purchase, don't make it. The most expensive clothes of all are the pieces you buy and don't wear.

Seasonal Color Chart		
Season	**Fabric**	**Colors to Wear**
Spring/ Summer	Silk Lighter weaves of cotton Linen	Lighter shades of brown, cream, white, off-white, lime, mint, apple, sea foam, red, pink (including brighter shades), orange, yellow, peach, coral, lighter shades of purple, lighter shades of blue and gray
Fall/Winter	Heavier weaves of cotton (flannel, corduroy) Heavier weaves of wool (cashmere, flannel)	Darker shades of brown, rust, gold, burnt orange, brick red, forest green, darker shades of olive, gray, and blue, maroon/burgundy, deep purple
Year-Round	Medium weaves of cotton, wool, silk, cashmere (or combinations)	Navy, medium gray, ecru (shirts), white (shirts), emerald green, olive, black, lighter shades of pink

Clothing Selection and Body Types

Be honest with yourself about the type of body you have as you build your wardrobe. Clothing that flatters your individual body type can completely change how you look and how you feel about yourself. A good tailor and proper clothing selection should make you look two inches taller and twenty pounds lighter.[3] The primary factors to consider are height, weight, and build.

Height

For the purposes of this book, let's define taller men as 6'2" and above and shorter men as 5'10" and below. Trousers for taller men should be hemmed long enough, with an indentation or "break" in the fabric of the cuff as it rests on the front of the shoe, and cloth resting ½" off the floor at the heel. Also, two- or three-button suits deemphasize the taller man's height. One-button, four-button, and double-breasted suits draw attention to it. Pinstriped suits aren't a good choice if you're tall; they'll make you look even taller. Solids work best; only a very subtle plaid or check will serve to balance the taller man's overall presentation. Shorter men likewise should avoid trousers that are hemmed too long. They should also choose two- or three-button suits, to visually lengthen the abbreviated torso. Vested suits also accomplish this lengthening effect and are a great look for the shorter man, particularly in the legal or financial profession. The shorter man also has better options in pattern selections. Pinstripes and subtle plaids make him appear taller. Checks or solids will also flatter him, if they are subtle and in colors that complement him.

Build

The components of a man's build are the bodily features he was born with. He may wish to accentuate some of them; others he will want to cover up. Examples of these features are arm length (sleeve length), leg length (inseam), and bone structure. For extreme inseams, either short or long, be especially sure to purchase slacks that are properly tailored. Trousers should fit loosely and move with you freely. They should be hemmed properly, with the break as described above. Likewise, purchase shirts with the proper sleeve length. When you put on your suit or sport coat over your shirt, it is proper for one-quarter to one-half inch of shirt cuff fabric to show. And the bottom of your shirt cuff should rest a touch below the bottom of your wrist, just at the beginning of your palm. If you have larger bone structure, stick with generously cut, pleated slacks for best fit. Avoid fitted shirts; they won't fit your broad shoulders and may also be too tight in the wrists and forearms. If you have smaller bone structure, many labels specialize in fitting smaller, thinner men. Please see the reference guides for brands in chapter 8 for some that will work for you. However, if all else fails and you just can't get a proper fit, go to a custom tailor or shirt maker. I discuss custom and made-to-measure clothing in chapter 5 and recommend a number of fine establishments in chapters 9 and 10.

Weight

Most men struggle to stay within 10 percent of ideal body weight. These men should wear clothing that makes them appear slimmer. Pleated slacks are one way of accomplishing this, particularly pants with one or two pleats at the waist. Flat-front pants should be avoided; they draw attention to the midriff area. Darker colored trousers are also a better choice for the larger man.[4] Flat-bottomed casual sweaters look best but are hard to find. If you must buy banded-bottom sweaters, select a generous cut or a bigger size. Casual and dress shirts also should have plenty of room. Do not buy fitted dress shirts; they will not flatter your physique and will be uncomfortable to wear. Larger men should avoid wearing horizontal stripes; these emphasize bulk as well. Finally, purchase suits cut in generous, classic styles that a competent tailor can shape to make you look thinner.

Conversely, if you're thin, avoid wearing loose clothing, since it will make you seem thinner. Flaunt your physique, and select tighter-fitting clothing and more modern styles and cuts of tailored clothing.

In this chapter you've gotten a preliminary road map indicating where and how to start looking for new clothing. I've given some simple guidelines for determining how best to complement your hair and skin tones and the body you were born with. Buying clothing that flatters you helps you build value into your wardrobe. You'll begin to select quality pieces that work for you, and you'll enhance your personal image.

3

Business Formal:
The Essential Wardrobe

This chapter covers the basics of building a business formal wardrobe. Business formal is defined as a situation in which it is proper to wear a tie. Since the wane of the high-tech revolution in the late 1990s, more and more businesses are requiring shirt and tie, and many require a coat as well. Many young men have never followed a dress code before and aren't sure what to wear or how and where to buy it. Many more are graduating from college or business school and may still be defining their style and looking for pointers. Below are some thoughts on the critical components of the essential business formal wardrobe. I've also added some suggestions on interesting items to add to your closet once you've got the basics.

Underwear: What Lies Beneath

Most men will want the comfort and assurance that comes from wearing underwear. In fact, a hundred years ago wearing underwear was a mark of distinction, because few people could afford it. The introduction of Jockey briefs in the 1930s made comfortable underwear with good support affordable for the average man.[5]

However, many men prefer boxer shorts for business dress and insist they're more comfortable. But remember, boxers work best with pleated trousers. They can disturb the flow of flat-front pants and often bunch up in a wad and make you uncomfortable. Boxers should be loose fitting, but avoid that annoying gap in the middle where certain personal accoutrements can—ahem—get away from you. A snap or regular button setup will do nicely. Many think boxers made of cotton are preferable, but some prefer silk because it feels more comfortable to them. Quality silk boxers should be hand washed and are often very expensive, making the choice of silk impractical for most. Boxers also come in more colors and patterns than briefs.

Briefs can be constricting, and who likes that? But they also render more support, for men who feel comfortable that way. If you wear briefs, you needn't be concerned with disturbing the drape of your trousers, and you can choose either pleated or flat-front slacks. However, you may want to avoid buying white briefs. They're somewhat old-fashioned and much harder to keep clean. Many other colors are available now from a number of different labels. It shows a great sense of style to match your underwear to the rest of your outfit. And it will impress the hell out of your love interest. Remember, putting outfits together is a skill few men have mastered.

Men have always debated the purpose and practicality of undershirts. Some always wear undershirts to protect their dress shirts from perspiration stains under the arms. However, buying antiperspirants and deodorants without aluminum is the best way to avoid these stains. White is usually the color of choice, but many more color options are available in undershirts today. Choose a color that does not show through your dress shirt. The choice of collar is irrelevant in business formal situations, as it will not show under a buttoned shirt.

Dress Shirts

If you select a navy or gray suit (later in this chapter), start by purchasing two white shirts. White means business everywhere, and it's good to have both a primary and a backup. Your next choice should be two soft blue shirts. Buy one with white collar and cuffs for style and variety if it won't look out of place at your office. Blue is always proper in corporate America and can actually look pretty distinctive paired with the right tie. A lighter shade of gray should round out your first five. If I recommend buying the olive suit for your coloring, purchase two ecru shirts. Ecru softens your look and is considered less formal. Ecru also actually matches more colors than white. Then purchase one white and one soft brown in color. If you have dark coloring, these choices match your palette particularly well. Then round out your first five by buying a more vibrant blue to be adventurous at least one day a week.

If you take your shirts to the laundry or dry cleaners, it's best to have ten, and rotate five from week to week. More diverse choices may be in order for the second five so you can begin defining your personal style. Try ecru, another shade of blue, muted pink or lavender, or a soft yellow, green, or orange for the navy or gray suit. For the olive suit buy a second white shirt, and select perhaps gray, beige, lavender, yellow, green, or orange. These second five shirts should be solid colors as well; solids are more versatile, and they match more items in your wardrobe. Refer to the Color Compatibility Chart in the previous chapter for the best options for you. Also see the Color Coordination Matrix at the end of this chapter for possible tie and shoe combinations to match your shirts.

Once you've gotten the minimum amount of ties, belts, shoes, and suits recommended later in the chapter, you'll probably want to purchase more dress shirts. Twenty should be enough; it's hard to wear more than that on a regular basis. These second ten shirt purchases will truly define your professional style. Buy carefully, and use some imagination; try stripes, tattersalls (Glossary, p. 323), unusual and perhaps darker solids that flatter your coloring, or even a subtle check or plaid. Put some color into your life and some individuality into your wardrobe!

There are many styles of dress shirts to choose from. Dress shirts can have a regular or European-style placket (Glossary, p. 321) and varied placement, appearance, and composition of buttons. They can also have a variety of pocket options to choose from, including buttons, pleats, flaps, or a combination of all three. The best dress shirts theoretically have no pockets, in order not to disturb the head-to-toe presentation of a business-clothing ensemble. But if you don't wear a coat all the time, having no shirt pocket to store things in will drive you nuts. Dress shirts also come with or without French or double cuffs. Accessorizing cuff links with French-cuffed shirts is a great way to further express individual style. I address cuff links in more detail in chapter 5.

Regarding collars, you can choose from several basic styles. What collar you select should be influenced by the environment you work in, what flatters your face, and personal preferences. There are four basic choices in collars: button-down, point, spread, and tab or snap (Glossary, p. 317). Button-down shirts flatter most faces and are a good choice for conservative business environments. They look best with sport coats and two-button suits. However, they're a stretch with three- or four-button suits, and they don't look right with double-breasted suits. Point collars look great in all professional situations. The longer the points on the collar, the more the shirt will flatter a man with a broader face. The shorter the points on the collar, the more the shirt fits a longer face. Point collars are proper with any suit or sport coat combination. Spread collars look best in more formal business situations. The wider the distance between points, the less it favors a broader-faced man, and vice versa. Also, a collar with a large spread looks best with a tie that produces a large knot, and with double-breasted suits. Tab- or snap-collared shirts are also appropriate in any business formal environment. They flatter most faces and look best with a smaller knot. However, an unbuttoned tab doesn't look good in casual situations, which limits the versatility of the shirt. Tab collars fit well with any single-breasted coat but look out of place with double-breasted suits.

Let's finish our discussion of dress shirts with a word on collar stays, shirt tails, and monograms. Collar stays are the small, tab-shaped pieces of plastic that fit inside the collar of spread- and point-collared shirts. Stays are vital in preserving the proper look and feel of a collar while being worn with a coat and tie. They are usually removable and should be taken out before the shirt is laundered. Washing machines and dry cleaning establishments are notorious for losing or destroying stays. If you need to replace yours, many men's stores give them away free with a small purchase. If you have problems keeping your shirt tails from flapping, tuck them into your underwear.[6] If you monogram your shirts, less is more. Choose a small, subtle design, and have it placed on your pocket or on a shirt cuff.

Ties

Colorful, distinctive ties add versatility to your business formal wardrobe.

As you build a business wardrobe, select at least one necktie to match each shirt as you purchase the shirt. Two is an even better idea. And the more items each tie matches in your wardrobe, the more dressing options you have. If you have ten ties that match each of your ten shirts, and also a suit, blazer, and sport coat, you have three hundred conceivable combinations before you repeat any given outfit. *That's* wardrobe versatility.

More combinations = more versatility = better value for your clothing dollar.

Buy colors you like and that flatter your complexion and hair color. Ties are especially good for highlighting colors in your eyes. If you don't think you can pull off a bold tie, stick to something more conservative. Seek assistance from a salesperson at your favorite local store; you should feel comfortable and confident wearing your ties in any business situation. Strive for balance between woven and prints, stripes, solids, and other patterns. Buy only top-quality ties; inferior-quality ties don't look or knot as well, and they wear out faster (see chapter 6, "How, When, and Where to Shop"). Silk ties look and tie the best, last the longest, and are therefore the best value for your money. However, a quality seasonal cotton, linen, or wool blend can work as well. At my website, www.MensSpecialtyRetail.com, you can find links to diagrams of how to tie the more popular knots. I recommend either the four-in-hand or half Windsor for thinner ties. For thicker ties, the four-in-hand works better. When a necktie is properly tied, its ends should be approximately the same length and should hang between the lowest exposed button on your shirt and the bottom of your belt buckle.

Bow ties are a snappy accessory to a man's business wardrobe. More lawyers and academics seem to favor them, and they seem more prevalent in the Deep South than other portions of the country. However, for serious business attire, bow ties aren't as widely accepted as neckties. They look best worn with single-breasted, two- or three-button suits or sport coats. If you choose to purchase a bow tie, it should require hand tying, not clipping on. On my website you can also find links to several Internet destinations that demonstrate bow tying.

Socks

Only over-the-calf socks are appropriate for business wear. It's tacky if others can see your hairy legs when you cross them in a meeting. Shaving your legs requires more effort than most of us are willing to take, and it may make people examine you for more than professional reasons. As a general guideline, you should have at least as many pairs of socks as you have shirts. However, as having enough socks minimizes laundry labor, I especially applaud men (like me) who buy more socks rather than doing their wash. Solid colors are boring. Purchase subtle stripes, patterns, or even argyles instead.

Shoes

Great looking cap toes (upper) and split toes (lower) from Laszlo Vass. See chapter 8's Shoe Reference Guide (p. 109) for more information.

Stylish shoes that fit well are of paramount importance. A professional-looking, well-shined pair of shoes is often the first thing a prospective client or employer looks for. And it's vitally important these shoes be comfortable to maintain the health of your feet. To begin building your shoe supply, buy two pairs of shoes for business wear—a brown or cordovan pair and a black pair. You may mix and match these with your clothes however you see fit; the rules for which color shoe matches which color suit have relaxed considerably over the last few years. I've given some basic pointers on what shoes to wear with various color combinations in the Color Coordination Matrix at the end of this chapter.

Conservative, lace-up shoes are considered proper in more conservative offices. However, stylish and even tasseled loafers are gaining acceptance in an increasing number of business environments. These can be dressed up or down, and they add versatility to your wardrobe. I also quarrel with the suggested practice of wearing only leather-soled shoes for business. Many stylish and professional rubber-soled alternatives now exist and can double as both business and casual shoes. Alternate shoes from day to day in order to minimize foot odor and maximize leather life. It's best to work up to five pairs when you can afford them, to allow your shoes to fully regain their shape and breathe properly before the next wearing.[7] Cedar shoe trees for each pair will also help absorb moisture and foot odor and preserve the leather.

Tailored Clothing

For the purposes of this book, tailored clothing refers to any garment that normally requires alteration—suits, sport coats, and dress slacks that are sold unhemmed. Your personal requirement for tailored clothing depends on your office's dress code. If you're required to wear a shirt and tie every day, you can get by with one suit and four pairs of dress pants. If you must also wear a coat, but

Two great but different combinations demonstrate your navy suit's versatility.

the same people will not see you every day, two or three suits will suffice. If coat, tie, and work with the same people are required each day, you're going to need to get five suits as soon as you can afford them. Luckily, this book will help you locate better-quality suits at more affordable prices. And the website will help you do it quickly and efficiently.

I think your first suit should be a solid-colored navy, gray, or olive, depending on your coloring (see the Color Compatibility Chart in chapter 2). Navy and gray are safe choices for any business environment. Olive complements a darker-colored man particularly well and

Glenn Laiken, proprietor of **ALANDALES** in Culver City, CA looks resplendent in this classic gray pinstripe.

Two equally fine looks show versatility in olive.

in my opinion offers more versatility than gray or navy. A single-breasted, two- or three-button style will remain fashionable longer, go with more combinations of shirts and ties, and maximize your investment. Choose a cut that flatters your build; it's imperative you get comfortable with a tailor in your area to assist with this process. A medium-weight, high-twist wool is best; this suit will move with you, resist wrinkles, and feel comfortable in more climates. Choosing a solid color allows you to wear striped, patterned, or solid ties as the mood strikes you. Solid, striped, or patterned shirts also all look great with solid suits.

More combinations = more versatility = better value for your clothing dollar.

Your first suit takes care of all life's little occasions that require you to dress up. You may now feel relaxed and confident in that interview, in an expensive restaurant, or at a friend's wedding. And, most important, you have a quality suit when it is required for business.

Dress slacks to accompany your navy suit might include gray, khaki, and black. But don't wear the black pants with the navy coat!

Some additional choices if you purchased the gray or olive suit are gray, olive, and black. Aim for versatility—do not buy gray to go with gray or olive to match olive. And the gray coat may not look right as a blazer—use your own judgment.

Begin building your wardrobe of dress slacks based on what you selected for your first suit. Dress slacks come in a myriad of colors. Choose pleated or flat-front slacks based on your build (see chapter 2). Generally, pleated trousers are cuffed while flat-front pants are not. If you bought a navy suit, select gray, khaki, and black dress slacks. Then choose olive pants, or a shade of brown appropriate to your coloring based on the chart in chapter 2. If you purchased a gray suit, buy black, navy, and olive trousers, and another shade of blue or brown that complements your color palette. If you selected an olive suit, buy navy, gray, black, and khaki or perhaps a shade of brown pants consulting the Color Compatibility Chart. A navy suit jacket can be worn as a blazer with every color of slacks in your wardrobe but black. In my opinion, gray suit jackets don't look right worn with different-colored trousers, and therefore gray suits aren't as versatile as the other two colors. But if your office dresses very conservatively, an olive suit may not be an option. The olive suit jacket will match all four pairs of trousers you've selected. Don't wear a suit jacket apart from its slacks as a regular practice because the suit can wear unevenly. Also, coats with patch or flap pockets (Glossary, p. 322) look best worn as blazers and may be difficult to find. But if you're not wearing your entire suit all day every time, and you're building your wardrobe from scratch, wearing your coat as a blazer is an acceptable, temporary way to squeeze more out of your clothing budget.

If you need two suits, buy whichever of the three solid colors you didn't buy the first time that fits your coloring best. Keep other details of the second suit close to those of the first: all-weather weight, two- or three-button, single-breasted style. If you want to change something, perhaps vary the cut or the vent style slightly with the advice of your tailor. If possible, don't wear the same suit on successive days. Rotate them to let them air out properly. Leave your suit out overnight, and let the fabric breathe before you put it back in the closet. Your suits will look better and last longer.

If you opt for a third suit, choose the remaining color—perhaps a slightly different suit from the first two, like an unusual texture or a subtle pinstripe or plaid. Or select a vested or double-breasted style. In my opinion, vests never go out of fashion, and you don't always have to wear the vest with the suit. And when double-breasted suits are supposedly "out," men with a timeless fashion sense will still wear them. If you live in a colder climate, buy a heavier wool or flannel fabric this time. If it's temperate where you live, choose a tropical-weight wool or a wool-linen or wool-silk blend. Your third suit expresses more personal style and individuality than what you've bought before. Select something more distinctive that you really like. If you purchase a fourth and fifth suit, choose even more variety and individual style. Perhaps you'll choose a three-piece, a double-breasted, and an unusual texture, stripe, pattern, or color that fits you well. Be more deliberate with each of these purchases; perhaps even spend a little more. Visit more stores, and view more clothing before making your final decisions. If you need any ideas, I have some style suggestions posted on my website, with links to other resources as well.

Fortunately, most labels make many more suits in navy, olive, and gray than other colors. You have an excellent chance of finding a good price on a quality suit if you know where to look. Don't settle for less than what you want. Use the "Online Shopping Guide" and the "Brick-and-Mortar Shopping Guide" (chapters 9 and 10) and www.MensSpecialtyRetail.com to help build a stylish and economical wardrobe of tailored clothing. For specifics of suit selection, please see "How, When, and Where to Shop" (chapter 6).

Necessary Accessories

The first essential accessory for business or casual wear is a pair of great-looking sunglasses. A good pair of shades defines your personal style inexpensively and effectively. If you can afford to, buy a second pair for variety and in case you lose one. Select something that complements the shape of your face and the hairstyle you're currently wearing. There are many excellent brands to choose from and many discount outlets for name-brand sunglasses.

A belt is your second necessary accessory. If you can, purchase one with brown *and* black leather, or buy two in colors that match your shoes. The color of your belt should match your shoes, unless you wish to draw the wrong kind of attention to yourself. Buy belts of medium width, with a simple but elegant clasp and a dull or matte finish to the leather. This style is appropriate for business or casual situations and will add to the versatility of your wardrobe. Remember the mantra:

More combinations = more versatility = better value for your clothing dollar.

The third essential accessory is a reliable, stylish wristwatch. A prospective employer often will glance at your wrist and partially evaluate you by your taste in wristwatches. Your choice in a watch says a lot about you and whether or not you're serious about your career. As with monograms, in watches less is more. Select a thin watch, preferably with a metal band. If you wear a large, ostentatious watch, your interviewer may think you don't need the job.[8]

The fourth needed accessory is a quality billfold or wallet. Your preference for wallet size may vary with your occupation and daily activities. You may opt for a larger, thicker wallet and keep it in one of your back pants pockets if you don't wear a suit. But if you spend a lot of time in a car or seated at a desk, a wallet in your back pocket will make you sit unevenly and cause lower back problems. If you wear a suit to work, purchase a slim, portfolio-style billfold to hold identification and credit cards. Keep this billfold in one of your suit's inner lapel pockets. Then buy a money clip for your cash, and keep it in one of the front pockets of your trousers. Money clips come in many interesting sizes and shapes and are another great way to express individual taste.

Overcoats and Foul Weather Gear

A well-dressed gentleman will also need an overcoat, unless he's fortunate enough to live where it's warm year-round and he doesn't travel. It makes no sense to hunt for bargains on quality suits if you don't protect them from inclement weather, and a stylish, well-chosen overcoat makes a great statement verifying your good fashion sense. Many books on men's haberdashery recommend a khaki-colored, cotton-blend coat with a removable lining. Such a coat can be used in any weather situation and is inexpensive to acquire. However, these coats don't show much individuality. Purchase something with a bit more flair. Choices here could include a charcoal gray, double-breasted wool-cashmere blend or perhaps a classic, single-breasted, tan camel hair. Use your imagination, and choose something that expresses your own sense of style. A matching muffler finishes the outfit perfectly if you live in a colder climate. Take more care choosing your overcoat than any suit; you'll wear it more often. If you've chosen wisely, you'll also own it longer.

Every well-dressed man should also have two or three serviceable umbrellas. Umbrellas are easily misplaced; it's best to have one each for your car, house, and office. That way you'll never be caught in a downpour when you're trying to look your best. Also, wear rubber-soled shoes in bad weather.

This chapter of *The Men's Clothing Guide* has given you some basic guidelines on how to stretch your clothing budget, emphasizing versatility and variety as you build a wardrobe that works for you in business formal situations.

Navy Suit

Color Coordination Matrix

Shirts

Shirts	TIES	Red	Navy	Green	Gold	Blue	Yellow	Orange	Burgundy	Pink	Purple
White		●	●	●	●	●	●	●	●	●	●
Soft Blue		●	●	●	●	●	●		●	●	●
Gray		●	●	●	●	●			●	●	●
Ecru		●	●			●	●	●			
Med. Blue		●		●	●	●	●	●	●	●	●
Pink		●			●				●	●	●
Lavender				●	●				●	●	●
Yellow		●		●	●		●		●		●
Green			●	●	●						●
Orange		●			●			●			

Knits

Knits	
Gray	●
Olive	●
Blue	●
Burgundy	●
Taupe	●
Camel	●

Shoes	
●	Chestnut
●	Brown
●	Cordovan
●	Black

Olive Suit

Color Coordination Matrix

Shirts	Ties: Black	Navy	Blue	Purple	Gray	Olive	Gold	Brown	Yellow	Orange
Ecru	●	●	●	●	●	●	●	●	●	●
White	●	●	●	●	●	●		●	●	●
Soft Blue	●	●	●					●		●
Med. Blue	●	●	●			●	●			●
Gray	●	●	●	●	●	●	●	●		
Beige	●	●	●			●		●		●
Lavender	●	●		●		●				●
Yellow	●	●	●	●			●		●	●
Green	●	●	●	●	●	●	●			●
Orange	●		●		●		●		●	●

Knits

Black	●
Gray	●
Navy	●
Ivory	●
Taupe	●
Camel	●

Shoes

●	Chestnut
●	Brown
●	Black

36

Gray Suit

Color Coordination Matrix

Shirts	TIES	Red	Gray	Navy	Black	Blue	Green	Burgundy	Pink	Purple
White		👞	👞	👞	👞	👞	👞	👞	👞	👞
Soft Blue		👞	👞	👞	👞	👞	👞	👞	👞	👞
Gray		👞	👞	👞	👞	👞	👞	👞	👞	👞
Ecru		👞	👞	👞	👞	👞	👞	👞	👞	👞
Med. Blue		👞	👞	👞	👞	👞	👞	👞	👞	👞
Pink			👞	👞	👞	👞		👞	👞	👞
Lavender			👞	👞	👞	👞			👞	👞
Green		👞	👞	👞	👞	👞				👞

Knits

Black	👞
Navy	👞
Blue	👞
Olive	👞
Burgundy	👞
Purple	👞

Shoes

👞	Brown
👞	Cordovan
👞	Black

4

Business Casual:
The Concept and the Wardrobe

The dot-com bubble burst long ago. Geek chic (Glossary, p. 323) is no longer fashionable or appropriate professional attire. Yet many men are still confused about proper business casual dress, especially in offices without a clearly defined dress code. I personally applaud the choice we now have whether or not to wear a tie every day. And I have a very simple guideline for appropriate business casual attire. If the outfit you've selected for a particular business day looks good worn under a tailored coat, it's proper business casual.[9] If it doesn't, it's better classified as weekend casual. This item may still be a great addition to your wardrobe; just wear it in the evenings or on the weekends. Here are some recommendations for the business and weekend casual wardrobe.

Underwear

As discussed in chapter 3, boxer shorts are very comfortable but can also billow and disturb the flow of an outfit. They're best worn with pleated slacks. Briefs or even boxer briefs (see Glossary, p. 315) look best when wearing flat-front pants or jeans.

Crew-neck T-shirts or undershirts in colors that complement casual outfits are a great way to express personal style. In addition to the thinner combed cotton usually found in undershirts, dressier

T-shirts can be woven of finer cotton, linen, or silk. They're also available in many more colors. They look great under a sweater or button-up shirt in the winter and add an extra layer of warmth and sophistication. In the warmer months, these T-shirts can be worn alone or under a tailored jacket for a casual yet dressy look. Because they are collarless, dressier T-shirts worn alone are often considered improper in business environments. Don't wear one to work unless you've seen your boss do it. Better still, wait until you've seen your boss's boss wear one.

I suggest buying black, gray, navy, and olive T-shirts for casual wear. Then choose another color or two that accentuate your individual palette (see the Color Compatibility Chart in chapter 2). If you prefer not to show a T-shirt under an open-collared shirt, buy V-necked undershirts. If you live in a colder climate, I recommend buying at least two undershirts for wearing under scratchy wool shirts or sweaters.

Casual Shirts

Today's man has many more options when choosing casual shirts. More colors, fabrics, and styles are available than ever before. And never before have so many choices been deemed appropriate for casual wear. For an explanation of any of the following terms, please see the Glossary.

Button-Up Shirts

Many button-up dress shirts can also be worn without a tie for business casual. Button-down-collared shirts certainly fall into this group. Point-collared shirts can also be dressed down by removing their collar stays. However, spread- and tab-collared shirts do not look appropriate in casual situations. Most shirts worn for business casual also look good for weekend casual. Purchase a minimum of two button-up shirts. One should be in heavier fabric; a soft cotton flannel does nicely for fall and winter wear. Choose a color or colors that flatter you, and match to the other items in your wardrobe (see chapter 2). The other shirt should be woven of lighter fabric, for wearing in spring and summer.

Sweaters with Ties

Cardigan sweaters (Glossary, p. 316) can be dressed up or down, worn with a tie or without, and they look great either way. They are also an acceptable substitute for a sport coat in many casual situations. They can be woven of cotton, wool, or cashmere and constructed with or without sleeves. Because of their versatility, they're a great addition to any man's wardrobe. Sweater vests also look sharp with a tie and can be worn under a sport coat to keep warm in the winter. They're also a smart way to accessorize any collared shirt. In sweater vests, V-necks are the predominant collar style. Sweater vests are also constructed of cotton, wool, or cashmere. The lighter fabrics and brighter colors work well during warm weather; heavier fabrics and darker colors are best when it's cold.

Sweaters without Ties

Crew-neck pullover sweaters appear in almost any weight, color, and design imaginable. Subtle crew necks in darker solid colors look great for casual wear to the office but are not usually considered proper in place of a sport coat. Brighter colors and lighter weaves work best in the evening or on weekends and during the summer months. Turtleneck sweaters (Glossary, p. 324) are usually made of wool or cashmere and are therefore impractical for wearing during warmer weather. Turtlenecks have a sleek, sophisticated look, perfect for stylish evenings out or fashionable cocktail parties. Many consider the turtleneck inappropriate for business wear. Ribbed turtlenecks don't look right tucked into slacks and therefore work best for weekend casual wear. But these sweaters are warm and comfortable, and they look great with a pair of jeans or corduroys (Glossary, p. 317) when it's cold.

Several sophisticated looks show the navy and olive suits adapted for business casual. The olive suit is paired with a black polo, yellow polo, and moss green dress T-shirt. The navy suit is paired with a gray mock, taupe mock, and the same yellow polo.

Knits

I define knits as solid-colored pullovers with either mock turtle-neck or polo collar styles (Glossary, p. 322). Knits are the corner-stone on which to build a business casual wardrobe that works. Finer weaves of cotton, silk, or wool are proper for work environments. Cotton piqué (Glossary, p. 321) or waffle knit fabrics are best left to the golf course. Long sleeves look better at the office, but in many climates the heat makes this impractical.[10] Again, dark colors look dressier and are best for business. Consult the Color Compatibility Chart in chapter 2, and if you bought the navy suit in chapter 3, purchase gray, olive, and two other colors that accentuate your natural palette. If you selected a gray suit, choose black, navy, olive, and at least one additional color that highlights your personal characteristics. If you purchased an olive suit in the last chapter, buy black, navy, gray, and at least one additional color that complements your coloring. Two of your knits should be lighter-weight fabrics for spring and summer. Then select two with heavier weaves for fall and winter. Balance your purchases between polo and mock collars, unless you prefer one style over the other or one style flatters your neck size and shape better. With polos, buttoning the placket completely is a more formal, elegant look that works best with darker colors. Darker knits also look sharp as evening wear at places with relaxed dress codes.

Socks

The socks you bought in chapter 3 to go with your suits can also be worn for business casual. Buy over-the-calf socks for casual wear as well; people aren't any more interested in your hairy legs in a less formal atmosphere. Brighter colors and more unusual designs are more appropriate for weekend casual. For business casual it's always best to wear socks. People aren't going to take you seriously in a business situation if you don't wear socks, unless you're in the movie industry and making a sales pitch on the beach in Malibu.

Shoes

Comfortable, preferably soft-soled shoes work best for casual wear. As mentioned in chapter 3, many soft-soled shoes look good enough to wear with suits as well. If you can find a pair containing both black and brown leather, they'll match everything in your wardrobe. Also buy an athletic shoe for the sport you play most or a good walking shoe if you're not into sports. Athletic shoes evolve more rapidly in style and function than can be covered properly in a book. If you want to purchase an athletic shoe for a particular purpose, it's best to purchase a magazine dedicated to the sport you want them for and evaluate several based on the magazine's recommendation. And if you're a golfer, choose a pair of soft spikes, as most courses now recommend them.

Tailored Clothing

I'm going to be controversial here, and tell you that the only sport coat you really need is a solid black. Black matches all the items in your wardrobe, looks great for evening wear, and goes well with jeans. A two- or three-button, single-breasted blazer has time-less style that won't go out of fashion. Match the weight of the fabric with the climate in which you'll be wearing it most often. A

Glenn from **ALANDALES** shows the versatility of the black blazer. Dress it up with a well-selected striped dress shirt and tie with a pair of very dark gray slacks underneath it. For a more casual look he chooses the same pants and a superbly colored blue polo that highlights his eyes, skin tone, and hair color.

tropical-weight wool works best if you live in a warm climate. A heavier wool, or even cashmere, is the best choice if you experience four seasons. You may want to buy the blazer in a rougher fabric texture than your suits and dress slacks. This will add more variety to your look, and your blazer will look better when dressed down.

More combinations = more versatility = better value for your clothing dollar.

If your office requires only shirt and tie, and I recommended four pairs of dress slacks for you in chapter 3, your dress slacks can also be used for business casual, and you need only one pair of cotton dress slacks. Don't buy the same khaki or blue color everyone else seems to have. Consult the color chart in chapter 2, and select a personally distinctive color you don't already have in wool. If you must wear coat

Slacks for wearing with a black blazer might include black, gray and khaki.

Glenn from ALANDALES demonstrates sophisticated business casual dressing. At left he wears dark gray slacks and a burgundy mock with black blazer. At right he's chosen the same knit and slacks with a coordinating plaid sport coat.

and tie to the office more often, or if your dress code is business casual, it's best to own two pairs of cotton slacks for more dressing options. Again, purchase colors that flatter your coloring and help individualize your style. Wool slacks are optimal for the office and for dressier casual occasions. Cotton slacks are appropriate for more relaxed situations, like outdoor barbecues and golf courses with dress codes. Finally, consider a pair of linen trousers for seasonal wear in spring and summer. Linen is notably comfortable against the skin and breathes even better than cotton. Many men (like me) initially don't like this fabric because it wrinkles so easily. But the wrinkles lend a roguish, rumpled air to your warm-weather outfits, and because your pants are supposed to look that way you don't have to iron as often, which is always a good thing. If you simply can't live with wrinkles, buy linen-rayon blends. They drape well and breathe almost as easily.

If your office has a business casual dress code, I still recommend buying one of the three suits described in chapter 3. In my opinion, every man should own a suit for an interview with a prospective new employer, dinner in a restaurant with a dress code, or a friend or family member's wedding. Buy two button-up shirts to wear with this suit, so you have at least two shirt and tie options. (Obviously you'll need two matching ties as well.) Purchase versatile shirts that can be dressed up or down—perhaps a white, blue, or pink button-down and a stripe or tattersall with a button-down collar or point collar with removable stays. These shirts can be worn with your suits, for business casual situations, and for weekend casual as well. Then buy two additional button-up shirts primarily for business casual and weekend wear. Again, one should be lighter fabric for spring and summer wear, and one a heavier weave for fall and winter. Make sure that all six of the button-up shirts you've selected will look appropriate under a sport coat. When added to the four knits I suggested earlier in this chapter, you now have ten business casual shirt options. Many men are able to wear casual shirts and knits more than one day between launderings. But if your casual shirts need to be cleaned more frequently, you have five to wear one week while you take the previous week's to the cleaners. For tailored clothing in addition to your black blazer and suit, I'd add a multicolored herringbone, checked, or plaid sport coat, two if you wear them often enough over your knits or button-up shirts. Consult the Color Compatibility Chart for a mix of colors that works with your individual characteristics. Darker colors again are dressier and more appropriate for business. And the more colors in the jacket, the more items it will match in your wardrobe and the more choices you will have on any given day.

More combinations = more versatility = better value for your clothing dollar.

You may also be able to purchase one or two solid-colored cardigans if your office considers them proper to wear in place of a sport coat. For slacks you have the two cotton choices suggested above as well as the wool choices recommended for purchase with the respective suits in chapter 3.

And of course you need a good, comfortable pair of jeans. Select soft cotton that fits well; tight jeans are a remnant of the disco era. Many choices of cuts, fits, and styles exist; find a pair that accentuates the positives of your physique. And purchasing a black rather than a blue pair will give you more options for evening wear. Select a belt that is appropriate for wear with jeans as discussed below. Finally, in my opinion, the well-dressed man never wears creases in his jeans.

Necessary Accessories

If you bought medium-width belts with a dull or matte leather finish for your business wardrobe, your belts are also appropriate for casual wear. If you didn't, buy a brown and black woven leather belt. Woven leather is a timeless style, and having both colors in your belt allows you to match your shoes without having to buy a second belt. Wider belts with metal tips and other stylish elements are great for casual wear. You may also want to buy a second, less expensive watch for casual wear. A watch with a second hand comes in particularly handy for timing presentations or cardiovascular workouts. It also helps to have two in case you leave one on someone's nightstand and don't want to retrieve it, or if one has to go in for repairs.

Outerwear

A stylish overcoat looks as good over a casual outfit as it does over a suit. However, if you have extra room in your budget, a shorter-length leather coat is a fashionable addition to your wardrobe. As with your overcoat, select a color that flatters you and a classic style. Also purchase something you can wear frequently, based on the climate where you live. Good leather is expensive; choose something you can wear for at least five years. And if you're outdoors a lot, you may want to purchase a jacket or coat that keeps you warm and dry. If you're pursuing a particular outdoor activity, do some research before your purchase in a magazine dedicated to that activity.

In this chapter, I've taken the mystery out of appropriate dress in business casual situations. I've also given some basic ideas for value and flexibility in filling this portion of your closet. You'll feel relaxed and confident when you know you're dressed properly for any business situation.

5

Fun Additions
to Your Wardrobe

Braces are a timelessly sophisticated addition to anyone's wardrobe.

This chapter is dedicated to discussing items that aren't essential to your wardrobe and may cost a little extra. However, they are fun to buy once you get a bit more money, and they are the little touches that really define your individual style.

Jewelry

With men's jewelry, less is more. If you get married (or if you are already), a simple wedding band is best. Signet rings also look great if they're not gaudy, as are college or graduate school class rings. I haven't ever worn any other jewelry and must therefore confess to a lack of objectivity. However, if you opt for a bracelet, chain, or pinkie ring, I would choose a simple gold or silver, perhaps with a small stone if a pinkie ring. Otherwise people may notice you for the jewelry you wear rather than the wonderful, charismatic person you are. The metal colors of the jewelry items you're wearing should match one another and your watch. The best way to ensure this is to buy a dress watch that contains both gold- and silver-colored metal.

Cuff Links

I'm a big fan of French, or double-cuffed, shirts and the cuff links required to fasten them. Cuff links can be coordinated to match your outfit, usually matching a color in your shirt or tie. They can also support the purpose of a business meeting. For example, if your client manages a public works plant, wear cuff links with a hot water faucet tap on one cuff and a cold water tap on the other. Or if you're calling on a golfer or a fisherman, you can wear cuff links with golf and fishing themes. There are hundreds of choices, and usually more than a thousand pairs are posted for sale on eBay on any given day. The Accessories Reference Guide in chapter 8 contains several other sources for cuff links, as does www.MensSpecialtyRetail.com. If you like cuff links, start with a simple gold or silver pair, perhaps a French knot or monogram. Buy quality sterling silver or fourteen-karat gold, and match the color of the metal in your dress watch. Then purchase a pair or two with precious stones of your favorite color or birthstone, again set in a metal that matches your watch. Decide on a budget, and acquire quality pieces as you can afford them.

Braces and Suspenders

Matching bands of leather or cloth that drape over a man's shoulders and attach to his dress slacks with buttons are called braces. If the bands attach to your pants with metal clips, you're wearing suspenders. Throw them out—now!

Braces, on the other hand, are an excellent way to show your style. They're more comfortable than belts, show off your pecs better if you like to work out, and make the line of a business suit flow more freely. Most braces are made of silk, but for your first pair leather is more practical. A sharp pair of brown or black leather will match your shoes and virtually anything else in your wardrobe. Leather braces cost more than silk, but by the time you've bought enough colors to match all your clothes, you may as well have bought the leather ones. When wearing braces, do not wear a belt; it's overkill.

Pocket Watches

Pocket watches are becoming popular again. These watches should be worn with a tailored vest that has functioning pockets or a good-quality cardigan sweater. They should also be in running condition, or the whole effect is achieved under false pretenses. Selecting an interesting chain to attach the watch to your vest further defines the look and individualizes your style. It's even more important to match metal colors with a watch chain and pocket watch. The chain connects directly to the watch, and it's more noticeable if the colors aren't the same. If you're feeling really adventurous, a distinctive watch fob (Glossary, p. 325) puts a nice finishing touch on the ensemble. If you're wearing a pocket watch, don't wear a wristwatch; it's repetitive.

Pocket Squares

Pocket squares are still another way of exhibiting personal style. A crisp, white linen pocket square is a timeless expression of elegance. A small monogram adds a nice touch, and white matches every suit in your wardrobe. Colored pocket squares are usually made of silk and are a very inexpensive way to express individual style. Solid squares look best with patterned suits, especially when highlighting a subtle color in a pinstripe or windowpane. Or match a solid square with one of the colors in your tie. Patterned pocket squares look best with solid suits or with sport coats on dressy casual occasions. Pocket squares should be worn not to attract attention but to help achieve an understated yet confident overall presentation. For instructions on how to fold a pocket square, see www.MensSpecialtyRetail.com.

Hats

A hat is an excellent and utilitarian way to accessorize an overcoat in cold climates, or it can be a flourishing finish to the perfect warm-weather ensemble. In cold weather, hats keep you warm by stopping heat loss through the top of your head, especially if you're losing hair. In a warmer environment, hats shield you from the harmful effects the sun can have on your face and head. Baseball caps are only for very casual wear and for outdoor activities. You can show the world much more creativity with a provocative porkpie or a fetching fedora perched atop your cranium. As with your shirt collar, choose a hat with a brim that flatters your face. A full-faced man looks better in a wider-brimmed hat. An angular face is better suited to a narrower brim. And the color of your hat should complement your coloring and the color of your outerwear.

Formal Wear

Few occasions today require formal evening attire for men. Don't buy a tuxedo unless you're going to wear it at least twice a year. Also, stay in shape. If purchasing, you'll need at least five years to recoup your investment. If you choose to rent a tuxedo, reserve one early for best selection. Here are some guidelines for proper formal wear evaluation and purchase.

A stylish tuxedo is usually black or midnight blue in color and is made of light- or medium-weight fabric. The events tuxedos are worn to are usually indoors and well heated. Tuxedo jackets can be single or double breasted and generally have shiny silk-faced or pebbled grosgrain, peaked lapels. Shiny-finished lapels are more appropriate for those who work in the entertainment industry. Grosgrain lapels are better suited for business executives who regularly attend formal events.[12] The trousers should match the jacket in color, with a plain silk stripe (called a braid) running down the outside of each pant leg. Tuxedo slacks are never cuffed; cuffs are considered informal. Formal shirts are always white, often with vertical or horizontal pleats to weigh the shirt down and keep it from bulging upward when its wearer sits down for a formal dinner. These shirts come with a variety of collar options; a wing collar is one of the more popular, and a personal favorite. Formal shirt cuffs always require cuff links, and the shirt may also have the option of using a stud set instead of buttons to fasten the torso. Any man who's gone to the trouble of purchasing a tuxedo should also consider a set of matching studs and cuff links to accompany it. These individualized pieces of jewelry are a great display of timeless elegance. Bow ties are always best black, but if you feel particularly adventurous you can try a different-colored tie and matching cummerbund. Be careful not to be gaudy; don't draw attention to yourself for the wrong reasons. Cummerbunds and vests as an option fade in and out of fashion. Cummerbunds are always worn with the pleats face up. Black patent leather shoes have traditionally completed the formal ensemble. However, many men today don't like the look of patent leather or won't buy shoes they can wear only a few evenings a year. For these men it's become as acceptable to wear a plain pair of black loafers with a good shine. Plain means plain; don't wear tasseled or penny loafers.[13]

Made-to-Measure

Most of this book is about how to get more and better clothes for less money. But once you've built your basic wardrobe and developed a good sense of style, you might want to express that style in a more unique manner. Perhaps you've come to really appreciate the art of dressing and the passion a great label and tailor bring to creating fine clothing. Having items made to measure allows you to express that appreciation and truly individualize your personal style. You can also select more unique items, which are a perfect, rather than just a great, fit. Made-to-measure and custom tailoring give you the ultimate satisfaction of having a garment made specifically for you by a true craftsperson, to your exact, personalized specifications. For an explanation of any unfamiliar terms below, please see the Glossary.

Most fine men's stores will have at least one brand of custom-stocked, made-to-measure, or custom shirt maker. Many have multiple shirt sources to offer you more variety and a better chance of finding something you like in your size and price range. A custom-stocked shirt is special-ordered for you in a style or size not normally carried by the store in ready-to-wear. These shirts are made with body measurements designed to fit most men in the size chosen, and they are constructed with uniform style characteristics. Your fitter will usually measure only your neck size and sleeve length and then order the proper size with your preference in collar and cuff styles. The fitter may also offer monogramming or may measure your chest and waist, if the shirt is fitted, to make sure the finished product will fit you properly. A made-to-measure shirt retailer will also measure your chest and waist, ask you whether or not you prefer a pocket, and often what style of pocket you prefer. This shirt fitter may occasionally allow you to choose the pleat and placket style for your shirt as well. A custom shirt seller will allow you to completely personalize the shirt and should make an individual paper pattern to create your shirts from.

Ties are rarely custom ordered because such a wide array of widths, designs, and styles are available ready-to-wear today. Consult The World's Best Labels and Where to Find Them in chapter 8 or my website for a list of made-to-measure tie makers.

More personalized tailored clothing from one or more labels is also available at most fine men's stores. These custom-stock or made-to-measure programs offer more choices than off-the-rack and allow specialty stores to offer a wider selection to their customers without the investment in inventory. Custom-stock programs are most popular when ordering trousers. The size availability, fabric weight, and style features of the pant are usually predetermined. You choose a color from a selection of fabric swatches, the store measures your waist, and then the slacks are hemmed to your specifications when the pants arrive. Made-to-measure trouser programs are rarer and will allow more options, depending on your choice of brand. You again select from an array of fabric swatches but can usually also choose pleat and pocket styles. Occasionally, you may choose pant leg width and waist rise as well. However, you are still limited to selections within that particular label's line and will have to stick to the choices offered in fabric, color, and style. Custom trousers are made from scratch, again usually from a paper pattern. A custom tailor will make you a completely unique pair of pants, with whatever features you want. You choose the exact rise in the pant, type and number of pleats, leg width, style of pocket, and cuffed or uncuffed hem. Your tailor will also take more measurements that will account for the peculiarities of your body.

Some stores offer suits and sport coats in custom-stock programs, which allow a quicker turnaround than made-to-measure. Again, the style and features of the garment are predetermined according to the brand you select. You choose the fabric from an array of swatches, and your clothing is made at a label's factory to a generic set of measurements designed to fit as many men in that size as possible. When the item arrives at your store of choice, their tailor then alters it to fit you. With made-to-measure suits and sport coats, you are offered more options, with much the same procedure described with trousers above. You again select a swatch and are usually allowed to choose number of buttons, number of vents, and a single- or double-breasted style. On occasion you may also be permitted to vary a lapel style or add a vest and determine the specifics of the vest's style. As with slacks, you will be limited to that particular brand's selections. Still, purchasing a made-to-measure suit is a thoroughly enjoyable shopping experience. Often the final touch of elegance is a tag sewn in the garment with your name and the date the piece was finished.

A good custom tailor will go one step further and make you a one-of-a-kind suit, giving you the ultimate expression of personal style. Custom tailors scour the world for the best fabrics and offer more selections from more mills than even the best ready-to-wear. A custom suit is created from scratch with a pattern, with many more measurements and fittings than a custom-stock or made-to-measure suit. A good tailor always stitches your private choice of label inside the garment. And custom-made clothing often does not cost any more than custom-stock or made-to-measure. Therefore, custom tailoring is the pinnacle of personal style if and when you can afford it. Several excellent custom tailors are listed as resources in chapter 10.

Because of the investment required to have a proper selection of shoes, many men's specialty stores do not have a shoe department, or they lease this service to a company that specializes in footwear. Therefore, custom-stock programs offer a much wider array of shoe styles and sizes than a retail store would normally inventory. Shoes are made to fit the average man's foot; the ability to select varying widths of finer shoes is adequate for most. Some shoe manufacturers, such as Edward Green of England (see the Shoe Reference Guide in chapter 8), make shoes to measure. The cobbler makes a wooden model of the average man's foot in a given size, called a last. The shoe is then created by hand around the last.

With custom shoes, each of your feet is painstakingly measured, and a last is made for each. Your shoes are then handcrafted to your specifications around the lasts. You choose the style, the leather, and materials used to construct and line the shoe. The result is a truly exquisite expression of personal style. Custom-made shoes are arguably more desirable than any other article of custom clothing because they contribute more comfort. You don't walk on your shirts or suits; you walk on your feet. And having comfortable shoes that fit you perfectly makes all the difference in the world. If you're going to spend the money on custom items for your wardrobe, consider beginning with a pair of shoes.

Have fun with the little details that define your individual style! You can enjoy distinctive accessories and still stay within your clothing budget. The accessories and made-to-measure portions of this chapter are not intended to encourage frivolous expenditures. Personalized, well-chosen items defining your individual taste tend to be kept and worn longer and are therefore still wise choices in the long run. For more on purchasing clothing that gives you value over an extended period of time, see the next chapter.

6

How, When,
and Where to Shop

How can you get the most value out of your clothing over a long period of time? Buy quality over quantity; you'll spend less money in the long run.

To understand how this works, let's take a look at your price per wearing. Let's say you buy a shirt for $50, but that shirt only lasts you two years. You wear it perhaps 25 times before it looks too ratty and needs to be discarded. Your price per wearing for this shirt is $2. Now let's say you buy a better-quality shirt for $100. This item will last more than twice as long; you wear it 60 times over five years. Although the shirt costs twice as much, the price per wearing is only $1.67, a savings of 17 percent. And you have the added satisfaction of wearing a better garment. *Over time, you pay less by buying more.*

The difference is even more dramatic with suits. If you pay $500 for a typical, midlevel brand suit, you'll be lucky if it lasts two years and you get to wear it 50 times. That's a price per wearing of $10. However, if you choose a better label and pay $1000, your suit will last a minimum of five years and 125 wearings. Your price per wearing is $8, a savings of 20 percent, *for better quality.* And I'm being conservative; I'm wearing suits now for the 150th time that are nine years old. And I've taken $500 suits to Goodwill after I wore them ten times because they were constructed so poorly no tailor could make them look right.

Should you pay full price? If you see a piece of clothing, perhaps the navy, gray, or olive suit I recommended in chapter 3, in a style and label you like, you'll still save 20 percent by paying retail. You take a calculated risk waiting for a sale. But that 20 percent savings can double or even triple if you're patient and find something that's been marked down. In my opinion, tailored clothing is always a buyer's market, particularly in a recession. Either way, you win by buying better-quality clothes. Conversely, don't buy something outside your wardrobe strategy just because it's on sale. If you're going to buy three suits on sale for $1000 and they don't quite fit right or are the wrong color for you, you've wasted your money. The most expensive clothes you own are those you don't wear. If a sale suit is not quite right for you, it's better to buy one at full price and enjoy the full useful life of your garment. The aim of this book is for you to wear out clothing you love rather than discard something because you got tired of it.

A high-quality wardrobe gives you the best value for your money over the long term. Wearing properly selected, stylish clothing adds mightily to your self-esteem, helping you radiate that confidence we talked about in chapter 2. My goal in writing this book is to minimize your price per wearing while maximizing your personal sense of style. You can accomplish this by using the resources provided in chapters 8 to 10 of this book and by visiting www.MensSpecialtyRetail.com for information in real time.

Overview: Service and Selection

A rude or inattentive salesperson can ruin an otherwise pleasant shopping trip. Conversely, a knowledgeable, friendly salesperson will always enhance your experience. Following is my opinion on service at retail establishments I visited nationwide.

Factory discount outlets have the most challenging task of delivering service among all retail establishments. These stores often do not pay salespeople as well as do other stores. Consequently, their sales forces are less experienced and tend to turn over faster than those in other retail situations. Accordingly, if you shop at outlet stores, be courteous and reasonable. After all, you'll be getting a great deal on some great clothes. Shopping at factory stores can also be tricky because merchandise moves in and out all the time. If you like a particular discount store, find out when its delivery arrives and shop on that day. Check often with a good idea of what you want in mind. And if you see something you like, snap it up. It's not likely to be there the next time you visit. When merchandise first arrives at an outlet store, prices generally are no better than at sales at department stores or boutiques. But if an item has been further marked down at the discount store, that's often the best price you'll find. In addition, most factory stores have stricter rules to follow if you want to make a return. Outlet stores also often mark the merchandise in some way, such as placing red or black marks on the garment label. And examine merchandise carefully if it's a second. You'll have to live for quite a while with marks on your labels and whatever flaws exist if you're building your wardrobe for the long term.

What about department stores? In my opinion the best reason for shopping at them is selection. Larger corporations have more financial resources and can afford to stock more inventory. However, you also have a better chance of seeing what you buy on someone else. This can be disconcerting when you're striving for individualized style. At department stores, service varies with the salesperson you deal with. If you encounter someone who isn't attentive or doesn't treat you respectfully, take your business elsewhere. My favorite department stores are Barney's, Saks Fifth Avenue, Nordstrom, and Neiman Marcus because they have the largest selections of my favorite merchandise. Depending on your tastes, you may also like shopping at Bloomingdale's (particularly the newer stores and the flagship in New York City), Macy's (especially the men's stores in Beverly Center/Los Angeles and San Francisco), and some of the Filene's and Marshall Field's locations.

I don't get to visit Barney's as often as I'd like because of where I live. Also, their website is not yet equipped for e-commerce. However, when I do visit a city that has a Barney's, I usually take time to drop in. The flagship store at Sixty-first and Madison in Manhattan is one of the first places I go when I'm in New York. Barney's always carries good selections from my favorite designers and very often has something I like on sale. And the Barney's house label stands for stylish, well-made merchandise. The service I've received in all locations has been excellent. Barney's also has a number of outlet stores throughout the United States, all of which have pretty good bargains on any given day.

The quality and selection of merchandise at Saks Fifth Avenue is usually first-rate. Be sure to work with a diligent associate in sportswear or furnishings. Saks corporate policy officially allows transfers between stores only of tailored clothing or higher-priced outerwear. Nevertheless, a good local salesperson will find a way to get an item to you with a minimum of hassle. And Saks will discount items more deeply and more often than its competitors. If you happen into the right store on the right day, you can find some great deals. Saks Off Fifth outlet stores have a lot of great values as well.

Nordstrom gives excellent service, particularly if you shop with a salesperson who has been with the company awhile. Nordstrom corporate culture is extremely customer service oriented; Nordstrom salespeople will find you an article if their store doesn't have it in your size. Nordstrom has a regional buying system, and the quality of its merchandise can vary greatly from store to store. Recently I've seen many first-quality items at Nordstrom, particularly at stores in urban, affluent areas. Nordstrom used to discount merchandise only three times a year. Now the company holds more frequent sales, and your chances of finding a bargain have greatly improved. Nordstrom Rack outlet stores are also good places to find great clothes at great prices.

For me, Neiman Marcus consistently has the best selection and service, if I can find the right associate to work with. Turnover is low, as associates are paid better and receive a better employee discount than at most other stores. I've shopped regularly with salespeople happy to locate merchandise I wanted in other locations, both on sale and at full price. Neiman's has a great inventory and shipping system. Merchandise is located almost instantly at another store and sent directly to the destination of your choosing for a minimum charge. Neiman Marcus has two sales per year, at the end of each season. You'll find great deals, particularly if you wait for the first day of the second markdown or "Last Call" portion of these sales. Neiman's also has outlet stores named Last Call, which are located throughout the United States.

Most of the experiences I've had shopping at label-owned boutique stores like Giorgio Armani, Polo Ralph Lauren, and Ermenegildo Zegna have been positive. The associates are very attentive and are interested in introducing customers to the finer nuances of the clothing line sold by their employer. You will find the largest and most varied selection from that particular designer but, understandably, nothing else. If you like to spread your purchases more evenly among several different labels, you're better off going to a different store with more designers to choose from. I've also found boutique stores will gladly transfer merchandise from other locations. And I've discovered great deals at these stores during end-of-season sales; discounts are routinely 30 to 60 percent. Most major designers have outlet stores; see chapter 10 or www.MensSpecialtyRetail.com for the nearest location of your particular favorite.

I like shopping everywhere and have been treated well at almost every store I've visited. But my best experiences have been at the independent men's stores listed in chapter 10. One hundred years ago, virtually everyone in America owned his or her own business and was an independent entrepreneur. In fact, that's how large department store chains like Neiman Marcus, Nordstrom, and Barney's all started. Americans still love that entrepreneurial spirit and like to support small businesses that give them great service.

Independent, or specialty, stores will go the extra mile for you; they won't stay in business any other way. I like their family atmosphere—getting to know the proprietor and having him or her get to know me. Many of these stores are also family-owned businesses and have been passed down from generation to generation. Surprisingly, retail prices at independent stores are about the same or lower than at department stores. Specialty stores also discount their merchandise at the end of the season, and their prices compare favorably with those I've found at outlet stores. You're more likely to find unique and unusual items that define your style at a local independent. The owner of a specialty store may even give you a discount on nonsale merchandise if he or she wants to establish a long-term relationship. Independent stores and custom tailors also often keep records of your purchases over the years and are a great help in building your wardrobe and developing individualized style. They'll help you minimize price per wearing and maximize the life of your wardrobe with clothes that work for you.

In conclusion, do not patronize stores with salespeople who show poor attitudes and give you substandard service. Your money is as good as anyone else's. You do not have to buy something just because you walk in a store. If a salesperson in any of the stores discussed above doesn't treat you respectfully, go somewhere else. If someone is pushy or taps their feet impatiently waiting for you to buy, take your business to a more relaxed environment. I have personally screened almost every store listed in chapter 10. If you have problems with any of these stores, please contact me; we will update our information. You've worked hard for the money you are going to spend, and you deserve to be treated well while spending it. Shop more with salespeople you grow comfortable with and at stores that carry things you like. Hopefully, the guides and reference tables in chapters 8 to 10 will assist you in this.

The rest of this chapter is devoted to the specifics of buying particular items in your wardrobe. My focus will again be on maximizing long-term value for your clothing expenditures.

Shirts, Dress and Casual

A good dress shirt should be 100 percent two-ply cotton (Glossary, p. 324), with at least a 100-thread count. Dress shirt choices are subjective and personal; the color, hand, and fit that are pleasing to one man may not be to another. Make sure you've chosen the right size! You'd be amazed how many people don't try shirts on before they buy them. If you've budgeted $50 for a dress shirt, wait for an end-of-season sale at one of the better specialty, department, or outlet stores listed in chapter 10. If you can afford more than $50, shirts with higher thread counts and more hand tailoring should cost you $70–120 at these same stores. If a shirt costs more than $125 retail, the stripes and patterns should line up from shoulder to sleeve. A quality dress shirt should last five years whether you launder it yourself or take it to the cleaners. You'll buy one quality shirt for every four or five inferior shirts you'd wear out. Think of your price per wearing: why buy anything but quality?

Casual shirts today are incredibly comfortable. They're made of light, high-twist fiber that breathes and moves with you and resists wrinkles. These fabrics work great for business if you choose a color and style that flatter you and fit well in your office environment. Fine casual shirts cost roughly the same as quality dress shirts, and you can find them at the same reputable stores in chapter 10. Once again, better fabric and hand detailing cost more. Quality casual shirts should also last five years.

Ties

Buy ties that will mix and match well with the rest of your wardrobe.

More combinations = more versatility = better value for your clothing dollar.

Rather than buying a cheaply made tie that retails for $40 or $50, buy quality on sale. A quality tie is made of fine silk, cotton, or wool. It should have a thick, reinforced loop of thread, similar in strength to high-test fishing line, sewn in each end to help secure the stitching down the middle and keep the tie from coming apart. Many quality ties also have a longer, thinner loop of thread extending from the smaller end. This line is used to straighten the fabric and lining, and sometimes to fasten the tie to a button on your shirt. Ties with self-fabric loops sewn into the back are optimal. The loops of fabric hold the smaller part of the tie in place after tying and keep your shirt and tie ensemble neat and in place. Ties made of two pieces of silk folded inward seven times (seven-fold ties) are the most stylish and durable and cost the most. As with shirts, aesthetic preferences in ties are highly personal. Fortunately, men today have a multitude of choices in colors, patterns, and styles. An occasional bow tie can even be a welcome change of pace. I suggest you balance your selections for versatility among solids, stripes, and patterns. Again, visit your local specialty, department, or outlet store regularly to hunt for values. There you will routinely find high-quality tie brands on sale for $50 or less. A well-selected, well-made tie can stay in style for two to three years and will last even longer. Opting to purchase quality ties is again an obvious choice.

Shoes

Always purchase comfortable shoes. If they look good but hurt your feet when you try them on, put them back. They will not feel better when they're broken in. You won't wear them often enough to justify your investment. Instead, choose style *and* comfort.

When you arrive at a store to buy shoes, try them on before you purchase them, and walk around in them as much as the store will let you. Buy shoes later in the day, because as the day progresses, your feet tend to swell and you want your shoes to be comfortable when your feet are at their largest.

Finding shoes that are both comfortable and stylish is a challenge. Some shoes are conservative and ideal for all business situations but hurt your feet like hell. Others have a reputation for comfort but just don't look right at the office. Some are known for cutting-edge fashion and are best worn in the evening or on the weekend. But ultimately, everyone's feet are different. If you find a brand or two you like that fit you well, keep buying their shoes.

Start looking for shoes at your favorite department or company-owned shoe store or a local specialty store if you know it has a good selection. Most department and specialty stores have good bargains on shoes at their end-of-season sales. If you arrive early in the sale, the selection is good and your chances of finding your size are greatest. Choice in sizes is more problematic in department store or designer discount outlets. But the prices are great if you can find what you want. Don't buy shoes from a catalog or website unless you've bought the exact size and style before and know how they will fit. You can't try these shoes on first, and returning them is often more trouble than it's worth.

Casual Slacks

If cotton or linen slacks are constructed poorly and retail for less than $50, they're a waste of money. I know—I've bought them and regretted it. These pants weren't durable, didn't launder well, or wouldn't stay colorfast. Sure, they were cheaper, but they didn't last long enough to justify even a minimal expenditure. These trousers wound up at Goodwill in two years or less.

Slacks that retail for more may seem expensive, but you can find them on sale for $50 to $125 at the end of each season. I've seen great values on chinos in every color and style imaginable in specialty stores, department stores, and outlet stores. My higher-priced purchases have held up well while looking and feeling much better. I still wear a pair I bought seven years ago for $65. Learn from my mistakes, and minimize your price per wearing. There's simply no substitute for quality in the long run.

I don't wear jeans every day, and only recently applied these same principles to purchasing denim. Quality fabric for jeans is softer and more comfortable than anything I've worn before. These jeans have superior style and fit, I got them for a great price, and I feel much better wearing them. I'm certain I'll be enjoying them five years from now. It's all about price per wearing and assembling elements of style you're happy with and can wear well for a long time.

Tailored Clothing

When selecting a pair of dress pants, refer to the Color Compatibility Chart in chapter 2 to determine what colors look good on you. Navy, gray, khaki, black, and olive work for almost anyone. All of these colors are usually available on sale if you're willing to be patient. Next, examine the fabric; it should feel soft and luxurious, not rough, to your hand. Ball the fabric gently, clench it in your fist, and see how quickly it springs back into shape. The better the fabric, the quicker this will happen. The more you shop, the better you'll get at differentiating fabrics. But in the beginning, visit several stores and take some time to feel the difference in fibers between slacks at varying prices. The fabric you select should be made of Super 100s wool (Glossary, p. 325) or better. The fabric should be the proper weight for its intended use, depending on where you live and what time of year you intend to wear it. Then make sure you like the style of the trousers. Unless you're thin and in good shape, a pleated pant with cuffed bottoms is your best bet. Finally, check the construction of the garment. The best dress slacks are always lined to the knee. A quality pair of dress slacks should retail for at least $150, but you can pay that or less for much more expensive trousers at end-of-season sales. I seem to have particularly good luck finding great values on dress slacks at specialty stores. And all the department stores listed in the overview above have good selections of dress pants at their sales. Once again, sizes and colors are more difficult to find at outlet stores, but the prices are great.

You can also regularly purchase top-quality suits and sport coats at semiannual sales. You should select a suit or sport coat by color, style, price, fabric, quality of construction, and cut and fit, in that order. If you are unfamiliar with any of the terms that follow, please consult the Glossary.

First, look for a color you like that fits your skin tones, hair, and eyes (see the Color Compatibility Chart, chapter 2). Examine the item more closely to determine if you like its style. For example, if you think two-button suits with center vents are too conservative for you, move on to something else. Alternatively, if the piece you noticed is a style you like, say a three-button, ventless model, you should investigate the garment further.

You should now find the price, to determine if it's within your budget. If the item is in your price range, feel its fabric. Like the trousers above, the garment should feel soft to your hand. You're probably better now at selecting quality fabrics, but you may still want to spend more time looking, particularly at suit fabrics. A suit is a major purchase and usually takes more shopping time before you're comfortable making a decision. Once again, select a fabric weight that will match its intended use, and make sure it's Super 100s weight wool or better.

For construction, check the piece for poorly sewed buttons or seams and loose threads. Also look for holes or stains in the fabric.

Matching suit slacks should be lined to the knee. Next, check that the lapels are aligned properly and lie flat against the body of the suit or sport coat. Last, and most important, make sure that the chest piece is made either with floating canvas or more modern fusing methods. Floating canvas refers to the process of sewing a piece of canvas into the lining of a coat and allowing it to float and adapt to its wearer's physique over time. Fusing is gluing the top layer of the chest to the coat lining or gluing the middle two layers together. Generally suits with floating canvas retail for $1500 and up, while decently fused suits cost $800 and up. The presence of floating canvas or the quality of the fusing can be detected by rolling the fabric of the coat's body between your thumb and forefinger. If the cloth moves easily, the coat is worthy of purchase. If the fabric on the chest piece doesn't move easily, the item has been made cheaply and should be avoided like the plague. A poorly glued suit or sport coat is more difficult to tailor properly, and its fabric will pucker after only a few visits to the dry cleaner. The result is a substantially shorter garment life, significantly less value for your hard-earned clothing dollar, and a much higher price per wearing.

Finally, try on the item; see if it fits properly and if the cut flatters you. If so, make your purchase. And remember, if you like everything about a piece of clothing but its price, chances are good it will eventually be marked down. That's what this book is all about—encouraging you to be patient and helping you find value for your money. *Remember, tailored clothing is always a buyer's market.* Some specialty stores give customers a discount on the spot if they want to make a sale. Others have beginning business wardrobe packages that allow you to buy clothes over time, interest free. Most associates at department stores will find a size for you at another store if you see something you want on sale. But if you see something you like at an outlet store, buy it now unless you know an additional markdown will happen in a week or less. These stores' inventories are designed to turn over completely every three weeks to a month, and you're really taking your chances if you wait longer than a week.

If you have less than $500 to spend on a suit, make it go as far as you can. Be patient and buy a high-quality label on sale rather than a poorly constructed, bargain basement waste of money. Purchase classic suits in a cut and style that never go out of fashion, and no one will know what season they're from. Getting a great deal on a quality suit makes you feel even more confident wearing your new suit into any business situation.

Accessories

For discounted belts, check virtually any end-of-season sale. Choices here would include specialty stores, department stores, and outlet stores. Company-owned retail and outlet shoe stores are also great destinations. Designer-owned boutiques often discount belts seasonally, too.

In watches, choose something subtle that has both gold- and silver-colored metal, so it will match any jewelry you choose to wear. If you elect to purchase a second watch, you don't need to spend as much and should think about a sport watch with a second hand. Finer jewelry stores will discount merchandise prior to major holidays like Christmas.

For pocket watches and vintage wristwatches, your best bet is eBay or your local antique store. Antique shows are another good place to look once you've checked all the antique shops in your surrounding area. You will find a chain or a fob to match your watch in the same manner.

Buy a good wallet as soon as you can afford one. You can pay $20 to $50 for an inexpensive leather wallet in a department or outlet store. However, I'm hard on wallets for some reason, and at one point I replaced one every six months. So I bit the bullet and bought a well-made billfold at full price. It lasted six years and had a far lower price per wearing than all the cheaper ones I used to wear out. For additional information on quality makers of wallets, please see the Accessories Reference Guide in chapter 8.

As with pocket watches, the best place to start your cuff link collection is online with eBay. Next try antique stores or shows. Your first few pairs should cost less than $50 each. When you can afford nicer cuff links, check the Accessories Reference Guide in chapter 8. Cuff links should always be worn with the decorative side facing out, but decoration on both sides looks best.

In braces, Trafalgar is the most popular brand in American men's stores. Their Limited Edition silk braces are woven on antique French looms with a limited amount of capacity, hence the name. These braces are pricey, but their quality of construction and timelessly elegant details make them a most desirable addition to anyone's wardrobe. They're also quite colorful and provide many options for matching suits and other accessories. Victor Talbots on Long Island has the best selection of Limited Edition braces I've seen anywhere; purchase them online at www.VictorTalbots.com. It's hard to find these braces at a discount; eBay is the best place to look. Nordstrom has the best overall selection of Trafalgar braces at retail price. You can find other varieties of Trafalgar braces on sale at many places during end-of-season sales, and most Nordstrom Racks usually have a good selection for around half price. Brooks Brothers, Polo Ralph Lauren, and Albert Thurston also make some great-looking braces. The former two discount them seasonally and at company outlet stores. Thurston usually has some on sale online at www.albertthurston.com. Please see the Accessories Reference Guide in chapter 8 for additional information.

If you like silk pocket squares, the best place to buy them is at Nordstrom Rack for around $6. Most Racks carry a good selection of solid colors at this price. Many department stores also carry solid colors of Asian silk for between $10 and $15. Italian silk squares cost about double that. Hand-rolled white Irish linen pocket squares are around $15 at most department and specialty stores.

You will occasionally see groups of silk or linen pocket squares for sale on eBay. You will rarely see pocket squares on sale at department or independent stores.

Overcoats, Umbrellas, and Hats

Obviously, the best time to shop for an overcoat is at the end of the winter season. It's therefore best to purchase something classic and not trendy. You will also frequently find great prices on outerwear at outlet stores, particularly those for department stores. I've often seen overcoats marked down 80 percent from original price. Umbrellas should cost at least $20; anything priced lower is a toy and will not last. However, if you're caught in an unexpected downpour, even the little ones sold on the streets of New York for $5 are better than nothing.

In my opinion the definitive authority on hats in America is Graham Thompson of Optimo Hats in Chicago (see directory, chapter 10). He is extremely passionate and knowledgeable about dress headwear. He's worked with hats since he was fifteen, and at the ripe "old" age of thirty-one is doing his best to keep the dying art of hat making alive. His products and services are of the utmost quality, and he and Kevin Fitzpatrick at Optimo are great to work with. If you're on a tighter budget, the JJ Hat Center in New York City is also a good place to shop. There you'll find a large and varied inventory and a knowledgeable and courteous sales staff. Both JJ and Optimo publish free catalogs and have information accessible online as well. Your local specialty store may also be able to help you if you're in the market for a hat. It's rare to see hats at a department store and even rarer to find a salesperson who knows enough about them to assist you in selecting one.

Formal Wear

Most department stores have a formal wear section. The larger the store, and the more affluent and urban the location, the more styles you will have to choose from. You can also occasionally get some outstanding buys at outlet stores. Formal wear that gets marked down gets marked way down. When purchasing formal wear, choose a classic style that will stay in fashion for a while. Most men simply don't wear formal wear enough to justify any other expenditure. Your local independent store is another good place to buy formal wear. The salespeople there will often have much more experience helping customers choose formal wear.

To conclude, bargain hunting now is good practice for the future. As your income increases, you will have more money to spend on clothes. The more stores you visit, the better chance you'll have of finding something that appeals to you. You'll know then what you like and where to find it. For any of the locations and stores I've discussed above, please consult chapters 9 and 10 or visit www.MensSpecialtyRetail.com.

7

Travel and Wardrobe Maintenance

Everyone travels for business sooner or later. I have some tips to make this often-laborious process much easier. If you're flying, and bringing a suit or sport coat, always carry it on in a garment bag. You'll usually be able to hang it up, and the garment will arrive with a minimum of wrinkles. The zippered bag you receive when purchasing tailored clothing at most stores will work perfectly. Then check the rest of your belongings in a bag with wheels. Rolling bags are essential for easy navigation through airport terminals and to ground transportation. Purchase a smaller bag if most of your business trips will be only up to three days in length. If your trips last three to seven days, select a medium-sized bag. If you travel frequently for a week or more, buy one of those steamer trunks on wheels. The well-dressed gentleman never travels light. It's hard to be away from your family and friends and the familiar comforts of home. Packing more of your favorite things will make you feel at ease and confident transacting business on the road. Bring backup clothes in case you soil or damage your first preference. Backup needs could include an extra shirt, tie, pair of trousers, or suit, depending on how important your meeting is and what you've experienced in the past.

With all the traveling I've done, I have yet to find a reliable way to pack shirts that will avoid wrinkles. I've tried packing them in plastic, folding them different ways, and hanging them in the shower to steam the wrinkles out. None of these methods has worked. Accordingly, I encourage you to become proficient with an iron, as I (sadly) have. Call ahead and make sure the place you're staying has an iron. You only have one chance to impress in a business meeting, and a freshly pressed shirt and suit always look crisp and professional. In contrast, most well-made knits will be wrinkle free in the morning if you hang them up the night before.

If you're driving, follow the same guidelines outlined above. If you travel routinely as part of your job, consider buying a backseat clothes rack to hang your clothes on. That way, it's easier to bring more of your wardrobe with you without worrying about it getting wrinkled. You never know how you're going to feel on any given day, and you want to have the right outfit for any given situation. When you drive a lot, you need to be comfortable and feel at home.

SOME MISCELLANEOUS TRAVEL TIPS

■ Make a list of things to take on every trip, based on its duration and primary purpose. To assist you with this, checklists are posted on www.MensSpecialtyRetail.com. There's nothing worse than forgetting something important on a trip.

■ Drink lots of water; it will keep you healthy and your mind focused. It's tempting to overuse caffeine when you're tired and to drink more alcohol when you've got a corporate expense account. Water helps your body counteract the effects of both.

■ Adopt an exercise regimen that doesn't require a lot of time or equipment. Regular exercise raises your endorphin levels and keeps your mind focused on the business at hand. Exercise also helps keep weight off.

■ When you're traveling, make frequent use of the store guide in chapter 10. It will expose you to more clothing and help you develop your own sense of style faster. Trust me—shopping is a lot more fun than sitting in your hotel room working on PowerPoint presentations.

■ Wear a suit coat as a blazer while traveling, particularly in business casual situations, and especially if you're building your wardrobe from scratch. Doing so minimizes space requirements during packing while maximizing outfit combinations.

■ Finally, to make packing for travel easier, have your closet organized by color. If you're color-blind, as are many men, get your roommate or significant other to help you arrange your closet. Many wardrobe consultants, custom clothiers, and specialty stores offer this service if you're a regular customer. Label your clothes (on the inside) if necessary to avoid any embarrassing combinations. Then packing for business trips is much easier, whether you're color-blind or not.

Maintaining Your Wardrobe

Maintaining your clothes properly from day to day, even when you're not traveling, is an important part of getting the most for your clothing dollar. At the end of the day, unknot your tie carefully, and hang it up to remove wrinkles and preserve its shape longer. Hang your other garments up as well, or they'll also wrinkle and you'll need to iron them before you can wear them again. No one likes ironing, and it shortens the life of your wardrobe. Let your clothes air out before returning them to your closet. Purchase a wooden valet, and hang them on it overnight. If possible, use a closet with louvered doors, which allow your clothes to breathe when they're not in use. I highly recommend cedar-lined closets, especially for storing and protecting the more expensive wool items in your wardrobe. Moths and other pests are attracted to odors, particularly sweeter smells like colognes or food you may have spilled on yourself. A cedar closet will absorb these odors and make them less detectable to pests. If you can, use a closet without windows; prolonged exposure to light will fade items in your wardrobe. Perspiration and dirt also break down the fibers in your clothes. Launder regularly what you can, according to the care instructions on the label of the garment. What you can't launder, take to a reputable dry cleaner (see below). Quality dry cleaning is expensive, so use the time-honored "sniff" method to determine when it's time to clean your clothes. But err on the side of caution; those around you will thank you for it. If you spill something on an item, the quicker you can get it to the cleaners, the better. That way the stain will have less chance to set and ruin your clothes.

Dry cleaning is the process of inserting a garment into a specially designed machine and infusing it with perchloroethylene solvent. The machine then heats the solvent and evaporates it rapidly, allowing the garment to emerge dry, hence the name. The newer dry-cleaning machines are computerized and use less of the solvent, making the process more sophisticated and easier on your clothes. However, if you still detect a chemical smell on your items, hang them outside for an hour or two before putting them away. And new technology is currently being developed that will use either water or carbon dioxide for dry cleaning and eliminate perchloroethylene from the process. Also, select a cleaner with Teflon on its finishing press and iron. This will prevent your clothes from developing a shiny finish from direct contact with metal over time. For the above reasons, the least expensive dry cleaner may not be the best. Choose someone who has newer equipment and will handle your wardrobe with care. This will be more economical in the long run. Below are some guidelines for care of individual pieces in your wardrobe.

Your overcoat should last at least ten years and should be dry cleaned at the end of each season. If you don't clean it before putting it away for the summer, it could have odors that attract pests, as described earlier. Store it in your cedar closet if you have one. If you don't, keep it wrapped in plastic to make pests travel through one more layer to damage the garment. Hang your coat away from the window, to avoid prolonged exposure to the light and fading of its original color.

Quality tailored clothing should last at least five years if properly maintained. I dry clean my wool slacks at least every third time they're worn. Otherwise they won't hold a decent crease. If you don't wear your suit coat as often, cleaning it every fifth or sixth wearing is sufficient. You may quarrel with this frequency, but I strongly advise cleaning your clothing at least every fifth wearing. If you don't, you risk having body odor detract from your overall presentation, and your perspiration will age your wardrobe prematurely.

I clean my cotton slacks every other time I wear them, again because they don't seem to hold a sharp crease when cleaned less frequently. I judge each situation with silk, cotton, or wool casual shirts differently. Some shirts seem to make me sweat more often; these go in after each wearing. For others it's generally every other time, unless I've worn them on a particularly warm day. Use your own judgment, and find a system that works for you. Just be sure to observe the five-day rule outlined above. You and those around you will thank you for it. All of the above wardrobe items should also last five years if cared for properly.

I like my dress shirts roomy and am therefore able to have them laundered professionally after each wearing (shirts can shrink with laundering). If you like yours more fitted, you may want to dry-clean them to avoid shrinkage. Dry cleaning will also help keep shirts colorfast longer. However, you'll still want to clean them after each wearing. Don't forget to remove your collar stays before cleaning them, whatever method you choose, since washing and dry cleaning machines have little regard for them. Again, it's a good idea to go to a finer men's store in your area and pick up some spare stays to have on hand. Ties should never need cleaning, unless you're using them for napkins. To avoid doing so, unbutton your shirt slightly when eating, and tuck the tie inside until you're finished. If you do accidentally soil your tie, take it to your local cleaners rather than trying to remove the stain yourself. Or if you prefer the ultimate specialist in tie care, contact Tiecrafters in New York City at (212)629-5800 or online at www.tiecrafters.com.

Shoes should always be clean and have a good shine. I recommend taking them to a local shoe repair shop for shining as soon as they become scuffed. A good shoe repair store will also be proactive in advising any needed refurbishment for your footwear. A local shop often can do any required work as well and may charge less than the shoe manufacturer's recommended repair depot.

Maintaining your clothes well, both at home and on the road, will increase their life, which decreases the price per wearing of each garment. It simply makes sense to pay as much attention to how you care for your clothes as it does to how you acquire them.

PART TWO

Reference Guides

The final three chapters of this book are full of resources to help you recognize and locate quality men's clothing. Labels alone cannot guarantee quality, but the companies standing behind them can. Many brands in these chapters have existed for a hundred years or more and have become time-honored standards of exemplary workmanship and classic good taste. The lists below are not meant to be exhaustive—that's impossible in a book, as labels come and go on a regular basis. The reference guides are also somewhat subjective, but they are comprised of brands I know, wear, and have come to appreciate over the years I've been interested in finer men's clothing. The prices listed are approximations; new information comes in almost daily on prices, labels, and styles. For even more current information, log on to www.MensSpecialtyRetail.com.

Following is a key to the abbreviations within the reference guides:

Cat	Catalog
COO	Company-Owned Outlet Store
COS	Company-Owned Store or Boutique
Saks	Saks Fifth Avenue
MSS	Men's Specialty Stores (For specifics on which stores carry which brands, consult chapter 10 or my website)
NM	Neiman Marcus
Nord	Nordstrom
OL	Available for purchase online

8

Clothing Designers

Buy quality over quantity. A well-known brand name does not always guarantee quality, but if a particular label has a reputation for stylish, well-made clothing, your chances of getting value for your purchase are greatly improved. Buying quality clothing minimizes your price per wearing. Select classic cuts and styles, and you'll acquire a wardrobe that will always be fashionable. Buying trendy clothing, even if it's made well, will cost you more because you have to replace it when it goes out of style. I discuss my favorite labels below, literally from A to Z, but the list is by no means exhaustive. New brands and additions to current labels' lines are introduced often.

Below you'll find some background information about each of these brands so you can have a better idea of who makes what and what styles might fit your tastes. Then I add some suggestions on where to find their products. Next you'll find a reference guide for shoes. Finally, there's a separate reference table for jewelry, primarily cuff links, and accessories such as braces, belts, and wallets. Again, please see my website for even more current information.

The World's Best Labels and Where to Find Them

7 for All Mankind *USA*. Casual Wear $125–180
Quality, modern fashion jeans primarily for the younger man.

Joseph Abboud *USA*. Casual Wear $75–300, Dress Shirts $75–200, Neckwear $75, Tailored Clothing $600–1,200
MSS, Nord, Saks
Great line with distinctive, updated classic style all its own. Many tailored clothing pieces done in earth tones with classic American structuring. One of the better sartorial choices for a young man straight out of business school. Higher-priced Black Label line is also a stylish selection for the more mature man.

Agnona *Italy*. Casual Wear $350–900
MSS, NM
www.agnona.it
Classic styling, primarily casual shirts and sweaters. Wonderful wool and cashmere fabrics. Part of the Zegna family of companies.

Allea *Italy*. Neckwear $75–90
MSS
Italian maker of neckwear. Simple but elegant designs, often in black-white combinations.

Altea *Italy*. Neckwear $50–75
MSS, Nord
Quality, value-priced ties. Known for sharp-looking polka dots.

Aquascutum *UK*. Casual Wear $60–200, Tailored Clothing $600–1,000, Outerwear $400–1,200
MSS
www.aquascutum.co.uk
Conservative cuts and styles in Super 100s wool give this brand classic elegance and give you a great value for the purchase price. Burberry and Aquascutum both claim to have invented the trench coat, and either is a stylish, if safe, purchase for business foul weather gear.

Giorgio Armani *Italy*. Casual Wear $80–800, Neckwear $70–125, Dress Shirts $110–400, Tailored Clothing $300–6,000, Outerwear $400–2,000, Shoes $450–600
MSS, NM, Nord, OL, Saks
www.giorgioarmani.com
Perhaps the most famous Italian label. Includes the following sublines: A/X (casual wear for the younger man, selections available online); Emporio Armani (casual and business wear); Mani (primarily business wear for the younger man); Armani Collezioni (large and varied selection), and Classico (also called Black Label—high-end line, mostly business wear). Noted for rich crepe fabrics with exceptional drape, in muted, unpretentious colors. Also does many modern pieces each season.

Sartoria Attolini *Italy*. Tailored Clothing $1,800–3,000

MSS
www.attolini.it
Very luxurious wool, cashmere, and blended fabrics for sport coats and suits. Exceptionally stylish, well-constructed tailored clothing.

Avon Celli *Italy*. Casual Wear $350–500
MSS
www.avoncelli.it
Primarily known for knits—cotton, silk, or cashmere. *Robb Report's* Best of the Best for 2002.

Axis *USA*. Casual Wear $60–300
MSS, Nord, Saks
Casual-wear maker—T-shirts, casual shirts, and sweaters. Moderate price, good quality.

Tommy Bahama *USA*. Casual Wear $50–135, Dress Shirts $50, Neckwear $50, Shoes $100–150, Tailored Clothing $150–250
COO, COS, MSS, NM, Nord, Saks
www.tommybahama.com
Tasteful brand, relaxed but refined island look that works great for weekends and in offices with relaxed dress codes. Includes Indigo Palms subline. Fabrics are modern—easy-care microfibers (rayon, Tencel) with a soft hand. Very comfortable jeans.

Ted Baker *UK*. Casual Wear $85–120, Dress Shirts $85–250, Tailored Clothing $500–900
COS, MSS, NM, Nord, OL
www.tedbaker.co.uk
Interesting styles and colors—sort of a funky, retro, Austin Powers–inspired motif. Baker's boutique in NYC's SoHo is a fun place to visit.

Ballin *Canada*. Dress Slacks $100–150
MSS, Nord
www.ballin.com
Second-generation family business. Founded in Montreal in 1946, primarily maker of dress slacks. Well constructed of quality fabric, and a particularly good value for the price.

Robert Barakett *Canada*. Casual Wear $95–150
MSS, Nord
www.robertbarakett.com
Maker of casual shirts in wrinkle-free fabrics or cotton with a soft hand. Moderate price, good value.

Barba *Italy*. Dress Shirts $225–300, Neckwear $105–125
MSS, NM, Nord
Italian maker of dress shirts and neckwear. Shirts are fitted, so you may want to buy a half-size larger than normal. Garments made with high thread count fabric, luxurious hand and appearance. Many unusual and thoughtful designs, with intricate, hand-finished details.

Scott Barber *USA*. Casual Wear $85–100
MSS
www.scottbarber.com
Casual shirts, usually of soft and comfortable cotton fabrics. Lots of colorful pieces, but some classics to choose from as well.

Luciano Barbera *Italy*. Casual Wear $250–600, Neckwear $125, Dress Shirts $225–300, Tailored Clothing $2,000–3,000
MSS, NM, Saks
www.lucianobarbera.it

Classic Italian style—sort of an Italian countryside look of relaxed sophistication. Suits and sport coats are composed of high-quality Super 120s or 150s wool and wool-cashmere blends in classic colors and designs. Shirts also excellent— high thread count broadcloth in classic stripes and solids. Ties are timeless, elegant stripes and patterns. *Robb Report's* Best of the Best 2002 for sportswear.

Barbour *UK*. Casual Wear $50–300, Overwear $65–400
MSS
www.barbour.co.uk
Good-quality wool and cashmere shirts, sweaters, and outerwear made of natural fabrics, usually wool or cashmere.

Jhane Barnes *USA*. Casual Wear $75–400, Neckwear $75–100, Tailored Clothing $700–1,200
COO, COS, MSS, NM, Nord, Saks
www.jhanebarnes.com
Has a singular, appealing look, primarily from the texture and color of the fabric used in her casual shirts and sweaters. Also has a unique means of transferring computerized designs to clothing, similar to an advanced form of silk screening.

Ike Behar *USA*. Casual Wear $75–300, Dress Shirts $75–135, Neckwear $75–90
COO, COS, MSS, NM, Nord, OL, Saks
www.ikebehar.com
Great-looking shirts and neckties; excellent variety of first quality fabrics. Custom and custom stock (C.E.O.) programs available at many places that sell the brand.

Discounted clothing is a particularly good value, and can be found seasonally at many stores that carry Ike Behar. Many outlet stores also have good selections of this brand.

Belvest *Italy*. Dress Slacks $75–110
MSS
Line of ready-to-wear tailored clothing from northern Italy. Clothing is cut to an average man's measurements in a certain size then assembled mostly by hand. Great fabrics with smooth drape and outstanding feel.

Berle *USA*. Dress Slacks $75–110
MSS
Quality cotton and wool dress slacks, traditional American styling.

Bills Khakis *USA*. Casual Wear $85–135. MSS, OL
www.billskhakis.com
Flat-front khakis made to American military WW II specs. Other styles of slacks and casual wear available as well.

Massimo Bizzocchi *Italy*. Neckwear $105–130
MSS, NM, Saks
High-quality, mostly woven Italian neckwear. Classic styles and colors.

Villa Bolgheri *Italy*. Neckwear $65–75
MSS, NM, Nord
Primarily printed Italian neckwear. Bolgheri makes many of Zegna's ties, recognized throughout the world for their quality and style.

Luigi Borrelli *Italy*. Casual Shirts $225–300, Neckwear $125–175,

Dress Shirts $225–400, Shoes
$500–900, Tailored Clothing
$1,800–2,800
COS, MSS, NM, Saks
www.luigiborrelli.com
A most celebrated shirt and necktie
maker. Each shirt is made almost
completely by hand and comes with
a booklet in four languages describ-
ing the eight steps involved in the
manufacturing process. Unusually
colored tattersalls are particularly
elegant; the hand and unusual
choice of colors are superb. Also
makes excellent ties, usually conservative designs in unusual colors that
are timeless classics. Recently introduced tailored clothing and shoes,
and opened boutiques in New York
and Palm Beach.

Hugo Boss *Germany.* Casual Wear
$75–500, Dress Shirts $90–250,
Neckwear $70–85, Shoes
$175–250, Tailored Clothing
$500–1,500, Outerwear
$500–2,500
COO, COS, MSS, NM, Nord, Saks
www.hugoboss.com
A different, sophisticated look for
almost any man in any price range.
The more affordable Red Label
features items made in the U.S.,
Hong Kong, and eastern Europe.
Black Label is made in Germany,
the U.S., and eastern Europe. The
higher end of the line is Baldessarini and is made in Italy. Tailored
clothing fits long and large and is a
great choice for the athletic man.
Expect some sleeve shrinkage from
the shirts made in Hong Kong.

Arnold Brant *Canada.* Tailored
Clothing $1,000–1,800

MSS, Saks
Tailored clothing with great fabrics
from some of the world's foremost
mills. Classic styling, well constructed. Excellent value for the price.

Breuer *France.* Dress Shirts $100–
150, Neckwear $85–105
MSS
Conservative ties, usually striped.
Also some great selections in
braces and dress shirts.

Barry Bricken *USA.* Casual Wear
$100–200, Tailored Clothing
$175–350
MSS, Nord
www.barrybricken.com
Affordable, distinctive, well-made
items.

Brioni *Italy.* Casual Wear
$200–800, Neckwear $135–300,
Dress Shirts $225–450, Tailored
Clothing $2,500 and up
COS, MSS, NM, Saks
www.brioni.com
Begun by a group of struggling tailors out of the ruins of Rome at the
end of World War II. Became a
not-so-well-kept secret when stars
of Hollywood's Golden Era began
ordering custom-made Brioni
suits in the fifties and sixties. Magnificent tailoring; only remaining
label with four-year tailor's school.
Interesting shirts with unusual
colors, and contrasting collar and
cuff combinations every season.
Many men also enjoy the elegant,
classic patterns and bold, baroque
prints in neckwear. Sportswear
line is also appealing; tends toward
the classic with vibrant color
combinations, but some unusual

unstructured pieces will also add panache to any wardrobe. Garments sized for tighter fit; buy a size or two larger than normal. Harder to find on sale, but many of the specialty men's stores discount them once or twice a year. Also appears at Neiman Marcus Last Call outlet stores on rare occasions.

Brooks Brothers *USA*. Casual Wear $50–250, Dress Shirts $50–100, Neckwear $30–55, Shoes $100–300, Outerwear $175–400, Tailored Clothing $350–600
Cat, COO, COS, OL
www.brooksbrothers.com
One of the oldest clothing makers, founded in New York in 1818. Long renowned for classic conservative business dress. Because of reputation for quality clothing at reasonable prices, can be a great starting point for a recent college or technical school graduate. Also make great braces.

Burberry *UK*. Casual Wear $75–450, Dress Shirts $95–150, Neckwear $85, Outerwear $600–800, Tailored Clothing $500–1,000
COO, COS, MSS, NM, Nord, Saks
www.burberry.com
Khaki-colored trench coat has long been a standard for outerwear. Also makes handsome flannel suits in traditional styles, with less traditional color accents. Sells fine dress and casual shirts as well—quality broadcloth in both traditional, British white-collar and contemporary styles. Recently added the Prorsum subline—higher priced,

more modern clothing for the younger man.

Canali *Italy*. Casual Wear $135–250, Dress Shirts $175–225, Neckwear $85–95, Shoes $350–700, Tailored Clothing $900–2,500, Outerwear $500–2,000
MSS, Saks
www.canali.it
Milanese brand of great quality. Suits have soft padded shoulders that will make any man's physique look terrific. Proposta subline has some beautiful fabrics and interesting updates to the classics every season. Shirts are an excellent value, constructed of fine fabric with superior construction and fit; not quite as roomy as a Zegna or Borrelli. Interesting neckwear, often refined interpretations in classic colors that will give your wardrobe subtle sophistication. Also makes first-rate sportswear and some really stylish shoes.

Caruso *Italy*. Tailored Clothing $700–1,500
MSS, Saks
Well-constructed, mostly handmade tailored clothing.

Casa Moda *Italy*. Casual Wear $75–150,
Dress Shirts $85–135
MSS
www.casamoda.com
Good-quality sportswear. Many colorful styles constructed of modern fabrics like rayon and Tencel as well as cotton.

Roberto Cavalli *Italy*. Casual Wear $150 and up

COS, MSS, NM, Saks
www.robertocavalli.it
Fashion-forward label with unusual, striking designs.

Davide Cenci *Italy.* Dress Shirts $150–200, Neckwear $90–110, Tailored Clothing $1,800–2,700
COS
www.davidecenci.com
Tasteful label headquartered in Milan, with spacious four-level store in New York. Great fabrics, particularly in dress shirts, cashmere sport coats, and cashmere-blend suits.

Cerruti/Cerruti 1881 *Italy.* Neckwear $80–100, Tailored Clothing $1,200–2,500
COS, MSS
Hundred-year-old fashion house and maker of fabrics. Great cloth, classic styling, with a few fashion-forward updates each season.

Ascot Chang *Hong Kong.* Dress Shirts $80 and up, Neckwear $120, Tailored Clothing $1,800 and up
COS, MSS
www.ascotchang.com
World-renowned custom shirts, and some tailored clothing as well.

Charleston Khakis *USA.* Casual Wear $65–125
MSS
Classic American styles in cotton dress slacks. Owned by Berle.

Charvet *France.* Dress Shirts $275–400, Neckwear $125–150
NM, Saks
A look of understated elegance all its own. Neckwear, both irides-
cently striped and textured, has a distinctive, European or continental appearance that looks resplendent on almost anyone. Shirts are usually constructed of exceptional-quality broadcloth; tend to fit snugly, so select a half-size larger than normal. Flagship store in Paris will also make neckwear to measure. Can be found on sale seasonally at Neiman Marcus, occasionally at Saks, and very occasionally at Last Call.

Cifonelli *Italy.* Casual Wear $175–300, Dress Shirts $200–250, Neckwear $95–125
MSS, NM, Saks
Terrific dress shirts with soft hands and lustrous finishes. Attractive sportswear and outerwear collections as well.

Kenneth Cole *USA.* Casual Wear $40–125, Dress Shirts $40–60, Neckwear $50–70, Shoes $150–200, Tailored Clothing $500
COO, COS, Nord, OL
www.kennethcole.com
Sleek and modern look with a decidedly urban feel. Includes Reaction subline. Clothing primarily for the younger man.

Como Sport *Italy.* Casual Wear $125–300
MSS, Saks
www.comosport.com
Quality golf and sportswear. Particularly handsome, finely woven polos for golf.

Robert Comstock *USA.* Outerwear $500–2,000
MSS, Nord, Saks

High-quality leather goods, primarily outerwear.

Coogi *Australia*. Casual Wear
$200–500
MSS, Saks
www.coogisweaters.com
Sweaters and polo shirts with colorful, distinctive look.

Coppley *Canada*. Tailored Clothing $500–1,100
MSS
www.coppley.com
Tailored clothing line made often of fabrics from Zegna mills, and made to measure at many specialty stores. Outstanding value for its price.

Corbin *USA*. Tailored Clothing $400–900
MSS
Good-quality, American-made tailored clothing and dress slacks. Traditional styling.

Corneliani *Italy*. Casual Wear $125–200, Neckwear $85–95, Dress Shirts $140–175, Tailored Clothing $1,000–1,500
MSS, Nord, Saks
www.corneliani.com
Softer shoulders and a slightly more conservative cut than many Italian brands. More unusually colored pinstripes or windowpanes in suits, and bolder-plaid sport coats. Dress shirts and ties are traditionally styled, well constructed of fine fabrics with good hands, and a great value for the price. Colorful, value-priced sportswear as well. Also makes tailored clothing for Polo Ralph Lauren.

CoSTUME NATIONAL *Italy*. Casual Wear $200–500, Shoes $350–600, Outerwear $600–1,800
COS, MSS
www.costumenational.com
Ennio Capasa named this label, co-founded with his brother Carlo in 1986, after a book on French military costume. Capasa's designs are noted for their superb cut and sharp silhouettes. The palette runs toward black, with blue, gray, and brown complements depending on the season.

Henry Cotton's *Italy*. Casual Wear $30–500
COS, MSS, Saks
www.henrycottons.com
Well-made casual wear, including some eye-catching colors and patterns. Great quality for the price, primarily for the younger man.

Brunello Cuccinelli *Italy*. Casual Wear $75–600
MSS, Saks
High-quality label for silk, cotton, wool, and cashmere knits.

Daks-Simpson *UK*. Casual Wear $75–120, Dress Shirts $75–120, Tailored Clothing $500–1,000
Nord
www.daks.com
Unusual, colorful designs. Slightly fitted; select a half-size larger.

Dalmine *Italy*. Casual Wear $100–450
MSS
Another high-quality brand of knitwear. Cashmere selections are particularly desirable.

Robert Daskal *USA.* Neckwear
$65–75
MSS, Nord, OL
www.robertdaskal.com
Hand-painted neckwear, signed by
the designer. Many unusual and
colorful designs.

d'Avenza *Italy.* Tailored Clothing
$1,200–3,000
MSS
www.davenza.com
Maker of exceptionally well constructed tailored clothing located
in Rome. Ready-to-wear is measured to average dimensions, then
handmade.

Diesel *Italy.* Casual Wear $100–300
COS, MSS, NM, Nord, Saks
www.diesel.com
Jeans and casual wear noted for
great style and fit.

Christian Dior *France.* Casual Wear
$150–1,000, Tailored Clothing
$1,200–2,000
COS, MSS
www.dior.com
Modern clothing in sleek, updated
classics by designer Hedi Slimane.

Dolce & Gabbana *Italy.* Casual
Wear $250–1,000, Shoes
$300–650, Tailored Clothing
$1,500–3,000
COO, COS, MSS, NM, Nord, Saks
www.dolcegabbana.com
Founded during the mid-1990s.
Fashion-forward, often colorful
and form fitting. Includes D&G
subline.

Dormeuil *France.*
www.dormeuil.com

Sixth-generation family-owned business founded in 1842. Fabrics world
famous for quality, and a popular
selection among custom tailors.

Duchamp *UK.* Neckwear $90–110
MSS, Nord, Saks
Colorful, well-made woven ties and
cuff links.

Alfred Dunhill *UK.* Casual Wear
$135–250, Dress Shirts
$150–250, Neckwear $110, Tailored Clothing $1,400 and up
COS
www.dunhill.com
Specializes in limited selections of
higher-end clothing and fine accessories aimed at the discerning gentleman. Many distinctive sterling
silver and leather items—pens, cuff
links, cigar cutters, briefcases, and
leather jackets. New York store
also takes custom orders for Savile
Row–style custom-tailored suits.

Eton *Sweden.* Dress Shirts
$140–200
MSS
www.etonshirts.com
Seventy-year-old manufacturer of
well-constructed, classically styled
shirts. Etastar™ cotton is world
renowned for ease of care and free-
dom from wrinkles.

ETRO *Italy.* Neckwear $75–100,
Dress Shirts $150–200, Tailored
Clothing $800–1,200
COO, COS, MSS, NM, Nord
www.etro.it
Another Milanese designer. Men's
collection is colorful and unusual,
with modern, often colorful twists
to classic clothing designs. Sizes

run very small; you'll usually need two sizes larger than normal.

Façonnable *France*. Casual Wear $45–150, Dress Shirts $90–115, Neckwear $80, Tailored Clothing $800–1,200, Outerwear $250–500
COS, Nord, OL.
www.nordstrom.com
Owned by Nordstrom and sold as one of its high-end house brands. Can be purchased on sale at many Racks; Nordstrom regularly discounts it in seasonal sales. Company-owned boutiques also carry great braces in unusual styles and colors. Excellent value for the money.

Ferrell Reed *UK*. Dress Shirts $50–100, Neckwear $50–100
MSS, Nord
Dress shirts, woven and printed ties. Roomy fit, traditional colors and styling.

Salvatore Ferragamo *Italy*. Casual Wear $125–600, Dress Shirts $150–300, Neckwear $110, Shoes $250–1,200, Tailored Clothing $1,200–1,800
COO, COS, MSS, NM, Nord, Saks
www.salvatoreferragamo.it
Suits and shirts are made of great fabric tailored in classic styles. Most famous for its brightly colored neckwear and stylish, comfortable shoes.

Gianfranco Ferré *Italy*. Neckwear $75–100, Tailored Clothing $1,000–3,500
COS, MSS, Saks
www.gianfrancoferre.com
A somewhat fashion forward

designer. Neckwear is interesting—always bold, black-and-white, baroque prints, or brazen solid colors. Also has some smart-looking tailored clothing, varying in price from the Studio 001 label to the higher-priced couture line. Discounted seasonally; ties and suits found occasionally at Saks Off Fifth.

Madeline Finn *USA*. Casual Wear $90–125
MSS
Well-made casual shirts; specializes in white button-downs.

Alan Flusser *USA*. Dress Shirts $125–250, Neckwear $95, Tailored Clothing $800–2,500
MSS
www.coppley.com
Made in Canada by Coppley. Highly influenced by English style—soft shoulders, trousers with no belt loops made to be worn with braces, or adjusted using sliding clasps on the side of the waist. Good quality for a reasonable price.

Forté *USA*. Casual Wear $300–500
MSS, OL
www.cashmere.com
Third-generation family business founded in 1917. Mongolian cashmere, first-rate quality.

Fray *Italy*. Casual Wear $200–350, Dress Shirts $350–500, Neckwear $125–200
MSS, NM
Maker of superior casual shirts, dress shirts, and neckwear. Dress shirts constructed of exceptionally soft, high thread count cotton. Casual shirts

also very comfortable with soft, luxurious hand. Shirts run about a half-size small.

Jean Paul Gaultier *France*. Casual Wear $150–1,000, Neckwear $60
MSS, NM, Saks
www.jeanpaulgaultier.com
Fashion-forward label with very interesting and unique designs. Famous for dressing men in skirts.

Romeo Gigli *Italy*. Dress Shirts $100–175, Neckwear $90–125
MSS, NM
www.romeogigli.it
Modern label with colorful and singular designs.

Gimo *Italy*. Outerwear $800–2,000
MSS
Fine, exceptionally soft leather outerwear.

Gitman Bros. *USA*. Casual Wear $65–200, Dress Shirts $65–125, Neckwear $65–80
MSS
www.gitmanco.com
High-quality clothing made in Pennsylvania since 1948. Traditional styling.

Golden Bear *USA*. Outerwear $550–1,750
MSS
www.goldenbearsportswear.com
Seventy-five-year-old family-owned company known for the outstanding quality of its leather outerwear.

Kenneth Gordon *USA*. Casual Wear $45–100, Dress Shirts $50–100
MSS, OL
www.kennethgordon.com

High-quality American label best known for its traditionally styled, durable dress shirts. Headquartered in Memphis.

Gran Sasso *Italy*. Casual Wear $75–500
MSS, Saks
www.gransasso.it
Quality knits made of natural fabrics and blends in a huge assortment of colors and styles. Great value for the price. Can be found frequently at seasonal sales.

Gucci *Italy*. Casual Wear $150–1,500, Dress Shirts $200–400, Neckwear $110–135, Shoes $250–1,000, Tailored Clothing $1,200–3,000
COO, COS, MSS, NM, Saks
www.gucci.com
Tom Ford is head designer for this label famous for its handbags, loafers, and the slim silhouettes of its updated classic suits.

Everett Hall *USA*. Tailored Clothing $600–1,500
COS, MSS
www.everetthalldesigns.com
Italian-made, sophisticated renderings of classic designs in natural fabrics. Family-owned business.

Hart, Schaffner & Marx *USA*. Tailored Clothing $500–900
MSS, Nord
www.hartschaffnermarx.com
Well-made, affordably priced tailored clothing. Primarily conservative cuts and traditional styles.

Haupt *Germany*. Casual Wear $85–125

MSS
Colorful, unusual shirts at reasonable prices. Usually made of easy-care, wrinkle-free fabrics.

Hermès *France*. Casual Wear $400 and up, Dress Shirts $225–400, Neckwear $115–175, Shoes $450–1,500
COS, MSS, NM, OL
www.hermes.com
A world-renowned brand established in 1837. Primarily known for magnificent women's scarves, men's ties, and briefcases. Exceptional quality; conservative, traditional designs.

Hickey Freeman *USA*. Casual Wear $75–125, Dress Shirts $75–125, Neckwear $80–100, Tailored Clothing $800–2,200
COO, COS, MSS, NM, Nord, Saks
www.hickeyfreeman.com
Clothing made in America, occasionally of imported fabric; known for quality construction and timelessly elegant style. Includes H. Freeman & Son subline.

Hilditch & Key *UK*. Dress Shirts $105–175, Neckwear $60
MSS, Saks
www.hilditch.co.uk
Classic British styling, known primarily for elegant, first-quality dress shirts.

Hilton/Nick Hilton/NH 1888 *USA*. Tailored Clothing $500–1,000
MSS
www.hartzco.com
Division of Hartz Company, one-hundred-year-old line of classically styled American clothing.

Holland & Sherry *UK*. Custom Fabrics for Tailored Clothing $1,200 and up for finished garment
MSS
www.hollandsherry.com
One-hundred-fifty-year-old purveyor of fine quality fabrics for bespoke clothing around the world.

Hubert *Italy*. Neckwear $70–85
MSS
Quality line of neckwear. Textured ties are particularly good-looking.

Incotex *Italy*. Casual Wear, Tailored Clothing $250–900
MSS, NM
First-quality label for casual and dress trousers made of cotton, wool, and cashmere.

Fabio Inghirami *Italy*. Dress Shirts $100–150
MSS, OL
www.fabioinghirami.com
Fifty-year-old clothing company, known primarily for high-quality fine cotton shirts.

Gianluca Isaia *Italy*. Dress Shirts $250–350, Neckwear $125–150, Tailored Clothing $1,500–3,500
MSS, NM, Nord, Saks
Located in Naples; famous for first-rate fabrics and tailoring. Suits are handcrafted of high-quality Super 120s or 150s wool or soft wool-cashmere blends. Also makes mostly handmade dress shirts of high-quality broadcloth and poplin with luxurious hands. Dress shirts are a bit fitted and run half to a full size small. Seven-fold neckties are also a highlight of the collection.

Italo Ferretti *Italy.* Neckwear
$125–150
MSS, Saks
Superior quality printed neckwear.
Owned by Brioni.

Marc Jacobs *USA.* Casual Wear
$150–500, Outerwear $500–1,000
COS
www.marcjacobs.com
Modern brand known primarily for
simplicity in outerwear and casual
wear designs.

Richard James *UK.* Dress Shirts
$250–325, Neckwear $100–125,
Tailored Clothing $1,000–1,500
NM, Saks
www.richardjames.co.uk
Design house founded in 1992, distinctive for its vibrantly colored, unusually patterned and textured dress
shirts and ties. Tailored clothing
features classic British styling and quality, with fresh, unusual color accents.

Jams World *USA.* Casual Wear
$60–80
MSS
www.jamsworld.com
Hawaiian company founded in
1964. Makes highly colorful,
unusually printed aloha shirts and
beachwear. Clothing usually composed of easy-care fabrics.

Bobby Jones *USA.* Casual Wear
$135–300, Outerwear $300–900
COO, COS, MSS, NM, Nord, OL, Saks
Owned by Hickey Freeman.
Sells high-quality golf and casual
wear. Golf shirts are finely woven
of Italian cotton and have exceptional hands. Casual shirts are
beautifully colored and made in

Italy and Portugal of first-quality
fabric. Can be found on sale at
many outlet stores.

Kahala *USA.* Casual Wear $60–80
MSS, Nord
One of the first makers of the aloha
shirt, handcrafted in Hawaii since
1936. Made of cotton or rayon.

Donna Karan *USA.* Casual Wear
$50–500, Dress Shirts $60–$175,
Neckwear $40–75, Tailored Cloth-
ing $600–1,200
COO, COS, NM, Saks
www.dkny.com
www.donnakaran.com
Brand with a sleek, urban look.
Makes many monochromatic
clothes with interesting and unusual
textures; interesting fabric mixes;
was one of the first to introduce
small amounts of Spandex to wool
suits for more comfortable movement and less wrinkling. Has two
distinct sublines, the lower-priced
DKNY and the more costly Italian-
made Donna Karan Signature.

Kilgour, French & Stanbury *UK.*
Dress Shirts $150–200, Neckwear
$90–125
MSS
www.8savilerow.com
Rich tradition of British Savile Row
tailoring. Three separate firms
merged over more than 100 years
to do business under the present
name since 1937. Licensing agree-
ment with Barneys New York since
1968. Excellent quality at compet-
itive prices.

Kiton *Italy.* Dress Shirts $325–550,
Neckwear $150–185, Tailored

Clothing $3,500 and up
MSS, NM, Saks
www.kiton.it
Rivals Brioni and Oxxford for the best ready-to-wear tailored clothing in the world. Suits are exquisite, made of the finest fabrics—often rare, limited-run fine Irish wools. Up to forty hours of hand tailoring goes into each suit. Dress shirts are of the highest thread count, softest cotton I've seen; they run about a half-size small. Also known for its seven-fold ties—conservative patterns and stripes with an occasional burst of vibrant color. Located in Naples.

Calvin Klein *USA*. Casual Wear $50–500, Dress Shirts $75–$200, Neckwear $50–75, Tailored Clothing $700–2,000, Outerwear $500–3,000
COO, COS, Saks
Probably most famous for underwear and jeans. Has two separate sublines: cK is less costly and usually American made; Calvin Klein Couture is priced higher and Italian made. The couture line has some great modern design items every season, and the flagship boutique in New York is a memorable, worthwhile visit.

Kolte *Italy*. Neckwear $50–75
MSS
Quality printed silk neckwear.

Krizia *Italy*. Casual Wear $125–200, Dress Shirts $150–200, Tailored Clothing $600–1,200
COS
Well-made, moderately priced

clothing label. Many unusual textures and colors.

Lacoste *France*. Casual Wear $50–125
COO, COS, MSS, NM, Saks
www.lacoste.com
René Lacoste was a tennis champion in the twenties and thirties who was the first to wear an external emblem on his clothing. Known primarily for its fine-quality golf and tennis wear.

Helmut Lang *Germany*. Casual Wear $150–1,000, Tailored Clothing $1,000–2,500
COS, MSS, NM, Saks
www.helmutlang.com
Minimalist designer. Uses modern, natural fibers blended with synthetics to achieve unusual, comfortable, and snug fit. Boutique in New York's SoHo is fascinating and a must-visit if you're in the city.

Lanvin *France*. Neckwear $80–110
MSS, Saks
Printed neckwear distinctively colored in high-quality printed silk. Exceptional dress shirts sold primarily in Europe.

Ralph Lauren *USA*. Casual Wear $20–1,000, Dress Shirts $60–225, Neckwear $50–125, Shoes $100–900, Tailored Clothing $200–2,500, Outerwear $400–2,500
COO, COS, NM, Nord, OL, Saks
www.polo.com
The person most responsible for introducing designer clothing to mainstream America, with the omnipresent appliquéd polo pony.

Timeless classics—soft cotton, wool, and cashmere sweaters, brightly colored polo shirts, and cotton shorts and trousers in every color of the rainbow. Dress slacks and suits also designed along classic lines. Has four sublines: Polo Sport (value priced for younger men, more fitted active wear); Chaps (a bit dressier, for business and business casual, less fitted); Polo (for an older and more affluent consumer—shoes are bench made in England by Crockett and Jones, some great silk braces, tailored clothing made in Italy by Corneliani—can fit snugly, so choose one size larger); and Purple Label (high end, made in Italy and England; casual shirts may be classic British linen or cotton, or bold and colorful Italian linen and silks; suits mostly handmade in Italy by Saint Andrews). All four lines stand for timeless elegance and impeccable good taste.

Leonard *France*. Neckwear
$135–175
MSS, NM
Neckwear made of first-quality silk, in bold tropical designs or brightly colored patterns. Timelessly fashionable, great choices for spring and summer or year-round in warmer climates. Not for the faint of heart and, like multicolored Brionis and Pancaldis, probably best worn with a conservative dress shirt.

Le Zetagi *Italy*. Casual Wear
$120–200
MSS, Saks
Well-made cotton trousers.

Jack Lipson *Canada*. Casual Wear
$50–125, Dress Shirts $50–125

MSS, Nord
www.lipsonshirts.com
Quality purveyor of shirts and boxer shorts. Twill dress shirts are an outstanding value for the price.

Lorenzini *Italy*. Casual Shirts
$200–275, Dress Shirts $225–350
MSS, NM, Saks
www.lorenzini.it
First-quality dress and casual shirts. Dress shirts are fully cut and made of high thread count broadcloth or more densely woven, lustrous cotton; distinctive because of their longer point collars and corresponding long, thin collar stays; also usually have a fold-over double seam on top of pockets.

Loro Piana *Italy*. Casual Wear
$250–1,000
COS, MSS, NM
www.loropiana.com
Noted for luxurious fabrics, particularly cashmere and cashmere blends. Also sells superior cotton sport shirts and wool sweaters. First-rate supplier of fabrics used by other labels and custom tailors as well.

Lubiam 1911 *Italy*. Tailored Clothing $500–1,200
MSS
www.lubiam.it
Well-made tailored clothing constructed of quality natural fabrics. Also makes some garments for Everett Hall and Arnold Zimberg.

Lucky Brand *USA*. Casual Wear
$50–100
COS, MSS, NM, Nord, Saks
Quality jeans and casual clothing.

MacCluer *USA.* Casual Wear
$50–100, Dress Shirts $50–100
MSS
The oldest, continuously operated, family shirt-making business in the U.S. (started in 1856). High-quality construction, traditional styling.

Malo *Italy.* Casual Wear
$350–1,500
COO, COS, MSS
www.malo.it
Premium-quality cashmere sweaters and knitwear.

Andrew Marc *USA.* Outerwear
$350–700
COO, COS, Nord, Saks
www.andrewmarc.com
Quality leather outerwear made in Korea and China.

Martin Margiela *Belgium.* Casual Wear $100–500, Outerwear $500–2,000
MSS
Martin Margiela is one of the original Antwerp Six who took the London fashion scene by storm in 1981, establishing Belgium as a fashion powerhouse. Considered at the forefront of avant-garde design, his collections are consistently original and generally explore the construction of clothing or how it is meant to be worn. He is famously secretive, to the point of never allowing himself to be photographed. His plain white label, showing only a series of numbers, and affixed at the four corners by plain white stitching, is worn as a badge of membership by fashion insiders. The

men's "10" collection is demarcated by the 10 being circled on the label.

Marinella *Italy.* Neckwear
$150–225
MSS
Third-generation, premium-quality maker of neckwear. Sold since 1914 out of a tiny store in Naples. One of the most desirable ties in the world to those in the know. Also one of few remaining places to have your tie made to measure.

Marzotto *Italy.* Casual Wear
$125–750, Tailored Clothing
$500–1,200
MSS, Saks
www.marzotto.it
Owned by Gianfranco Ferré clothing group. Well constructed with classic Italian styling. Lab line for sportswear, Sartoriale line for tailored clothing.

Mavi *Turkey.* Casual Wear $50–100
MSS, Nord
Value-priced quality jeans for the younger man.

Missoni *Italy.* Casual Wear
$25–200, Tailored Clothing
$125–800
MSS, Saks
www.missoni.com
Also part of Ferré group. Good quality, modern designs.

Moreno Martini Da Firenze *Italy.*
Casual Wear $150–500
MSS, Saks
Colorful, trendy casual wear. Sizes tend to run at least a size small.

Luciano Moresco *Italy*. Casual Wear
$125–200, Dress Shirts $140–200
MSS
www.lucianomoresco.com
Dress shirts and casual wear constructed of lustrous fabrics with
outstanding hands.

Moschino *Italy*. Casual Wear
$95–300, Neckwear $80–120, Tailored Clothing $500–1,200
COS, MSS, Saks
www.moschino.it
Fashion-forward label known for
whimsical, colorful clothing.

Thierry Mugler *France*. Tailored
Clothing $1,200–2,000
MSS
www.thierrymugler.com
Modern designer uses updated fabrics and sleek styles to achieve
sophisticated, continental look.

Nat Nast *USA*. Casual Wear
$75–200
MSS, Saks
www.natnast.com
Family-owned label founded in
1946 in Kansas City, MO. Known
mostly for silk sport shirts with '50s
retro styling.

New England *USA*. Casual Wear
$75–125
MSS
Quality label for casual wear,
tending toward more traditional
styling.

New & Lingwood *UK*. Dress Shirts
$165–210, Neckwear $60–85,
Shoes $375–1,000
OL
www.newandlingwood.com

First-quality shirts, ties, accessories,
and shoes from venerable, well-
respected British clothier. Company established in Eton in 1865 and
became official supplier of clothing
for the school and college.

Nicky/Nicky's of Milan *Italy*. Neckwear $125–150
MSS
Handmade neckwear, often unusually colored stripe combinations.

Normandy & Monroe *USA*. Casual
Wear $250–350, Outerwear
$250–350
MSS
www.normandyandmonroe.com
Khakis and jackets made of
durable, high-quality cotton fabric.

H. Oritsky *USA*. Tailored Clothing
$400–800
MSS
Quality tailored clothing with tra-
ditional styling.

Oxxford *USA*. Dress Shirts
$250–350, Neckwear $125–175,
Tailored Clothing $500–3,500+,
Outerwear $1,500–3,000
COS, MSS, NM, Saks
www.oxxfordclothes.com
The last American haberdasher to
tailor garments almost completely
by hand. Possibly the best-looking
gray flannel suit in the world.
Dress shirts and ties also of superb
quality. Conservative, traditional
styling and fit.

Vitaliano Pancaldi *Italy*. Neckwear
$100–150
MSS, OL
www.pancaldities.com

First-quality, brilliantly colored printed silk neckwear, made in Bologna by hand for over fifty years. Company is part of group that owns Dalmine knits and Moresco shirts. Some conservative woven ties and dress shirts as well.

Paper, Denim, & Cloth *USA*. Casual Wear $150–200
MSS, Saks
First-quality, couture-style jeans with slight flare at the bottom to fit over boots.

Paul & Shark *Italy*. Casual Wear $125–750
COS, MSS
www.paulshark.it
Sportswear inspired by yachting and incorporating the latest in weatherproof fabrics. Excellent choice for foul weather gear. Also nice casual shirts with soft hands.

Thomas Pink *UK*. Casual Shirts $100–150, Dress Shirts $125–195, Neckwear $60–100
Cat, COS, OL
www.thomaspink.com
Shirts are made in Ireland of high-quality broadcloth and super high quality, 170-thread count cotton. Colors are vibrant and distinctive with the signature color, of course, being pink. Shirts are fitted; buy a half-size larger. Casual shirts are also great looking and well made, particularly the linens. Great selection of brightly colored printed and woven ties and cuff links to coordinate with your shirt purchase. Ties are a bit narrow, which is British custom. If you can, visit one of the stores in per-

son; they look and smell great. Everyone in retail should use Pink's aromatherapist.

Prada *Italy*. Casual Wear $150–1,000, Dress Shirts $200–350, Neckwear $100–125, Shoes $450–900, Tailored Clothing $1,200–3,000
COS, NM, Saks
www.prada.com
Modern designer label known for high fashion and trademark red vertical stripe. Stylish shoes are a highlight of the collection. Includes Prada Sport subline.

Pringle of Scotland *UK*. Casual Wear $250–600
MSS
www.pringle–of–scotland.co.uk
Sweaters made of fine wool and cashmere. Classic styles, and also some particularly flamboyant argyles each season.

Raffi *Italy*. Casual Wear $100–500
MSS
High-quality knits and casual wear.

Ravazzolo *Italy*. Tailored Clothing $1,000–2,500
MSS
www.ravazzolo.it
Sixth generation of family making exceptional tailored clothing. Known primarily for high-twist, lightweight fabrics and excellent made-to-measure program.

Redaelli *Italy*. Tailored Clothing $700–1,500
MSS
www.redaelli.com
First-quality fabrics and construction.

Austin Reed *UK*. Tailored Clothing
$500–1,500
MSS, Nord
www.austinreed.co.uk
British menswear line headquartered
on Regent Street in London since
1900. Quality-made garments with
traditional styling.

Remy *USA*. Tailored Clothing
$500–1,000, Outerwear
$500–1,000
MSS
Soft, quality leather outerwear man-
ufactured in the U.S. of primarily
Italian and New Zealand lamb hides.

Reyn Spooner *USA*. Casual Wear
$70–115
MSS, Nord, OL, Saks
www.reyns.com
Has been making more conservative (if there is such a thing)
Hawaiian shirts since the early
1950s. Shirts are usually made of
spun rayon—durable and colorfast. More conservative styles often
made of soft cotton polyester
blends. Can often be found at
great prices at Nordstrom Rack
and Saks Off Fifth.

Stefano Ricci *Italy*. Dress Shirts $400
and up, Neckwear $135 and up,
Tailored Clothing $1,500 and up
COS, MSS, NM, Saks
www.stefanoricci.it
Distinguished Florentine designer
known for luxurious, extremely high
quality clothing. Dress shirts are
mostly handmade, of outstanding
quality, and consequently quite
pricey. Ties are printed silk and also
very well made in unique patterns
and baroque prints. Ties are dis-

counted seasonally at Saks Fifth
Avenue and Neiman Marcus and can
occasionally be spotted at Off Fifth.

Tori Richard *USA*. Casual Wear
$50–100
MSS, Nord
www.toririchard.com
Made in Hawaii since 1956. Colorful prints, usually made of colorfast rayon.

Richel *Spain*. Neckwear $75–100
MSS
Founded in Barcelona, Spain, in
1948. Ties are uniquely colored
prints fashioned of fine-quality silk.

Riscatto Portofino *USA*. Casual
Wear $75–200
MSS, Nord
Quality European-inspired, Italian-
made casual shirts made by Merrill
Sharpe Inc., a family-owned busi-
ness founded in 1944.

Jeff Rose *USA*. Casual Wear
$85–200
MSS, Nord
Good-quality, Italian-made cotton
casual shirts and knits. Great-looking finely woven golf shirts.

Georg Roth *Germany*. Casual Wear
$125–175
MSS
Unusual, brightly colored, abstract
shirts, made in Italy of cotton,
rayon, or multifiber blends.

Samuelsohn *Canada*. Casual Wear
$125–200, Tailored Clothing
$500–1,100
MSS
www.samuelsohn.com

Family-owned producer of quality suits at reasonable prices for almost eighty years. Fabrics are Super 100s, 110s, and 120s wools purchased from English and Italian mills then constructed in Canada. Styles are subtle variations on classic pinstripes, solids, and windowpanes. Made-to-measure suit available for the same price as ready-to-wear in approximately four weeks.

Scabal *Belgium*. Fabrics for custom-tailored clothing $3,000 and up for finished garment
MSS
www.scabal.com
Manufacturer of some of the finest fabrics in the world. Company founded in 1938. Fabrics known for innovative technology and the finest quality.

Serica Elite *Italy*. Neckwear $60–90
MSS
Quality printed silk neckwear.

Signum *Germany*. Casual Wear $125–175
MSS
Casual shirts with unusual, thought-provoking designs. Usually constructed of cotton; tend to run a little large, so buy a size smaller.

John Smedley *UK*. Casual Wear $100–500
MSS, Nord, OL
www.johnsmedley.co.uk
The oldest family-owned business surveyed here, begun as a cotton mill in 1784. Known primarily for first-quality cotton and New Zealand merino wool knitwear.

Paul Smith *UK*. Casual Wear $135–700, Dress Shirts $135–350, Shoes $200–500, Tailored Clothing $1,000–2,200
COS, MSS, NM
www.paulsmith.co.uk
Designer best known for brightly colored striped shirts and coordinating ties. Label also features tailored clothing in classic British styling, with unusual color accents. Shirts are very fitted; you'll need two sizes larger than normal. Interesting cuff link collection. Smith pieces are great to add a little fun to your wardrobe.

Southwick *USA*. Tailored Clothing $400–1,000
MSS
www.southwickclothing.com
Family-owned business begun in 1929. Quality tailored clothing in traditional, soft-shouldered style.

St. Croix *USA*. Casual Wear $125–450, Outerwear $400–800
COS, MSS, OL
www.stcroixshops.com
Handcrafted, hand-finished casual shirts, sweaters, and knitwear.

Robert Talbott *USA*. Casual Wear $125 and up, Dress Shirts $135–350, Neckwear $60–195
COO, COS, MSS, NM, Nord, Saks
www.roberttalbott.com
Family-owned business begun on Monterey peninsula in California in 1950. Distinctive, first-quality merchandise. Cashmere casual shirts voted *Robb Report's* Best of the Best for 2002. Website features diagrams on how to tie bow ties and neckties. Many retail locations feature custom stock programs.

Tallia *USA*. Tailored Clothing
$400–800
MSS, Nord
www.hartzco.com
Quality-constructed, value-priced
tailored clothing. Label is a division of Hartz Company.

Bob Timberlake *USA*. Casual Wear
$65–150, Shoes $100–150
MSS
Well-made, comfortable clothing.

Tino Cosma *Italy*. Casual Wear
$125–175, Neckwear $80–100,
Dress Shirts $125–175
COS, MSS
www.tinocosma.com
Company begun in 1946. Beautiful textures in dress and casual
shirts. Equally smart looking, subtle woven and print designs in
neckwear. Found primarily in independent men's specialty stores.

Tombolini *Italy*. Tailored Clothing
$800–2,000
MSS
www.tombolini.it
Second-generation family business
known mostly for tailored clothing.

Torras *Spain*. Outerwear
$500–2,000
MSS
www.torras.com
Well-made, quality leather outerwear.

Tricots St. Raphael *USA*. Casual
Wear $50–250
MSS, Nord
Tasteful, multicolored sweaters for
business casual and weekend wear.
Also has a fine assortment of solid-

color T-shirts, polos, and sweaters
in a myriad of great colors.

Linnea Trussini *USA*. Tailored
Clothing $600–1,600
MSS
Italian-made tailored clothing line
distributed by Boyd's of Philadelphia.
Nice fabrics, well-constructed clothing with classic European styling.

Tundra *Canada*. Casual Wear
$60–300
MSS
Brightly colored, well-made
sweaters in cotton and wool. Some
casual shirts as well.

Turnbull & Asser *UK*. Casual Shirts
$200 and up, Dress Shirts $175
and up, Neckwear $110
COS, NM
www.turnbullandasser.com
First-quality English haberdasher
since 1885. Prince Charles's shirt
maker by royal appointment.
Known for distinctive stripes with
traditional banker's white collars
and cuffs. Also sells neckwear,
accessories, and some items of formal wear and tailored clothing.
Discussed in 2002 *GQ* article on
sources for best custom shirts, surprisingly affordable, if you know
when to shop for them; check
Neiman Marcus First Call and Last
Call sales. Will also replace collars,
cuffs, or make repairs on your
shirts for around $50 each time.

Valentino *Italy*. Dress Shirts
$80–200, Neckwear $80–100, Tailored Clothing $1,200–1,800
COS, MSS
www.valentino.it

Known for bold colors, intriguing items in red and white, and unusual twists on classic designs. Also has a higher-priced couture line intended primarily for women and sold at its four American boutiques, but you can find interesting and appealing men's clothing in these stores as well.

Dries van Noten *Belgium*. Casual Wear $150–1,000, Outerwear $500–1,200, Shoes $250–400
MSS, Saks
Dries van Noten showed his first collection in 1985; collections are heavily influenced by costume, and his attention to texture and pattern makes his pieces a perennial favorite among the fashion set. Recent collections have had a hippie-ish appeal, tending toward a palette of earth colors and washed fabrics.

John Varvatos *USA*. Casual Wear $100–800, Dress Shirts $200–300, Neckwear $80–100, Shoes $300–650, Tailored Clothing $1,200–1,800, Outerwear $500–2,000
COS, MSS, NM, Saks
www.johnvarvatos.com
Label debuted in fall 2000. Clothes are eclectic, mixing luxurious fabrics with casual styling to create a look of easy elegance.

Gianni Versace *Italy*. Casual Wear $400–2,000, Dress Shirts $300–500, Neckwear $110–150, Tailored Clothing $1,200 and up, Outerwear $2,000 and up
COO, COS, MSS, NM, Saks
www.versace.com
Impressive collection of clothing,

perhaps most famous for silk casual shirts in bold, dramatic designs. Also makes interesting, fashion-forward suits and sport coats in distinctive colors and styles. Colorful ties have prominently featured trademark Medusa head. Jeans are very comfortable and are available in a number of styles and eye-popping colors. Outlets usually have some great deals on representative selections, although it's a challenge finding bigger sizes. Versace tends to run a size or more small.

Vestimenta *Italy*. Dress Shirts $200–250, Tailored Clothing $800–1,600
MSS, Saks
www.vestimenta.com
Noted for wool crepe tailored clothing with superior performance, texture, and drape. Dress and casual shirts are also of exceptional, soft cotton. Also makes clothing for other labels such as Giorgio Armani.

Jack Victor *Canada*. Tailored Clothing $150–850
MSS
www.jackvictor.com
Third-generation family business begun in 1913. Line covers primarily traditional styles of tailored clothing.

Viyella *UK*. Casual Wear $90–150
MSS
www.coats–viyella.com
Comfortable wool and cotton casual shirts in traditional styles. British company founded as thread manufacturer in India in 1784.

Xacus *Italy.* Dress Shirts $60–125
MSS
www.xacus.com
Somewhat fashion forward label
for casual and dress shirts. Unusual
and distinctive fabrics.

XMI *USA.* Casual Shirts $60–135,
Dress Shirts $65–125, Neckwear
$60–110
MSS, Nord
www.xmi.com
Label is owned by experienced
designer Bert Pulitzer with wife,
Betsy, and brother-in-law, John
Sazama. Dress shirts are made in
Portugal and Hong Kong with
fabrics from the finest mills in the
world. XMI shirts have a lustrous
appearance and drape well because
of a great fit. Ties are handmade in
Chippewa Falls, WI. Platinum
Series ties are mostly wovens from
imported British and Italian silks;
about 25% are printed fabrics from
Italy. XMI ties are known for their
great knotting ability and long
dimple at the knot.

Yves St. Laurent *France.* Neckwear
$90–115, Tailored Clothing
$2,000–3,000
COS
www.yslonline.com
Design house established in 1962.
Rive Gauche subline for men is
headed by Tom Ford and is known
for sleek, modern updates of classic
designs.

Yohji Yamamoto *Japan.* Casual Wear
$250–1,500, Tailored Clothing
$1,200 and up
COS, MSS
www.yohjiyamamoto.com

Fashion-forward designer with
many striking pieces. SoHo boutique is an ethereal experience that
includes incredible music and furnishings not to be missed if you're
in New York.

Zanella *Italy.* Casual Wear
$125–300, Dress Shirts $125–175,
Tailored Clothing $175–700
MSS, NM, Nord, Saks
Originated in Vicenza, Italy, in
the late fifties. Specializes in dress
slacks of high-quality wool, available in many styles, cuts, and colors. Clothing can occasionally be
found at great prices at end-of-season sales and outlet stores.

Zanetti *Italy.* Casual Wear
$75–150, Dress Shirts $70–125,
Tailored Clothing $500–1,000
MSS
Suits tend to be more fashion forward, particularly the Extrema
subline, and thus may be more
suitable for the younger man.
Made of excellent fabrics, many
milled by Ermenegildo Zegna.
Designs add a distinctive flair to a
more conservative style, like a subtle pink-on-gray pinstripe.

Zanone *Italy.* Casual Wear
$150–600
MSS
www.zanone.it
Known mostly for high-quality
cotton and wool knitwear.

Ermenegildo Zegna *Italy.* Casual
Wear $75–1,000, Dress Shirts
$175–450, Neckwear $110–175,
Shoes $300–700, Tailored Cloth-
ing $500–3,500, Outerwear

$1,500-3,500
COO, COS, MSS, NM, Nord, Saks
www.zegna.com
Famous clothing and fabric label, founded in 1910 and currently run by the family's fourth generation. Zegna clothing features many interesting and distinctive pieces with new colors, styles, and fabrics each season. Tailored in classic European style with somewhat structured shoulder. Four sublines: Zegna Sport—casual and active wear for the younger man; Zegna Soft—less structured, more affordable clothing primarily for business casual; Ermenegildo Zegna—full collection; and Napoli Couture—higher priced, ultrafine fabrics and hand construction for business formal dress. Zegna is also the largest producer of fine fabrics in the world and is often used by other clothing brands and custom tailors. Widely available online, at specialty stores, Zegna company and outlet stores, department stores, and outlet stores. Can be found on sale frequently at most of these locations.

Pal Zileri *Italy.* Casual Wear $200–275, Dress Shirts $100–300, Neckwear $85, Tailored Clothing $1,000–2,500
COS, MSS, Nord, Saks
www.palzileri.com
Known primarily for tailored clothing with distinctive updates in colors and cuts of classic European styling. Sartoriale subline features great fabrics and many hand-finished details.

Arnold Zimberg *Italy.* Casual Wear $125–200, Tailored Clothing

$800–1,500
MSS
www.lubiam.it
Tailored clothing line made in Italy by Lubiam. Well constructed of fine wools and cashmeres, traditional styling.

Bernard Zins *France.* Tailored Clothing (Slacks) $150–350
MSS, Nord
High-quality cotton and wool dress pants.

Shoe Reference Guide

The companies below are primarily shoemakers. Clothing lines that include shoes have been covered in the previous table.

Alden *USA*. $175–425
COS, MSS, OL, Saks
www.aldenshoe.com
www.aldenshop.com
Durable, conservatively styled shoe. Ideal for business.

Allen-Edmonds *USA*. $175–400
Cat, COO, COS, MSS, Nord, OL
www.allenedmonds.com
Durable classic, for business and casual dress. Can be factory refurbished for under $100.

Bally *Switzerland*. $275–1,200
COO, COS
www.bally.com
Classic shoe with great reputation and styles for all occasions.

Lorenzo Banfi *Italy*. $275–600
MSS
www.lorenzobanfi.com
Sleek, well-made shoe. Appropriate for business or casual wear.

Borgioli *Italy*. $175–300
MSS
Great-looking footwear well made and reasonably priced. Styles appropriate for all occasions.

Church's *UK*. $250–500
OL, COS
www.churchsshoes.com
Bench made in England. Great quality, conservative styling, primarily for business.

Cole Haan *USA*. $175–900
COO, COS, MSS, NM, Nord, OL, Saks
www.colehaan.com
Well-made, comfortable shoes. Can be worn casually or to work.

Crockett & Jones *UK*. $275–700
MSS
www.crockettandjones.co.uk
Venerable British shoemaker established in 1879. Hand grade considered to be one of the better constructed shoes in the world. Styles available for all occasions.

Fratelli Rossetti *Italy*. $300–450
COS, MSS
Classically styled, comfortable shoe. Styles available for all occasions.

Gravati *Italy*. $400–1,200
MSS
www.gravati.it
Very stylish, comfortable shoes. Available in styles appropriate for business and casual situations.

Edward Green *UK*. $300–750
MSS
www.edwardgreen.co.uk
Bench made in the UK. Primarily for business wear, but some casual styles. Refurbishing program.

Peter Huber *Italy*. $185–1,000
MSS, OL
www.peterhuber.com
Classically styled shoe. Models

available that work in business and casual situations.

Johnston & Murphy *USA*. $100–900
Cat, COO, COS, MSS, OL
www.johnstonmurphy.com
Well-constructed, comfortable shoes. Many styles, appropriate in all situations.

Silvano Lattanzi $1,800–3,000
MSS, NM
www.zintala.it
Superb, luxurious handmade shoe, perhaps the best footwear in the world. Styles appropriate for business or casual dress.

John Lobb *UK*. $500–1,500
COS, NM, MSS
www.johnlobb.com
Lobb's Handmade by Custom Fit are also considered by many to be the finest shoes in the world. Primarily for the office, but some casual styles.

Bruno Magli *Italy*. $235–500
COO, COS, MSS, NM, Saks
www.brunomagli.com
Great for both business and casual applications.

Mauri *Italy*. $600–1,200
MSS
www.maurishoes.com
Primarily exotic leathers and many unusual colors. Good selection in larger sizes available through Friedman's in Atlanta—store popular with larger men and professional athletes.

Mephisto *Italy*. $240–350
COS, MSS

www.mephisto.com
Reputed to be among the most comfortable in the world. Viewed as more casual shoe, but styles available for business as well. Factory refurbishment also available for less than $100 per pair.

Mezlan *Spain*. $175–400
MSS, Nord
www.mezlanshoes.com
Great value for the price. Some fashion-forward styles may not be appropriate in all office environments.

Moreschi *Italy*. $275–800
MSS
www.moreschi.it
Well-made, stylish shoe. Available in business and casual styles.

Cesare Paciotti *Italy*. $350–1,200
MSS
Mostly fashion-forward styles more appropriate for casual wear.

Donald J. Pliner *USA*. $200–350
COO, COS, MSS, Saks
www.donaldjpliner.com
Smart-looking, comfortable shoe. Italian made. More casual styles available, but some of the line works for business as well.

Sergio Rossi *Italy*. $350–800
COS, MSS
www.sergiorossi.it
Stylish, great-looking shoe made in styles that fit all occasions.

Santoni *Italy*. $350–800
COS, MSS, Nord
Classically styled, comfortable shoe. Primarily for the office, but some casual styles.

Sutor Mantellassi *Italy.* $250–800
MSS, NM, Saks
www.sutormantellassi.com
Great-looking shoe made in styles
that fit all occasions.

Terra Plana *UK.* $175–300
MSS
www.terraplana.com
Very comfortable shoe. Best
for casual and business casual
applications.

a. testoni *Italy.* $350–1,400
COS, MSS, NM
www.testoniusa.com
Well-made, stylish shoe, equally at
home in office or casual situations.

To Boot New York *USA.* $200–275
MSS, NM, Nord, OL
www.toboot.com
Italian-made shoes. Business or
casual applications.

Tod's *Italy.* $250–1,200
COO, COS, MSS, NM
www.tods.com
Extremely comfortable footwear.
Best known for driving and casual
shoes. However, many stylish shoes
for the office as well.

Michael Toschi *Italy.* $300–500
MSS
www.toschi.com
Extremely comfortable shoes with
high-tech, shock-absorber soles.
Unusual as well as traditional colors and styles appropriate for all
occasions.

H.S. Trask *USA.* $135–230
MSS, Nord, OL
www.hstrask.com

Very comfortable shoes made from
bison, elk, and longhorn sheep hides.
Economical factory refurbishment.
No leather-soled shoes—more for
casual and business casual occasions.

Laszlo Vass *Hungary.* $650–950
MSS
In the beginning of the last century
the master shoemakers of Budapest
were famous the world over. Today,
that great tradition lives on in the
hand-sewn shoes of Laszlo Vass,
author of the definitive book
Handmade Shoes for Men. The Vass
ready-to-wear and demi-custom
lines are completely handcrafted in
exactly the same manner as world-
class bespoke shoes. Styles appropriate for business and casual applications. Info@vass-shoes.com.

J. M. Weston *France.* $500–1,200
COS, MSS
Bench-made shoe, renowned for quality construction and superb fit. Styles
proper for office and casual wear.

Accessories Reference Guide

Below are additional resources for accessories such as belts, braces, hosiery (socks), jewelry (including cuff links), underwear, and leather goods (card cases, wallets, and so forth). The brands listed below specialize in the categories in which they are listed. Clothing lines that include accessories are covered in the World's Best Labels table earlier in the chapter.

2⁽ˣ⁾ist *USA*. Underwear $10–40
MSS, NM, Nord, Saks
www.2xist.com
Modern designs, reasonable pricing.

Bresciani *Italy*. Hosiery $20–30
MSS
www.bresciani.it
Well-made socks available in many different fabrics and stylish designs.

Byford *UK*. Hosiery $10–20
MSS
www.byfordsock.com
Quality socks, more conservative selection.

Coach *USA*. Belts and Leather Goods $50–275
COO, COS, Nord, Saks, OL
www.coach.com
Brand well known for quality and durability.

Crookhorn *USA*. Belts, Braces, and Hosiery $15–150
MSS, Nord
www.crookhorn.com
Great quality, reasonably priced.

Martin Dingman *USA*. Belts and Leather Goods, $50 and up
MSS, NM, Nord
www.martindingman.com

First quality, *Robb Report* Best of the Best for Furnishings, 2002.

Dolan & Bullock *USA*. Jewelry, $250–1,000
NM, Nord, Saks
www.colibri.com
Well-made cuff links and fine jewelry.

Dooney and Bourke *USA*. Belts and Leather Goods, $80–250
COO, COS, Nord, OL
www.dooneyandbourke.com
Long-lasting, well-constructed items.

Ghurka *USA*. Leather Goods $50–200
COO, COS, MSS, OL
www.ghurka.com
Label is known for rugged construction, durability, and classic style.

Hanro *Switzerland*. Underwear $40–70
NM
First-quality brand known for its soft cotton and superior fit.

John Hardy *Bali*. Jewelry, $100–700
NM, Saks

www.johnbali.com
Well-crafted, distinctive jewelry with signature armadillo texture and tropical themes.

Kieselstein-Cord *USA*. Jewelry, $250 and up
COS, NM, Saks
www.kieselstein-cord.com
Distinctive fine quality jewelry and cuff links featuring alligators and world peace themes in sterling silver.

Bill Lavin *USA*. Belts $75–140
MSS
Stylish, hand-tied belts for any occasion. Great quality.

Links of London *UK*. Jewelry, $100–300
OL
www.linksoflondon.com
Outstanding selection of attractive cuff links.

Colonel Littleton *USA*. Belts, Jewelry, Leather Goods $75–500
Cat, MSS, OL
www.colonellittleton.com

Nancy and Risé *USA*. Jewelry, $100–350
MSS, Nord
Quality cuff links in distinctive styles.

Pantherella *UK*. Hosiery, $20–50
MSS, NM, Nord
www.pantherella.co.uk
Great socks made in a wide assortment of fabrics and styles.

Robin Rotenier *USA*. Jewelry, $150–1,000
MSS, NM, Saks
www.robinrotenier.com

Impressive selection of whimsical novelty cuff links.

Jack Spade *USA*. Leather Goods $50–100
NM, Nord
www.jackspade.com
Affordable, quality leather goods, many with signature orange trim.

Robert Tateossian *UK*. Jewelry $100–3,000
MSS, Nord, OL, Saks
www.tateossian.co.uk
Impressive assortment of attractive cuff links and unusual jewelry.

Albert Thurston *UK*. Belts and Braces, $40–120
MSS, OL
www.albertthurston.com
Famous quality at affordable prices. Some items usually on sale at website.

Tiffany *USA*. Jewelry, $100 and up
COS, OL
www.tiffany.com
World-renowned name is synonymous with luxury. Simple silver cuff links, key rings, and money clips are affordable and are a great way to express timeless style.

Torino *USA*. Belts and Braces $40–400
MSS
www.torinobelts.com
Impressive assortment of great quality belts and braces. Exotic skins are a highlight of the collection.

Trafalgar *USA*. Belts and Braces, $50–200

COO, COS, MSS, NM, Nord, Saks
Popular, affordable, well-made
braces.

H.S. Trask *USA*. Belts and Leather
Goods, $50–75
Cat, MSS, OL
www.hstrask.com
Durable, well-made products. Usu-
ally some great Internet specials.

Louis Vuitton *France*. Belts, Jewelry,
and Leather Goods, $100 and up
COS, NM, Saks
www.louisvuitton.com
Products known the world over for
luxury, quality of construction,
and style. May be purchased online
at eLuxury (see chapter 9).

David Yurman *USA*. Jewelry, $250
and up
COS, NM, Saks
www.davidyurman.com
Attractive cuff links and jewelry
featuring signature cables combin-
ing fine quality gold and sterling
silver.

Zimmerli *Switzerland*. Underwear,
$50–70
MSS
www.zimmerlitextil.ch
World famous for luxury undergarments made with only the finest
cotton.

9

Online Shopping Guide

I've put together a list below of independent clothing stores, Internet-only retailers, and department stores who sell quality clothing over the Internet. Brands or designers designated in chapter 8 as OL (for online capability) are not relisted here. Also, I did not list any independent clothing stores or websites that did not also have e-commerce capability. Specialty store sites that are informational only are listed in chapter 10. I have not purchased items from most of the sites listed in this table; let the buyer beware.

When buying clothes over the Internet it's important to deal with a reputable company. If you're unsure about the firm you're dealing with, ask for and check references. When shopping at eBay, be sure to review feedback on the seller. If your Internet privacy is important to you, review the site's policy, and determine whether or not you're comfortable with it. Also make sure of the size and fit, and don't buy items you can't return. Your time is your most precious asset, and if you're not saving any by shopping online, and actually creating aggravation for yourself, then what's the point? When looking to purchase clothes online, visit www.MensSpecialty Retail.com often, where information will be more current.

Nevertheless, I've gotten some pretty good deals online, particularly at eBay, and am pleased to share what I've found below.

Following is a key to the terms used in chapter 9:

Accessories Includes listings for braces, belts, cuff links, formal wear, hosiery (socks), jewelry, pocket squares, swimwear, outerwear, toiletries, and undergarments. Bow ties are included in this category rather than neckwear because relatively few stores sell them. Anything of interest that normally wouldn't be listed in the other categories.

Casual Wear Button-up or pullover shirts (See Glossary, pp. 316, 322) jeans, knits, sweaters, and casual slacks (all trousers not made predominantly of wool or cashmere).

Dress Shirts Button-up shirts normally worn with a tie in a business formal situation.

Neckwear Neckties.

Shoes Leather (usually) items normally worn on your feet.

Tailored Clothing Suits, sport coats, cashmere or wool trousers sold unhemmed.

Custom Garment created exclusively for you, using your exact personal measurements. See chapter 5 for more detailed explanation.

M2M Made-to-Measure. See chapter 5 for more detailed explanation.

Independent Establishment that specializes in menswear but sells several different labels and types of clothing.

Outlet Store Retail outlet specializing in discounted merchandise.

2C Clothes

www.2cclothes.com
Nice selection of mostly casual
clothing for golf and weekend wear.
Some selections also appropriate for
business casual. Usually some items
on sale. Store hosted by Yahoo.

Casual Wear Joseph Abboud,
Tommy Bahama, Tundra

Maurice Abrahams

www.menswear.ie
Reasonable prices, although none
listed for neckwear as of this writing.

Dress Shirts Maurice Abrahams
Neckwear Maurice Abrahams,
Cerruti 1881, Ermenegildo Zegna
Tailored Clothing Cerruti, Cerruti
1881

Ashworth

www.ashworth.com
Also occasionally some quality
selections of discounted name-
brand ties. Check site frequently
for current selections.

Accessories Jewelry

Bauman's

www.baumans.com
Quality website from first-class
specialty store located in Little
Rock, AR (see chapter 10).
Interesting and distinctive items,
also online wardrobe consulting.

Accessories Art of Shaving toiletries;
Robert Talbott cuff links;
Pantherella hosiery; Martin
Dingman leather goods;
Normandy & Monroe outerwear
Casual Wear Bobby Jones, Jeff
Rose, Normandy & Monroe
Dress Shirts Robert Talbott
Shoes Alden, Allen Edmonds,

Mephisto, Santoni
Tailored Clothing Zanella,
Ermenegildo Zegna

Blue Fly

www.bluefly.com
The Internet's outlet store. Many
reputable brands available depend-
ing on when you visit. Merchandise
included from following labels:
Joseph Abboud, Giorgio Armani,
Jhane Barnes, Hugo Boss, Canali,
Cerruti, Kenneth Cole, Diesel,
Dolce & Gabbana, Alfred Dunhill,
Salvatore Ferragamo, Bobby Jones,
Donna Karan/DKNY, Calvin
Klein, Helmut Lang, Ralph Lauren,
Malo, Moreschi, Tateossian,
a. testoni, Tod's, Vestimenta,
Ermenegildo Zegna

Sizes are frequently limited; visit
often for best selection. Finding
larger sizes in particular can be
challenging. Prices are especially
good with coupons or when items
are in the clearance section. Great
return policy.

*Accessories, Casual Wear, Dress
Shirts, Neckwear, Shoes, Tailored
Clothing*

Christophier Custom Clothiers

www.christophier.com
Internet destination for Christophier
Custom Clothiers in Cleveland, OH
(see chapter 10). Some unique,
first-quality selections at reasonable prices.

Accessories Christophier belts; cuff
links; leather goods; pocket squares
Casual Wear Christophier
Dress Shirts Christophier private
label
Neckwear Genesis, Kolte, Richel

Dann-Online Men's Clothing

www.dann-online.com

Online independent store located in Indianapolis, IN. Interesting representative selections of many types of merchandise. Reasonable prices.

Accessories Ferrell Reed braces; Dann and Southwick formal wear; pocket squares
Casual Wear Bills Khakis, Dann
Dress Shirts Ferrell Reed
Neckwear Ferrell Reed
Shoes Alden
Tailored Clothing Joseph Abboud, Dann, Southwick

Direct Clothiers

www.directclothiers.com

Website founded by two former principal employees of Bullock & Jones specialty store in San Francisco. Best selection of Robert Talbott clothing available online. Also only online retail destination for Brioni and Oxxford.

Accessories Trafalgar belts; Robert Talbott bow ties; Hickey Freeman formal wear; Robert Talbott formal wear and outerwear; Byford hosiery
Dress Shirts Robert Talbott
Neckwear Robert Talbott
Tailored Clothing Brioni, Hickey Freeman, Oxxford

eBay

www.ebay.com

The Internet's thrift store. Selections from a myriad of reputable brands can be expected at the World's Online Marketplace™— Giorgio Armani, Luciano Barbera, Luigi Borrelli, Brioni, Dolce & Gabbana, Gucci, Gianluca Isaia, Kiton, Ralph Lauren, Lorenzini,

Oxxford, Prada, Ermenegildo Zegna, to name just a few. In my opinion the best values on the web. Many items are available new if you don't like used clothing. Knowing your size is very helpful; see my website for instructions on how to take proper measurements. Visit eBay often for best results.

Accessories, Casual Wear, Dress Shirts, Neckwear, Shoes, Tailored Clothing

Esuit

www.esuit.com

Great selection, lots of helpful information, and some great values for the young man who is building his wardrobe. Good return policy. Check frequently for best selection.

Accessories Many value-priced formal wear and outerwear options
Tailored Clothing Joseph Abboud, Hugo Boss, Kenneth Cole, DKNY, Hickey Freeman, cK Calvin Klein

eLuxury

www.eluxury.com

Official e-commerce site for brands listed; merchandise usually sold at full price. Selections offered change frequently; visit often for best results.

Accessories DKNY belts; Louis Vuitton leather goods
Casual Wear 7 for All Mankind, Hugo Boss, Marc Jacobs
Shoes Samsonite

Family Britches

www.familybritches.com

Online destination for two great New York area stores (see chapter 10).

Accessories Aquarius and Trafalgar belts; Robert Talbott cuff links, outerwear, and pocket squares; Rainforest outerwear
Casual Wear Bills Khakis
Dress Shirts Robert Talbott, Ermenegildo Zegna
Neckwear Robert Talbott

Forzieri
www.forzieri.com
Great Italian site for ties—large selections of modern designs you won't see anywhere else. Prices are reasonable.

Accessories Gianfranco Ferré belts; Forzieri bow ties and pocket squares
Neckwear Bagutta (nice selection of knits); Villa Bolgheri (more interesting and distinctive selections than usually seen in the U.S.), Roberto Cavalli, Dolce & Gabbana, Forzieri, Jean Paul Gaultier, Gucci, Leonard, Moschino, Valentino, Versace

Friedman's Shoes
www.largefeet.com
Excellent website for shoes, particularly in large sizes. Huge selection, first-rate customer service, frequent Internet price specials. Brick-and-mortar store is located in Atlanta, GA (see chapter 10).

Accessories Large selection of belts and socks to match purchased shoes
Shoes Bacco Bucci, Kenneth Cole, Mauri, Mezlan, Paolo de Marco, Donald J. Pliner

Franco's
www.francos.com
Excellent web destination. Fine

specialty store location in the Richmond, VA, area (see chapter 10) has posted a significant portion of its inventory on the Internet for convenient shopping for first-quality items. Shoe selection in particular is a highlight.

Accessories Assorted colognes; Torino and Trafalgar belts; Trafalgar leather braces; J.J. Weston cuff links; Barbour and Robert Talbott outerwear
Casual Wear Tommy Bahama, Barbour, Canali, Henry Cotton's, Bobby Jones, Paul & Shark, St. Croix, Tundra
Dress Shirts Canali, Gitman Bros., Robert Talbott, Ermenegildo Zegna
Neckwear Tommy Bahama, Breuer, Brioni, Burberry, Tino Cosma, Fabergé, Pancaldi, Robert Talbott
Shoes Allen Edmonds, Tommy Bahama, Lorenzo Banfi, Borgioli, Cole Haan, Gravati, Moreschi, Santoni
Tailored Clothing Tommy Bahama, Arnold Brant, Burberry, Canali, Hart, Schaffner & Marx, Hickey Freeman, Oxxford, Ermenegildo Zegna

Get Real Clothes
www.getrealclothes.com
Website for specialty stores that belong to the DLS Outfitters group. Added feature that directs shoppers to stores in their local area.

Accessories Torino belts; Gitman Bros. formal shirts; Viyella robes; Axis, Golden Bear, Johnston & Murphy, Remy outerwear
Casual Wear Tommy Bahama, Robert Barakett, Ike Behar,

Madeline Finn, Haupt, Keithmoor,
Lacoste, McKenzie Tribe, Raffi,
Tricots St. Raphael, Victorinox,
Viyella
Neckwear Bob Goodman & Co.
Tailored Clothing Joseph Abboud,
Ballin, Kenneth Cole, Keithmoor,
Lauren by Ralph Lauren, Tallia

Gifts2Gift
www.gifts2gift.com
Good selection of unusual, value-
priced items.

Accessories Bow ties; large selection
of cuff links and stud sets
Neckwear Lee Allison, Robert
Daskal, Genesis, Kolte, Richel

Granger Owings
www.grangerowings.com
Website for specialty store located
in Columbia, SC. Specializes in
updated traditional clothing.

Accessories Martin Dingman belts;
Royal Label formal wear; Colonel
Littleton gentleman's accessories
Casual Wear Granger Owings
Dress Shirts Kenneth Gordon
Neckwear Robert Talbott
Shoes Alden, Allen Edmonds
Tailored Clothing Granger Owings,
Royal Label

H. Herzfeld Clothiers
www.herzfeldonline.com
Internet destination for H. Herzfeld specialty store in Manhattan
(see chapter 10). Great selection of
distinctive accessories.

Accessories Nice selection of
Trafalgar Limited Edition braces;
Herzfeld and Tateossian cuff links;
Zimmerli undergarments

His Room
www.hisroom.com
Specializes in athletic socks and
underwear.

Accessories 2(x)ist, Hanro, and
Zimmerli undergarments

Maus and Hoffman
www.mausandhoffman.com
Website for Maus and Hoffman
specialty stores in Florida (see
chapter 10). E-commerce through
Catalog City. Many interesting and
unique items. Emphasis on resort
and warm weather wear.

Accessories Brioni, Maus and
Hoffman (good selection of exotic
leather) belts; Maus and Hoffman
hosiery; Paul and Shark outerwear;
Maus and Hoffman, Paul and
Shark swimwear; Maus and
Hoffman (pajamas also), Zimmerli
undergarments
Casual Wear Bobby Jones, Maus
and Hoffman, Paul and Shark
Neckwear Maus and Hoffman
(good selection of solid silk and
knit ties), Robert Talbott
Shoes Cole Haan, Bruno Magli,
Maus and Hoffman, Mephisto
Tailored Clothing Brioni, Hickey
Freeman, Maus and Hoffman

Men's Apparel
www.mensapparel.com
Site is managed through Yahoo.
Many value-priced items for traditional tastes.

Accessories Torino belts; Gitman
Bros. and Kenneth Gordon formal
wear; Colonel Littleton gentleman's accessories; Byford hosiery;
Aquascutum outerwear

Shoes Allen Edmonds, Magnanni, Mezlan
Casual Wear Kenneth Gordon
Dress Shirts Gitman Bros., Kenneth Gordon, MacCluer
Tailored Clothing H. Freeman & Sons, Southwick

Neiman Marcus
www.neimanmarcus.com
LARGE selection of interesting, quality items. Selection varies from season to season; visit often for best results.

Accessories Martin Dingman, Salvatore Ferragamo, Prada belts; Trafalgar Limited Edition braces; various colognes; Kieselstein-Cord, John Hardy, Robin Rotenier, David Yurman cuff links; Burberry, Salvatore Ferragamo, Prada, Jack Spade leather goods; Tommy Bahama, Hugo Boss, Burberry, Bobby Jones, Loro Piana, Polo Ralph Lauren, Ermenegildo Zegna, Zegna Sport outerwear; Kiehl's toiletries; 2(x)ist and Hanro undergarments
Casual Wear 7 for All Mankind, Tommy Bahama, Jhane Barnes, Burberry, Hugo Boss, Diesel, Bobby Jones, Loro Piana, Lucky Brand, Polo Ralph Lauren, Ermenegildo Zegna, Zegna Sport
Neckwear Brioni, Burberry, Charvet, Salvatore Ferragamo, Ermenegildo Zegna
Shoes Burberry, Cole Haan, Salvatore Ferragamo, Prada, Prada Sport
Tailored Clothing Zanella

Nordstrom
www.nordstrom.com
GREAT selection of value-priced merchandise, particularly shoes.

Assortment of merchandise changes from season to season; check regularly for best results.

Accessories Tommy Bahama, Cole Haan, Martin Dingman, Trafalgar belts; Joseph Abboud formal wear; Cole Haan hosiery; Jack Spade leather goods; Kenneth Cole, Façonnable, Bruno Magli, Andrew Marc, Remy outerwear; Façonnable swimwear, Polo Ralph Lauren undergarments
Casual Wear Joseph Abboud, Tommy Bahama, Hugo Boss, Burberry, Kenneth Cole, Diescl, Façonnable, Bobby Jones, Lucky Brand, Mavi, Polo Jeans Co., Polo Ralph Lauren, Tricots St. Raphael
Neckwear Robert Talbott
Shoes Tommy Bahama, Kenneth Cole, Cole Haan, Allen Edmonds, Johnston & Murphy, Bruno Magli, Mephisto, Mezlan, Polo Ralph Lauren
Tailored Clothing Joseph Abboud

Raffaello
www.raffaelloties.com
Italian website with large and varied selection from prestigious modern European labels. Merchandise discounted somewhat. Selection varies; visit often for best results.

Accessories Gucci, Prada, Versace belts; Raffaello cuff links; Dolce & Gabbana, Gucci, Prada, Raffaello, Versace leather goods; Dolce & Gabbana, Paul Smith undergarments
Casual Wear Gucci
Dress Shirts Gucci, Dolce & Gabbana, Prada, Raffaello, Versace, Ermenegildo Zegna
Neckwear Giorgio Armani, Canali, Corneliani, Leonard, Moschino, Versace, Ermenegildo Zegna

Shoes CoSTUME NATIONAL, Gucci, Bruno Magli, Cesare Paciotti, Prada, Raffaello, Tod's, Versace

Saks Fifth Avenue
www.saksfifthavenue.com
Huge selection of interesting, quality items. Selection varies from season to season, some items usually on sale; visit often for best results.

Accessories Cole Haan, Salvatore Ferragamo belts; Alfred Dunhill collar stays and cuff links, John Hardy cuff links and jewelry; Hugo Boss, Ermenegildo Zegna formal wear; Brioni hosiery; Bobby Jones outerwear; Hugo Boss, Moschino, Victorinox, Zegna Sport swimwear; Art of Shaving toiletries; 2(x)ist and Hanro undergarments
Casual Wear Joseph Abboud, Ike Behar, Hugo Boss, Burberry, Corneliani, Gran Sasso, Moschino, Tricots St. Raphael, John Varvatos, Victorinox, Ermenegildo Zegna, Zegna Sport
Dress Shirts Hugo Boss, Corneliani, Dolce & Gabbana, Ermenegildo Zegna
Neckwear Brioni, Burberry, Canali, Salvatore Ferragamo, Hickey Freeman, Ermenegildo Zegna
Shoes Tommy Bahama, Kenneth Cole, Cole Haan, Salvatore Ferragamo, Bruno Magli, Donald J. Pliner, To Boot New York, John Varvatos
Tailored Clothing Joseph Abboud, Hugo Boss, Canali, Corneliani, Hickey Freeman, Ermenegildo Zegna

Mark Shale
www.markshale.com

Excellent website for the Mark Shale chain of specialty stores, headquartered in the Chicago area (see chapter 10). Great selection of knits for business casual. Check seasonal sales and clearance section for outstanding values.

Accessories Cole Haan, Mark Shale belts; Robert Talbott cuff links; Cole Haan, Pantherella hosiery; Andrew Marc, Mark Shale outerwear; Tommy Bahama, Victorinox swimwear
Casual Wear Tommy Bahama, Ballin, Robert Barakett, Scott Barber, Ted Baker, Burberry, Gran Sasso, Keithmoor, Mani, Nat Nast, Mark Shale, Robert Talbott, Tricots St. Raphael, Zanella, Ermenegildo Zegna
Dress Shirts Joseph Abboud, Ike Behar, Mani, Robert Talbott, Ermenegildo Zegna
Neckwear Joseph Abboud, Ike Behar, Robert Talbott, Ermenegildo Zegna
Shoes Cole Haan, Donald J. Pliner
Tailored Clothing Joseph Abboud, Corneliani, Mani, Zanella

Seize Sur Vingt
www.16sur20.com
Internet destination featuring ready-to-wear shirts from this Manhattan store, featured in *GQ* in 2002 as one of the world's best choices for custom shirts.

Dress Shirts Seize Sur Vingt

Ben Silver
www.bensilver.com
Remarkable selection of quality items at this web address for renowned London and Charleston,

SC, specialty store. Great values at online factory outlet.

Accessories Huge selection of bow ties; huge selection of Ben Silver cuff links and jewelry; Ben Silver formal wear; Ben Silver hosiery; Aquascutum, Barbour, Ben Silver outerwear; Creed toiletries
Casual Wear Scott Barber, Ike Behar, Bills Khakis, Charleston Khakis, Lacoste, Ben Silver, Viyella
Dress Shirts Hilditch & Key, Ben Silver
Neckwear Fabergé, Kiton, Leonard, Ben Silver
Shoes Alden, Crockett & Jones
Tailored Clothing Aquascutum, Nick Hilton, Loro Piana, Oxxford, Ben Silver

Suit Yourself
www.suityourself.com
Internet destination for Fairfield Clothiers of Fairfield, CT (see chapter 10).

Accessories Mezlan belts; Brixton & Gill, Duchamp cuff links; Ferrell Reed, Gitman Bros., Kenneth Gordon, Jack Victor formal wear; Cardinal of Canada outerwear; Ferrell Reed pocket squares, Gitman Bros. undergarments
Casual Wear Dalmine, Kenneth Gordon, Nick Hilton
Dress Shirts Ferrell Reed, Gitman Bros., Kenneth Gordon
Neckwear Duchamp
Shoes Alden, Magnanni, Mezlan
Tailored Clothing Belvest, Hilton, Keithmoor, H. Oritsky, Tallia, Jack Victor, M2M Ermenegildo Zegna

Victor Talbots
www.victortalbots.com

Website for Victor Talbots specialty store in Greenvale, NY (see chapter 10). Incredible selection of evening and formal wear. Largest, most complete selection of Trafalgar Limited Edition braces available anywhere.

Accessories Moreschi, Victor Talbot exotic leather belts; Victor Talbot and Trafalgar Limited Edition braces; Hugo Boss, Brioni, Luigi Borrelli, d'Avenza, Eton, Kiton, Ralph Lauren Purple Label, Polo Ralph Lauren, Victor Talbot formal wear; Ralph Lauren Purple Label overcoats; alligator leather goods; assorted pocket squares; satin smoking jackets; walking sticks
Neckwear Formal wear bow ties and neckties by Hugo Boss Couture, Gianfranco Ferré Couture, Leonard, Ralph Lauren Purple Label, Pancaldi, Victor Talbot Couture, Yves St. Laurent Couture
Shoes Cole Haan, Bruno Magli, Moreschi, Victor Talbot exotic leathers

The Custom Shop
www.customshop.com
Internet destination for various Custom Shop locations around the U.S. (see chapter 10).

Accessories Belts and wallets, including exotic skins; cuff links; Allen Edmonds socks and belts
Casual Wear Custom Shop
Dress Shirts Custom Shop
Neckwear Genesis, Kolte, Richel

Ties.Com
www.ties.com
Excellent assortment of discounted Ferré, Pancaldi, and Versace.

Neckwear Lee Allison, Altea, Villa
Bolgheri, Duchamp, Timothy
Everest (Daks-Simpson), Fabergé,
Gianfranco Ferré, Hubert,
Pancaldi, Versace, XMI, YSL

Tip Top Shoes

www.tiptopshoes.com
Internet destination for this independent New York City shoe store.

Shoes Kenneth Cole, Cole Haan,
Diesel, Allen Edmonds, Johnston
& Murphy, Mephisto

YooX

www.yoox.com
Great website for those interested
in modern labels, which might
include Hugo Boss, CoSTUME
NATIONAL, Dolce & Gabbana,
ETRO, Gucci, Helmut Lang,
Prada, Jil Sander, Paul Smith,
Yohji Yamamoto, Yves St. Laurent,
or Ermenegildo Zegna. Check
often for best results.

*Accessories, Casual Wear, Dress
Shirts, Neckwear, Shoes, Tailored
Clothing*

Zappos.Com

www.zappos.com
Large selection of Tommy Bahama
and Donald J. Pliner footwear.

Accessories Tommy Bahama,
Mezlan belts
Shoes Bacco Bucci, Tommy Bahama,
Kenneth Cole, Diesel, Bruno
Magli, Mezlan, Donald J. Pliner

10

Brick-and-Mortar Shopping Guide

The final chapter of *The Men's Clothing Guide* contains information to help you physically locate your favorite quality clothing. Unfortunately, I wasn't able to visit every store or every metropolitan area in America. But you will find over 1200 stores that I visited *personally* to bring you firsthand information about aesthetics, quality of service, and merchandise mix. I've alphabetized according to the most common use of the label or brand name rather than by first name. Stores are arranged alphabetically in the following order:

- Metro Area
- State (where applicable)
- City
- Name of mall or store
- Alphabetically within the mall (where applicable)

Store types are not added where I believe you're familiar enough with the store's brand to know what type of store it is. Examples of this would be Nordstrom or Neiman Marcus for department stores, or Ralph Lauren or Lucky Brand Dungarees for company-owned boutiques. If you're still unsure how to categorize a store, search the database at www.MensSpecialtyRetail.com for details. These establishments are sorted into more than 35 metropolitan areas and include about 300 independent specialty stores. The descriptions of brands listed are according to my most recent visit or verification prior to publication. In rare cases, descriptions are omitted, meaning I haven't visited the store yet but felt it was important for you to know about the store based on its reputation. As I continue to travel and change information, I will update my website; log on to www.MensSpecialtyRetail.com for the most current data. If you have a favorite that I missed, there's a place on my site to submit store information.

Following is a key to the terms used in chapter 10, and repeated from chapter 9 for your convenience:

Accessories Includes listings for braces, belts, cuff links, formal wear, hosiery (socks), jewelry, pocket squares, swimwear, outerwear, toiletries, and undergarments. Bow ties are included in this category rather than neckwear because relatively few stores sell them. Anything of interest that normally wouldn't be listed in the other categories.

Casual Wear Button-up or pullover shirts (see glossary, pp. 316, 322), jeans, knits, sweaters, and casual slacks (all trousers not made predominantly of wool or cashmere).

Dress Shirts Button-up shirts normally worn with a tie in a business formal situation.

Neckwear Neckties.

Shoes Leather (usually) items normally worn on your feet.

Tailored Clothing Suits, sport coats, cashmere or wool trousers sold unhemmed.

Custom Garment created exclusively for you, using your exact personal measurements. See chapter 5 for more detailed explanation.

M2M Made-to-Measure. See chapter 5 for more detailed explanation.

Independent Establishment that specializes in menswear but sells several different labels and types of clothing.

Outlet Store Retail outlet specializing in discounted merchandise.

Metro Area: Atlanta

H. Stockton, North Point
Independent
7300 Northpoint Pkwy., Alpharetta,
GA 30022 (770)772-0800
Attractive store in great location.
Excellent customer service. Clothing
for both European and updated
traditional tastes.

Accessories Good selection of bow
ties, cuff links, Barbour outerwear,
and Robert Comstock leather out-
erwear
Casual Wear Scott Barber, Barbour,
Ike Behar, Bills Khakis, Jeff Rose,
H. Stockton, Robert Talbott,
Zanella
Dress Shirts Ike Behar, H. Stockton,
Robert Talbott
Neckwear Breuer, Ferragamo,
H. Stockton, Robert Talbott
Shoes Alden, Cole Haan
Tailored Clothing Canali, Hickey
Freeman, Samuelsohn, Southwick,
H. Stockton, Jack Victor

Dick Ferguson's
Independent
Dick Ferguson, Proprietor/
Lee Allen, Sales
Beechwood Shopping Center,
Athens, GA 30606 (706) 548-7246
www.dickfergusons.com
Family business begun in 1934.
Great-looking store in convenient
location. Helpful, polite sales staff.
Clothing primarily for updated tra-
ditional tastes.

Accessories Trafalgar belts and
braces; good selection of cuff links
and pocket squares; Colonel
Littleton gentleman's accessories;
Bosca leather goods

Casual Wear Bills Khakis, Bobby
Jones, Lacoste, Polo by Ralph
Lauren
Dress Shirts Dick Ferguson, Polo
by Ralph Lauren, Robert Talbott
Neckwear Robert Talbott
Shoes Cole Haan, Johnston &
Murphy, H.S. Trask
Tailored Clothing Hart, Schaffner
& Marx, Samuelsohn (also M2M),
Southwick, Jack Victor

George Gibson's Men's Wear
Independent
Andy Gibson, Proprietor
Colonial Promenade Beechwood, 196
Alps Rd., Athens, GA 30606 (706) 548-
4663 www.georgegibsons.com
Family business begun in 1964.
Large, attractive store in great
location. Excellent customer serv-
ice. Clothing primarily for updated
traditional tastes. Mr. Gibson is a
pleasure to deal with.

Accessories Brighton and Allen
Edmonds belts; Crookhorn braces;
nice selection of cuff links and
pocket squares; LB Evans slippers
Casual Wear Joseph Abboud, Axis,
Tommy Bahama, Ike Behar, Berle,
Bills Khakis, Burberry, Cutter &
Buck, Gitman Bros., Kenneth
Gordon, Lacoste, Riscatto
Portofino, Jeff Rose
Dress Shirts Ike Behar, Enro,
Gitman Bros., Kenneth Gordon,
XMI
Neckwear Joseph Abboud,
Fabergé, Ferrell Reed, Countess
Mara, JZ Richards, XMI
Shoes Clarks, Allen Edmonds,
Sebago, H.S. Trask, Zelli
Tailored Clothing Joseph Abboud,
Berle, Burberry, Chaps by Ralph

Lauren, Coppley, Corbin, Haspel, Lauren by Ralph Lauren, Majer, Austin Reed, Zanella

Andrew
Independent
Andrew Capron, Owner
1545 Peachtree Rd., N.E., Atlanta, GA 30309 (404)607-1747
www.andrewatlanta.com
Hip, energetic boutique with great shopping atmosphere and informed, friendly salespeople. Also a women's store. Unique and interesting collections.

Accessories Paul Smith and Tateossian cuff links
Casual Wear Avon Celli, ETRO, Paul Smith
Dress Shirts Ergasterium of Napoli, ETRO, Paul Smith
Neckwear Ergasterium of Napoli, Paul Smith
Shoes J. Finnestrier, Paul Smith
Tailored Clothing Ergasterium of Napoli M2M, Paul Smith
Sales Semiannual

Custom Clothing of Atlanta
Independent
Al Kleber, President
6095 Barfield Rd., N.E., Ste. 110, Atlanta, GA 30328 (404)843-3765
Mr. Kleber is a congenial and knowledgeable third-generation tailor. His fabrics are exquisite, with a huge selection to choose from. I viewed garments in various stages of assembly and can vouch for Custom's first-rate construction. This establishment has been voted one of the thirty best tailor's shops in the U.S. by *Town & Country* magazine, and the best

custom tailor in Atlanta by *Atlanta* magazine.

Accessories Good selection of cuff links and pocket squares; great selection of Breuer, Crookhorn, Durango, and Albert Thurston braces
Casual Wear Avon Celli, Custom
Dress Shirts Custom, Oxxford
Neckwear Best selection on hand of any custom store I've seen— Dormeuil, Charles Hill, Michelson's, Robert Talbott, Venanzi, XMI

Friedman's Shoes
Independent
Bruce Teilhaber, Owner
209 Mitchell St., Atlanta, GA 30303 (404)524-1311 www.largefeet.com
(see chapter 9)
World-famous shoe emporium. Huge selection of shoes in every style, shape, color, and size imaginable. Exotic skins like ostrich, alligator, crocodile, and lizard. Athletic shoes on ground floor; closeout shoes are on second floor at enormous markdowns. Current season's stock on third floor, as well as marked-down exotic leathers. Highly recommended.

Shoes Davanzanti, Mauri, Mezlan, Paolo de Marco, Donald J. Pliner

Guffey's
Independent
Don Guffey and Neil Guffey, Owners
Tower Place 100 Building, 3340 Peachtree Rd., Atlanta, GA 30326 (404)231-0044 www.guffeys.com
Spacious, elegant store with first-rate customer service. The Guffeys have 50 years' experience in the retail business, and their staff is

very knowledgeable as well. Also a barbershop in the rear of the establishment.

Accessories Belts; Trafalgar braces (including great selection of Limited Edition); Colonel Littleton gentleman's accessories; leather outerwear
Casual Wear Axis, Scott Barber, Bills Khakis, Barry Bricken, Burma Bibas, Robert Comstock, Gran Sasso, Bobby Jones, John McCoy, One of a Kind (Guffey's house label), Jeff Rose
Dress Shirts Ike Behar, Gitman Bros., Kenneth Gordon, Robert Talbott, Geneva and Gambert Custom
Neckwear Villa Bolgheri, Countess Mara, R. Hanauer, Fumigalli's
Shoes Cole Haan
Tailored Clothing Belvest, Hickey Freeman, Alan Lebow, One of a Kind, Oxxford, Saint Andrews, Jack Victor, Zanella, custom fabrics by Scabal, Dormeuil, Loro Piana, Schofield & Smith
Sales Semiannual

LENOX SQUARE MALL
Location and Stores:
3393 Peachtree Rd., N.E., Atlanta, GA 30326 www.shopsimon.com

Bally
(404)231-0327 www.bally.com

Bernini
(404)841-6664 www.bernini.com
Accessories Interesting selection of custom leather outerwear and exotic leather shoes
Casual Wear Ermenegildo Zegna

BOSS Hugo Boss
(404)841-9320 www.hugoboss.com

Brooks Brothers
(404)237-7000
www.brooksbrothers.com

Burberry
(404)231-5550 www.burberry.com

Coach
(404)237-6297 www.coach.com

Hermès
(404)233-1011 www.hermes.com

Johnston & Murphy
(404)261-6529
www.johnstonmurphy.com

Lacoste
(404)842-9353 www.lacoste.com

Ralph Lauren
(404)261-2663 www.polo.com

Neiman Marcus
(404)266-8200
www.neimanmarcus.com
Very nice store, great inventory and customer service. LARGE Polo Ralph Lauren, Ermenegildo Zegna, and Giorgio Armani selections and in-store boutiques.

Casual Wear Giorgio Armani, Jhane Barnes, Brioni, Diesel, Dolce & Gabbana, Polo Ralph Lauren, Ermenegildo Zegna
Dress Shirts Giorgio Armani, Luigi Borrelli, Brioni, Kiton, Turnbull & Asser, Ermenegildo Zegna
Neckwear Giorgio Armani, Massimo Bizzocchi, Brioni, Salvatore Ferragamo, Ermenegildo Zegna
Tailored Clothing Giorgio

Armani, Brioni, Hickey
Freeman, Kiton, Oxxford, Polo
Ralph Lauren, Ermenegildo
Zegna

Mark Shale
Independent
(404)231-0600 www.markshale.com
Large store with ample selection. Sales staff knowledgeable
and congenial.

Casual Wear Ted Baker, Scott
Barber, Mark Shale, Tricots
St. Raphael, Ermenegildo Zegna
Dress Shirts Joseph Abboud, Ike
Behar, Hugo Boss, Mark Shale,
Ermenegildo Zegna
Neckwear Joseph Abboud,
Luciano Barbera, Massimo
Bizzocchi, Robert Talbott,
Ermenegildo Zegna
Shoes Cole Haan, Donald J.
Pliner, To Boot New York,
Ermenegildo Zegna
Tailored Clothing Joseph
Abboud, Hugo Boss, Corneliani,
Mark Shale, Ermenegildo Zegna,
Pal Zileri
Sales Semiannual

H. Stockton
Independent
(404)233-1608
Attractive store in great location. Excellent customer service.
Clothing for both European and
updated traditional tastes.

Accessories Good selection of
bow ties, cuff links, Barbour
outerwear, and Robert
Comstock leather outerwear
Casual Wear Scott Barber,
Barbour, Ike Behar, Bills Khakis,
Jeff Rose, H. Stockton, Robert

Talbott, Zanella
Dress Shirts Ike Behar,
H. Stockton, Robert Talbott
Neckwear Breuer, Ferragamo,
H. Stockton, Robert Talbott
Shoes Alden, Cole Haan
Tailored Clothing Canali, Hickey
Freeman, Samuelsohn,
Southwick, H. Stockton, Jack
Victor

Versace Jeans Couture
(404)848-1435 www.versace.com

Louis Vuitton
(404)266-3674
www.louisvuitton.com

PERIMETER MALL
Location and Stores:
4400 Ashford Dunwoody Rd., Atlanta,
GA 30346 www.perimetermall.com

Brooks Brothers
(770)394-9051
www.brooksbrothers.com

Coach
(770)393-9303 www.coach.com

Johnston & Murphy
(770)393-8297
www.johnstonmurphy.com

Nordstrom
(770)394-1141 www.nordstrom.com

Casual Wear Joseph Abboud,
Jhane Barnes, Ermenegildo
Zegna
Dress Shirts Ike Behar, Robert
Talbott
Neckwear Robert Talbott, XMI,
Ermenegildo Zegna
Tailored Clothing Corneliani,
Ermenegildo Zegna

PHIPPS PLAZA
Location and Stores:
3500 Peachtree Rd., N.E., Atlanta, GA
30326 www.shopsimon.com

A/X Armani Exchange
(404)365-9765
www.giorgioarmani.com

Kenneth Cole
(404)261-2653
www.kennethcole.com

Cole Haan
(404)233-6634 www.colehaan.com

Gucci
(404)233-4899 www.gucci.com

Saks Fifth Avenue
(404)261-7234
www.saksfifthavenue.com
Large store with atypical, interesting inventory. Giorgio Armani, Prada, and Ermenegildo Zegna in-store boutiques.

Casual Wear Giorgio Armani, Henry Cotton's, Polo Ralph Lauren, Prada, Ermenegildo Zegna
Dress Shirts Giorgio Armani, Prada, Ermenegildo Zegna
Neckwear Giorgio Armani, Brioni, Prada, Stefano Ricci, Ermenegildo Zegna
Tailored Clothing Giorgio Armani, Corneliani, Prada, Vestimenta, Ermenegildo Zegna

Jil Sander
(404)237-8300 www.jilsander.com

St. Croix
(404)816-8393
www.stcroixshop.com

Gianni Versace
(404)814-0664 www.versace.com

Sebastian's Closet
Independent
Bob Kuchenbecker, President/Jerry Lemno, Store Manager
3222 Peachtree Rd., N.E., Atlanta, GA
30305 (404)365-9033
Caters to the sophisticated Atlanta male and features many great updates on classic ideas, as well as fresh ideas for upscale dressing. Excellent customer service.

Accessories Art of Shaving toiletries
Casual Wear Alberto, Axis, Haupt, Marzotto Lab, Nat Nast, Georg Roth, Signum, Zanella, Bernard Zins
Dress Shirts Canali, Eton, Lorenzini
Neckwear Sevica, Tino Cosma, Daniel Craig
Shoes Donald J. Pliner
Tailored Clothing Canali, Vestimenta, Zanella, Pal Zileri

H. Stockton, Downtown
Independent
191 Peachtree Rd., N.E., Suite 130, Atlanta, GA 30303 (800)923-7741 or (404)523-7741
Across from Macy's. Attractive store in great location. Excellent customer service. Clothing for both European and updated traditional tastes.

Accessories Good selection of bow ties, cuff links, Barbour outerwear, and Robert Comstock leather outerwear
Casual Wear Scott Barber, Barbour, Ike Behar, Bills Khakis, Jeff Rose, H. Stockton, Robert Talbott, Zanella

Dress Shirts Ike Behar, H. Stockton, Robert Talbott
Neckwear Breuer, Ferragamo, H. Stockton, Robert Talbott
Shoes Alden, Cole Haan
Tailored Clothing Canali, Hickey Freeman, Samuelsohn, Southwick, H. Stockton, Jack Victor

H. Stockton, Overton Park
Independent
Overton Park, 3625 Cumberland Blvd., Suite 100, Atlanta, GA 30339
(770)984-1111
Located at intersection of Cumberland Blvd. and I-75. Drive-up parking. Attractive store in great location. Excellent customer service. Clothing for both European and updated traditional tastes.

Accessories Good selection of bow ties, cuff links, Barbour outerwear, and Robert Comstock leather outerwear
Casual Wear Scott Barber, Barbour, Ike Behar, Bills Khakis, Jeff Rose, H. Stockton, Robert Talbott, Zanella
Dress Shirts Ike Behar, H. Stockton, Robert Talbott
Neckwear Breuer, Ferragamo, H. Stockton, Robert Talbott
Shoes Alden, Cole Haan
Tailored Clothing Canali, Hickey Freeman, Samuelsohn, Southwick, H. Stockton, Jack Victor

H. Stockton, Park Place
Independent
4505 Ashford Dunwoody Rd., Atlanta, GA 30346 (770)396-1300
Great-looking store in convenient location. Excellent customer serv-

ice. Clothing for both European and updated traditional tastes.

Accessories Good selection of bow ties, cuff links, Barbour outerwear, and Robert Comstock leather outerwear
Casual Wear Scott Barber, Barbour, Ike Behar, Bills Khakis, Jeff Rose, H. Stockton, Robert Talbott, Zanella
Dress Shirts Ike Behar, H. Stockton, Robert Talbott
Neckwear Breuer, Ferragamo, H. Stockton, Robert Talbott
Shoes Alden, Cole Haan
Tailored Clothing Canali, Hickey Freeman, Samuelsohn, Southwick, H. Stockton, Jack Victor

NORTH GEORGIA PREMIUM OUTLETS
Location and Stores:
800 Highway 400 South, Dawsonville, GA 30534 www.premiumoutlets.com

Brooks Brothers
(706)216-2865
www.brooksbrothers.com

Kenneth Cole
(706)216-8315
www.kennethcole.com

Cole Haan
(706)216-8160 www.colehaan.com

Hugo Boss
(706)265-8150 www.hugoboss.com

Johnston & Murphy
(706)216-4252
www.johnstonmurphy.com

Polo Ralph Lauren Factory Store
(706)216-6618 www.polo.com

Saks Off Fifth
(706)216-4087
www.saksfifthavenue.com

Casual Wear Kenneth Cole, Diesel, La Zetagi, Lucky Brand, Moreno Martini Da Firenze, Ermenegildo Zegna, Zegna Sport
Dress Shirts Ike Behar, Hugo Boss, Burberry
Neckwear Hugo Boss, Burberry, Gianfranco Ferré, Ermenegildo Zegna
Tailored Clothing Joseph Abboud, Giorgio Armani, Hugo Boss, Corneliani, Dolce & Gabbana, Zanella

Metro Area: Austin

By George
Independent
Matt & Kathy Culmo, Owners
524 N. Lamar Blvd., Austin, TX 78703
(512)472-5951
Hip, attractive shopping environment with many fresh and unique new clothing lines. Prompt personable customer service; the Culmos are great to work with.

Accessories Paul Smith cuff links; Janine Payer jewelry
Casual Wear Coast, CoSTUME NATIONAL, Levi's Premium, Poggianti, Paul Smith
Dress Shirts Liberty, Orlando, Poggianti
Neckwear Gallieni
Shoes Buttero, CoSTUME NATIONAL, Dries Van Noten

Capra & Cavelli
Independent
Jeff Friedman, Owner/

Kenneth Miller, Sales
3500 Jefferson, #110, Austin, TX 78731
(512)450-1919 www.capracavelli.com
Attractive, pleasant shopping environment. Friendly and helpful sales staff. Women's store carrying Vestimenta and Bernard Zins as well.

Accessories Good selection of cuff links; Colonel Littleton gentleman's accessories; Ghurka leather goods; Robert Comstock, Jose Luis, Remy and Sanyo leather outerwear
Casual Wear Anthology, Ted Baker, Jhane Barnes, Casa Moda, Dalmine, Andrea Fenzi, Gran Sasso, Haupt, Per Lui, Quick Reflex, Arnold Zimberg
Dress Shirts Ike Behar, Tino Cosma
Neckwear Altea, Jhane Barnes, Tino Cosma, Robert Talbott, XMI
Shoes Cole Haan, Magnanni, Santoni, To Boot New York, Zelli
Tailored Clothing Belvest (also M2M), Hugo Boss, Corneliani (also M2M), Marzotto Lab, Oxxford M2M, Ravazzollo (also M2M), Tallia, Linnea Trussini, Vestimenta (also M2M)
Sales Semiannual, January and July

Estrella Tailors
Independent
Buddy Estrella, Proprietor
3801 N. Capital of Texas Hwy., Ste. 160, Austin, TX 78746 (512)327-2567
www.gatlinestrella.com
Attractive store—high-quality inventory of updated traditional clothing. Mr. Estrella was most hospitable; it was a pleasure to visit his establishment.

Accessories William E. Hill cuff links; Golden Bear leather outerwear

Casual Wear Acorn, Tommy Bahama, Scott Barber, Ike Behar, Berle, Charleston Khakis, Hickey Freeman, Raffi, St. Croix, Reyn Spooner, Tricots St. Raphael, Viyella, Zanella
Dress Shirts Ike Behar (also M2M), Eton, Thomas Mason (M2M), Oxxford
Neckwear Jhane Barnes, Oxxford, Ferrell Reed, Richel, Robert Talbott, XMI
Shoes Tommy Bahama, Cole Haan, Allen Edmonds, Zilli
Tailored Clothing Hickey Freeman (also M2M), Oxxford (also M2M), Tallia (also M2M)

Johnstone Made to Measure Men's Clothing
Independent
James Johnstone, Owner
2905 San Gabriel Ave., Ste. 201, Austin, TX 78705 (512)478-5637
Very attractive, wood-lined store. Mr. Johnstone is very knowledgeable about custom clothing and was a pleasure to talk with.

Accessories Brioni, Oxxford, and Carrot & Gibb formal wear
Casual Wear Bella Collezioni, Madeline Finn, Fred Perry, Robert Talbott, XMI
Dress Shirts Robert Talbott ready-to-wear and custom, Hamilton custom
Neckwear Brioni, Carrot & Gibb, Oxxford, Robert Talbott
Shoes Polo Ralph Lauren
Tailored Clothing Brioni, Oxxford, Southwick, all also M2M

Keepers
Independent
Chuck Haidet, Managing Partner/

Ed Hite and Tanya Robinson, Sales
1004 W. 38th St., Austin, TX 78705 (512)302-3664
www.keepersclothing.com
Excellent store with quality merchandise and first-rate customer service.

Accessories Custom belts and buckles; cuff links; Ike Behar formal shirts; Comstock leather outerwear
Casual Wear Joseph Abboud, Acorn, Axis, Jhane Barnes, Hugo Boss, Barry Bricken, Dalmine, Equilibrio, ISDA & Co., Bobby Jones, Jeff Rose, St. Croix, Ermenegildo Zegna, Zegna Sport
Dress Shirts Joseph Abboud, Acorn, Ike Behar (also M2M), Eton, Rodin, Robert Talbott, Ermenegildo Zegna
Neckwear Joseph Abboud, Jhane Barnes, Ike Behar, Tino Cosma, Hubert, Robert Talbott, Ermenegildo Zegna
Shoes Cole Haan, Bruno Magli, Donald J. Plincr
Tailored Clothing Joseph Abboud, Jhane Barnes (also M2M), Burberry (also M2M), Rodin, Tallia, Tombolini, Zanella, Ermenegildo Zegna (also M2M), Zegna Soft

Neiman Marcus Last Call
Brodie Oaks Shopping Center, 4115 Capital of Texas Hwy. South, Austin, TX 78704 (512)447-0701
www.neimanmarcus.com
One of the best Last Calls I visited. Excellent assortment of quality merchandise at great discounts.

Casual Wear Brioni, Ralph Lauren Purple Label, Vestimenta, Ermenegildo Zegna

Dress Shirts Ike Behar, Luigi
Borrelli, Lorenzini
Neckwear Ermenegildo Zegna
Tailored Clothing Armani, Jhane
Barnes, Corneliani, Polo Ralph
Lauren, Ermenegildo Zegna

Texas Clothiers
Independent
Dain Higdon, Owner
2905 San Gabriel, Ste. 102, Austin, TX
78705 (512)478-4956
Mr. Higdon prides himself on the
unique accessories he carries. He
likes to inventory clothes that take
the Texas heat into account—
structured but unlined and super-
lightweight fabrics. The accessories
alone are worth a visit to this great
store.
Accessories Almost too numerous
to mention—exotic leather belts;
custom-made silver belt buckles;
Trafalgar braces (including Limited
Edition); cuff links made from
Republic of Texas antique army
and navy buttons, and other
unusual cuff links; a fine assortment of cummerbunds and unusual matching bow ties; Colonel
Littleton gentleman's accessories;
Panamanian straw hats in the summer; Swiss Army knives; great
selection of pocket squares; a great
selection of lightweight and
Comstock leather outerwear; a
good selection of Hawaiian shirts;
and handmade walking sticks
Casual Wear Acorn, Axis, Scott
Barber, Burma Bibas, Kahala, Nat
Nast, Tori Richard, Reyn Spooner,
Texas Clothiers, Tulliano
Dress Shirts Ike Behar, Luigi
Borrelli, Canali, Hickey Freeman,
Kenneth Gordon, Venanzi,

Zanella, Independent custom
Neckwear Ike Behar, Canali,
Hickey Freeman, Ferrell Reed,
yAprè
Shoes Alden, Allen Edmonds (spe-
cial order), Cole Haan, Bruno
Magli, Mezlan (special order),
H.S. Trask
Tailored Clothing Aquascutum,
Canali, Coppley (also M2M),
Hickey Freeman (also M2M)

THE ARBORETUM
Location and Stores:
Market 9722 Great Hills Trail, Austin,
TX 78759

Tommy Bahama
(512)241-1888
www.tommybahama.com
Large inventory, spacious store,
pleasant shopping experience.

Coach
(512)345-0610 www.coach.com

Saks Fifth Avenue
(512)231-3700
www.saksfifthavenue.com
No tailored clothing at this Saks
location.
Casual Wear Giorgio Armani,
Jhane Barnes, Hugo Boss,
Henry Cotton's, Ermenegildo
Zegna
Dress Shirts Giorgio Armani,
Hugo Boss, Ermenegildo Zegna
Neckwear Giorgio Armani,
Hugo Boss, Ermenegildo Zegna

PRIME OUTLETS SAN MARCOS
Locations and Stores:
3939 IH-35 South, #900, San Marcos,
TX 78666 www.primeoutlets.com

A/X Armani Exchange
Outlet Store
(512)805-9330
www.giorgioarmani.com

Brooks Brothers
Outlet Store
(512)396-3753
www.brooksbrothers.com

Cole Haan
Outlet Store
(512)396-0404 www.colehaan.com

Johnston & Murphy
Outlet Store
(512)392-2766
www.johnstonmurphy.com

Polo Ralph Lauren Factory Store
Outlet Store
(512)396-9180
www.polo.com

Saks Off Fifth
Outlet Store
(512)392-7916
www.saksfifthavenue.com
Casual Wear Robert Talbott,
Lorenzini
Dress Shirts Ermenegildo Zegna
Neckwear Ermenegildo Zegna
Tailored Clothing Canali,
Ermenegildo Zegna, Zegna Soft

Metro Area: Birmingham

Plain Clothes
Independent
Martha and Stephen Fazio, Owners
2820 Linden Ave., Birmingham, AL
35209 (205)871-3391

Fascinating and aesthetically pleasing store—spacious, presents merchandise extremely well. Also a tasteful women's department. Mr. and Mrs. Fazio also have a signature cologne that smells great!

Accessories Good selection of bow ties and cuff links
Casual Wear Brunello Cuccinelli, Jeff Rose, Guy Rover, John Smedley
Dress Shirts Barba, Guy Rover
Neckwear Barba, Nicky
Shoes Alden
Tailored Clothing Incotex, Gianluca Isaia (also M2M), Samuelsohn (also M2M)
Sales Semiannual

Shaia's
Independent
J. L., Leo, and Ken Shaia, Owners/Greg Flowers, Sales
2818 18th St. South, Birmingham, AL 35209 (205)871-1312 www.shaias.com
Large store with informative, congenial sales staff. Remarkable selection in made-to-measure tailored clothing. Shaia's is a fourth-generation family business and has been a Birmingham tradition since 1922.

Accessories Colonel Littleton gentleman's accessories; Ghurka leather goods; Art of Shaving toiletries
Casual Wear Giorgio Armani, Tommy Bahama, Robert Barakett, Scott Barber, Luciano Barbera, Brioni, Cifonelli, Henry Cotton's, Corneliani, Salvatore Ferragamo, Hiltl, Nat Nast, Paul & Shark, Robert Talbott, Ermenegildo Zegna
Dress Shirts Giorgio Armani, Luigi Borrelli, Canali, Gitman Bros.,

Lorenzini, Robert Talbott, Ermenegildo Zegna
Neckwear Giorgio Armani, Brioni, Canali, Salvatore Ferragamo, Robert Talbott, Ermenegildo Zegna
Shoes Cole Haan, Salvatore Ferragamo, Gravati, J.B. Hill boots (also custom), Paraboot, To Boot New York
Tailored Clothing Giorgio Armani, Brioni, Canali, Coppley, Kiton, Ermenegildo Zegna
Sales Semiannual, January and July

THE SUMMIT
Location and Stores:
129 Summit Blvd., Birmingham, AL 35243 www.thesummitonline.com

Tommy Bahama
(205)967-8389
www.tommybahama.com

Saks Fifth Avenue
(205)298-8550
www.saksfifthavenue.com

Metro Area: Boston

KAPS The Men's Store
Independent
Jim and JohnKapelson, Owners/ Kevin Moriarity, Sales
5 Main St., Andover, MA 01810
(978)475-3905
Attractive retail space with friendly and informed salespeople. Great selection of high-quality labels.

Accessories Bow ties; Robert Talbott cuff links; some formal wear
Casual Wear Joseph Abboud, Tommy Bahama, Canali, Corneliani, Brunello Cuccinelli, KAPS, John Smedley, Vestimenta,

Jack Victor, Zanella, Ermenegildo Zegna
Dress Shirts Eton, Canali, Hickey Freeman, KAPS, Lorenzini, Vestimenta, Ermenegildo Zegna, Custom shirtmakers
Neckwear Tino Cosma, Ferrell Reed, Robert Talbott, Vestimenta, Ermenegildo Zegna
Shoes Cole Haan, Bruno Magli, Mezlan
Tailored Clothing Canali, Corneliani, Hickey Freeman (also M2M), KAPS, Vestimenta, Jack Victor, Zanella, Ermenegildo Zegna, Zegna Soft

Kenneth Cole
128 Newbury St., Boston, MA 02116
(617)867-0836 www.kennethcole.com

Cole Haan
109 Newbury St., Boston, MA 02116
(617)536-7826 www.colehaan.com

COPLEY PLACE
Location and Stores:
2 Copley Place #100, Boston, MA 02116 www.shopcopleyplace.com

A/X Armani Exchange
(617)927-0451
www.giorgioarmani.com

Bally
(617)437-1910 www.bally.com

BOSS Hugo Boss
(617)266-7492 www.hugoboss.com

Coach
(617)262-2063 www.coach.com

Kenneth Cole
(617)867-9580
www.kennethcole.com

Gucci
(617)247-3000 www.gucci.com

Neiman Marcus
(617)536-3660
www.neimanmarcus.com
Casual Wear Giorgio Armani,
Hugo Boss, Burberry, Loro
Piana, Polo Ralph Lauren, Ralph
Lauren Purple Label,
Ermenegildo Zegna
Dress Shirts Giorgio Armani,
Brioni, Ike Behar, Luigi Borrelli,
Charvet, Turnbull & Asser,
Ermenegildo Zegna
Neckwear Massimo Bizzocchi,
Brioni, Salvatore Ferragamo,
Hermès, Turnbull & Asser
Ermenegildo Zegna
Tailored Clothing Ermenegildo
Zegna, Giorgio Armani, Hugo
Boss, Burberry, Prada

Thomas Pink
(617)267-0447
www.thomaspink.com

St. Croix
(617)247-5353
www.stcroixshop.com

Emporio Armani
210–214 Newbury St., Boston, MA
02116 (617)262-7300
www.giorgioarmani.com

Johnston & Murphy
292 Washington St., Boston, MA
02116 (617)426-8086
www.johnstonmurphy.com

Ralph Lauren
93–95 Newbury St., Boston, MA
02116 (617)424-1124 www.polo.com

Louis Boston
Independent
234 Berkeley St. (Corner of Newbury),
Boston, MA 02116 (617)262-6100
www.louisboston.com
Five-star emporium—perhaps the
most attractively presented merchandise I've seen. Features quality, not quantity, of collections.
Merchandise arranged in store-in-
store format. Also some of the best
salespeople in the retail business.
Robb Report Best of the Best
men's specialty store for 2002.

Accessories Some bow ties; great
selection of leather outerwear;
some formal wear
Casual Wear Luciano Barbera,
Neil Barrett, Brioni, Kiton,
Lorenzini, Loro Piana, Rogan,
Duffer St. George, Dries Van
Noten
Dress Shirts Luciano Barbera, Luigi
Borrelli, Brioni, Kiton
Neckwear Luciano Barbera,
Massimo Bizzocchi, Kiton
Shoes Henry Beguelin, Church's,
Silvano Lattanzi, Sutor
Mantellassi, Prada, J.M. Weston
Tailored Clothing Luciano Barbera,
Belvest, Brioni, Kiton
Sales Semiannual

Thomas Pink
280 Washington St., Boston, MA
02108 (617)426-7859
www.thomaspink.com

Saks Fifth Avenue
800 Boylston St., Boston, MA 02199
(617)262-8500
www.saksfifthavenue.com
Great store in convenient Back Bay
location across bridge from Copley
Square. In-store boutiques by

Giorgio Armani, Gucci, and
Ermenegildo Zegna.

Casual Wear Joseph Abboud,
Giorgio Armani, Hugo Boss, Polo
Ralph Lauren, Ermenegildo Zegna
Dress Shirts Ike Behar, Hugo Boss,
Hickey Freeman, Lorenzini,
Ermenegildo Zegna, Zegna Soft
Neckwear Hugo Boss, Brioni,
Burberry, Canali, Ermenegildo
Zegna
Tailored Clothing Joseph Abboud,
Giorgio Armani, Hugo Boss,
Gucci, Hickey Freeman, Polo
Ralph Lauren, Ermenegildo
Zegna, Zegna Soft

Riccardi
Independent
116 Newbury St., Boston, MA 02116
(617)266-3158
Hip boutique for the man who
prefers modern clothing.

Casual Wear Roberto Cavalli,
Dolce & Gabbana, Miu Miu,
Thierry Mugler, Prada

Ermenegildo Zegna
39 Newbury St., Boston, MA 02116
(617)424-9300 www.zegna.com

KAPS The Men's Store
Independent
Jim and John Kapelson, Owners
Burlington Mall, 75 Middlesex St.,
Burlington, MA 01803 (781)273-3164
Attractive retail space with friendly
and informed salespeople. Great
selection of high-quality labels.

Accessories Bow ties; Robert Talbott
cuff links; some formal wear
Casual Wear Joseph Abboud,
Tommy Bahama, Canali, Corneliani, Brunello Cuccinelli, KAPS,

John Smedley, Vestimenta, Jack
Victor, Zanella, Ermenegildo
Zegna
Dress Shirts Eton, Canali, Hickey
Freeman, KAPS, Lorenzini,
Vestimenta, Ermenegildo Zegna,
Custom shirtmakers
Neckwear Tino Cosma, Ferrell
Reed, Robert Talbott, Vestimenta,
Ermenegildo Zegna
Shoes Cole Haan, Bruno Magli,
Mezlan
Tailored Clothing Canali,
Corneliani, Hickey Freeman (also
M2M), KAPS, Vestimenta, Jack
Victor, Zanella, Ermenegildo
Zegna, Zegna Soft

Stonestreets
Independent
William Hootstein, Owner
1276 Massachusetts Ave.,
Cambridge, MA 02138 (617)547-3245
Delightful store, well worth stopping by. Great customer service
and lots of interesting, tasteful
accessories you won't find elsewhere in Boston.

Accessories Italian berets; Borsalino
headwear; Allegri outerwear;
Schneider outerwear (Salzburg,
Austria)
Casual Wear Avon Celli, Biella,
Bills Khakis, Brunello Cuccinelli,
Coast, Madeline Finn, Lorenzini,
Malo, New England, Vestimenta,
Via Petra (Stonestreets)
Dress Shirts Barba, Luigi Borrelli,
Lorenzini
Neckwear Massimo Bizzocchi,
Nick Hilton
Shoes Paraboot
Tailored Clothing Biela, Caruso,
Vestimenta

KAPS The Men's Store
Independent
Jim and John Kapelson, Owners
22 Atlantic Ave., Marblehead, MA
01945 (781)639-4377
Attractive retail space with friendly
and informed salespeople. Great
selection of high-quality labels.

Accessories Bow ties; Robert Talbott
cuff links; some formal wear
Casual Wear Joseph Abboud,
Tommy Bahama, Canali,
Corneliani, Brunello Cuccinelli,
KAPS, John Smedley, Vestimenta,
Jack Victor, Zanella, Ermenegildo
Zegna
Dress Shirts Eton, Canali, Hickey
Freeman, KAPS, Lorenzini,
Vestimenta, Ermenegildo Zegna,
Custom shirtmakers
Neckwear Tino Cosma, Ferrell
Reed, Robert Talbott, Vestimenta,
Ermenegildo Zegna
Shoes Cole Haan, Bruno Magli,
Mezlan
Tailored Clothing Canali,
Corneliani, Hickey Freeman (also
M2M), KAPS, Vestimenta, Jack
Victor, Zanella, Ermenegildo
Zegna, Zegna Soft

Mosher's Men's Store
Independent
Dana Mosher, President
1221 Centre St., Newton Centre, MA
02459 (617)527-3121
Caters toward the more traditional
dresser. Mr. Mosher was cordial
and informative.

Casual Wear Robert Barakett,
Gillio, Hickey Freeman, Jack
Lipson, Mosher's, Oxxford, Raffi,
St. Croix, Robert Talbott
Dress Shirts Burberry, Hickey

Freeman, Mosher's (fabric by
Ermenegildo Zegna), Robert
Talbott
Neckwear Hickey Freeman,
Oxxford, Robert Talbott
Tailored Clothing Coppley, Hickey
Freeman (also M2M), Mosher's
(also M2M), Oxxford (also M2M)

Mr. Sid
Independent
Barry Segel, Vice President
1211 Centre St., Newton Centre, MA
02459 (617)969-4540 www.mrsid.com
Very attractive, wood-filled retail
space. Mr. Segel was very informative and gracious. Mr. Sid's is a
first-class shopping destination.

Accessories Good selection of belts;
very nice formal wear section
Casual Wear Giorgio Armani,
Tommy Bahama, Luigi Borrelli,
Brioni, Polo Ralph Lauren, Gran
Sasso, Robert Talbott, Zanella,
Ermenegildo Zegna and Zegna
Soft, Zegna Sport
Dress Shirts Giorgio Armani, Luigi
Borrelli, Brioni, Ermenegildo Zegna
Neckwear Altea, Brioni, Robert
Talbott, Ermenegildo Zegna
Shoes Salvatore Ferragamo, Bruno
Magli, Moreschi, Santoni, J.M.
Weston
Tailored Clothing Giorgio Armani,
Brioni, Canali, Corneliani, Hickey
Freeman, Polo Ralph Lauren,
Ermenegildo Zegna, Zegna Napoli
Couture, Zegna Soft
Sales Semiannual

KAPS The Men's Store
Independent
Jim and John Kapelson, Owners
54 Central St., Wellesley, MA 02482
(781)235-1401

Attractive retail space with friendly and informed salespeople. Great selection of high-quality labels.

Accessories Bow ties; Robert Talbott cuff links; some formal wear
Casual Wear Joseph Abboud, Tommy Bahama, Canali, Corneliani, Brunello Cuccinelli, KAPS, John Smedley, Vestimenta, Jack Victor, Zanella, Ermenegildo Zegna
Dress Shirts Eton, Canali, Hickey Freeman, KAPS, Lorenzini, Vestimenta, Ermenegildo Zegna, Custom shirtmakers
Neckwear Tino Cosma, Ferrell Reed, Robert Talbott, Vestimenta, Ermenegildo Zegna
Shoes Cole Haan, Bruno Magli, Mezlan
Tailored Clothing Canali, Corneliani, Hickey Freeman (also M2M), KAPS, Vestimenta, Jack Victor, Zanella, Ermenegildo Zegna, Zegna Soft

Saks Off Fifth
Outlet Store
Worcester Commons, 110 Front St., Worcester, MA 01608 (508)757-4666
www.saksfifthavenue.com
Off Fifth clearance center. Broken lots, items can be damaged and stained, but GREAT prices.

Casual Wear Giorgio Armani, Luciano Barbera, Ermenegildo Zegna
Neckwear Giorgio Armani, Gianfranco Ferré, Ermenegildo Zegna
Tailored Clothing Giorgio Armani, Chester Barrie, Hugo Boss, Ermenegildo Zegna

WRENTHAM VILLAGE PREMIUM OUTLETS
Location and Stores:
One Premium Outlets Blvd., Wrentham, MA 02093
www.premiumoutlets.com

Joseph Abboud
Outlet Store
(508)384-0124

Barney's New York
Outlet Store
(508)384-7077 www.barneys.com

Hugo Boss
Outlet Store
(508)384-0358 www.hugoboss.com

Brooks Brothers
Outlet Store
(508)384-9864
www.brooksbrothers.com

Kenneth Cole
Outlet Store
(508)384-7049
www.kennethcole.com

Calvin Klein
Outlet Store
(508)384-0997

Andrew Marc
Outlet Store
(508)384-0968
www.andrewmarc.com

Polo Ralph Lauren Factory Store
Outlet Store
(508)384-1843 www.polo.com

Saks Off Fifth
Outlet Store
(508)384-9309

www.saksfifthavenue.com
One of better sportswear selections I've seen in an Off Fifth.

Casual Wear Giorgio Armani, Luciano Barbera, Salvatore Ferragamo, Vestimenta, Ermenegildo Zegna
Dress Shirts Ike Behar, Ermenegildo Zegna
Neckwear Versace, Ermenegildo Zegna
Tailored Clothing Joseph Abboud, Hugo Boss, Hickey Freeman, Zanella, Zegna Soft

Versace
Outlet Store
(508)384-2254 www.versace.com

Metro Area: Charlotte

Fairclough & Company
Independent
Paul Haddock, Owner/John Bryant, Manager
102 Middleton Dr., Charlotte, NC 28207 (704)331-0001
www.faircloughonline.com
The quintessential neighborhood specialty store. While visiting, I observed several families dropping by, all of whom Mr. Bryant knew by name. Mr. Haddock and Mr. Bryant were generous sharing time with me as well. Fairclough's caters to the updated traditional dresser. I highly recommend this establishment.

Accessories Nice selection of Martin Dingman belts, bow ties, and cuff links
Casual Wear Scott Barber, Bills Khakis, British Apparel, Fairclough & Co., Madeline Finn, Nick Hilton, Lacoste, Jeff Rose

Dress Shirts Gitman Bros., Fairclough, Kenneth Gordon, MacCluer, individualized custom
Neckwear Breuer, Dormeuil, Fabergé, Fairclough (J.Z. Richards)
Shoes Alden
Tailored Clothing Ballin, Corbin, Fairclough, Hilton-Oakloom, Majer, Oliver, H. Oritsky Samuelsohn (also M2M), Dormeuil M2M
Sales Semiannual

Paul Simon
Independent
Jon Simon, Manager
Morrocroft Village, 3900 Colony Rd. #E, Charlotte, NC 28211 (704)366-4523
www.paulsimonco.com
Pleasant shopping environment. Good inventory of quality items. More formal looking store at this location, with elegant, winding staircase to second floor.

Accessories Martin Dingman belts; some cuff links; formal wear section; and leather outerwear
Casual Wear Scott Barber, Luciano Barbera, Barry Bricken, Bobby Jones, Alexander Julian, Hickey Freeman, Maxx H., Moreno Martini Da Firenze, New England, Jeff Rose, Paul Simon, Ermenegildo Zegna, Zegna Sport
Dress Shirts Brioni, Gitman Bros., Robert Talbott, Ermenegildo Zegna, custom
Neckwear Salvatore Ferragamo, Robert Talbott
Shoes Allen Edmonds, Cole Haan, Bruno Magli, Zegna Sport
Tailored Clothing Barry Bricken, Brioni, Coppley M2M, Hickey Freeman (also M2M), Samuelsohn

(also M2M), Ermenegildo Zegna, Zegna Soft
Sales Semiannual

Paul Simon
Independent
Larry Blankenship, Manager
Myers Park Center, 1027 Providence Rd., Charlotte, NC 28207
(704)372-6842
www.paulsimonco.com
Pleasant shopping environment. Good inventory of quality items. Also a women's store, and a separate entrance for sportswear at this location.

Accessories Martin Dingman belts; some cuff links; formal wear section; and leather outerwear
Casual Wear Scott Barber, Luciano Barbera, Barry Bricken, Bobby Jones, Alexander Julian, Hickey Freeman, Maxx H., Moreno Martini Da Firenze, New England, Jeff Rose, Paul Simon, Ermenegildo Zegna, Zegna Sport
Dress Shirts Brioni, Gitman Bros., Robert Talbott, Ermenegildo Zegna, custom
Neckwear Salvatore Ferragamo, Robert Talbott
Shoes Allen Edmonds, Cole Haan, Bruno Magli, Zegna Sport
Tailored Clothing Barry Bricken, Brioni, Coppley M2M, Hickey Freeman (also M2M), Samuelsohn (also M2M), Ermenegildo Zegna, Zegna Soft
Sales Semiannual

Taylor, Richards & Conger
Independent
Lyn Conger, Partner
South Park Specialty Shops, 6401

Morrison Blvd., #6A, Charlotte, NC 28211 (704)366-9092 www.trcstyle.com
Excellent store, attractive dark wood fixtures filled with tasteful, first-rate inventory. Selection of shoes is particularly noteworthy. Mr. Conger was very gracious while showing me around his establishment.

Accessories Great selection of Tateossian cuff links
Casual Wear Brunello Cuccinelli, ISDA & Co., Ralph Lauren Purple Label, Tricots St. Raphael, Ermenegildo Zegna
Dress Shirts Bagutta, Luigi Borrelli, Lorenzini, Ermenegildo Zegna
Neckwear Giorgio Armani, Massimo Bizzocchi, Canali, Taylor, Richards & Conger, Ermenegildo Zegna
Shoes Canali, Salvatore Ferragamo, Bruno Magli, To Boot New York, J.M. Weston
Tailored Clothing Giorgio Armani, Canali, Kiton (also M2M), Polo Ralph Lauren, Ermenegildo Zegna, Zegna Soft
Sales Semiannual

Saks Off Fifth
Outlet Store
Concord Mills, 8281 Concord Mills Blvd., Concord, NC 28027 (704)979-6000 www.saksfifthavenue.com

Casual Wear Diesel, Moreno Martini Da Firenze, Robert Talbott, Versace, Ermenegildo Zegna
Dress Shirts Ike Behar, Hugo Boss, Burberry, Ermenegildo Zegna
Neckwear Giorgio Armani, Hugo Boss, Salvatore Ferragamo, Gianfranco Ferré, Ermenegildo

Zegna
Tailored Clothing Joseph Abboud,
Hugo Boss, Corneliani, Mani,
Polo Ralph Lauren

Taylor, Richards & Conger
Independent
Chris Estridge, Manager
Shops on the Green, 20220 Knox
Road, Cornelius, NC 28031
(704)895-2081 www.trcstyle.com
Same quality product mix and
superb customer service as South
Park location. Slightly smaller
venue.

Accessories Great selection of
Tateossian cuff links
Casual Wear Brunello Cuccinelli,
ISDA & Co., Ralph Lauren Purple
Label, Tricots St. Raphael,
Ermenegildo Zegna
Dress Shirts Bagutta, Luigi Borrelli,
Lorenzini, Ermenegildo Zegna
Neckwear Giorgio Armani,
Massimo Bizzocchi, Canali, Taylor,
Richards & Conger, Ermenegildo
Zegna
Shoes Canali, Salvatore Ferragamo,
Bruno Magli, To Boot New York,
J.M. Weston
Tailored Clothing Giorgio Armani,
Canali, Kiton (also M2M), Polo
Ralph Lauren, Ermenegildo
Zegna, Zegna Soft
Sales Semiannual

Metro Area: Chicago
BJ's
Independent
Bill Patterson, Proprietor
931 Main St., Antioch, IL 60002
(847)395-6212
Pleasant shopping environment
with great inventory of reputable

brands. Helpful, informative sales
staff.

Accessories Good selection from
overcoats to pocket squares
Casual Wear Tommy Bahama,
Carlo Colucci, Gillio, Riscatto
Portofino, Zanella
Dress Shirts Ike Behar, Hugo Boss,
Eton
Neckwear Jhane Barnes, Leonard,
Pancaldi
Shoes Allen Edmonds, H.S. Trask
Tailored Clothing Hugo Boss,
Arnold Brant, Samuelsohn (also
M2M), Tallia, Jack Victor, Zanella
Sales Semiannual

Chuck Hines
Independent
141 W. Main St., Barrington, IL 60010
(847)381-6616
Spacious store filled with appealing
wood fixtures. Great inventory of
quality clothing lines. Women's
department as well.

Casual Wear Joseph Abboud, Axis,
Tommy Bahama, Robert Barakett,
Gran Sasso, Robert Talbott,
Tricots St. Raphael, Viyella
Dress Shirts Joseph Abboud, Klauss
Bohler, Robert Talbott, XMI
Neckwear Joseph Abboud, Robert
Talbott, XMI
Shoes Allen Edmonds, Cole Haan
Tailored Clothing Joseph Abboud,
Burberry, Oliver, Tallia
Sales Semiannual

Peter Daniel
Independent
Ice House Mall, 200 Applebee St.,
Barrington, IL 60010 (847)382-6676
Attractive shopping environment
with cordial customer service. Also
a women's department.

Casual Wear Gran Sasso, Toscano, Tricots St. Raphael, Tundra, Victorinox
Dress Shirts Ike Behar, Klauss Bohler, MacCluer, Robert Talbott
Neckwear Jhane Barnes, Robert Talbott, XMI
Shoes Cole Haan, Mephisto, Donald J. Pliner
Tailored Clothing Oliver, Tallia, Jack Victor, Zanella
Sales Semiannual

900 N. MICHIGAN SHOPS
Location and Stores:
900 N. Michigan Ave., Chicago, IL 60611 www.shop900.com

Coach
(312)440-1777 www.coach.com

Davis for Men
Independent
Stephen Davis, Owner/
Steven Palazzolo, Manager
(312)440-0016
www.davisformen.com
Top-notch merchandise and helpful sales staff. Mr. Davis and Mr. Palazzolo are knowledge-able and great to deal with. One of Chicago's finest men's stores for over 60 years.

Casual Wear Gran Sasso, Iceberg, Versace, Zanella
Dress Shirts Luigi Borrelli, Eton, Lorenzini, Marol
Neckwear Tino Cosma, Leonard, Pancaldi, Stefano Ricci
Shoes Cole Haan, Bruno Magli, Mezlan, Donald J. Pliner
Tailored Clothing Brioni, Cerruti 1881, Edwin Nazario, Ravazzolo, John Varvatos,

Versace, Vestimenta
Sales Semiannual

Gucci
(312)664-5504
www.gucci.com

Mark Shale
Independent
(312)440-0720
www.markshale.com
Attractive store, great selection and customer service.

Casual Wear Anthology, Scott Barber, Burberry, Gran Sasso, Mark Shale, Ermenegildo Zegna
Dress Shirts Joseph Abboud, Ike Behar, Robert Talbott
Neckwear Robert Talbott, XMI
Shoes Kenneth Cole, Cole Haan, Donald J. Pliner, Mark Shale
Tailored Clothing Hugo Boss, Burberry, Corneliani, Mani, Ermenegildo Zegna
Sales Semiannual

St. Croix
(312)787-2888
www.stcroixshop.com

Allen Edmonds
541 North Michigan Avenue, Chicago, IL 60611 (312)755-9306
www.allenedmonds.com

Apartment Number 9
Independent
Amy and Sarah Blessing, Owners
1804 N. Damen Ave., Chicago, IL 60647 (773)395-2999
Pleasant, modern boutique filled with items you won't find any-where else in Chicago. First-rate customer service; the Blessings are a delight to deal with.

Accessories Art of Shaving toiletries, cuff links, vintage T-shirts
Casual Wear Bills Khakis, Andrew Dibben, Levi's, Fred Perry, Paul Smith, John Smedley
Dress Shirts Paul Smith
Neckwear Lee Allison
Shoes Paul Smith

Barney's New York
25 E. Oak St., Chicago, IL 60611
(312)587-1700 www.barneys.com
Nice men's selection, with some particularly unique collections I didn't see elsewhere in Chicago.

Casual Wear Barney's, Fray, Moreno Martini Da Firenze, Ermenegildo Zegna
Dress Shirts Barney's, Brioni, Fray, Lorenzini, Ermenegildo Zegna
Shoes Barney's
Tailored Clothing Barney's, Ermenegildo Zegna

Burberry
633 N. Michigan Ave., Chicago, IL 60611 (312)787-2500
www.burberry.com

Chasalla
Independent
70 E. Oak St., Chicago, IL 60611
(312)640-1940
www.oakstreetchicago.com
Cozy, hip boutique for shopper seeking more modern designs.

Casual Wear Hugo Boss, Roberto Cavalli, Dolce & Gabbana, Versace

Kenneth Cole
540 N. Michigan Ave., Chicago, IL 60611 (312)644-1163
www.kennethcole.com

Cole Haan
673 N. Michigan Ave., Chicago, IL 60611 (312)642-8995
www.colehaan.com

Davis for Men
Independent
Stephen Davis, Owner/
Shelly Weingarten, Manager
824 W. North Ave., Chicago, IL 60622
(312)266-9599
www.davisformen.com
Top-notch merchandise and helpful sales staff. Mr. Davis and Mr. Weingarten are knowledgeable and great to deal with. One of Chicago's finest men's stores for over 60 years.

Casual Wear AJ by Giorgio Armani, Gran Sasso, Versace, Zanella
Dress Shirts Luigi Borrelli, Eton, Lorenzini, Marol
Neckwear Tino Cosma, Leonard, Pancaldi, Stefano Ricci
Shoes Cole Haan, Bruno Magli, Mezlan, Donald J. Pliner
Tailored Clothing Brioni, Cerruti 1881, Edwin Nazario, Ravazzolo, John Varvatos, Versace, Vestimenta
Sales Semiannual

Diesel
923 Rush St., Chicago, IL 60611
(312)255-0157 www.diesel.com

Alfred Dunhill
Tom Flint, Manager
55 E. Oak St., Chicago, IL 60611
(312)943-9030 www.dunhill.com

Salvatore Ferragamo
645 N. Michigan Ave., Chicago, IL 60611 (312)397-0464
www.salvatoreferragamo.it
Spacious boutique with great inventory and helpful sales staff.

George Greene

Independent
Edmund Paszylk, John Moran, John Jones, Proprietors
49 E. Oak St., Chicago, IL 60611
(312)654-2490
Attractive, intimate boutique filled with top-notch merchandise and excellent customer service.

Casual Wear Luciano Barbera, Chrome Hearts, Brunello Cuccinelli, Christian Dior, La Matta, Missoni, Moreno Martini Da Firenze, Yohji Yamamoto, Ermenegildo Zegna
Dress Shirts Luciano Barbera, Kiton, Lorenzini, Ermenegildo Zegna
Neckwear Luciano Barbera, Massimo Bizzocchi, Kiton, Nicky's of Milan
Shoes Silvano Lattanzi
Tailored Clothing Kiton, Oxxford, Vestimenta, Ermenegildo Zegna

Hanig's Footwear

Independent
660 North Michigan Ave., Chicago, IL 60611 (800)621-2384 or (312)642-5330
www.hanigs.com
Family owned and operated for more than 50 years. Great service and selection.

Shoes Alden, Kenneth Cole, Ecco, Johnston & Murphy, Mephisto, Mezlan

In Chicago for Men and Women

Independent
David Perlow
72 E. Oak St., Chicago, IL 60611
(312)787-9557
Great store with unique, quality items and good customer service.

Women's department also.

Accessories Pelle Pelle leather outerwear
Casual Wear Hugo Boss, Byblos, Versace, Zanella
Dress Shirts Hugo Boss
Neckwear Hugo Boss, Tino Cosma, Versace
Shoes Cesare Paciotti, Versace
Tailored Clothing Everett Hall, Verri, Versace, Zanella
Sales Semiannual, January/February and after July 4

Syd Jerome

Independent
Sid and Scott Shapiro, Owners
2 N. LaSalle St., Chicago, IL 60620
(312)346-0333
Extremely well stocked with many great designers and pieces. I shop here whenever I'm in Chicago. Scott is one of my favorite salespeople—very knowledgeable and helpful—and I highly recommend Syd Jerome.

Accessories Cole Haan, Salvatore Ferragamo, Mezlan, A. Testoni belts and leather goods
Casual Wear Giorgio Armani, Hugo Boss, Brioni, Gran Sasso, Syd Jerome, Versace, Ermenegildo Zegna, Pal Zileri
Dress Shirts Luigi Borrelli, Hugo Boss, Brioni, Canali, Fray, Fabio Inghirami, Ermenegildo Zegna
Neckwear Jhane Barnes, Brioni, Tino Cosma, Syd Jerome, Ermenegildo Zegna
Shoes Cole Haan, Salvatore Ferragamo, Mezlan, a. testoni, Sutor Mantellassi
Tailored Clothing Giorgio Armani, Oxxford, Gianluca Isaia, Saint

Andrews, Zanella, Ermenegildo
Zegna, Pal Zileri
Sales Semiannual, January/February and after July 4

Loro Piana
45 E. Oak St., Chicago, IL 60611
(312)664-6644

Ralph Lauren
750 N. Michigan Ave., Chicago, IL
60611 (312)280-1655 www.polo.com
Largest Polo Ralph Lauren location. Excellent customer service.
Café also on premises.

Johnston & Murphy
625 N. Michigan Ave., Chicago, IL
60611 (312)751-1630
www.johnstonmurphy.com

**Mazzei Montopoli & Strahorn
Custom Tailoring**
Independent
*Jeff Landis, Clothier and Image
Consultant*
625 N. Michigan Ave., Ste. 205,
Chicago, IL 60611 (312)642-1221
In business since 1897. Experienced
old-world tailors; coat maker has
been in the tailoring industry for
40 years. Elegant wood furnishings
with bolts upon bolts of first-quality fabrics. Mr. Landis is knowledgeable, personable, and great to
deal with.

Dress Shirts Custom
Neckwear Dormeuil, Robert
Talbott
Tailored Clothing Custom

Morris & Sons
Independent
Gary Rosenbaum, President

555 W Roosevelt Rd., Chicago, IL
60607 (800)943-5635 or (312)243-5635
www.morrisandsons.com
One of Chicago's best-kept secrets
for over 50 years. Morris & Sons
carries men's and women's current-season merchandise purchased
directly from Europe—the majority from Italy—from many of the
world's best designers. At the
store's request I do not mention
specific names because Morris &
Sons is the only store allowed to
discount this incredible merchandise.

Neiman Marcus
737 N. Michigan Ave., Chicago, IL
60611 (312)642-5900
www.neimanmarcus.com
Excellent selection of Brioni and
Oxxford tailored clothing.

Casual Wear Giorgio Armani,
Brioni, Burberry, Gucci, Dolce &
Gabbana, Loro Piana, Polo Ralph
Lauren, Prada, Ralph Lauren
Purple Label, Ermenegildo Zegna,
Zegna Sport
Dress Shirts Giorgio Armani, Luigi
Borrelli, Brioni, Lorenzini, Paul
Smith, Turnbull & Asser,
Ermenegildo Zegna
Neckwear Villa Bolgheri, Brioni,
Charvet, Salvatore Ferragamo,
Hermès, Stefano Ricci, Paul Smith,
Turnbull & Asser, Ermenegildo
Zegna
Tailored Clothing Giorgio Armani,
Brioni, Gianluca Isaia, Oxxford,
Paul Smith, Ermenegildo Zegna

Optimo Hats
Independent
*Graham Thompson, Owner/Kevin
Fitzpatrick, Sales*

10215 S. Western Ave., Chicago, IL
60643 (773)238-2999
www.optimohats.com
The finest hats in the world (see
chapter 5). All hats are handmade;
the process takes about one month.
The felt, leather, and even the silk
lining for the hats are custom-made
by Optimo from the finest sources
around the world. Also an extremely reliable resource for hat blocking
and cleaning. Mr. Thompson owns
many machines that are no longer
made and are essential to the fine
art of hat making. Optimo has
excellent customer service; Mr.
Thompson and Mr. Fitzpatrick are
both great to work with.

Accessories Handmade hats

Saks Fifth Avenue
717 N. Michigan Ave., Chicago, IL
60611 (312)944-6500
www.saksfifthavenue.com
Huge, stand-alone men's store. One
of top five Saks in America. Only
Saks with Kiton in-store boutique.

Casual Wear Joseph Abboud,
Giorgio Armani, Luciano Barbera,
John Barrett, Cifonelli, Kiton,
Michael Kors, Helmut Lang, Polo
Ralph Lauren, John Varvatos,
Yohji Yamamoto, Ermenegildo
Zegna, Zegna Sport
Dress Shirts Joseph Abboud,
Giorgio Armani, Ike Behar, Luigi
Borrelli, Hugo Boss, Charvet,
Hickey Freeman, Kiton, Lorenzini,
Vestimenta, Ermenegildo Zegna
Neckwear Giorgio Armani,
Luciano Barbera, Massimo
Bizzocchi, Hugo Boss, Charvet,
Kiton, Stefano Ricci, Ermenegildo
Zegna

Tailored Clothing Giorgio Armani,
Hugo Boss, Canali, Kiton,
Oxxford, John Varvatos,
Ermenegildo Zegna, Zegna Soft

Paul Stuart
Independent
John Hancock Center, 875 N.
Michigan Ave., Chicago, IL 60611
(312)640-2650 www.paulstuart.com
Attractive store with first-quality,
primarily privately labeled merchandise. For the more traditional
dresser.

Accessories Great selection of bow
ties, braces, and cuff links
Sales Semiannual

Tessuti
Independent
Robert Green, Buyer
50 E. Oak St., Chicago, IL 60611
(312)266-4949
www.oakstreetchicago.com
Great-looking store known for
selling clothing with fine fabrics
and soft hands. Merchandise
arranged appealingly; courteous,
personable sales staff.

Casual Wear Gran Sasso
Dress Shirts Tino Cosma, Xacus
Neckwear Tino Cosma
Tailored Clothing Mabro, Pal Zileri

THE SHOPS AT NORTH BRIDGE
Location and Stores:
520 N. Michigan Ave. Chicago, IL
60611 www.northbridgechicago.com

A/X Armani Exchange
(312)467-5702
www.giorgioarmani.com

Avventura
(312)337-3700 www.avventura.com

Bernini
(312)943-8786 www.bernini.com

BOSS Hugo Boss
(312)660-0056 www.hugoboss.com

Brass Boot
(312)464-1604

Lucky Brand Dungarees
(312)464-0829
www.luckybrandjeans.com

Nordstrom
(312)464-1515 www.nordstrom.com
Casual Wear Joseph Abboud, Burberry, Mani, Ermenegildo Zegna
Dress Shirts Giorgio Armani, Ike Behar, Hugo Boss, Jack Lipson, Robert Talbott, Ermenegildo Zegna
Neckwear Robert Talbott, XMI, Ermenegildo Zegna
Tailored Clothing Giorgio Armani, Hugo Boss, Burberry, Façonnable, Hart, Schaffner & Marx, Hickey Freeman, Zanella, Ermenegildo Zegna, Pal Zileri, Bernard Zins

WATER TOWER PLACE
Location and Stores:
909 N. Michigan Ave Chicago, IL 60611 www.shopwatertower.com

Fratelli Rosetti
(312)337-5496 www.rossetti.it

Louis Vuitton
(312)944-2010
www.louisvuitton.com

Ermenegildo Zegna
645 N. Michigan Ave., Chicago, IL

60611 (312)587-9660 www.zegna.com
Large boutique with excellent selection and first-rate salespeople.

Leonard's
Independent
Bill Patterson, Owner/Jym Becker, Sales
144 N. York St., Elmhurst, IL 60126
(630)833-8900
Spacious, pleasant shopping environment with some great clothing lines. Mr. Patterson and Mr. Becker were helpful and congenial.

Accessories Good selection from overcoats to pocket squares
Casual Wear Tommy Bahama, Carlo Colucci, Gillio, Riscatto Portofino, Timberland, Zanella
Dress Shirts Ike Behar, Hugo Boss, Eton
Neckwear Jhane Barnes, Leonard, Pancaldi
Shoes Allen Edmonds, H.S. Trask
Tailored Clothing Hugo Boss, Arnold Brant, Samuelsohn (also M2M), Tallia, Jack Victor, Zanella
Sales Semiannual

Robert Grasselle
Independent
Robert Grasselle, Owner
2720 N. Harlem Ave., Elmwood Park, IL 60707 (708)456-7700
Founded in 1957. Interesting store with unique circular layout of sales floor and stuffed shark over the entrance. Good inventory of interesting, quality items. Attentive, helpful salespeople.

Accessories St. Croix Limited Edition sweaters each winter season
Casual Wear Haupt, St. Croix
Dress Shirts Robert Grasselle

Neckwear Stefano Ricci
Shoes Santoni
Tailored Clothing Robert Grasselle, Samuelsohn (also M2M)
Sales Semiannual

Raymond Levine
Independent
Jeff Glick, President/
Lynne DiLorenzo, Sales
Hickory Creek Market Square, 19919 S. LaGrange Rd., Frankfort, IL 60423
(877)251-5567 or (815)464-5766
www.raymondlevine.com
Third-generation family business begun in 1924. Visually appealing store with well-presented, first-quality merchandise. Congenial and helpful sales staff.

Accessories Remy leather outerwear; Sanyo outerwear
Casual Wear Tommy Bahama, Carlo Colucci, Dalmine, Gran Sasso, St. Croix
Dress Shirts Canali, Eton, Robert Talbott
Neckwear Altea, Brioni, Canali, Tino Cosma, Leonard, Pancaldi, Robert Talbott
Shoes Mezlan
Tailored Clothing Brioni, Canali, Kenneth Cole, Coppley M2M, Linnea Trussini, Pal Zileri
Sales Semiannual

GURNEE MILLS
Location and Stores:
6170 West Grand Ave., Ste. 527, Gurnee, IL 60031
www.gurneemills.com

Polo Jeans Company
Outlet Store
(847)856-0897 www.polo.com

Saks Off Fifth
Outlet Store
(847)662-098
www.saksfifthavenue.com

Casual Wear Burberry, Polo Ralph Lauren, Tricots St. Raphael, Ermenegildo Zegna
Dress Shirts Ike Behar, Hugo Boss, Versace, Ermenegildo Zegna (good selection)
Tailored Clothing Hugo Boss, Gianfranco Ferré Studio, Mani, Zegna Soft, Pal Zileri

Saks Fifth Avenue
1849 Green Bay Rd., Highland Park, IL 60035 (847)681-5100
www.saksfifthavenue.com

Casual Wear Joseph Abboud, Giorgio Armani, Hugo Boss, Polo Ralph Lauren, Ermenegildo Zegna
Dress Shirts Giorgio Armani, Ike Behar, Canali, Ermenegildo Zegna
Neckwear Giorgio Armani, Ike Behar, Canali, Charvet, Ermenegildo Zegna
Tailored Clothing Giorgio Armani, Canali, Ermenegildo Zegna

Hinsdale Clothiers
Independent
Steven Potter and Ed Lipscomb, Proprietors
Gateway Square, 777 N. York Rd., Hinsdale, IL 60521 (630)323-1858
Large establishment with great feel for attractive presentation of merchandise. Hinsdale Clothiers prides itself on accommodating the hard-to-fit customer. Mr. Potter and Mr. Lipscomb have 75 years of experience in the clothing industry and are great to work with.

Accessories Good selection of cuff

links and outerwear
Casual Wear Axis, Tommy
Bahama, Ballin, Robert Barakett,
Scott Barber, Bills Khakis, Pringle,
Raffi, Zanella
Dress Shirts Joseph Abboud, Ike
Behar, Robert Talbott
Neckwear Joseph Abboud, Robert
Talbott
Tailored Clothing Arnold Brant,
Coppley, Corneliani, Tallia
Sales Semiannual

William Michael
Independent
Don Gill and Marty Robbins,
Owners
11 E. 1st St., Hinsdale, IL 60521
(630)920-8502
Spacious, attractive store with well-
arranged, first-quality merchandise.
Exceptional, come-to-you customer
service. Mr. Gill and Mr. Robbins
were formerly employed with leg-
endary Chicago retailer Biggsby &
Kruthers.

Casual Wear Joseph Abboud,
Robert Barakett, Scott Barber,
Luciano Barbera, Gran Sasso,
Haupt, ISDA & Co., Nat Nast,
Robert Talbott
Dress Shirts Ike Behar, Robert
Talbott, custom
Neckwear Robert Talbott
Tailored Clothing Joseph Abboud,
William Michael, Vestimenta
Sales Semiannual

Argyle's
Independent
Joseph Costanza, Owner
950 N. Western Ave., Lake Forest, IL
60045 (847)295-0200
Pleasant store with attractive wood
furnishings directed toward updated

traditional dresser. Great customer
service, tailor on premises.

Casual Wear Bills Khakis, Bobby
Jones Pringle, Viyella
Dress Shirts Ike Behar, Kenneth
Gordon
Neckwear Robert Talbott;
B,C & G
Tailored Clothing Hickey Freeman,
Samuelsohn
Sales Semiannual

Smith's Men's Store
Independent
John Tadel, Owner
770 N. Western Ave., Lake Forest, IL
60045 (847)234-6483
Store founded in 1937. Pleasant
shopping environment with quality
inventory of clothing for the traditional dresser. Mr. Tadel is a pleasure to deal with.

Casual Wear Bills Khakis, MacCluer,
Corbin, Viyella
Dress Shirts Gitman Bros.
Neckwear Robert Talbott
Tailored Clothing Corbin, Southwick
Sales Semiannual

Robert Vance Ltd.
Independent
Jack Shniderman, Proprietor
Village Green of Lincolnshire, 185 N.
Milwaukee Ave., Ste. 150,
Lincolnshire, IL 60069 (847)478-0988
Delightful store, in business since
1973. Large, well-presented inven-
tory nicely divided between
European and updated traditional
tastes. Robert Vance's staff has
over 125 years' experience in
retail. Also great women's section.

Accessories Good selection of belts;
braces, including Trafalgar Limited

Edition; and cuff links
Casual Wear Tommy Bahama,
Robert Barakett, Jhane Barnes,
Bills Khakis, Gitman Bros., Gran
Sasso, MacKenzie Tribe, Zanella
Dress Shirts Kenneth Gordon,
Robert Talbott, Robert Vance
(Jack Lipson)
Neckwear Robert Talbott, XMI
Shoes Cole Haan, Bruno Magli,
Mezlan, H.S. Trask
Tailored Clothing Joseph Abboud,
Ballin, Jhane Barnes, Hugo Boss,
Alan Flusser, Hickey Freeman,
Zanella
Sales Semiannual

NORTHBROOK COURT
Location and Stores:
2171 Northbrook Ct., Northbrook, IL
60062
www.shopnorthbrookcourt.com

Brooks Brothers
(847)272-3800
www.brooksbrothers.com

Coach
(847)272-7195 www.coach.com

Johnston & Murphy
(847)480-1636
www.johnstonmurphy.com

Neiman Marcus
(847)564-0300
www.neimanmarcus.com
In my opinion, one of top five
Neiman Marcus men's departments in America. Excellent
merchandise mix and customer
service.

Casual Wear Joseph Abboud,
Giorgio Armani, Avon Celli,

Brioni, Burberry, Diesel, Loro
Piana, Polo Ralph Lauren,
Ermenegildo Zegna
Dress Shirts Giorgio Armani, Ike
Behar, Luigi Borrelli, Hugo
Boss, Brioni, Fray, Kiton,
Lorenzini Ermenegildo Zegna
Neckwear Giorgio Armani, Villa
Bolgheri, Brioni, Burberry,
Salvatore Ferragamo, Hermès,
Ermenegildo Zegna
Tailored Clothing Giorgio
Armani, Brioni, Kiton, Incotex,
Gianluca Isaia, Oxxford,
Ermenegildo Zegna

Mark Shale
Independent
(847)272-3860
www.markshale.com
Attractive store, with the great
customer service one can always
expect from Mark Shale.

Casual Wear Anthology, Scott
Barber, Burberry, Gran Sasso,
Mark Shale, Ermenegildo Zegna
Dress Shirts Joseph Abboud, Ike
Behar, Robert Talbott
Neckwear Robert Talbott, XMI
Shoes Kenneth Cole, Cole Haan,
Donald J. Pliner, Mark Shale
Tailored Clothing Hugo Boss,
Burberry, Corneliani, Mani,
Ermenegildo Zegna
Sales Semiannual

Louis Vuitton
(847)714-1004
www.louisvuitton.com

Nordstrom Rack
Outlet Store
199 Skokie Blvd., Northbrook, IL
60062 (847)205-0890
www.nordstrom.com

Casual Wear Tommy Bahama, Jack Lipson, Robert Talbott
Dress Shirts Ike Behar, Robert Talbott
Neckwear Joseph Abboud, XMI, Ermenegildo Zegna
Tailored Clothing Joseph Abboud, Joseph Abboud Black Label, Corneliani, Vestimenta, Pal Zileri

OAK BROOK CENTER
Location and Stores:
100 Oakbrook Ctr., Oak Brook, IL 60523 www.oakbrookcenter.com

Brooks Brothers
(630)571-0700
www.brooksbrothers.com

Burberry
(630)571-6400 www.burberry.com

Coach
(630)572-1772 www.coach.com

Kenneth Cole
(630)645-0020
www.kennethcole.com

Johnston & Murphy
(630)574-9040
www.johnstonmurphy.com

Lucky Brand Dungarees
(630)368-0151
www.luckybrandjeans.com

Neiman Marcus
(630)572-1500
www.neimanmarcus.com
Casual Wear Joseph Abboud, Giorgio Armani, Jhane Barnes, Burberry, Polo Ralph Lauren, Ermenegildo Zegna

Dress Shirts Giorgio Armani, Ike Behar, Brioni, Lorenzini, Ermenegildo Zegna
Neckwear Giorgio Armani, Ike Behar, Villa Bolgheri, Charvet, Hermès, Oxxford, Ermenegildo Zegna
Tailored Clothing Giorgio Armani, Hugo Boss, Oxxford, Ermenegildo Zegna

Nordstrom
(630)571-2121 www.nordstrom.com
Magnificent men's department, in my opinion one of five best in the U.S.!
Casual Wear Giorgio Armani, Jhane Barnes, Ermenegildo Zegna
Dress Shirts Barba, Ike Behar, Façonnable, Jack Lipson, Robert Talbott, Ermenegildo Zegna
Neckwear Joseph Abboud, Hugo Boss, Façonnable, Pancaldi, Robert Talbott, XMI Platinum, Ermenegildo Zegna
Tailored Clothing Joseph Abboud, Giorgio Armani, Ballin, Hugo Boss, Burberry, Hart, Schaffner & Marx, Hickey Freeman, Marzotto, Zanella, Ermenegildo Zegna, Pal Zileri, Bernard Zins

Mark Shale
Independent
(630)571-9440
www.markshale.com
Large, new store with excellent inventory and first-rate customer service.

Accessories Some Trafalgar Braces, including Limited Edition

Casual Wear Tommy Bahama, Scott Barber, Gran Sasso, North 44, Mark Shale, Robert Talbott, Ermenegildo Zegna
Dress Shirts Joseph Abboud, Ike Behar, Mark Shale, Robert Talbott, Ermenegildo Zegna
Neckwear Joseph Abboud, Luciano Barbera, Mark Shale, Robert Talbott, XMI, Ermenegildo Zegna
Shoes Cole Haan, Mark Shale
Tailored Clothing Joseph Abboud, Hugo Boss, Corneliani, Mani, Jack Victor, Ermenegildo Zegna

Nordstrom Rack
Outlet Store
The Shops at Oakbrook Place, 2155 W. 22nd St., Oak Brook, IL 60521 (630)572-1212 www.nordstrom.com

Casual Wear Robert Talbott, Tricots St. Raphael
Dress Shirts Ike Behar, Robert Talbott, XMI
Neckwear Robert Talbott, XMI
Tailored Clothing Ballin, Hugo Boss, Corneliani, Hart, Schaffner & Marx, Tallia, Zanella, Pal Zileri

Spaulding's Fine Apparel for Men and Women
Independent
Don Micheli, Owner
110 N. Marion St., Oak Park, IL 60301 (708)386-1802
Spacious, attractive store filled with first-quality merchandise. Women's section as well.

Casual Wear Axis, Tommy Bahama, Robert Barakett, Gran Sasso, Haupt, ISDA & Co., Tricots St. Raphael, Zanella,

Ermenegildo Zegna
Dress Shirts Ike Behar, Klauss Bohler
Neckwear Canali, Robert Talbott, Ermenegildo Zegna
Tailored Clothing Joseph Abboud, Canali, Samuelsohn, Jack Victor, Pal Zileri, Ermenegildo Zegna
Sales Semiannual

Executive Clothiers
Independent
Ollie Galam, Proprietor
6 N. Elmhurst Rd., Ste. A, Prospect Heights, IL 60070 (847)253-3800
Great store, which unique, first-rate merchandise mix. Mr. Galam is a pleasure to deal with.

Accessories Good selection of cuff links; Gimo leather outerwear
Casual Wear Tommy Bahama, Robert Barakett, Jhane Barnes, Brioni, Canali, Charleston Khakis, Eton, Gran Sasso, Minos, Robert Talbott, XMI, Zanella
Dress Shirts Joseph Abboud, Klauss Bohler, Eton, Executive Clothiers, Robert Talbott (also M2M)
Neckwear Giorgio Armani, Tino Cosma, Robert Talbott, XMI
Shoes Allen Edmonds, Johnston & Murphy, Bruno Magli, Mezlan, Donald J. Pliner
Tailored Clothing Joseph Abboud, Canali, Coppley, Executive Clothiers, Hart, Schaffner & Marx (also M2M), Hilton, Mani, Zanella, Pal Zileri
Sales Semiannual

WOODFIELD SHOPPING CENTER
Location and Stores:
5 Woodfield Shopping Center, Schaumburg, IL 60173
www.shopwoodfield.com

Bernini
Beth Leitter, Store Manager
(847)330-1786 www.bernini.com

Brooks Brothers
Donna Selagea, Store Manager
(847)240-1949
www.brooksbrothers.com

Coach
Chris Hefel, Store Manager
(847)330-1772 www.coach.com

Johnston & Murphy
Deborah Smith, Store Manager
(847)619-2929
www.johnstonmurphy.com

Lucky Brand Dungarees
David Dawson, Store Manager
(847)619-0209
www.luckybrandjeans.com

Nordstrom
Marybeth Gaffney, Store Manager
(847)605-2121 www.nordstrom.com

Casual Wear Joseph Abboud, Robert Barakett, Zanella, Ermenegildo Zegna
Dress Shirts Ike Behar, Jack Lipson, Robert Talbott
Neckwear Robert Talbott, XMI, Ermenegildo Zegna
Tailored Clothing Joseph Abboud, Hart, Schaffner & Marx, Hickey Freeman, Zanella, Pal Zileri

WOODFIELD VILLAGE GREEN SHOPPING CENTER
Location and Stores:
1520 E. Golf Rd., Schaumburg, IL 60173

Nordstrom Rack
Outlet Store
(847)413-2121 www.nordstrom.com

Casual Wear Robert Barakett, Tricots St. Raphael
Dress Shirts Ike Behar, Robert Talbott
Neckwear Robert Talbott, XMI
Tailored Clothing Joseph Abboud, Joseph Abboud Black Label, Corneliani, Façonnable Hickey Freeman, Pal Zileri

Saks Off Fifth
Outlet Store
(847)413-8803
www.saksfifthavenue.com

Casual Wear Joseph Abboud, Giorgio Armani, Jhane Barnes, Burberry, Diesel, Polo Ralph Lauren, Tricots St. Raphael, Ermenegildo Zegna
Dress Shirts Ermenegildo Zegna
Neckwear Giorgio Armani, Versace, Ermenegildo Zegna
Tailored Clothing Joseph Abboud, Joseph Abboud Black Label, Jhane Barnes, Gianfranco Ferré Studio, Polo Ralph Lauren, Vestimenta, Zanella, Zegna Soft

OLD ORCHARD CENTER
Location and Stores:
34 Old Orchard Ctr., Skokie, IL 60077
www.westfield.com

Brooks Brothers
(847)679-9090
www.brooksbrothers.com

Coach
(847)329-1772 www.coach.com

Nordstrom
(847)677-2121 www.nordstrom.com
Attractive store with first-rate selection, particularly in casual wear and tailored clothing.

Casual Wear Robert Barakett, Ike Behar, Burberry, Diesel, Hiltl, Ermenegildo Zegna
Dress Shirts Joseph Abboud, Ike Behar, Jack Lipson Robert Talbott
Neckwear Joseph Abboud, Robert Talbott, XMI, Ermenegildo Zegna
Tailored Clothing Joseph Abboud, Hickey Freeman, Ermenegildo Zegna, Zegna Soft, Pal Zileri

Saks Fifth Avenue
(847)676-3450
www.saksfifthavenue.com
No tailored clothing at this location.

Casual Wear Giorgio Armani, Hugo Boss, Henry Cotton's, Levi's, Polo Ralph Lauren, Theory, Ermenegildo Zegna
Neckwear Joseph Abboud, Robert Talbott, Ermenegildo Zegna

Gaede's
Independent
Bill Gaede, Owner
124 N. Hale St., Wheaton, IL 60187
(630)653-6770
Large store filled with quality merchandise. Also a women's department. For shopper with updated traditional tastes.

Accessories Good selection of pocket squares and leather outerwear
Casual Wear Joseph Abboud, Bills Khakis, Forsyth, Gitman Bros., Gran Sasso, Raffi, Zanella
Dress Shirts Joseph Abboud, Gitman Bros., Kenneth Gordon
Neckwear Joseph Abboud, JZ Richards, Robert Talbott, XMI
Tailored Clothing Joseph Abboud, Coppley (also M2M), Hart, Schaffner & Marx (also M2M), Lauren by Ralph Lauren, Jack Victor, Zanella, Pal Zileri
Sales Semiannual

PLAZA DEL LAGO
Location and Stores:
1515 Sheridan Rd., Wilmette, IL 60091

Hanig's Footwear
Independent
(847)256-3545 www.hanigs.com
Family owned and operated for more than 50 years. Great service and selection.

Shoes Alden, Ecco, Johnston & Murphy, Mephisto

Huntley's Ltd.
Independent
Irwin Lips, Owner/Richard Foltos, Sales/Rusty Martin, Sales
(847)853-0666
Very attractive, spacious store in choice location along Lake Michigan. Quality inventory from well-known manufacturers, including: Joseph Abboud, Tommy Bahama, Barbour, Belford, Burberry, Bills Khakis, Corbin, Gitman Bros., Royall Fragrance, Southwick, St. Croix, Robert Talbott, True Grit, Viyella, Zanella, and many more. Great customer service. Honors all major credit cards.

Sales Semiannual

Mr. Eddie
Independent
114 Skokie Blvd., Wilmette, IL 60091
(847)251-0500
Attractive store with quality clothing lines.

Casual Wear Giorgio Armani,
Tommy Bahama, Jhane Barnes,
Brunello Cuccinelli, Gran Sasso
Dress Shirts Giorgio Armani, Ike
Behar, Lorenzini
Neckwear Giorgio Armani, Jhane
Barnes
Shoes Mezlan
Tailored Clothing Giorgio Armani,
Canali, Jack Victor

The Fell Company
Independent
David Fell, President
511 Lincoln Ave., Winnetka, IL 60093
(847)446-8983
Ninety-year-old, third-generation
family business. Large, cheery store
filled with great merchandise for
the updated traditional dresser. Mr.
Fell and his staff are a pleasure to
deal with. Women's section as well.

Casual Wear Joseph Abboud,
Tommy Bahama, Barbour, Bills
Khakis, Gran Sasso, Lacoste,
Patagonia, Toscano, Viyella, Zanella
Dress Shirts Joseph Abboud,
Kenneth Gordon
Neckwear Piatelli, Robert Talbott
Shoes Mezlan, H.S. Trask
Tailored Clothing Joseph Abboud,
Ballin, Hickey Freeman, Oliver,
Jack Victor, Zanella
Sales Semiannual

Trooping the Colour
Independent
Howard Smith, Owner/Ray James,

Sales
896 Green Bay Rd., Winnetka, IL
60093 (847)446-6360
Great merchandise for the updated
traditional dresser. Friendly, helpful
sales staff. Also a women's section.

Casual Wear Forté cashmere,
Haupt, Gran Sasso, Robert
Talbott, Viyella
Dress Shirts Kenneth Gordon
Neckwear Robert Talbott, XMI
Tailored Clothing Coppley, Oliver,
Jack Victor
Sales Semiannual

Metro Area: Cleveland

AURORA PREMIUM OUTLETS
Location and Stores:
549 S. Chillicothe Rd., Aurora, OH
44202 www.premiumoutlets.com

Brooks Brothers
Outlet Store
(330)562-1122
www.brooksbrothers.com

DKNY Jeans
Outlet Store
(330)995-3385 www.dkny.com

Polo Ralph Lauren Factory Store
Outlet Store
(330)995-8855 www.polo.com

Saks Off Fifth
Outlet Store
(330)995-0665
www.saksfifthavenue.com

Casual Wear Henry Cotton's,
Vestimenta, Ermenegildo Zegna
Dress Shirts Ike Behar
Neckwear Brioni, ETRO,
Ermenegildo Zegna

Tailored Clothing Joseph
Abboud, Hugo Boss, Canali,
Vestimenta

BEACHWOOD PLACE
Location and Stores:
26300 Beachwood Rd., Beachwood,
OH 44122
www.beachwoodplace.com

Brooks Brothers
(216)292-6852
www.brooksbrothers.com

Coach
(216)591-1772 www.coach.com

Johnston & Murphy
(216)292-3097
www.johnstonmurphy.com

Nordstrom
(216)378-2121 www.nordstrom.com

Accessories Great selection of
Trafalgar braces
Casual Wear Jhane Barnes,
Ermenegildo Zegna (limited)
Dress Shirts Ike Behar
Neckwear Robert Talbott, XMI,
Ermenegildo Zegna
Tailored Clothing Joseph
Abboud, Jhane Barnes (limited),
Pal Zileri (limited)

Saks Fifth Avenue
(216)292-5500
www.saksfifthavenue.com
Good-sized Giorgio Armani,
Ermenegildo Zegna boutiques.

Casual Wear Giorgio Armani,
Jhane Barnes, Polo Ralph
Lauren, Ermenegildo Zegna
Dress Shirts Ike Behar, Hickey
Freeman, Ermenegildo Zegna

Neckwear Giorgio Armani,
Hugo Boss, Brioni,
Ermenegildo Zegna
Tailored Clothing Joseph
Abboud, Giorgio Armani, Hugo
Boss, Corneliani, Ermenegildo
Zegna

Ticknors
Independent
(216)514-7848
Good assortment of value-priced
merchandise for the younger man.

Casual Wear Jhane Barnes,
Tundra
Dress Shirts Ike Behar, Kenneth
Cole, DKNY
Neckwear Jhane Barnes
Tailored Clothing Jhane Barnes,
Kenneth Cole, DKNY

Cuffs Clothing Company
Independent
Rodger Kowall, Owner
18 East Orange St., Chagrin Falls, OH
44022 (440)247-2828
Distinctive store filled with unique,
tasteful items. Located in a remodeled house.

Casual Wear Cuffs, Fray
Dress Shirts Luigi Borrelli, Brioni,
Charvet, Cuffs
Neckwear Charvet, Hermès, Kiton
Tailored Clothing Belvest, Brioni,
Kiton

Peter's of Chagrin Falls
Independent
Peter Di Biasi, Owner
40 N. Main St., Chagrin Falls, OH
44022 (440)247-8462
Peter's customers prefer its custom
line of tailored clothing, made of
exceptional Italian fabrics.

Accessories Trafalgar braces;
Robert Talbott cuff links; nice
selection of Peter's brand leather
outerwear
Casual Wear Axis, Tommy
Bahama, Robert Barakett, Jhane
Barnes, Barry Bricken, Burberry,
Dalmine, Kenneth Gordon,
Peter's, Raffi, Sartori, Robert
Talbott, Viyella, XMI
Dress Shirts Joseph Abboud, Ike
Behar, Gitman Bros., Kenneth
Gordon, Hickey Freeman, Luciano
Moresco, Robert Talbott
Neckwear Fabergé, Pancaldi,
Robert Talbott, XMI
Tailored Clothing Joseph Abboud,
Luciano Moresco, Peter's,
Ravazzolo, Pal Zileri (including
Sartoriale line)

Christopher's Clothier's Co., Ltd.
Independent
Bob Genovese, President/
Peter Tarnay, Vice President
BP Building Atrium, 200 Public
Square, Cleveland, OH 44114
(216)621-6333.
Hospitable establishment in con-
venient downtown location. Nice
inventory of quality, reasonably
priced merchandise.

Casual Wear Riscatto Portofino,
Tricots St. Raphael
Dress Shirts XMI
Neckwear XMI
Shoes Alden
Tailored Clothing DKNY, Ralph
Lauren, Tallia

Christophier Custom Clothiers
Independent
Maurice Christophier, Owner
10435 Clifton Blvd., Cleveland, OH

44102 (216)961-5555 or (877)216-8686
www.christophier.com
(see chapter 9)
Classy, intimate emporium with
interesting inventory of ready-
made items as well as great fabrics
for custom clothing.

Casual Wear Avon Celli, Dalmine,
Equilibrio, Haupt, Bernard Zins
Dress Shirts Custom
Neckwear Allea, Tino Cosma,
Pancaldi
Shoes Allen Edmonds, Bresciani,
Bruno Magli, Mezlan, Donald J.
Pliner
Tailored Clothing Custom, fabrics
primarily from Loro Piana and
Ermenegildo Zegna

Joseph Scafidi
Custom Tailors and Shirtmakers
Independent
Joseph Scafidi, Owner/President
One Huntington Building Arcade, 925
Fuclid Ave., Cleveland, OH 44115
(216)579-9500
www.scafiditailors.com
Impressive tailor's shop with many
unique ready-to-wear items as
well. Mr. Scafidi was gracious with
his time and highly knowledgeable
about the clothing industry. I highly recommend his establishment.

Accessories Excellent selection of
braces, including Trafalgar Limited
Edition. Also good selection of
unusual cuff links
Casual Wear Burberry, Gran Sasso,
Robert Talbott
Dress Shirts Custom
Neckwear Italo Ferretti, Pancaldi,
Robert Talbott
Shoes Allen Edmonds
Tailored Clothing Custom fabrics

from Dormeuil, Holland & Sherry,
Loro Piana, Schofield & Smith,
Scabal, Ermenegildo Zegna

Kilgore Trout
Independent
Walter Naymon, Owner
28601 Chagrin Blvd., Cleveland, OH
44122 (216)831-0488
Ermenegildo Zegna store-in-store.
Large, attractive store in great
location.

Accessories Gimo's outerwear
Casual Wear Giorgio Armani,
Zanella, Zanone, Ermenegildo
Zegna, Zegna Sport
Dress Shirts Brioni, Eton, Kilgore
Trout, Kiton, Ermenegildo Zegna
Neckwear Robert Talbott,
Ermenegildo Zegna
Tailored Clothing Giorgio Armani,
Brioni, Canali, Dolce & Gabbana,
Kiton, Ermenegildo Zegna

Riley's
Independent
*Jeff Riley, Owner/George Corrado,
Sales*
100 N. Main St., Hudson, OH 44236
(888)468-8584 or (330)656-3343
Mr. Corrado has 60 years' experience in retail—more than any
other person I interviewed—and is
gracious with his time and expertise. Tasteful boutique with unusual
and unique merchandise arranged
appealingly. Updated traditional
inventory; also a good-sized
women's section.

Accessories Trafalgar braces (including Limited Edition); good selection of cuff links; Cleveland
Indians leather baseball jackets;
Guy Laroche leather outerwear

Casual Wear Ike Behar, Casa
Moda, Dalmine, Gitman Bros.,
Gran Sasso, Hickey Freeman,
Raffi, Tricots St. Raphael, Tundra,
Viyella
Dress Shirts Ike Behar, Gitman
Bros., Hickey Freeman, Robert
Talbott
Neckwear Pancaldi, Robert Talbott
Shoes Allen Edmonds, Cole Haan
Tailored Clothing Joseph Abboud,
Aquascutum, Coppley (also
M2M), Corbin, Hickey Freeman,
Samuelsohn (also M2M), Jack
Victor

James Clothiers
Independent
Joe Paster, Manager
30679 Pinetree Rd., Pepper Pike, OH
44124 (216)831-6470
Pleasant store with merchandise
arranged appealingly and helpful,
attentive customer service.

Accessories Some braces and formal
wear; nice selection of pocket
squares
Casual Wear Scott Barber, Gran
Sasso, Haupt, St. Croix, Robert
Talbott
Dress Shirts Ike Behar, Eton,
Robert Talbott
Neckwear Jhane Barnes, Brioni,
Robert Talbott
Tailored Clothing Jhane Barnes,
Corneliani, Zanella, Pal Zileri

Adesso
Independent
*Domenico DiCristofaro, Owner/
Dan Varnadoe, Store Manager/
Joe Zodda, Assistant Manager*
Hahn Plaza, 19920 Detroit Rd., Rocky
River, OH 44116 (440)333-4778
www.adessofashions.com

Excellent store operated by third generation of tailors. Mr. DiCristofaro and his staff give old-world, personalized service and truly make one feel at home. One of two U.S. locations I visited that sells Marinella ties.

Accessories Allegri, Gallotti, and Longhi outerwear
Casual Wear Berretta, Brioni, Gran Sasso, Dalmine, Paul & Shark
Dress Shirts Luigi Borrelli, Eton, Kiton, Lorenzini
Neckwear Kiton, Marinella
Shoes Bruno Magli, a. testoni
Tailored Clothing Gianluca Isaia, Kiton, Gianluca Napoli, Pal Zileri
Sales Semiannual

Ford's Clothier
Independent
19821 Detroit Rd., Rocky River, OH 44116 (440)333-2355
Good inventory of quality items for the traditional dresser. Friendly, helpful sales staff.

Casual Wear Joseph Abboud, Bills Khakis, Burberry, Tricots St. Raphael, Tundra, Viyella
Dress Shirts Burberry, Kenneth Cole, MacCluer, Robert Talbott
Neckwear Robert Talbott, XMI
Tailored Clothing Burberry, Coppley, Hickey Freeman, Tallia

Giovanni Carrelli Clothier
Independent
Giovanni Carrelli, Owner
The Promenade of Westlake, 30187 Detroit Rd., Westlake, OH 44145 (440)899-5454
www.giovannicarrelli.com
Marvelous store filled with quality merchandise arranged in a most

appealing manner. Mr. Carrelli is extremely knowledgeable about the clothing profession and is always generous in sharing his time and expertise.

Accessories Canali, Salvatore Ferragamo, and Paul & Shark outerwear
Casual Wear Avon Celli, Dalmine, Gran Sasso, Salvatore Ferragamo, Paul & Shark
Dress Shirts Ike Behar, Brioni, Canali
Shoes Salvatore Ferragamo
Tailored Clothing Brioni (also custom), Canali, Corneliani, Oxxford (also custom)
Sales Semiannual

RR Freestyle
Independent
Rick Rasgaitis, Owner
30175 Detroit Rd., Westlake, OH 44145 (440)356-0100 www.rrfreestyle.com
Attractive store with sleek, modern look. One of the better selections of Jhane Barnes items you'll find anywhere.

Accessories Raz cuff links, Leegin leather outerwear
Casual Wear Jhane Barnes, Equilibrio, Jack Lipson, Riscatto Portofino, Gran Sasso
Dress Shirts RR Freestyle
Neckwear Jhane Barnes, Pavone, Nicole Miller
Tailored Clothing Joseph Abboud, Jhane Barnes, Arnold Brant, Coppley
Sales Semiannual

Metro Area: Columbus
COLUMBUS CITY CENTER
Location and Stores:

111 S. Third St., Columbus, OH 43215
www.shopcitycenter.com

Christian St. John
Independent
(614)228-7000
Hospitable store in convenient
location. Courteous, helpful
sales associates.

Accessories Stetson hats; Andres
leather outerwear
Casual Wear Ballin, Jhane
Barnes, Barry Bricken, Gillio,
Jack Lipson, Raffi, Tricots St.
Raphael, Toscano, Tulliano,
Tundra
Dress Shirts Ike Behar, Hugo
Boss, Rodin, XMI, Zanetti
Neckwear Burberry, Robert
Daskal, XMI
Shoes Cole Haan, Mezlan,
Santoni
Tailored Clothing Jhane Barnes,
Burberry, Coppley, Corneliani,
DKNY, Jack Victor, Zanetti

Brooks Brothers
(614)228-1964
www.brooksbrothers.com

Johnston & Murphy
(614)224-8725
www.johnstonmurphy.com

Nordstrom
Easton Towncenter, 4000 Worth Ave.,
Columbus, OH 43219 (614)416-7111
www.nordstrom.com

Casual Wear Ermenegildo Zegna
Dress Shirts Joseph Abboud, Ike
Behar, Robert Talbott
Neckwear XMI, Ermenegildo
Zegna
Tailored Clothing Joseph Abboud,

Jhane Barnes, Corneliani, Jack
Victor

Woodhouse Lynch Clothiers
Independent
Tom Lynch, Owner
146 E. Broad St., Columbus, OH 43215
(614)228-7200
Appealing store with some really
unique items, especially for the
holidays. Mr. Lynch was great to
shop with. Clothing caters to the
traditional customer.

Casual Wear Riscatto Portofino,
Bob Timberlake, Tricots St.
Raphael
Dress Shirts Gitman Bros., Kenneth
Gordon, MacCluer, Woodhouse
Lynch, Versailles Custom
Neckwear Ferrell Reed,
Woodhouse Lynch, XMI
Tailored Clothing Ballin, Bronzetta
(Hickey Freeman), Corbin, Hilton
Sales Semiannual

Godfrys Columbus
Independent
Heinz Ellrod, President/
Michael Landin, Manager
92 Worthington Mall, Worthington,
OH 43085 (614)433-0101
www.godfrys.com
Elegant and exquisite store in
excellent location. First-class presentation of merchandise, including
brand-new Ermenegildo Zegna
shop-in-shop, the first of its kind
in the U.S.

Accessories Ballenasia, Martin
Dingman, Paulo De Pointe, Nancy
and Risé, Tateossian, Cristom/
Gentili luxury boxes
Casual Wear Giorgio Armani,
Luciano Barbera, Brioni, Canali,

Dalmine, Brunello Cuccinelli,
Eton, Gran Sasso, Haupt, St.
Croix, Robert Talbott, Zanella,
Ermenegildo Zegna, Pal Zileri
Dress Shirts Canali, Eton, Brioni,
Ermenegildo Zegna, Marol
Neckwear Brioni, Canali, Tino
Cosma, Fabergé, Pancaldi, Robert
Talbott, yAprè, Ermenegildo
Zegna
Shoes Salvatore Ferragamo, Bruno
Magli, Mezlan, Donald J. Pliner,
Zegna Sport
Tailored Clothing Giorgio Armani,
Luciano Barbera, Brioni, Canali,
Ermenegildo Zegna, Pal Zileri
Sales Semiannual

Metro Area: Dallas

Culwell and Son
Independent
*Michael Culwell, Charlie and Jay
Burgin, Owners*
6319 Hillcrest Ave., Dallas, TX 75205
(214)522-7000
Huge, unique store, family-owned
business since 1920. Fifteen-seat
barbershop, laundry, and dry
cleaner on the premises. Caters to
the updated traditional dresser.
Also some nice introductory packages for business school graduates.

Accessories Trafalgar braces, including Limited Edition; good selection of cuff links; large formal wear
dept.; Colonel Littleton gentleman's accessories; Robert Talbott
leather outerwear
Casual Wear Scott Barber, Ike
Behar, Bills Khakis, Barry Bricken,
Burberry, Cifonelli, Henry
Cotton's, Culwell and Son,
Dalmine, Gitman Bros., Kenneth

Gordon, Gran Sasso, Hickey
Freeman, ISDA & Co., Lacoste,
Majer, Raffi, Royal Label, Bob
Timberlake, Robert Talbott, XMI
Dress Shirts Ike Behar (also M2M),
Culwell and Son, Ferrell Reed,
Hickey Freeman, Robert Talbott
(also M2M), custom
Neckwear Brioni, Burberry, Ferrell
Reed, Polo Ralph Lauren, Robert
Talbott, Venanzi
Shoes Alden, Cole Haan, Donald J.
Pliner, Royal Label, H.S. Trask,
Zelli
Tailored Clothing Axis, Corbin,
Culwell and Son, Hickey Freeman
(also M2M), Hilton (M2M),
Mabro, NH 1881, Oxxford (also
M2M), Polo Ralph Lauren,
Southwick (M2M)

DALLAS GALLERIA
Location and Stores:
13355 Noel Rd., Dallas, TX 75240
www.dallasgalleria.com

A/X Armani Exchange
(972)701-9743
www.giorgioarmani.com

BOSS Hugo Boss
(972)702-7100 www.hugoboss.com

Brass Boot
(972)702-7100 www.brassboot.com

Brooks Brothers
(972)960-6200
www.brooksbrothers.com

Coach
(972)392-1772 www.coach.com

Kenneth Cole
(972)458-6822
www.kennethcole.com

Gucci
(972)387-3357 www.gucci.com

Johnston & Murphy
(972)387-7934
www.johnstonmurphy.com

Nordstrom
(972)702-0055 www.nordstrom.com

Dress Shirts Robert Talbott, Zanella
Neckwear Robert Talbott, XMI
Tailored Clothing Joseph Abboud, Hugo Boss, Corneliani, Vestimenta, Zanella, Pal Zileri

Thomas Pink
(972)759-0207
www.thomaspink.com

Saks Fifth Avenue
(972)458-7000
www.saksfifthavenue.com
Giorgio Armani store in-store.

Casual Wear Giorgio Armani, Hugo Boss, Ermenegildo Zegna
Dress Shirts Ike Behar, Hugo Boss, Canali, Hickey Freeman, Lorenzini, Ermenegildo Zegna
Neckwear Giorgio Armani, Hugo Boss, Ermenegildo Zegna
Tailored Clothing Canali, Vestimenta, Ermenegildo Zegna

Gianni Versace
(972)385-9155 www.versace.com

Versace Jeans Couture
(972)503-6220 www.versace.com

Louis Vuitton
(972)934-3637
www.louisvuitton.com

Daniel Taylor
Independent
Danny Taylor, Owner
West Village, 3699 McKinney, Ste. 313, Dallas, TX 75204 (214)521-0433
Attractive store catering to the traditional shopper. Mr. Taylor is great to shop with.

Accessories Some unique belts and cuff links
Casual Wear Acorn, Ike Behar, Berle, Como Sport, Gillio, Raffi, Samuelsohn, St. Croix
Dress Shirts Ike Behar
Neckwear Ferrell Reed, Robert Talbott, Daniel Taylor
Shoes Alden, Cole Haan, H.S. Trask, Zelli
Tailored Clothing Coppley (also M2M), Tallia, Samuelsohn (also M2M)

Ken's
Independent
Ken Helfman, Owner
309 Preston Royal, Dallas, TX 75230 (214)369-5367
Homey store with lots of windows and light. Uses antiques to add to store's atmosphere and present merchandise. Complimentary collar stays.

Accessories Tateossian cuff links; Robert Comstock and Vestimenta leather outerwear
Casual Wear Jhane Barnes, Ike Behar, Coast, Equilibrio, Ken's, Moreno Martini Da Firenze, Rodin, Jeff Rose, White Shirt/Blue Jean
Dress Shirts Eton, Ken's, Zanella
Neckwear Altea, Jhane Barnes, Ken's
Shoes Mezlan

Tailored Clothing Jhane Barnes, Ken's, Rodin, Zanella, Pal Zileri

Kent Shop
Independent
Scot Harris, Owner/Rod Trapp, Sales
5342 Belt Line Rd., Dallas, TX 75240
(972)233-1752
Attractive shopping environment with large, varied inventory of quality items. Sales staff attentive and helpful.

Accessories Good selection of belts, cuff links, and pocket squares; some formal wear, and a great variety of leather outerwear as well
Casual Wear Allegré, Axis, Ballin, Robert Barakett, Ike Behar, Bills Khakis, Barry Bricken, Dalmine, Georgio Danielli, Equilibrio, Gran Sasso, Haupt, Riscatto Portofino, St. Croix, Tricots St. Raphael, XMI
Dress Shirts Ike Behar (also M2M), XMI, Thomas Mason M2M
Neckwear Villa Bolgheri, Tino Cosma, Luciano Moresco, Pancaldi, Robert Talbott, XMI
Shoes Cole Haan, Bruno Magli, Donald J. Pliner
Tailored Clothing Ballin, Jhane Barnes, Canali, Coppley, Tallia, Jack Victor, Zanella

Neiman Marcus
One Marcus Square, 1618 Main St., Dallas, TX 75201 (214)741-6911
www.neimanmarcus.com

Casual Wear Giorgio Armani, Jhane Barnes, Polo Ralph Lauren, Ermenegildo Zegna
Dress Shirts Giorgio Armani, Luigi Borrelli, Lorenzini, Turnbull & Asser, Ermenegildo Zegna
Neckwear Giorgio Armani, Brioni, Salvatore Ferragamo, Turnbull & Asser, Ermenegildo Zegna
Tailored Clothing Giorgio Armani, Hugo Boss, Brioni, Hickey Freeman, Kiton, Oxxford, Ermenegildo Zegna

NORTH PARK MALL
Location and Stores:
400 NorthPark Center, Dallas, TX 75201

Bally
(214)368-6535 www.bally.com

Brooks Brothers
(214)363-2196
www.brooksbrothers.com

Burberry
(214)369-1100 www.burberry.com

Kenneth Cole
(214)369-2663
www.kennethcole.com

Façonnable
(214)369-9611 www.nordstrom.com

Johnston & Murphy
(214)363-0698
www.johnstonmurphy.com

Neiman Marcus
(214)363-8311
www.neimanmarcus.com
Company's largest store.

Casual Wear Giorgio Armani, Jhane Barnes, DKNY, Loro Piana, Polo Ralph Lauren, Ralph Lauren Purple Label, Ermenegildo Zegna

Dress Shirts Giorgio Armani, Ike Behar, Luigi Borrelli, Brioni, Charvet, Lorenzini, Turnbull & Asser, Ermenegildo Zegna
Neckwear Giorgio Armani, Luigi Borrelli, Brioni, Charvet, Salvatore Ferragamo, Kiton, Turnbull & Asser, Ermenegildo Zegna
Tailored Clothing Giorgio Armani, Hugo Boss, Brioni, Hickey Freeman, Incotex, Oxxford, Polo Ralph Lauren, Ermenegildo Zegna

Pockets Menswear
Independent
David Smith, Owner
9669 N. Central Expy., Dallas, TX 75231 (214)368-1167
Great store—open, airy, with lots of wood. Ermenegildo Zegna store-in-store. Mr. Smith is great to work with.

Accessories Good selection of Trafalgar braces; cuff links
Casual Wear Tommy Bahama, Luciano Barbera, Barry Bricken, Gran Sasso, Lorenzini, Marzotto Lab, Ermenegildo Zegna, Zegna Sport
Dress Shirts Barba, Luciano Barbera, Ike Behar, Canali, Lorenzini, Robert Talbott, Ermenegildo Zegna
Neckwear Allea, Jhane Barnes, Canali, Robert Talbott, XMI, Ermenegildo Zegna
Shoes Cole Haan, Gravati, Moreschi, Santoni, Ermenegildo Zegna
Tailored Clothing Ballin, Luciano Barbera, Arnold Brant, Canali, Cifonelli, Coppley, Corneliani,

Samuelsohn, Linnea Trussini, Zanella, Ermenegildo Zegna (also M2M), Zegna Soft, Bernard Zins

Robert Talbott
Highland Park Village, 87 Highland Park Village, Dallas, TX 75205
(214)526-6800 www.roberttalbott.com

Sebastian's Closet
Independent
Cass Niru, Sales
Village on the Parkway, 5100 Belt Line Rd., Ste. 540, Dallas, TX 75240
(972)387-0888
Tasteful store with cordial, responsive customer service.

Casual Wear Axis, Tommy Bahama, Haupt, Marzotto Lab, Nat Nast, Georg Roth, Signum, Zanella
Dress Shirts Acorn, Eton, Lorenzini
Neckwear Tino Cosma, Daniel Craig
Shoes Donald J. Pliner
Tailored Clothing Lubiam 1911, Vestimenta, Zanella, Pal Zileri

Stanley Korshak
Independent
Gary Murray, Sales
500 Crescent Court, Ste. 100, Dallas, TX 75201 (214)871-3645
www.stanleykorshak.com
Magnificent store, perennially voted one of best in the country by the *Robb Report*. Large Giorgio Armani and Kiton store-in-stores. Mr. Murray was very attentive and helpful.

Accessories Robert Comstock leather outerwear and others too numerous to mention

Casual Wear Agnona, Avon Celli, Luigi Borrelli, Burberry, Lorenzini, Loro Piana
Dress Shirts Giorgio Armani, Luigi Borrelli, Charvet, Kiton, Lorenzini
Neckwear Giorgio Armani, Luciano Barbera, Charvet, Kiton
Tailored Clothing Giorgio Armani, Luciano Barbera, Belvest, Kiton

Neiman Marcus
Ridgmar Mall, 2100 Green Oaks Rd., Fort Worth, TX 76116 (817)738-3581
www.neimanmarcus.com
Casual Wear Giorgio Armani, Tommy Bahama, Hugo Boss, Polo Ralph Lauren, Ermenegildo Zegna
Dress Shirts Giorgio Armani, Ike Behar, Luigi Borrelli, Lorenzini, Turnbull & Asser, Ermenegildo Zegna
Neckwear Giorgio Armani, Salvatore Ferragamo, Turnbull & Asser, Ermenegildo Zegna
Tailored Clothing Hugo Boss, Hickey Freeman, Oxxford, Ermenegildo Zegna

GRAPEVINE MILLS
Location and Stores:
3000 Grapevine Mills Pkwy., Grapevine, TX 76051
www.grapevinemills.com

Brooks Brothers
Outlet Store
(972)724-6904
www.brooksbrothers.com

Off Rodeo Drive
Outlet Store
(972)724-7860 www.bernini.com
Large store with good selection.

Polo Jeans Company
Outlet Store
(972)874-3445 www.polo.com

Saks Off Fifth
Outlet Store
(972)724-3500
www.saksfifthavenue.com

Dress Shirts Ermenegildo Zegna
Neckwear Ermenegildo Zegna
Tailored Clothing Joseph Abboud, Hugo Boss, Burberry, DKNY, Mani

NORTHEAST MALL
Location and Stores:
1101 Melbourne Rd., Hurst, TX 75053
www.shopsimon.com

Nordstrom
(817)590-2599 www.nordstrom.com
Casual Wear Jhane Barnes, Zanella
Neckwear Robert Talbott, XMI
Tailored Clothing Joseph Abboud, Jhane Barnes, Corneliani, Zanella, Pal Zileri

Saks Fifth Avenue
(817)590-3500
www.saksfifthavenue.com
Casual Wear Polo Ralph Lauren

Nordstrom Rack
Outlet Store
Northeast Mall, 861 N.E. Mall Blvd., Hurst, TX 75053 (817)590-8877
www.nordstrom.com
Tailored Clothing Joseph Abboud, Hugo Boss, Tallia

Circa 2000
Independent
Mike Zack, Owner
5800 Legacy, Ste. C5, Plano, TX 75024
(972)673-0920
Pleasant shopping destination. Merchandise is presented well, and

customer service is friendly and helpful.

Casual Wear Jhane Barnes, Haupt
Tailored Clothing Jhane Barnes, Tallia, Jack Victor

Nordstrom Rack
Outlet Store
1701 D-1 Preston Rd., Plano, TX 75093
(972)267-1414
www.nordstrom.com

THE SHOPS AT WILLOW BEND
Location and Stores:
6121 W. Park Blvd., Plano, TX 75093
www.shopwillowbend.com

Allen Edmonds
Richard Curry, Store Manager
(469)366-0020
www.allenedmonds.com

Armani Collezioni
Collette Hummel, Store Manager
(972)202-8813
www.giorgioarmani.com

Bernini
Linda Azhari, Store Manager
(469)366-0786 www.bernini.com

Dress Shirts Barba, Brioni

BOSS Hugo Boss
(972)202-5559 www.hugoboss.com
Large, beautiful store. If you're a Boss fan, this boutique is definitely worth checking out.

Burberry
(972)202-5500 www.burberry.com

Coach
(972)202-5511 www.coach.com

Diesel
(469)366-1055 www.diesel.com

Johnston & Murphy
Leonard Hernandez, Store Manager
(469)366-1076
www.johnstonmurphy.com

Lucky Brand Dungarees
(469)366-4483
www.luckyjeans.com

Bruno Magli
(469)366-0650
www.brunomagli.com

Neiman Marcus
(972)629-1700
www.neimanmarcus.com
Brand-new, attractive store. Giorgio Armani and Ermenegildo Zegna in-store boutiques.

Casual Wear Giorgio Armani, Ermenegildo Zegna
Dress Shirts Giorgio Armani, Ike Behar, Hugo Boss, Ermenegildo Zegna
Neckwear Giorgio Armani, Hermès, Fabergé
Tailored Clothing Giorgio Armani, Hugo Boss, Brioni, Gianluca Isaia, Ermenegildo Zegna

Rangoni Firenze
(469)366-1032
www.rangonishoes.com
Shoes Bally, Cole Haan, Johnston & Murphy, Moreschi, Mephisto, Donald J. Pliner

Metro Area: Denver
FLATIRON CROSSING
Location and Stores:
One W. Flatiron Circle, Broomfield, CO 80021 www.flatironcrossing.com

Coach
(303)460-7634 www.coach.com

Nordstrom
(720)887-0333 www.nordstrom.com

Dress Shirts Ike Behar
Neckwear Robert Talbott, XMI,
Ermenegildo Zegna
Tailored Clothing Joseph
Abboud, Hickey Freeman

Nordstrom Rack
Outlet Store
Flatiron Marketplace, 130 E. Flatiron
Circle, Broomfield, CO 80021
(720)887-3588 www.nordstrom.com

Kinsley and Company
Independent
Court Dixon and Edward Kapson,
Owners/Pete Giffin, Sales
1155 13th St., Boulder, CO 80302
(303)442-6204
www.kinsleyoutfitters.com
Excellent, 54-year-old store with
great selection of quality merchandise. Informed and friendly sales
staff. Adjoining women's boutique
and Orvis fly-fishing outfitting
capability make Kinsley an even
more interesting destination.

Accessories Belts, bow ties, braces,
cuff links, cummerbund sets, hats,
luggage, large selection of interest-
ing socks, wallets
Casual Wear Barba, Scott Barber,
Luciano Barbera, Bills Khakis,
Hugo Boss, Bruli, DeSanto,
ETRO, Gran Sasso, New England,
Ermenegildo Zegna
Dress Shirts Giorgio Armani,
Barba, Luciano Barbera, Luigi
Borrelli, Hugo Boss, Ermenegildo
Zegna

Neckwear Luciano Barbera, Hugo
Boss, Carrot & Gibbs, Ferrell
Reed, Ermenegildo Zegna
Shoes Allen Edmonds, Gravati,
Paraboot, Bruno Magli
Tailored Clothing Luciano Barbera,
Hugo Boss, Arnold Brant, Hickey
Freeman, Gianluca Isaia, Zanella,
Ermenegildo Zegna
Sales Semiannual, January and July

Weekends
Independent
1101 Pearl St., Boulder, CO 80302
(303)444-4231
Great place to shop for upscale
casual and business casual wear.

Accessories Golden Bear leathers
Casual Wear Axis, Tommy
Bahama, Scott Barber, Hugo Boss,
Haupt
Dress Shirts Hugo Boss
Neckwear Jhane Barnes
Shoes Cole Haan, H.S. Trask
Tailored Clothing Hugo Boss,
Tallia
Sales Semiannual, January and July

Andrisen Morton Co.
Independent
Bob Schultz, Buyer
280 St. Paul St., Denver, CO 80206
(303)377-8488
Spacious, open emporium with
excellent arrangement of invento-
ry. One of largest Ermenegildo
Zegna store-in-stores among inde-
pendent retail outlets in the U.S.
Amicable and responsive staff; Mr.
Schultz was a pleasure to talk to.

Accessories Some cuff links;
Ermenegildo Zegna leather coats
Casual Wear Giorgio Armani,
Tommy Bahama, Barba, Brioni,

Gran Sasso, Haupt, Bobby Jones,
Loro Piana
Dress Shirts Andrisen Morton,
Baldessarini, Luigi Borrelli, Brioni,
Canali, Gianluca Isaia,
Ermenegildo Zegna
Neckwear Barba, Brioni, Canali,
Robert Talbott, Ermenegildo
Zegna
Shoes Cole Haan, Salvatore
Ferragamo, Gucci, Gravati, Terra
Plana
Tailored Clothing Andrisen
Morton, Brioni, Canali, Gianluca
Isaia, Samuelsohn, Ermenegildo
Zegna
Sales Semiannual, January and July

Bolderdash
Independent
2721 E. Third Ave., Denver, CO 80206
(303)399-3940
For the younger casual and business casual dresser. Clothes for
men and women.

Casual Wear Axis, Tommy
Bahama, Jhane Barnes, Diesel,
DKNY, Tricots St. Raphael,
Tundra
Shoes Cole Haan, H.S. Trask
Sales Semiannual, January and July

CHERRY CREEK SHOPPING CENTER
Location and Stores:
3000 E. First Ave., Denver, CO 80206
www.shopcherrycreek.com

BOSS Hugo Boss
(720)945-1101 www.hugoboss.com

Burberry
(303)388-2700 www.burberry.com

Coach
(303)393-1772 www.coach.com

Diesel
(303)355-9555 www.diesel.com

DKNY
(303)333-9400 www.dkny.com

Johnston & Murphy
(303)320-4925
www.johnstonmurphy.com

Ralph Lauren
(303)355-7656 www.polo.com

Lucky Brand Dungarees
(303)320-9771
www.luckyjeans.com

Neiman Marcus
(303)329-2600
www.neimanmarcus.com
Spacious, attractive men's
department. Helpful, patient
salespeople who handled a difficult exchange in a very professional manner.

Dress Shirts Giorgio Armani, Ike
Behar, Brioni, Lorenzini,
Ermenegildo Zegna
Neckwear Giorgio Armani,
Brioni, Ermenegildo Zegna
Tailored Clothing Giorgio
Armani, Hickey Freeman,
Oxxford, Ermenegildo Zegna

Saks Fifth Avenue
(303)393-6333
www.saksfifthavenue.com

Casual Wear Joseph Abboud,
Ermenegildo Zegna
Dress Shirts Giorgio Armani,
Hugo Boss, Ermenegildo Zegna
Neckwear Giorgio Armani,
Ermenegildo Zegna
Tailored Clothing Giorgio

Armani, Canali, Ermenegildo
Zegna

Louis Vuitton
(303)388-0033
www.louisvuitton.com

Lawrence Covell
Independent
Lawrence, Joe, and Cathy Covell,
Proprietors
225 Steele St., Denver, CO 80206
(303)320-1023
Named as one of *Robb Report*'s
top menswear stores in the U.S.
Sumptuous hardwood floors and
luxurious furnishings. Joe was very
knowledgeable and fun to talk
with.

Accessories Colombo and Luciano
Barbera outerwear; Art of Shaving
and Acqua Di Parma toiletries
Casual Wear Luciano Barbera,
ETRO, Lorenzini, Avon Celli,
Malo, Kiton, John Varvatos,
Vestimenta, Ermenegildo Zegna
Dress Shirts Luigi Borrelli, Kiton,
Ermenegildo Zegna
Neckwear Luciano Barbera, Luigi
Borrelli, Kiton, Ermenegildo
Zegna
Shoes Stefano Bi, Car Shoe, John
Lobb, J.M. Weston
Tailored Clothing Luciano Barbera,
Luigi Borrelli, Raffaele Caruso,
Kiton, Oxxford, Vestimenta,
Ermenegildo Zegna
Sales Semiannual, January and July

Homer Reed Ltd.
Independent
Mark Reed, Owner
303 University Blvd., Denver, CO
80206 (303)322-9480

Well-appointed, wood-lined retail
space with traditional feel. Helpful
and friendly customer service.
Carries inventory directed primarily toward the traditional dresser.

Accessories Good selection of bow
ties, cuff links, and pocket squares
Casual Wear Scott Barber, Homer
Reed, Reyn Spooner, Tricots St.
Raphael
Dress Shirts Corbin, Kenneth
Gordon, Homer Reed, Robert
Talbott
Neckwear Robert Talbott, XMI
Shoes Cole Haan, Trask
Tailored Clothing Corbin, Hickey
Freeman, Southwick
Sales Semiannual, January and July

Homer Reed Ltd.
Independent
Mark Reed, Owner
1717 Tremont Place, Denver, CO
80202 (303)298-1301
Helpful and friendly customer
service. Inventory directed primarily toward the traditional dresser.

Accessories Good selection of bow
ties, cuff links, and pocket squares
Casual Wear Scott Barber, Homer
Reed, Reyn Spooner, Tricots St.
Raphael
Dress Shirts Corbin, Kenneth
Gordon, Homer Reed, Robert
Talbott
Neckwear Robert Talbott, XMI
Shoes Cole Haan, Trask
Tailored Clothing Corbin, Hickey
Freeman, Southwick
Sales Semiannual, January and July

Homer Reed Ltd.
Independent
Mark Reed, Owner

Belleview Promenade, 8000 E.
Belleview, Denver, CO 80206
(303)322-9480
Well-appointed, wood-lined retail
space with traditional feel. Helpful
and friendly customer service.
Carries inventory directed primarily toward the traditional dresser.

Accessories Good selection of bow
ties, cuff links, and pocket squares
Casual Wear Scott Barber, Homer
Reed, Reyn Spooner, Tricots St.
Raphael
Dress Shirts Corbin, Kenneth
Gordon, Homer Reed, Robert
Talbott
Neckwear Robert Talbott, XMI
Shoes Cole Haan, Trask
Tailored Clothing Corbin, Hickey
Freeman, Southwick
Sales Semiannual, January and July

St. Croix
2445 E. Third Ave., #1, Denver, CO
80206 (303)331-9807
www.stcroixshops.com

PARK MEADOWS MALL
Location and Stores:
8401 Park Meadows Center Dr.,
Littleton, CO 80125
www.parkmeadows.com

A/X Armani Exchange
(303)799-9060
www.giorgioarmani.com

Brooks Brothers
(303)792-2683
www.brooksbrothers.com

Nordstrom
(303)799-3400 www.nordstrom.com
Casual Wear Ermenegildo
Zegna

Dress Shirts Ike Behar, Robert
Talbott
Neckwear Robert Talbott, XMI,
Ermenegildo Zegna
Tailored Clothing Hugo Boss,
Corneliani, Façonnable, Zanella

Nordstrom Rack
Outlet Store
Meadows Marketplace, 8676 Park
Meadows Center Dr., Littleton, CO
80124 (303)706-0035
www.nordstrom.com

Dress Shirts Ike Behar, Robert
Talbott
Neckwear Robert Talbott, XMI,
Ermenegildo Zegna

Metro Area: Detroit
Van Boven
Independent
Gary Clark, Manager/
Hank Schoch, Sales
326 S. South St., Ann Arbor, MI 48104
(734)665-7228
Good inventory of quality lines.
Prompt personable customer serv-
ice. Mr. Clark and Mr. Schoch
were a pleasure to work with. For
updated traditional tastes.

Accessories Braces and some cuff
links
Casual Wear Tommy Bahama,
Scott Barber, Bills Khakis, Gran
Sasso, Raffi, Robert Talbott,
Tricots St. Raphael
Dress Shirts Ike Behar, Robert
Talbott
Neckwear Tino Cosma, Robert
Talbott
Tailored Clothing Joseph Abboud,
Coppley, Jack Victor, Zanella
Sales Semiannual

GREAT LAKES CROSSING
Location and Stores:
4000 Baldwin Rd., Auburn Hills, MI
48326
www.shopgreatlakescrossing.com

Brooks Brothers
Outlet Store
Marlene Weber, Store Manager
(248)333-1811
www.brooksbrothers.com

DKNY
Outlet Store
Kathy DuBois, Store Manager
(248)745-9339 www.dkny.com

Neiman Marcus Last Call
Outlet Store
Marla Wald, Store Manager
(248)745-6868
www.neimanmarcus.com
One of the better Last Calls I
visited in the U.S.

Casual Wear Brioni, Diesel,
Loro Piana, Polo Ralph Lauren,
Ralph Lauren Purple Label,
John Varvatos, Versace,
Ermenegildo Zegna
Dress Shirts Ike Behar, Brioni,
Lorenzini, Ermenegildo Zegna
Tailored Clothing Giorgio
Armani, Bergdorf Goodman,
Corneliani, Hickey Freeman,
Richard James, Polo Ralph
Lauren, John Varvatos,
Ermenegildo Zegna, Zegna Soft

Saks Off Fifth
Outlet Store
Scott Smith, Store Manager
(248)334-3819
www.saksfifthavenue.com

Casual Wear Burberry, Como
Sport, Bobby Jones, Robert

Talbott, Ermenegildo Zegna
Dress Shirts Ike Behar, Hugo
Boss, Ermenegildo Zegna
Neckwear Hugo Boss, Versace,
Ermenegildo Zegna
Tailored Clothing Jhane Barnes,
Gianfranco Ferré Studio, Mani,
Missoni, Ermenegildo Zegna,
Zegna Soft

Carl Sterr
Independent
Carl Sterr II, Owner/
Dan Culbertson, Manager
742 N. Old Woodward, Birmingham,
MI 48009 (248)645-6675
Brand-new, custom-designed store
specializing in natural-shoulder
European-tailored clothing. Excel-
lent selection of top-notch cloth-
ing lines. Mr. Sterr and Mr. Culbert-
son are a delight to deal with.

Accessories Crescent belts (exotic
skins); bow ties; Trafalgar braces
(including Limited Edition);
Cifonelli outerwear
Casual Wear Luciano Barbera,
Luigi Borrelli, Brioni, Coast,
Cifonelli, Colombo, Gran Sasso,
John Smedley
Dress Shirts Luigi Borrelli, Marol,
Robert Talbott, Truzzi
Neckwear Luigi Borrelli, Brioni,
Tino Cosma, Nicky's of Milan,
Robert Talbott
Shoes Alden, Sutor Mantellassi
Tailored Clothing Luciano Barbera,
Luigi Borrelli, Brioni, Cifonelli,
Dormeuil (M2M), Incotex,
Gianluca Isaia, Samuelsohn (also
M2M)
Sales Semiannual

Paul Cicchini Custom Clothier
Independent

*Rick Depanicis, Owner/Herman
Masters, Manager/Sheila Blum,
Sales*
180 S. Old Woodward Ave.,
Birmingham, MI 48009 (248)646-0535
Spacious, elegant store in downtown Birmingham. Custom-made
clothing for men and women with
special attention to personal service, quality, and style. Something
for every budget. Nine master tailors right on the premises.

Accessories Nice selection of belts;
braces, cuff links, leather accessories; and outerwear
Casual Wear The finest cashmere
sweaters for men and women as
well as many mock necks, cable
knits, and Polo Ralph Laurens
Dress Shirts Custom; choose from
a large number of fabrics, including broadcloths, pima cottons, and
pure silks
Neckwear Hundreds to choose
from, including hand-painted; also
custom-ordered ties with matching
braces and cummerbunds
Shoes Alden, Allen Edmonds,
Bruno Magli, Mezlan, Moreschi
Tailored Clothing Men's and
women's custom suits, sport coats,
pants, topcoats, and tuxedos
Sales Semiannual

The Claymore Shop
Independent
Allen Skiba, Vice President
908 S. Adams Rd., Birmingham, MI
48009 (248)642-7755
Huge, excellent retail establishment for the updated traditional
dresser. Incredible number of fabric selections for custom and
made-to-measure clothing to fit

any budget. Mr. Skiba and his staff
are focused on serving their customer's needs for a lifetime of building and maintaining personal style.

Accessories Great selection of
braces, cuff links, pocket squares,
and outerwear, including Robert
Talbott
Casual Wear Tommy Bahama,
Scott Barber, Bills Khakis, Forsyth,
Lacoste, McKenzie Tribe, Polo
Ralph Lauren, Tricots St. Raphael
Dress Shirts Ike Behar, Forsyth,
Gitman Bros., Robert Talbott
Neckwear Breuer, Polo Ralph
Lauren, Robert Talbott
Shoes Alden, Magnanni, Mezlan
Tailored Clothing Coppley, Hickey
Freeman (also M2M), Oxxford
(also M2M), Polo Ralph Lauren
(also M2M), Samuelsohn (also
M2M), Southwick
Sales Semiannual

The Custom Shop
Independent
Stuart Silbert, Sales
223 S. Old Woodward Ave., Birmingham, MI 48009 (248)642-0460
www.customshop.com
(see chapter 9)
First-rate customer service. Great
quality fabrics and exceptional tailoring at reasonable prices. An
excellent place to build one's
wardrobe and develop individualized style.

Accessories Custom Shop
Casual Wear Custom Shop
Dress Shirts Custom Shop
Neckwear Custom Shop, Kolte,
Genesis, Richel, Pancaldi, Pavone
Shoes Allen Edmonds
Tailored Clothing Custom Shop

Manno Clothing and Tailoring
Independent
Pat Manno, Owner
23810 Michigan Ave., Dearborn, MI
48124 (313)5461-1419
Staffed by European tailors. Great
selection of fabrics for made-to-
measure garments. First-quality
customer service; Mr. Manno is
great to deal with.

Accessories Great selection of
Italian silk ties
Casual Wear Gillio, Riscatto
Portofino, Tundra
Dress Shirts Enro, Hickey
Freeman, Tallia
Shoes Johnston & Murphy
Tailored Clothing Hart, Schaffner,
& Marx (also M2M), Hickey
Freeman (also M2M), Tommy
Hilfiger, Tallia, Austin Reed
Sales Semiannual

Saks Off Fifth
Outlet Store
Lee Garling, Store Manager
Fairlane Town Center, 18900
Michigan Ave., Dearborn, MI 48126
(313)336-3070
www.saksfifthavenue.com
One of the better Off Fifths I visit-
ed; located in a converted Saks
Fifth Avenue store.

Casual Wear Joseph Abboud,
Giorgio Armani, Burberry, Caruso,
Henry Cotton's, Diesel, Le Zetagi,
Polo Ralph Lauren, Versace,
Ermenegildo Zegna
Dress Shirts Ike Behar, Hugo Boss,
Ermenegildo Zegna
Neckwear Giorgio Armani, Hugo
Boss, Gianfranco Ferré, Gucci,
Versace, Ermenegildo Zegna
Tailored Clothing Joseph Abboud,

Giorgio Armani, Burberry,
Corneliani, Mani, Zanella,
Ermenegildo Zegna

Hickey's Walton Pierce Clothiers
Independent
William Huntington, President
17140 Kercheval Ave., Grosse Pointe,
MI 48230 (313)882-8970
Founded in 1900. Nice store, fine
clothing lines directed toward tra-
ditional tastes. Women's section
(Walton Pierce) added to men's
business seven years ago. Mr.
Huntington and his staff are a
pleasure to work with.

Accessories Colored belts; some
braces; nautically themed khakis
Casual Wear Scott Barber, Polo
Ralph Lauren, Raffi, Robert
Talbott, and many others
Dress Shirts Kenneth Gordon,
MacCluer, Robert Talbott M2M
Neckwear Robert Talbott
Shoes Allen Edmonds, Cole Haan
Tailored Clothing Corbin, Hickey
Freeman (also M2M), Hickey's,
Oritsky, Oxxford (also M2M),
Southwick (also M2M),
Samuelsohn (also M2M)
Sales Semiannual

Gebran's Men's Clothing
Independent
Pete Collias, Owner
81 Macomb Place, Mt. Clemens, MI
48043 (586)465-5410
Pleasant, spacious store with quality inventory of clothes for the
updated traditional dresser. Mr.
Collias and his staff were knowledgeable and helpful.

Accessories Good selection of Cole
Haan, Crookhorn, Mezlan, and

Torino belts; some braces; cuff links; formal wear; nice selection of pocket squares; Rubin outerwear
Casual Wear Anthology, Axis, Tommy Bahama, Robert Barakett, Bills Khakis, Bugatchi, Gillio, Gran Sasso, Hickey Freeman, Marcello, Raffi, Riscatto Portofino, St. Croix, Zanella
Dress Shirts Jack Victor, Ike Behar, Hickey Freeman, Lorenzo
Neckwear Hickey Freeman, JZ Richards, Serica Elite
Shoes Allen Edmonds, Cole Haan, Mezlan
Tailored Clothing Ballin, Coppley, Hickey Freeman, Rubin, Tallia, Jack Victor, Zanella
Sales Semiannual

LeConte Ltd.
Independent
Michael and Suzanne Browe, Owners/Judy Johnson, Sales
3086 Walton Blvd., Rochester Hills, MI 48309 (248)375-5577
Large store filled with quality clothing for the updated traditional dresser. Mr. Browe and his staff are great to work with.

Accessories Some cuff links and pocket squares
Casual Wear Anthology, Tommy Bahama, Scott Barber, Gitman Bros., Jack Lipson, Tricots St. Raphael
Dress Shirts Gitman Bros.
Neckwear Robert Talbott, XMI
Shoes Cole Haan
Tailored Clothing Oliver, Tallia, Jack Victor, Samuelsohn (also M2M), Zanella
Sales Semiannual

Mitzelfeld's
Independent
Monty Mitzelfeld, Manager
312 S. Main St., Rochester, MI 48307 (248)651-8171
One of a vanishing breed, the family-owned independent department store. The menswear staff has lots of experience and provide great customer service.

Accessories Trafalgar braces
Casual Wear Gillio, Raffi, Riscatto Portofino, Tricots St. Raphael
Dress Shirts Joseph Abboud, MacCluer, Robert Talbott
Neckwear Joseph Abboud, JZ Richards, Robert Talbott
Tailored Clothing Hickey Freeman, Lauren by Ralph Lauren, Silverstone, Tallia
Sales Semiannual

SOMERSET COLLECTION
Location and Stores:
2800 W. Big Beaver Rd., Troy, MI 48084
www.thesomersetcollection.com

A/X Armani Exchange
(248)637-0080
www.giorgioarmani.com

Bernini
(248)816-7869 www.bernini.com
Casual Wear Hugo Boss, Bernini, Iceberg, Ermenegildo Zegna
Dress Shirts Bernini
Neckwear Bernini, Ermenegildo Zegna
Tailored Clothing Canali, Gianfranco Ferré, Versace

BOSS Hugo Boss
(248)822-0600 www.hugoboss.com

Brooks Brothers
(248)643-6888
www.brooksbrothers.com

Coach
(248)649-4877 www.coach.com

Kenneth Cole
(248)816-8300
www.kennethcole.com

Cole Haan
(248)816-6947 www.colehaan.com

Johnston & Murphy
(248)643-0950
www.johnstonmurphy.com

Neiman Marcus
(248)643-3300
www.neimanmarcus.com

Casual Wear Giorgio Armani, Jhane Barnes, Brioni, Burberry, Roberto Cavalli, Diesel, Loro Piana, Polo Ralph Lauren, Ralph Lauren Purple Label, Ermenegildo Zegna, Zegna Sport
Dress Shirts Giorgio Armani, Luigi Borrelli, Hugo Boss, Brioni, Lorenzini, Turnbull & Asser, Ermenegildo Zegna
Neckwear Brioni, Charvet, Hermès, Salvatore Ferragamo, Ermenegildo Zegna
Tailored Clothing Giorgio Armani, Hugo Boss, Brioni, Dolce & Gabbana, ETRO, Zanella, Ermenegildo Zegna

Nordstrom
(248)816-5100 www.nordstrom.com

Casual Wear Burberry, Tricots St. Raphael, XMI, Ermenegildo Zegna
Dress Shirts Joseph Abboud, Ike Behar, Jack Lipson, Robert Talbott
Neckwear Joseph Abboud, Robert Talbott, XMI, Ermenegildo Zegna
Tailored Clothing Burberry, Kenneth Cole, Hart, Schaffner & Marx

Saks Fifth Avenue
(248)643-9000
www.saksfifthavenue.com

Casual Wear Hugo Boss, Burberry, Brunello Cuccinelli, Dolce & Gabbana, Hickey Freeman, Prada, Ralph Lauren Purple Label, Ermenegildo Zegna, Zegna Sport
Dress Shirts Joseph Abboud, Giorgio Armani, Canali, Hickey Freeman, Lorenzini, John Varvatos, Ermenegildo Zegna
Neckwear Joseph Abboud, Giorgio Armani, Hugo Boss, Salvatore Ferragamo, Gucci, Ermenegildo Zegna
Tailored Clothing Giorgio Armani, Canali, Corneliani, Dolce & Gabbana, Hickey Freeman, Oxxford, Prada, John Varvatos, Ermenegildo Zegna

St. Croix
(248)816-1390
www.stcroixshop.com

Louis Vuitton
(248)643-8930
www.louisvuitton.com

Nordstrom Rack
Outlet Store
Troy Marketplace, 822 E. Big Beaver

Rd., Troy, MI 48083 (248)764-2121
www.nordstrom.com

Dress Shirts Joseph Abboud, Ike
Behar, Robert Talbott
Neckwear Audrey Bruckner, XMI,
Robert Talbott
Tailored Clothing Joseph Abboud,
Hugo Boss, Corneliani, Hart,
Schaffner & Marx, Zegna Soft, Pal
Zileri

Metro Area: Greensboro

Goforth Fine Clothing
Independent
2417A Lawndale Dr., Greensboro, NC
27408 (336)282-7990
For updated traditional tastes. Lots
of colorful selections for dress
shirts and neckwear. Aesthetically
appealing floors and furnishings.
Women's section as well.

Accessories Some cuff links
Casual Wear Acorn, Gran Sasso,
Lacoste, Minos, Robert Talbott
Dress Shirts Robert Talbott
Neckwear Robert Talbott
Tailored Clothing Aquascutum,
Hickey Freeman, Mabro, NH,
Jack Victor
Sales Semiannual

Norman Stockton
Independent
State Street Crossing Shopping
Center, 2104 Georgia St., #104,
Greensboro, NC 27408.
(336)333-2353
www.normanstockton.com
Fine clothier in business since
1909. Nice selection of first-quali-
ty lines. Pleasant atmosphere.
Cordial, helpful sales staff.

Casual Wear Bills Khakis, Canali,
Gitman Bros., Bobby Jones,
Alexander Julian Estate, McKenzie
Tribe, St. Croix, Bob Timberlake,
Tricots St. Raphael, Ermenegildo
Zegna
Dress Shirts Canali, Gitman Bros.,
Robert Talbott, Ermenegildo
Zegna
Neckwear Breuer, Canali, Robert
Talbott, Ermenegildo Zegna
Shoes Cole Haan, Santoni, H.S.
Trask
Tailored Clothing Aquascutum,
Canali, Hickey Freeman, Jack
Victor, Ermenegildo Zegna, Zegna
Soft
Sales Semiannual

O'Kennedy's Fine Clothiers
Independent
Chesley Kennedy, Owner
500h W. Cornwallis Dr., Greensboro,
NC 27408 (336)272-9388
www.okclothes.com
Tasteful boutique specializing in
classic and updated traditional
clothing. Great customer service;
Mr. O'Kennedy was knowledgeable and friendly. Also a fine
women's section.

Accessories Good selection of
Nancy and Risé cuff links
Casual Wear Scott Barber, Ike
Behar, Henry Cotton's
Dress Shirts Ike Behar (stock and
custom stock), custom
Neckwear Dormeuil
Shoes Zelli (by catalog)
Sales Semiannual

Lindsay Odom
Independent
Lindsay Odom, President

1501 N. Main St., High Point, NC
27262 (336)885-8500
Elegant, attractive venue. Women's
section as well. Mr. Odom was
very informed and helpful.

Casual Wear Tommy Bahama,
Casa Moda, Gitman Bros.,
Raffi, St. Croix, Robert Talbott,
Tulliano
Dress Shirts Ike Behar, Gitman
Bros., Robert Talbott
Neckwear Jhane Barnes, Lindsay
Odom, Robert Talbott
Shoes Cole Haan, H.S. Trask
Tailored Clothing Corbin, Hickey
Freeman (also M2M), Samuelsohn
(also M2M), Tallia
Sales Semiannual

Norman Stockton
Independent
249 S. Stratford Rd., Winston Salem,
NC 27103 (336)723-1079
www.normanstockton.com
Fine clothier, in business since
1909. This location includes a
women's section as well. Nice
selection of first-quality lines.
Pleasant atmosphere. Cordial,
helpful sales staff.

Casual Wear Bills Khakis, Canali,
Gitman Bros., Bobby Jones,
Alexander Julian Estate, McKenzie
Tribe, St. Croix, Bob Timberlake,
Tricots St. Raphael, Ermenegildo
Zegna
Dress Shirts Canali, Gitman Bros.,
Robert Talbott, Ermenegildo
Zegna
Neckwear Breuer, Canali, Robert
Talbott, Ermenegildo Zegna
Shoes Cole Haan, Santoni, H.S.
Trask
Tailored Clothing Aquascutum,

Canali, Hickey Freeman, Jack
Victor, Ermenegildo Zegna, Zegna
Soft
Sales Semiannual

Metro Area: Hampton Roads, Va.

beecroft & bull
Independent
*Craig and Bryan Beecroft,
Proprietors*
Hilton Village, 10325 Warwick Blvd.,
Newport News, VA 23601
(757)596-0951
www.beecroftandbull.com
Excellent family-owned small chain
of stores specializing in providing
men with clothing that works over
a lifetime of dressing. Great starter
wardrobe packages for the young
man beginning his business career.

Accessories Good selection of bow
ties, braces, and cuff links
Casual Wear Tommy Bahama,
Scott Barber, Luciano Barbera,
beecroft & bull, Ike Behar, Bills
Khakis, Gran Sasso, Lacoste,
Lucky Brand, Robert Talbott,
Tricots St. Raphael, Ermenegildo
Zegna, Zegna Sport, Bernard Zins
Dress Shirts beecroft & bull,
Canali, Robert Talbott (also
M2M), Ermenegildo Zegna
Neckwear beecroft & bull, Breuer,
Tino Cosma, NH 1888, Robert
Talbott, Ermenegildo Zegna
Shoes Alden, Cole Haan
Tailored Clothing Ballin, Arnold
Brant, Burberry (also M2M),
Canali, Corbin, Samuelsohn (also
M2M), Southwick (also M2M),
Jack Victor, Zanella, Zegna

beecroft & bull

Independent
Craig and Bryan Beecroft,
Proprietors
Selden Arcade, 200 E. Main St.,
Norfolk, VA 23510 (757)625-5597
www.beecroftandbull.com
Excellent family-owned small chain
of stores specializing in providing
men with clothing that works over
a lifetime of dressing. Great starter
wardrobe packages for the young
man beginning his business career.

Accessories Good selection of bow
ties, braces, and cuff links
Casual Wear Tommy Bahama,
Scott Barber, Luciano Barbera,
beecroft & bull, Ike Behar, Bill's
Khakis, Gran Sasso, Lacoste,
Lucky Brand, Robert Talbott,
Tricots St. Raphael, Ermenegildo
Zegna, Zegna Sport, Bernard Zins
Dress Shirts beecroft & bulll,
Canali, Robert Talbott (also
M2M), Ermenegildo Zegna
Neckwear beecroft & bull, Breuer,
Tino Cosma, NH 1888, Robert
Talbott, Ermenegildo Zegna
Shoes Alden, Cole Haan
Tailored Clothing Ballin, Arnold
Brant, Burberry (also M2M),
Canali, Corbin, Samuelsohn (also
M2M), Southwick (also M2M),
Jack Victor, Zanella, Zegna

beecroft & bull

Independent
Craig and Bryan Beecroft,
Proprietors
Pacific Place, 3198 Pacific Ave.,
Virginia Beach, VA 23451
(757)422-1961
www.beecroftandbull.com
Excellent family-owned small chain

of stores specializing in providing
men with clothing that works over
a lifetime of dressing. Great starter
wardrobe packages for the young
man beginning his business career.

Accessories Good selection of bow
ties, braces, and cuff links
Casual Wear Tommy Bahama,
Scott Barber, Luciano Barbera,
beecroft & bull, Ike Behar, Bill's
Khakis, Gran Sasso, Lacoste,
Lucky Brand, Robert Talbott,
Tricots St. Raphael, Ermenegildo
Zegna, Zegna Sport, Bernard Zins
Dress Shirts beecroft & bull,
Canali, Robert Talbott (also
M2M), Ermenegildo Zegna
Neckwear beecroft & bull, Breuer,
Tino Cosma, NH 1888, Robert
Talbott, Ermenegildo Zegna
Shoes Alden, Cole Haan
Tailored Clothing Ballin, Arnold
Brant, Burberry (also M2M),
Canali, Corbin, Samuelsohn (also
M2M), Southwick (also M2M),
Jack Victor, Zanella, Zegna

Metro Area: Houston

A. Taghi

Independent
Ali and Hushang Taghi, Owners
5116 Westheimer Rd., Houston, TX
77056 (713)963-0884
Impressive store. Large, well-
stocked shoe department. Made-
to-measure Stefano Ricci formal
wear. Also a spacious Brioni store-
in-store.

Accessories Bruno Magli belts;
Nancy and Risé cuff links; good
selection of pocket squares
Casual Wear Hugo Boss, Dalmine,
A. Taghi, Versace, Zanella

Dress Shirts Brioni, Fabio
Inghirami, A. Taghi
Neckwear Brioni, Hubert,
Pancaldi, Stefano Ricci, Santo
Stefano, Versace
Shoes Chellani, Bruno Magli,
a. testoni
Tailored Clothing Belvest (also
M2M), Brioni (also M2M),
Zanella, Pal Zileri

Harolds in the Heights
Independent
*Michael, Darryl, and Harold
Wiesenthal, Owners/Johnny Mykoff,
Shoes*
305 W. 19th St., Houston, TX 77008
(713)864-2647
Third-generation family business.
Johnny Mykoff, the manager of
the shoe department, is one of the
more knowledgeable shoe salespeople I've met. When I visited
the store, the sportswear was
arranged by colors in one of the
more appealing displays I've ever
seen. Newly added Robert Talbott
in-store boutique. Also has a fine
women's store.

Accessories Moreschi and Torino
belts; good selection of cuff links;
formal wear alcove; pen section
Casual Wear Axis, Tommy
Bahama, Ike Behar, Barry Bricken,
Casa Moda, Gran Sasso, Haupt,
Hickey Freeman, Bobby Jones,
Luciano Moresco, Riscatto, Georg
Roth, Tricots St. Raphael, St.
Croix, Tundra
Dress Shirts Ike Behar (also M2M),
Canali, Eton, Hickey Freeman,
Robert Talbott (also M2M)
Neckwear Jhane Barnes, Canali,
Hickey Freeman, Oxxford,
Pancaldi, Robert Talbott, yAprè

Shoes Allen Edmonds, Salvatore
Ferragamo, Gravati, Mephisto,
Moreschi, Santoni, Michael Toschi
Tailored Clothing Arnold Brant,
Canali, Coppley (also M2M),
Hickey Freeman (also M2M),
Oxxford (also M2M), Jack Victor,
Pal Zileri

HOUSTON GALLERIA
Location and Stores:
5075 Westheimer Rd., Houston, TX
77056 www.shopsimon.com

A/X Armani Exchange
(713)850-1995
www.giorgioarmani.com

Bally
(713)629-4180 www.bally.com

Brass Boot
(713)622-3412 www.brassboot.com

Brooks Brothers
(713)627-2057
www.brooksbrothers.com

Church's English Shoes
(713)960-9363
www.churchsshoes.com

Coach
(713)877-8737 www.coach.com

Kenneth Cole
(713)626-2490
www.kennethcole.com

The Custom Shop
Independent
Eric Kirn and Jim Bruce, Sales
(713)621-5538
www.customshop.com
(see chapter 9)
First-rate customer service.

Great quality fabrics and exceptional tailoring at reasonable prices. An excellent place to build one's wardrobe and develop individualized style.

Accessories Custom Shop
Casual Wear Custom Shop
Dress Shirts Custom Shop
Neckwear Custom Shop, Kolte, Genesis, Richel, Pancaldi, Pavone
Shoes Allen Edmonds
Tailored Clothing Custom Shop

Alfred Dunhill
Warren Liebman, Manager
(713)961-4661 www.dunhill.com

Emporio Armani
(713)599-0044
www.giorgioarmani.com
Gucci
(713)961-0778 www.gucci.com

Johnston & Murphy
(713)961-0025
www.johnstonmurphy.com

Lacoste
(713)850-7316 www.lacoste.com

Ralph Lauren
(713)850-9330 www.polo.com

Neiman Marcus
(713)621-7100
www.neimanmarcus.com

Casual Wear Giorgio Armani, Jhane Barnes, Brioni, Polo Ralph Lauren, Ralph Lauren Purple Label, Ermenegildo Zegna
Dress Shirts Giorgio Armani, Ike Behar, Luigi Borrelli, Brioni,

Lorenzini, Turnbull & Asser, Ermenegildo Zegna
Neckwear Giorgio Armani, Brioni, Charvet, Salvatore Ferragamo, Turnbull & Asser, Ermenegildo Zegna
Tailored Clothing Giorgio Armani, Hugo Boss, Brioni, Hickey Freeman, Oxxford, Ermenegildo Zegna

Saks Fifth Avenue
(713)627-0500
www.saksfifthavenue.com
Great men's department. Designed like a wagon wheel with the center a café and spokes containing in-store boutiques by various designers.

Casual Wear Joseph Abboud, Giorgio Armani, Jhane Barnes, Hugo Boss, Ralph Lauren Purple Label, Ermenegildo Zegna
Dress Shirts Giorgio Armani, Baldessarini, Ike Behar, Hugo Boss, Brioni, Lorenzini, Ermenegildo Zegna
Neckwear Giorgio Armani, Brioni, Ermenegildo Zegna
Tailored Clothing Joseph Abboud, Giorgio Armani, Baldessarini, Hugo Boss, Canali, Hickey Freeman, Ermenegildo Zegna

Velleriano
Independent
Patricia Porto, President/Ana Salmon, Public Relations
(713)552-1188
Attractive store with helpful, friendly management and sales staff. Interesting selection of

clothing from first-rate brands.

Accessories Pal Zileri outerwear
Casual Wear Hugo Boss, Dolce
& Gabbana, Moschino
Dress Shirts Luigi Borrelli,
Canali, Gianfranco Ferré Studio,
Moschino, Verri
Neckwear Brioni, Italo Ferretti,
Valentino
Tailored Clothing Belvest,
Canali, Gianfranco Ferré Studio,
Zanella, Pal Zileri

Gianni Versace
(713)623-8220 www.versace.com

KATY MILLS
Location and Stores:
5000 Katy Mills Circle, Katy, TX 77494
www.katymills.com

Brook Brothers
Outlet Store
(281)644-2525
www.brooksbrothers.com

Cole Haan
Outlet Store
(281)644-6300 www.colehaan.com

Hugo Boss
Outlet Store
(281)644-5800 www.hugoboss.com

Kenneth Cole
Outlet Store
(281)644-2088
www.kennethcole.com

M. Penner
Independent
Morris Penner, Owner
2950 Kirby Dr., Houston, TX 77098
(713)527-8200

Large, great-looking, comfortable
store with distinctive inventory of
first-quality items. Mr. Penner and
his entire staff are very knowledgeable and easy to talk with. A don't-
miss Houston destination!

Accessories Good selection of jewel-
ry and personal leather goods
Casual Wear Armani Collezioni,
Luciano Barbera, Levi's, Loro
Piana, M Penner, Paul Smith,
Ermenegildo Zegna, Zegna Sport
Dress Shirts Ike Behar (stock siz-
ing), Luigi Borrelli, Lorenzini,
Ermenegildo Zegna
Neckwear Giorgio Armani, Brioni,
Charvet, Ermenegildo Zegna
Shoes Giorgio Armani, Salvatore
Ferragamo, Gravati, Ermenegildo
Zegna
Tailored Clothing Giorgio Armani
(also M2M), Luciano Barbera,
Canali, Kiton (also M2M), Paul
Smith, Vestimenta (also M2M),
Zanella, Ermenegildo Zegna (also
M2M), Bernard Zins

R. Rose Clothier
Independent
Bob Rose, Owner
722 Travis St., Ste. 150, Houston, TX
77002 (713)222-7673
Boutiquelike store serving the traditional dresser in downtown
Houston. Mr. Rose knows his
clothing and is happy to share his
expertise. A great place to shop.

Accessories Great selection of bow
ties; Trafalgar belts and braces
(including Limited Edition); and J.
Weston cuff links
Casual Wear Ferrell Reed,
Madeline Finn, Gitman Bros.,
Samuelsohn, Robert Talbott,

Tricots St. Raphael, XMI, Viyella
Dress Shirts Gitman Bros., Ferrell
Reed
Tailored Clothing Corbin, NH
1888, Samuelsohn (also M2M)

Neiman Marcus
Town and Country, 10615 Town &
Country Way, Houston, TX 77024
(713)984-2100
www.neimanmarcus.com
Also includes a Last Call outlet
store that had no men's clothing
the day I visited.

Casual Wear Giorgio Armani,
Jhane Barnes, Polo Ralph Lauren,
Ermenegildo Zegna
Dress Shirts Giorgio Armani, Ike
Behar, Hickey Freeman, Turnbull
& Asser, Ermenegildo Zegna
Neckwear Giorgio Armani,
Turnbull & Asser, Ermenegildo
Zegna
Tailored Clothing Giorgio Armani,
Hugo Boss, Ermenegildo Zegna

Metro Area: Knoxville

M.S. McClellan & Co.
Independent
Matthew McClellan and
Bob Mc Clellan, Proprietors/
Dan Kocks, Sales
5614 Kingston Pike, Knoxville, TN
37919 (865)584-3492
Business begun in 1966. Pleasant
shopping environment, including
an attractive women's section.
Sales staff cordial and helpful; the
McClellans provide a wealth of
information about the clothing
industry.
Accessories Bow ties; Trafalgar
braces (including Limited

Edition); good selection of cuff
links; pocket squares
Casual Wear Barry Bricken, Forté
Cashmere, Gran Sasso, Bobby
Jones, Jeff Rose, Ermenegildo
Zegna
Dress Shirts Ike Behar, Luigi
Borrelli, Canali, Robert Talbott,
Ermenegildo Zegna
Neckwear Altea, Breuer, Brioni,
Robert Talbott, Ermenegildo
Zegna
Shoes Allen Edmonds, Cole Haan,
Mezlan
Tailored Clothing Ballin, Canali,
Hickey Freeman (also M2M),
Oxxford (also M2M), Samuelsohn
(also M2M), Southwick, Linnea
Trussini, Zanella, Ermenegildo
Zegna
Sales Semiannual

Metro Area: Las Vegas

BELLAGIO HOTEL
Location and Stores:
3600 Las Vegas Blvd. South, Las
Vegas, NV 89109

Giorgio Armani
(702)893-8327
www.giorgioarmani.com

Gucci
(702)732-9300 www.gucci.com

Prada
(702)866-6886 www.prada.com

D Fine
Independent
Mirage Hotel and Casino, 3400 Las
Vegas Blvd. South, Las Vegas, NV
89109 (702)792-7760
Great store with unique, first-

quality merchandise presented attractively.

Accessories Nice selection of cuff links
Casual Wear Tommy Bahama, Jhane Barnes, D. Fine, Haupt, Georg Roth, Arnold Zimberg
Dress Shirts Brioni, D. Fine
Neckwear Brioni, D. Fine, Leonard, Pancaldi
Shoes Fratelli Rosetti, Moreschi
Tailored Clothing Brioni, Canali, D. Fine, Arnold Zimberg

DESERT PASSAGES/ ALADDIN HOTEL AND CASINO
Location and Stores:
3663 Las Vegas Blvd. South, Ste. 840, Las Vegas, NV 89109

Allegre
Independent
(702)362-2882
Attractive store with techno look and black fixtures. Selected inventory of unique, colorful clothing. Oriented more toward casual dresser; sport coats and dress slacks only.

Casual Wear Bertone, Versace
Dress Shirts Bertone, Pancaldi, Versace
Tailored Clothing Bertone, Redaelli
Sales Semiannual, January and July

Tommy Bahama
(702)731-3988
www.tommybahama.com

Jhane Barnes
(702)866-0080
www.jhanebarnes.com

HUGO Hugo Boss
(702)732-4272 www.hugoboss.com

Lucky Brand Dungarees
(702)733-6613
www.luckyjeans.com

Melwani's
Independent
(702)733-6676
Good selection and attractive presentation of merchandise with wood fixtures. Aimed at younger, more casual dresser. Helpful, courteous staff.

Casual Wear Georg Roth, Signum, Versace V2
Dress Shirts Versace V2
Neckwear Pancaldi, Versace V2
Shoes Versace V2
Tailored Clothing Versace V2

Napoleon
Independent
(702)733-6005
www.napoleonfashions.com
Largest Napoleon retail outlet. One of the best selections of Leonard ties I've seen in the U.S. Attractive store with a large assortment of colorful, one-of-a kind items you won't find elsewhere.

Accessories Good selection of cuff links
Casual Wear Napoleon
Dress Shirts Brioni, Napoleon, Stefano Ricci
Neckwear Brioni, Leonard, Pancaldi
Shoes Versace
Tailored Clothing Brioni, Napoleon
Sales Semiannual, January and July

St. Croix
Zoreh Ramsey, Store Manager
(702)892-9140
www.stcroixshop.com

FASHION SHOW MALL
Location and Stores:
3200 Las Vegas Blvd. South, Las
Vegas, NV 89109
www.thefashionshow.com

Bally
(702)737-1968 www.bally.com

Johnston & Murphy
(702)737-0114
www.johnstonmurphy.com

Neiman Marcus
(702)731-3636
www.neimanmarcus.com
Casual Wear Giorgio Armani,
Hugo Boss, Brioni, Prada,
Ermenegildo Zegna
Dress Shirts Giorgio Armani, Ike
Behar, Brioni, Ermenegildo
Zegna
Neckwear Giorgio Armani,
Brioni, Salvatore Ferragamo,
Ermenegildo Zegna
Tailored Clothing Giorgio
Armani, Brioni, Incotex,
Ermenegildo Zegna

Saks Fifth Avenue
(702)733-8300
www.saksfifthavenue.com
Casual Wear Giorgio Armani,
Jhane Barnes, Hugo Boss,
Ermenegildo Zegna
Dress Shirts Giorgio Armani,
Hugo Boss, Ermenegildo Zegna
Neckwear Giorgio Armani,
Hugo Boss, Brioni,
Ermenegildo Zegna

Tailored Clothing Giorgio
Armani, Hugo Boss,
Ermenegildo Zegna

St. Croix
(702)794-4333
www.stcroixshop.com

Louis Vuitton
(702)731-9860
www.louisvuitton.com

THE FORUM AT CAESAR'S PALACE
Location and Stores:
3500 Las Vegas Blvd. South, Las
Vegas, NV 89109

A/X Armani Exchange
(702)733-1666
www.giorgioarmani.com

Bernini
Douglas Jones, Store Manager
(702)892-1786 www.bernini.com
One of my favorite and more
spacious Bernini locations in the
U.S. Large and varied selection.
Many unusual items, such as
Brioni silk monochromatic shirt
and tie sets and one-of-a-kind
leather coats and jackets.

BOSS Hugo Boss
(702)696-9444 www.hugoboss.com

Kenneth Cole
(702)794-2653
www.kennethcole.com
Largest Kenneth Cole location
in Las Vegas with best selection.

Cuzzens
Independent
Sanjay Jhuraney, Assistant
Manager
(702)732-1329

Very appealing store with nicely presented merchandise arranged in wood fixtures. Private-label tailored clothing made of great fabric with nice hand. Mr. Jhuraney was very helpful.

Accessories Good selection of cuff links
Casual Wear Cuzzens, Georg Roth, Paul Smith
Dress Shirts Cuzzens, Luciano Moresco
Neckwear Brioni, Pancaldi
Shoes Cuzzens
Tailored Clothing Mabro for Cuzzens
Sales Semiannual, January and July

Alfred Dunhill
Carrie Robertson, Store Manager
(702)650-2292 www.dunhill.com

Diesel
(702)791-5927 www.diesel.com

DKNY
(702)650-9670 www.dkny.com
Largest Donna Karan outlet in Las Vegas with best selection.

Emporio Armani
(702)650-5200
www.giorgioarmani.com

Salvatore Ferragamo
(800)856-9743
www.salvatoreferragamo.it

Gucci
(702)369-7333 www.gucci.com

Lacoste
(702)791-7616 www.lacoste.com

Ralph Lauren
(702)650-5656 www.polo.com

Vasari
Independent
(702)792-2476
Attractive store with techno look, black fixtures. Large inventory of unusual, colorful clothing. More oriented toward casual dresser—sport coats and dress slacks only.

Casual Wear Bertone
Neckwear Bertone, Pancaldi, Versace
Tailored Clothing Bertone, Redaelli
Sales Semiannual, January and July

Gianni Versace
(702)796-7222
www.versace.com
Great-looking store with ample selection, particularly in the larger sizes. Lots of colorful and distinctive Versace pieces.

Louis Vuitton
(702)732-1227
www.louisvuitton.com

Versace Jeans Couture
(702)796-7332 www.versace.com

THE GRAND CANAL SHOPPES AT THE VENETIAN HOTEL
Location and Stores:
3355 Las Vegas Blvd. South, Las Vegas, NV 89109

Bertone
Independent
(702)733-4011

New store with lots of unusual, colorful clothing. More oriented toward casual dresser.

Casual Wear Bertone
Neckwear Bertone, Pancaldi, Versace
Tailored Clothing Bertone, Redaelli
Sales Semiannual, January and July

Burberry
(702)735-2600 www.burberry.com

Kenneth Cole
(702)836-1916
www.kennethcole.com

Tino Cosma
(702)732-2424
Attractive boutique filled with appealing wood fixtures and precise arrangement of merchandise. Best selection of Cosma shirts, ties, and cuff links to be found anywhere.

Lior
Independent
(702)650-9005
Fascinating showroom filled with well-arranged, unusual items. Selection tends toward those preferring more modern clothing. If you're looking for something unique and trendy, this is the shop for you.

Casual Wear Lior, Lorenzini, Missoni, Thierry Mugler
Dress Shirts Lorenzini
Sales Semiannual, January and July

Pal Zileri
(702)732-2100

Large, very appealing storefront filled with Zileri merchandise equally divided between business and casual dress. You'll find the largest, best-presented selection of this label in the U.S.

FASHION OUTLET OF LAS VEGAS
Location and Stores:
32100 Las Vegas Blvd. South, Primm, NV 89019
www.fashionoutletlasvegas.com

Tommy Bahama
Outlet Store
(702)874-5388
www.tommybahama.com

Bally
Outlet Store
(702)874-2288 www.bally.com

Jhane Barnes Xtras
Outlet Store
(702)874-1222
www.jhanebarnes.com

Brooks Brothers
Outlet Store
(702)874-2272
www.brooksbrothers.com

Burberry
Outlet Store
(702)874-2244 www.burberry.com

Coach
Outlet Store
(702)874-1171 www.coach.com

Kenneth Cole
Outlet Store
(702)874-1987
www.kennethcole.com

Cole Haan
Outlet Store
(702)874-1908 www.colehaan.com

DKNY
Outlet Store
(702)874-1950 www.dkny.com

Johnston & Murphy
Outlet Store
(702)874-1455
www.johnstonmurphy.com

Calvin Klein
Outlet Store
(702)874-1806

Lacoste
Outlet Store
(702)874-1833 www.lacoste.com

Neiman Marcus Last Call
Outlet Store
(702)874-2100
www.neimanmarcus.com
Largest Last Call in the U.S.

Polo Ralph Lauren Factory Store
Outlet Store
(702)874-2144 www.polo.com

Tod's
Outlet Store
(702)874-2191 www.tods.com

Versace
Outlet Store
(702)874-2266 www.versace.com

Metro Area: Little Rock

Bauman's
Independent
L. Wayne Ratcliff, Owner/
Rick Maldonado, Store Manager/
Josh Lynn, Ermenegildo Zegna &

Custom Clothing Specialist/
Sean Cullers, Sportswear Specialist
Pavilion in the Park, 8201 Cantrell,
#150, Little Rock, AR 72227
(800)231-0086 or (501)227-8797
www.baumans.com *(see chapter 9)*
Impressive emporium with open
feeling—lots of glass and burnished steel fixtures to visually
expand the space. Giorgio Armani,
Hugo Boss, and Ermenegildo
Zegna store-in-stores. Also has an
excellent wardrobe-building pro-
gram, the Bauman's Club, for the
younger man to begin his business
career. Mr. Lynn and Mr. Ratcliff
were very gracious and helpful.
Accessories Good selection of bow
ties and cuff links; some Borsalino
hats
Casual Wear Giorgio Armani,
Avon Celli, Luciano Barbera, Luigi
Borrelli, Hugo Boss, Salvatore
Ferragamo, Gran Sasso, Bobby
Jones, Loro Piana, Nat Nast,
Normandy and Monroe, Oxxford,
Jeff Rose, St. Croix, Robert
Talbott, Zanella, Ermenegildo
Zegna
Dress Shirts Giorgio Armani, Luigi
Borrelli, Hugo Boss, Hamilton
(M2M only), Robert Talbott
Neckwear Luciano Barbera, Brioni,
Salvatore Ferragamo, Kiton,
Oxxford, Stefano Ricci, Robert
Talbott, Ermenegildo Zegna
Shoes Alden, Allen Edmonds, Cole
Haan, Salvatore Ferragamo,
Gravati, Mephisto, Santoni
Tailored Clothing Giorgio Armani,
Bauman's, Hugo Boss, Arnold
Brant, Brioni, Coppley, Oxxford
(also M2M), Samuelsohn (also
M2M), Zanella, Ermenegildo
Zegna

The Men's Clothing Guide

Sales Semiannual at end of seasons, event-driven monthly

Mr. Wicks
Independent
Mark and Chuck Carroll,
Owners/Curtis Jones, Sales
5924 R St., Little Rock, AR 72207
(501)664-3062
Hospitable store with very friendly, knowledgeable salespeople. Business began in 1960 by Charles F. Carroll, the current owners' father. Clothing selections here are directed toward the traditional dresser.

Accessories Good selection of bow ties and braces
Casual Wear Scott Barber, Bills Khakis, Charleston Khakis, Forté, Gitman Bros., Kenneth Gordon, Gran Sasso, Bobby Jones, MacCluer, Jeff Rose, Robert Talbott, Tricots St. Raphael
Dress Shirts Gitman Bros., Kenneth Gordon, Robert Talbott (also M2M)
Neckwear Robert Talbott
Shoes Alden
Tailored Clothing Aquascutum, Ballin, Corbin, H. Oritsky, Samuelsohn (also M2M), Southwick, Jack Victor, Mr. Wicks

Metro Area: Los Angeles

Orsini
Independent
Abdullah Mojadidi, Proprietor
Santa Anita Fashion Square, 400 S. Baldwin Ave., Arcadia, CA 92821
(626)254-8786
Tasteful store with some unusual and distinctive pieces.

Accessories Some cuff links; interesting selection of leather outerwear
Casual Wear Leonard, Versace
Dress Shirts Tino Cosma, Gianfranco Ferré, Gorena
Neckwear Leonard, Versace
Shoes Magnanni, Versace
Tailored Clothing d'Avenza, Versace

Amir
Independent
Beverly Hills Hotel, 9641 Sunset Blvd., Beverly Hills, CA 90210
(310)858-8589
Impressive boutique located in the lower shopping arcade of the Beverly Hills Hotel. Everything is custom-made and of the highest quality.

Anto Distinctive Shirtmakers/ Nat Wise
Independent
Jack and Ken Sepetjian, Proprietors
268 N. Beverly Dr., Beverly Hills, CA 90210 (310)278-4500
In business since 1976. Bolts upon bolts of sumptuous, colorful shirting fabrics to choose from. Anto makes shirts for many movies, celebrities, and important businessmen from around the world. All items are handmade on the premises from paper patterns. Featured in *GQ* in 2002 as one of the finest custom shirts available in the world. The Sepetjians are extremely knowledgeable and pleasant to deal with.

Giorgio Armani
436 N. Rodeo Dr., Beverly Hills, CA 90210 (310)271-5555

www.giorgioarmani.com
Large store with fine selection of Armani favorites.

Ascot Chang
9551 Wilshire Blvd., Beverly Hills, CA 90210 (310)550-1339
www.ascotchang.com

Bally
340 N. Rodeo Dr., Beverly Hills, CA 90210 (310)271-0666 www.bally.com

Barney's New York
9570 Wilshire Blvd., Beverly Hills, CA 90212 (310)276-4400
www.barneys.com
Largest Barney's after flagship store in Manhattan. Large men's department with excellent selection.

Casual Wear Giorgio Armani, Battistoni, Luciano Barbera, Fray, Lorenzini, Ermenegildo Zegna
Dress Shirts Barney's, Fratelli, Ermenegildo Zegna
Neckwear Luciano Barbera, ETRO, Ermenegildo Zegna
Tailored Clothing Giorgio Armani, Hugo Boss, Vestimenta, Ermenegildo Zegna

Bernini Classic
344–346 Rodeo Dr., Beverly Hills, CA 90210 (310)278-6287
www.bernini.com

Dress Shirts Baldessarini, Bernini, Brioni, Luigi Borrelli
Neckwear Bernini, Brioni, Pancaldi, Ermenegildo Zegna, Zilli
Shoes Bally, Belvedere, Salvatore Ferragamo, Lucchese, Mezlan
Tailored Clothing Brioni, Bernini, Canali, d'Avenza, Ermenegildo Zegna, Arnold Zimberg

Bernini Couture
362 N. Rodeo Drive, Beverly Hills, CA 90210 (310)273-8786
www.bernini.com

Dress Shirts Baldessarini, Bernini, Brioni, Luigi Borrelli
Neckwear Bernini, Brioni, Pancaldi, Ermenegildo Zegna, Zilli
Shoes Bally, Belvedere, Salvatore Ferragamo, Lucchese, Mezlan
Tailored Clothing Brioni, Bernini, Canali, d'Avenza, Ermenegildo Zegna, Arnold Zimberg

BOSS Hugo Boss
414 N. Rodeo Dr., Beverly Hills, CA 90210 (310)859-2888
www.hugoboss.com

Brioni
337 N. Rodeo Dr., Beverly Hills, CA 90210 (310)271-1300 www.brioni.com
Large, sumptuous boutique filled with Brioni's best wares.

Carroll & Co.
Independent
425 N. Canon Dr., Beverly Hills, CA 90210 (310) 273-9060
Large, well-appointed store with prompt, helpful customer service. Selection fairly evenly divided between updated traditional and European tastes.

Accessories Great selection of belts, braces, cuff links
Casual Wear Carroll & Co.
Dress Shirts Carroll & Co., Ermenegildo Zegna
Neckwear Carroll & Co., Robert Talbott, Ermenegildo Zegna
Shoes Alden
Tailored Clothing Carroll & Co., Oxxford, Samuelsohn, Ermenegildo Zegna

Emporio Armani
9533 Brighton Way, Beverly Hills, CA
90210 (310)271-7790
www.giorgioarmani.com

G. B. Harb & Son
Independent
George Harb, Owner/Varouj
Krikorian and Tom Curry, Sales
336 N. Camden Dr., Beverly Hills, CA
90210 (310)274-8466
Spacious, pleasant store with quality merchandise. Friendly and helpful staff.

Accessories Trafalgar braces, Bruno Magli and Remy leather outerwear
Casual Wear Robert Barakett, Scott Barber, Ike Behar, Bills Khakis, Dalmine, Gran Sasso, Paul & Shark, Robert Talbott, Ermenegildo Zegna
Dress Shirts Ike Behar, Robert Talbott
Neckwear Robert Talbott, Ermenegildo Zegna
Shoes Alden, Moreschi
Tailored Clothing Hickey Freeman, Samuelsohn, Vestimenta, Ermenegildo Zegna
Sales Semiannual

Salvatore Ferragamo
357 N. Rodeo Dr., Beverly Hills, CA
90210 (310)273-9990 or (800)822-1956
www.salvatoreferragamo.it

Gianfranco Ferré
270 N. Rodeo Dr., Beverly Hills, CA
90210 (310)273-3211
www.gianfrancoferre.com

Gucci
347 N. Rodeo Dr., Beverly Hills, CA
90210 (310)278-3451 www.gucci.com

Neiman Marcus
9700 Wilshire Blvd., Beverly Hills, CA
90212 (310)550-5900
www.neimanmarcus.com
Excellent selection of merchandise. Many items by modern brands that aren't inventoried at other Neiman Marcus locations.

Casual Wear Giorgio Armani, Roberto Cavalli, Gucci, Bobby Jones, Issey Miyake, Prada, Ermenegildo Zegna
Dress Shirts Giorgio Armani, Ike Behar, Luigi Borrelli, Hugo Boss, Brioni, Charvet, Fray, Lorenzini, Paul Smith, Turnbull & Asser, Ermenegildo Zegna
Neckwear Giorgio Armani, Massimo Bizzocchi, Luigi Borrelli, Hugo Boss, Brioni, Charvet Stefano Ricci, Turnbull & Asser, Ermenegildo Zegna
Tailored Clothing Giorgio Armani, Hugo Boss, Brioni, Dolce & Gabbana, Prada, Paul Smith Ermenegildo Zegna

Prada
343 N. Rodeo Dr., Beverly Hills, CA
90210 (310)385-5959 www.prada.com

Stefano Ricci
431 N. Rodeo Dr., Beverly Hills, CA
90210 (310)858-9595
www.stefanoricci.com
Impressive retail space. Only Ricci boutique in U.S.

Saks Fifth Avenue
9600 Wilshire Blvd., Beverly Hills, CA
90210 (310)275-4211
www.saksfifthavenue.com
Large men's department in separate building. Excellent selection

of tailored clothing. Largest formal wear section of any Saks store I visited. Brioni, Giorgio Armani, and Ermenegildo Zegna boutiques.

Casual Wear Giorgio Armani, Brioni, Brunello Cuccinelli, Ralph Lauren Purple Label, John Varvatos, Vestimenta, Zanella, Ermenegildo Zegna
Dress Shirts Luciano Barbera, Luigi Borrelli, Brioni, Canali
Neckwear Luciano Barbera, Duchamp, Paul Smith, Vestimenta, Ermenegildo Zegna
Tailored Clothing Giorgio Armani, Baldessarini, Luciano Barbera, Brioni, Donna Karan, Oxxford, Vestimenta, Ermenegildo Zegna

Jack Taylor
Independent
Jack Taylor, Owner
341 N. Camden Dr., Beverly Hills, CA 90210 (310)274-7276
One of oldest and most well respected custom tailors in the U.S. Mr. Taylor was generous with his time and extensive knowledge of the men's clothing industry.

a. testoni
365 N. Rodeo Dr., Beverly Hills, CA 90210 (310) 273-5558
www.atestoni.com

Theodore Man
Independent
451 N. Rodeo Dr., Beverly Hills, CA 90210 (310)274-8029
Most merchandise self-labeled. For the man who prefers a more modern look. Good prices, quality fabrics and construction.

Turnbull & Asser
Robert Salter, Store Manager
9633 Brighton Way, Beverly Hills, CA 90210 (310) 550-7600
www. turnbullandasser.com
Brand-new location opened April 2003.

Vestiti
Independent
Tony Lonzano, Owner
143 S. Beverly Dr., Beverly Hills, CA 90212 (310)275-8668
Brand-new location, choice inventory of top-notch merchandise. Excellent customer service.

Accessories Borsalino hats
Casual Wear Brunello Cuccinelli
Dress Shirts Barba, Luigi Borrelli, Brioni
Neckwear Brioni, Kiton
Tailored Clothing Sartoria Attolini, Kiton, Arnold Zimberg
Sales Semiannual

Ermenegildo Zegna
301 N. Rodeo Dr., Beverly Hills, CA 90210 (310)247-8827 www.zegna.com
Good-sized Ermenegildo Zegna boutique, excellent selection.

Zegna Sport
305 N. Rodeo Dr., Beverly Hills, CA 90210 (310)247-9566 www.zegna.com

Art's Fashion for Men
Independent
1010 E. Imperial Hwy., Ste. B-3, Brea, CA 92821 (714)529-4888
Best selection of Haupt and Roth shirts of any store I visited in the U.S.

Casual Wear Haupt, Georg Roth
Dress Shirts Jack Lipson

Tailored Clothing Jhane Barnes,
Lubiam 1911, Zanetti
Sales Semiannual

BREA MALL
Location and Stores:
1065 Brea Mall Rd., Brea, CA 92821
www.shopsimon.com

B & G
Independent
Abdullah Mojadidi, Proprietor
(714)671-1700
Tasteful store with some unusual
and distinctive pieces.

Accessories Some cuff links; inter-
esting selection of leather outer-
wear
Casual Wear Tino Cosma,
Gianfranco Ferré, Gorena
Neckwear Leonard, Versace
Shoes Magnanni, Versace
Tailored Clothing d'Avenza,
Versace

Coach
(714)257-0772 www.coach.com

Guccini
Independent
Abdullah Mojadidi, Proprietor
(714)671-2072
Tasteful store with some unusual
and distinctive pieces. Rodeo
Drive–quality items can be
found here without having to
make the trip.

Accessories Cuff links, interesting
selection of leather outerwear
Casual Wear Tino Cosma,
Gianfranco Ferré, Gorena
Neckwear Leonard, Versace
Shoes Magnanni, Versace
Tailored Clothing d'Avenza,
Versace

Lucky Brand Dungarees
(714)672-0701
www.luckyjeans.com

Nordstrom
(714)529-0123 www.nordstrom.com

Nordstrom Rack
Outlet Store
Brea Union Plaza, 2345 E. Imperial
Hwy., Brea, CA 92821 (714)529-4222
www.nordstrom.com
Excellent selection of tailored
clothing the day I visited.

Dress Shirts Ike Behar, Hugo Boss,
Robert Talbott
Tailored Clothing Joseph Abboud,
Coppley, Ermenegildo Zegna

DESERT HILLS PREMIUM OUTLETS
Location and Stores:
48400 Seminole Dr., Cabazon, CA
92230 www.premiumoutlets.com

A/X Armani Exchange
Outlet Store
(909)922-2333
www.giorgioarmani.com

Armani General Store
Outlet Store
(909)922-3400
www.giorgioarmani.com
Excellent selection. Merchandise
is also often discounted further.

Jhane Barnes Xtras
Outlet Store
(909)922-2866
www.jhanebarnes.com
Great selection, helpful sales staff.

Barney's New York
Outlet Store
(909)849-1600 www.barneys.com

Hugo Boss
Outlet Store
(909)849-2223 www.hugoboss.com

Brooks Brothers
Outlet Store
(909)849-0072
www.brooksbrothers.com

Kenneth Cole
Outlet Store
(909)922-2492
www.kennethcole.com

Salvatore Ferragamo
Outlet Store
(909)922-9883
www.salvatoreferragamo.it

Gucci
Outlet Store
(909)849-7430 www.gucci.com

Donna Karan
Outlet Store
(909)922-9862
www.donnakaran.com

Lacoste
Outlet Store
(909)922-2138 www.lacoste.com

Lucky Brand
Outlet Store
(909)922-2600
www.luckyjeans.com

Polo Ralph Lauren Factory Store
Outlet Store
(909)849-8446 www.polo.com

Polo Jeans Company
Outlet Store
(909)922-2535 www.polo.com

Saks Off Fifth
Outlet Store
(909)849-8415
www.saksfiftavenue.com

Casual Wear Joseph Abboud,
Hugo Boss, Como Sport, Gucci
(limited selection), Ermenegildo
Zegna
Dress Shirts Ike Behar,
Ermenegildo Zegna
Neckwear Salvatore Ferragamo,
Gianfranco Ferré, Ermenegildo
Zegna
Tailored Clothing Giorgio
Armani, Caruso, Mani, Versace

Versace
Outlet Store
(909)922-9111 www.versace.com

Ermenegildo Zegna Outlet Store
*Jennifer Delao, General
Manager/Tina Weston, Sales*
(909)849-8383 www.zegna.com
Great selection, particularly in
business casual basics the day I
visited. Ms. Delao and Ms.
Weston are two of the better
customer service people I've
worked with.

CAMARILLO PREMIUM OUTLETS
Location and Stores:
740 E. Ventura Blvd., Camarillo, CA
93010 www.premiumoutlets.com

Jhane Barnes Xtras
Outlet Store
(805)484-0409
www.jhanebarnes.com

Barney's New York
Outlet Store
(805)445-1123 www.barneys.com

Casual Wear Diesel, Moreno
Martini Da Firenze

Neckwear Diesel, Gianfranco
Ferré
Tailored Clothing Hugo Boss,
Donna Karan Signature

Hugo Boss
Outlet Store
(805)388-6060 www.hugoboss.com

Brooks Brothers
Outlet Store
(805)383-6225
www.brooksbrothers.com

Kenneth Cole
Outlet Store
(805)445-8779
www.kennethcole.com

Cole Haan
Outlet Store
(805)987-8448 www.colehaan.com

Donna Karan
Outlet Store
(805)482-2663
www.donnakaran.com

Calvin Klein
Outlet Store
(805)484-4008

Polo Ralph Lauren Factory Store
Outlet Store
(805)383-2772 www.polo.com

Polo Jeans Company
Outlet Store
(805)383-6353 www.polo.com

Saks Off Fifth
Outlet Store
(805)987-4475
www.saksfifthavenue.com

Casual Wear Giorgio Armani,
Diesel, Bobby Jones, Nat Nast,
Theory, John Varvatos
Dress Shirts Ike Behar, Hugo
Boss, Ermenegildo Zegna
Neckwear Salvatore Ferragamo,
Versace
Tailored Clothing Joseph
Abboud, Hugo Boss, Hickey
Freeman, Mani, Missoni, Zegna
Soft

Nordstrom
Topanga Plaza, 6602 Topanga Canyon
Blvd., Canoga Park, CA 91303
(818)884-7900
www.nordstrom.com

Casual Wear Joseph Abboud,
Robert Barakett, Riscatto
Portofino, Ermenegildo Zegna
Dress Shirts Hugo Boss, Robert
Talbott, Ermenegildo Zegna
Neckwear Robert Talbott, XMI
Platinum, Ermenegildo Zegna
Tailored Clothing Joseph Abboud,
Hugo Boss, Corneliani, Zanella

Orsini
Independent
Abdullah Mojadidi, Proprietor
Los Cerritos Shopping Center, 239 Los
Cerritos Center, Cerritos, CA 90703
(562)809-3308
Tasteful store with some unusual
and distinctive pieces.

Accessories Some cuff links; inter-
esting selection of leather outer-
wear
Casual Wear Tino Cosma,
Gianfranco Ferré, Gorena
Neckwear Leonard, Versace
Shoes Magnanni, Versace
Tailored Clothing d'Avenza,
Versace

Nordstrom Rack
Outlet Store
Spectrum Town Center, 3849 Grand
Ave., Chino, CA 91710 (909)591-0551
www.nordstrom.com
Excellent selection of tailored
clothing the day I visited.

Dress Shirts Ike Behar, Robert
Talbott
Neckwear Robert Daskal Robert
Talbott, XMI
Tailored Clothing Joseph Abboud,
Coppley, Ermenegildo Zegna

Xerxes
Independent
*Afsanen Farzad and Arman
Ariane, Owners/Jason Dunnahoe,
Sales*
319 Yale Ave., Claremont, CA 91711
(909)482-1111
Xerxes uses three tailors who specialize in various phases of sculpt-
ing garments, ensuring a great fit
every time. Sales staff extremely
helpful and friendly. Complimentary pamphlets from Robert Talbott
on how to tie a tie.

Accessories Great selection of neck-
wear; Bruno Magli outerwear
Dress Shirts Ike Behar, Robert
Talbott
Neckwear Villa Bolgheri, Robert
Talbott, XMI, Ermenegildo Zegna
Shoes Allen Edmonds, Bruno
Magli, Mezlan
Tailored Clothing Coppley (also
M2M), Hickey Freeman (also
M2M), Tallia

Renzi Custom Tailors
Independent
Rod Baker, President
2183 Fairview Rd., Ste. 212, Costa

Mesa, CA 92626 (949)515-1180
www.renzicustom.com
All clothes are custom-made and
privately labeled by Renzi. If
you've decided you're ready for a
custom tailor, I highly recommend
Renzi Tailoring. Mr. Baker was
most generous with his time,
including information on
wardrobe makeovers and wardrobe
building from the ground up.

SOUTH COAST PLAZA
Location and Stores:
3333 Bristol St., Costa Mesa, CA
92626 www.southcoastplaza.com

A/X Armani Exchange
(714)556-8842
www.giorgioarmani.com

Giorgio Armani
(714)546-9377
www.giorgioarmani.com

Avventura
(714)979-9900 www.avventura.com
Shoes Lorenzo Banfi

Bally
(714)557-1914 www.bally.com

Bernini
(714)432-1786 www.bernini.com
Casual Wear Ermenegildo
Zegna
Dress Shirts Barba, Brioni
Tailored Clothing Belvest, Canali

BOSS Hugo Boss
(714)791-9100 www.hugoboss.com

Burberry
(714)556-8110 www.burberry.com

Coach
(714)979-1771 www.coach.com

DKNY
(714)557-4408 www.dkny.com

Alfred Dunhill
(714)641-0521 www.dunhill.com

Emporio Armani
(714)754-1200
www.giorgioarmani.com

Façonnable
(714)966-1140 www.nordstrom.com

Salvatore Ferragamo
(714)979-7654
www.salvatoreferragamo.it

Gucci
(714)557-9600 www.gucci.com

Hermès
(714)437-1725 www.hermes.com
John Lobb shoe store-in-store.

BOSS Hugo Boss
(714)641-8661 www.hugoboss.com

Donna Karan
(714)549-1053
www.donnakaran.com

Johnston & Murphy
(714)549-1833
www.johnstonmurphy.com

Lacoste
(714)641-1730 www.lacoste.com

Bruno Magli
(714)966-2600
www.brunomagli.com

Nordstrom
(714)549-9300 www.nordstrom.com

Casual Wear Joseph Abboud,
Giorgio Armani, Jeff Rose,
Ermenegildo Zegna
Dress Shirts Giorgio Armani,
Barba, XMI, Ermenegildo
Zegna
Neckwear Robert Talbott, XMI
Platinum, Ermenegildo Zegna
Tailored Clothing Joseph
Abboud, Hickey Freeman,
Ermenegildo Zegna

Polo Sport
(714)556-7656 www.polo.com

Prada
(714)979-3003 www.prada.com

Rangoni Firenze
(714)751-3195
www.rangonishoes.com

Sergio Rossi
(714)751-7311
www.sergiorossi.com

Saks Fifth Avenue
(714)540-3233
www.saksfifthavenue.com

Casual Wear Giorgio Armani,
Hugo Boss, Ermenegildo Zegna
Dress Shirts Giorgio Armani,
Hugo Boss, Ermenegildo Zegna
Neckwear Giorgio Armani,
Ermenegildo Zegna
Tailored Clothing Giorgio
Armani, Hugo Boss, Arnold
Brant, Ermenegildo Zegna

Gianni Versace
(714)751-7473 www.versace.com

Louis Vuitton
(714)662-6907
www.louisvuitton.com

Ermenegildo Zegna
(714)444-1534 www.zegna.com

Nordstrom Rack
Outlet Store
METRO Pointe, 901 South Coast Dr.,
Ste. C, Costa Mesa, CA 92626
(714)751-5901 www.nordstrom.com

Dress Shirts Ike Behar, Façonnable,
Robert Talbott
Neckwear ETRO, Robert Talbott,
XMI, Ermenegildo Zegna
Tailored Clothing Corneliani,
Hickey Freeman, Zanella

Glenn Laiken A L A N D A L E S
Independent
Glenn Laiken, Owner/Stan Blunck,
Mike Dubinski, Bobby Yosten, Sales
9715 Washington Blvd., Culver City,
CA 90232 (310)838-5100
www.alandales.com
A L A N D A L E S specializes in
providing total service to men,
including excellent on-site tailoring and in-store hair styling. This
establishment helps clients select
clothing that fits their coloring and
body type as well. The sales staff
also assists customers in selecting
clothing that allows them to make
as many combinations as possible
with items in their wardrobe. Most
A L A N D A L E S clothing is
constructed of highly twisted yarns,
creating multiseasonal, fluid fabrics
that drape well and resist wrinkles.
I highly recommend this store.

Accessories Bill Lavin hand-tied belts
Casual Wear Alberto jeans and

pants, Axis, Tommy Bahama,
Hugo Boss, Nat Nast, True Grit,
Arnold Zimberg
Dress Shirts Glenn Laiken
A L A N D A L E S private label
Neckwear Glenn Laiken
A L A N D A L E S private label,
Lee Allison, Altea, Villa Bolgheri,
Hugo Boss, Robert Daskal, Kolte,
Tino Cosma
Shoes Donald J. Pliner
Tailored Clothing Glenn Laiken
A L A N D A L E S private label,
Hugo Boss Black Label,
Vestimenta
Sales Semiannual, occasional pro-
motions

Mel Fox
Independent
17255 Ventura Blvd., Encino, CA
91316 (818)995-1264
Spacious store filled with quality
inventory of reputable brands.

Accessories Some cuff links
Casual Wear Alberto, Tommy
Bahama, Canali, Diesel, Gran
Sasso, Haupt, Lucky Brand, Nat
Nast, Polo Ralph Lauren, Paul &
Shark, True Grit, White
Shirt/Blue Jean, Zanella
Dress Shirts Hugo Boss, Canali,
Eton, Robert Talbott,
Ermenegildo Zegna
Neckwear Jhane Barnes, Canali,
Tino Cosma, Mel Fox
Shoes Tommy Bahama, Relax
Sales Semiannual

Nordstrom Rack
Outlet Store
Glendale Fashion Center, 227 N.
Glendale Ave., Glendale, CA 91206
(818)240-2404
www.nordstrom.com

Casual Wear Tricots St. Raphael
Neckwear Robert Talbott, XMI
Tailored Clothing Joseph Abboud,
Hugo Boss

American Rag Compagnie
Independent
Mark Wertz, Owner
150 S. La Brea Ave., Los Angeles, CA
90036 (323)935-3154
Hip, interesting shopping environment for the man looking for vintage and trendy clothing.

Accessories Large selection of vin-
tage clothing
Casual Wear Comme Des
Garçons, Diesel, Levi's,
J. Lindeberg
Shoes Samsonite, Paul Smith

Avedon
Independent
8620 Melrose Ave., Los Angeles, CA
90069 (310)659-9606
Spacious, attractive store. Cordial,
attentive customer service.

Accessories Gimo leather outerwear
Casual Wear 120% Linen, Bagutta,
ETRO, Moreno Martini Da
Firenze
Dress Shirts Cerruti 1881, ETRO
Neckwear Tino Cosma
Tailored Clothing Cerruti 1881,
Vestimenta

BEVERLY CENTER
Location and Stores:
8500 Beverly Center, Los Angeles, CA
90048 www.beverlycenter.com

A/X Armani Exchange
(310)289-3610
www.giorgioarmani.com

Bernini
*Greg Peters, Coordinator of
Studio Services*
(310)855-1786 www.bernini.com
One of larger Bernini stores
with good selection of clothing.
Greg was a pleasure to talk with.

Casual Wear Hugo Boss, Brioni,
Versace, Ermenegildo Zegna
Dress Shirts Brioni, Canali
Neckwear Brioni, Canali, Dolce
& Gabbana, Versace,
Ermenegildo Zegna
Tailored Clothing Belvest,
Canali, Hugo Boss

BOSS Hugo Boss
(310)657-0011 www.hugoboss.com

Coach
Helen Lee, Store Manager
(310)659-1772 www.coach.com

D & G
(310)360-7282
www.dolcegabbana.com

Diesel
Adam Garris, Store Manager
(310)652-5504 www.diesel.com

DKNY
Armand Geneseo, Store Manager
(310)289-9787 www.dkny.com

Lucky Brand Dungarees
Melissa Reed, Store Manager
(310)360-9796
www.luckyjeans.com

Macy's Men's Store
(310)854-6655 www.macys.com

Casual Wear Diesel, Iceberg
Shoes Hugo Boss, Salvatore
Ferragamo

Politix
Independent
Barre Gray, Store Manager
(310)659-1964
www.politixstore.com
Cool, unusual items you won't find elsewhere. Primarily for the younger man.

Accessories Some vintage T-shirts
Casual Wear Diesel, Andrew Mackenzie, Paper, Denim & Cloth

Traffic
Independent
Nadia Shapiro/Sara Dovan, Store Managers
(310)659-4313
Ultrahip boutique in prime location. MANY items epitomizing L.A. style you won't find anywhere else.

Accessories Shearling car coats; funky hats; good selection of leather outerwear
Casual Wear John Bartlett, Comme Des Garcons, CoSTUME NATIONAL, Dolce & Gabbana, Jean Paul Gaultier, Helmut Lang, Levi's, Andrew Mackenzie, Moschino, Paper, Denim & Cloth, Dirk Schonberger, Paul Smith, Romeo Gigli, Vivienne Westwood

Louis Vuitton
Marie Hoyt, Store Manager
(310)360-1506
www.louisvuitton.com

CENTURY CITY SHOPPING CENTER
Location and Stores:
10250 Santa Monica Blvd., Los Angeles, CA 90067
www.westfield.com

Bernini
(310)551-1786 www.bernini.com

Casual Wear Tommy Bahama, Canali, Ermenegildo Zegna
Dress Shirts Canali, Versace, Ermenegildo Zegna
Neckwear Canali, Pancaldi, Ermenegildo Zegna
Shoes Salvatore Ferragamo, Sutor Mantellassi
Tailored Clothing Canali

BOSS Hugo Boss
(310)553-7171 www.hugoboss.com

Brooks Brothers
(310)553-3335
www.brooksbrothers.com

Coach
(310)282-0772 www.coach.com

Kenneth Cole
(310)282-8535
www.kennethcole.com

Cole Haan
(310)553-4800 www.colehaan.com

Dooney & Bourke
(310)201-6556
www.dooneyandbourke.com

Alfred Dunhill
Mark Petroski, Manager
(310)551-6536 www.dunhill.com

Johnston & Murphy
(310)551-2656
www.johnstonmurphy.com

Politix
Independent
Kwaku Aidoo, Store Manager
(310)203-0464

www.politixstore.com
Cool, unusual items you won't
find elsewhere. Primarily for the
younger man.

Accessories Some vintage T-shirts
Casual Wear Diesel, Andrew
Mackenzie, Paper, Denim &
Cloth

Louis Vuitton
(310)551-0090
www.louisvuitton.com

G. B. Harb & Son
Independent
George Harb, Owner
500 S. Grand Ave., Los Angeles, CA
90071 (213)892-0283
Attractive store with great quality
merchandise. Prompt and pleasant
customer service.

Accessories Trafalgar braces; Bruno
Magli and Remy leather outerwear
Casual Wear Robert Barakett,
Scott Barber, Ike Behar, Bills
Khakis, Dalmine, Gran Sasso, Paul
& Shark, Robert Talbott,
Ermenegildo Zegna
Dress Shirts Ike Behar, Robert Talbott
Neckwear Robert Talbott,
Ermenegildo Zegna
Shoes Alden, Moreschi
Tailored Clothing Hickey Freeman,
Samuelsohn, Vestimenta,
Ermenegildo Zegna
Sales Semiannual

Ron Herman/Fred Segal
Independent
8100 Melrose Ave., Los Angeles, CA
90046 (323)651-4129
World-famous, intriguing, hip
store for the man looking for the
latest trends in fashion.

Accessories Large selection of
brightly colored vintage Levi's
cords and vintage T-shirts
Casual Wear Ted Baker, Michael
Brandon, Comme Des Garçons,
Dries Van Noten, Oliver Spencer,
Theory
Tailored Clothing Ted Baker

Scott Hill
Independent
*Jeff Fox, Executive Vice President &
Operating Partner*
100 S. Robertson Blvd., Los Angeles,
CA 90048 (310)777-1190
Excellent establishment filled with
first quality merchandise you won't
find anywhere else. Scott Hill also
designs and merchandises its own
outstanding private label clothing.
Inventory is well presented using
some antique fixtures. Mr. Fox has
very discriminating taste as a buyer
and is knowledgeable and helpful.

Accessories Tateossian and some
antique cuff links; Oliver Peoples
eyewear; La Matta leather outer-
wear; Allegri, Luciano Barbera,
and Persol outerwear
Casual Wear 120% Linen, Avon
Celli, Barba, Luciano Barbera,
Cividini, Coast, Brunello
Cuccinelli, Heritage, Kiton,
Lorenzini, Mason's, Moreno
Martini Da Firenze, Maria Sartini,
Stone Island, Two Flowers
Dress Shirts Barba, Luigi Borrelli,
Kiton, Lorenzini
Neckwear Luciano Barbera, Kiton
Shoes Gravati, Silvano Lattanzi,
Sutor Mantellasi, Samsonite,
Terra Plana
Tailored Clothing Luciano Barbera,
Kiton (also M2M), Incotex,

Brick-and-Mortar Shopping Guide

Vestimenta (also M2M)
Sales Semiannual

Lisa Kline Men
Independent
Nicole Sargent, Manager
123 S. Robertson Blvd., #B, Los
Angeles, CA 90048 (310)385-7113
www.lisakline.com
Eclectic, comfortable store for the
younger man who prefers modern
designs and brands.

Accessories Cool, kitschy cuff links,
Vintage Zippo lighters and T-shirts
Casual Wear Paper, Denim &
Cloth, James Perse, Levi's, Oliver
Smith, Paul Smith, Oliver Spencer,
Theory

Maxfield
Independent
Deirdre Wheaton, Manager
8825 Melrose Ave., Los Angeles, CA
90069 (310)274-8800
Impressively decorated emporium
resembles an art gallery in its
unique presentation of merchandise. Excellent customer service.
Many celebrities shop regularly at
Maxfield's for unique, tasteful
ensembles.

Casual Wear Comme Des
Garçons, Helmut Lang, Martin
Margiela, Yohji Yamamoto
Neckwear Giorgio Armani, Gucci
Tailored Clothing Giorgio Armani
Black Label, Prada, Yohji
Yamamoto

Maxfield Bleu
Outlet Store
151 N. Robertson Blvd., Los Angeles,
CA 90048 (310)275-7007
Maxfield's Outlet Store

Casual Wear Comme Des
Garçons, Helmut Lang, Martin
Margiela, Yohji Yamamoto
Neckwear Giorgio Armani, Gucci
Tailored Clothing Giorgio Armani
Black Label, Prada, Yohji
Yamamoto

Nordstrom Rack
Outlet Store
Promenade at Howard Hughes
Center, 6081 Center Dr., Los Angeles,
CA 90045 (310)641-4046
www.nordstrom.com

Casual Wear Mavi jeans, Robert
Talbott
Dress Shirts Joseph Abboud, Ike
Behar, Dak's, Fratelli Moda,
Robert Talbott, XMI Platinum
Neckwear XMI, Robert Talbott
Tailored Clothing Joseph Abboud,
Jhane Barnes, Hugo Boss, Dak's,
Façonnable, Tallia, Ermenegildo
Zegna, Bernard Zins

On Beverly Blvd. for Men
Independent
8601 Beverly Blvd., Los Angeles, CA
90048 (310)652-5522
Attractive, impressive storefront.
Many unique, quality items you
won't find elsewhere in L.A.

Casual Wear Brunello Cuccinelli
(GREAT selection), Moreno
Martini Da Firenze
Dress Shirts Bagutta, Moreno
Martini Da Firenze
Neckwear Dolce & Gabbana
Tailored Clothing Mabro, Oliver
Sales Semiannual

Scott & Co.
Independent
Scott Hill, Proprietor

8710 Sunset Blvd., Los Angeles, CA 90069 (310)659-5829
Attractive, tastefully decorated store with great assortment of first-quality merchandise.

Accessories Some cuff links; leather car-length coats
Casual Wear Giorgio Armani, Incotex, New England, Scott & Co., John Varvatos, Arnold Zimberg
Dress Shirts Giorgio Armani, Sartoria Attolini, Gianluca Isaia, Lorenzini, Truzzi
Neckwear Giorgio Armani, Gianluca Isaia, Nicky's of Milan
Shoes Borgioli, Certo, Sutor Mantellassi, John Varvatos
Tailored Clothing Giorgio Armani, Sartoria Attolini, Belvest, Gianluca Isaia, Calvin Klein, Incotex
Sales Semiannual

THE GROVE
Location and Stores:
189 The Grove Dr., Los Angeles, CA 90036 www.shopthegrove.com

Tommy Bahama
(323)930-2888
www.tommybahama.com

Nordstrom
(323)930-2230 www.nordstrom.com
Excellent Nordstrom location for fashionable men's wear.

Casual Wear Robert Barakett, D & G, Riscatto Portofino, Ermenegildo Zegna
Dress Shirts Ike Behar, Robert Talbott, Ermenegildo Zegna
Neckwear Robert Talbott, XMI, Ermenegildo Zegna
Tailored Clothing Joseph

Abboud, Giorgio Armani, Hugo Boss, Hickey Freeman, Ermenegildo Zegna, Zegna Soft, Pal Zileri

Giacomo Trabalza Custom Tailoring
Independent
Giacomo Trabalza, Proprietor
723 N. La Cienega Blvd., Los Angeles, CA 90069 (310)652-6396
Recently observed their 40th anniversary. Many choices in exclusive fabrics such as Cerruti, Dormeuil, Holland & Sherry, Jodex, and Ermenegildo Zegna. Superb old-world service with handcrafted attention to detail. All garments are handmade from paper patterns on the premises. Mr. Trabalza has a notable client list and also frequently makes clothes for motion pictures. He is a real joy to talk with as well. I highly recommend his establishment.

Nordstrom
Westside Pavilion, 10830 W. Pico Blvd., Los Angeles, CA 90064 (310)470-6155 www.nordstrom.com

Casual Wear Ermenegildo Zegna
Dress Shirts Ike Behar, Robert Talbott, Ermenegildo Zegna
Neckwear Robert Talbott, XMI, Ermenegildo Zegna
Tailored Clothing Joseph Abboud, Hugo Boss, Hickey Freeman, Pal Zileri

Island Sport
Independent
Gene Muntean, Owner/
Joseph Cipolla, General Manager/
Herb Wagner, Manager

221 Manhattan Beach Blvd.,
Manhattan Beach, CA 90266
(310)546-7173
Good destination for casual/beach
wear. Great customer service.

Casual Wear Tommy Bahama,
Michael Brandon, Koko Island,
Paradise Found, Tori Richard,
Riscatto Portofino, Reyn Spooner

Mark Michaels
Independent
Mark Friedman, Owner
4672 Admiralty Way, Marina Del Rey,
CA 90292 (310)822-1707
Very pleasant shopping environ-
ment. Lots of wood and light.
The merchandise is arranged
appealingly as well. Great customer
service.

Accessories Nice selection of belts,
cuff links, and leather outerwear
Casual Wear Acorn, Avon Celli,
Tommy Bahama, Equilibrio,
Forte, Paul & Shark, Zanella,
Ermenegildo Zegna
Dress Shirts Canali
Neckwear Giorgio Armani,
Pancaldi, Ermenegildo Zegna
Tailored Clothing Giorgio Armani,
Canali, Zanella, Ermenegildo
Zegna
Sales Semiannual

THE SHOPS AT MISSION VIEJO
Location and Stores:
555 The Shops at Mission Viejo,
Mission Viejo, CA 92691
www.shopsimon.com

A/X Armani Exchange
(949)364-2772
www.giorgioarmani.com

Coach
(949)365-0771 www.coach.com

DKNY
(949)364-1313 www.dkny.com

Gary's Studio
Independent
John and Dick Braeger, Owners
(949)364-9686
www.garysonline.com
Like the Fashion Island location
in Newport Beach, a top-notch
selection of fine designer clothing. Tommy Bahama store-in-
store.

Casual Wear Tommy Bahama,
Hugo Boss, Gary's, Gran Sasso,
Haupt, Georg Roth,
Ermenegildo Zegna
Dress Shirts Hugo Boss, Canali,
Robert Talbott, Ermenegildo
Zegna
Neckwear Hugo Boss, Brioni,
Robert Talbott, Ermenegildo
Zegna
Shoes Cole Haan, Hugo Boss,
Moreschi, Donald J. Pliner,
Terra Plana
Tailored Clothing Hugo Boss
Canali, Ermenegildo Zegna
Sales Semiannual, January and
July

Lucky Brand Dungarees
(949)347-6790
www.luckyjeans.com

Nordstrom
(949)347-2710 www.nordstrom.com

Saks Fifth Avenue
(949)347-5100
www.saksfifthavenue.com

FASHION ISLAND
Location and Stores:
579 Newport Center Dr., Newport
Beach, CA 92660
www.shopfashionisland.com

At Ease
Independent
(949)759-7979
Spacious, comfortable store,
filled with dark wood and over-
sized leather chairs. Also has a
large room with a huge selection
of Hawaiian shirts. Unique
assortment of handmade walking sticks.

Accessories Robert Comstock
leathers; handmade walking
sticks
Casual Wear Axis, Ike Behar,
Barry Bricken, Bobby Jones,
Riscatto Portofino, Reyn
Spooner, Tricots St. Raphael,
Zanella
Dress Shirts Ike Behar (also
M2M)
Neckwear Tino Cosma, XMI
Tailored Clothing Aquascutum,
Tallia, Zanella
Sales Semiannual, January and
July

Gary's and Company
Independent
*John and Dick Braeger,
Owners/John Greene, Store
Manager*
(949)759-1622
www.garysonline.com
Has a separate home and beach
wear store (Gary's Island/
Dick's Last Resort), a women's
store (Gary's Per Donna), and
Cole Haan and Hugo Boss store

in Fashion Island. All are impressive. Huge, well-presented selections of merchandise you won't
find anywhere else. Also a denim
section and a good selection of
leather outerwear.

Accessories Breuer braces;
bow ties; great selection of
cuff links, Art of Shaving
toiletries
Casual Wear Hugo Boss,
Gary's, Gran Sasso, Haupt,
Georg Roth, Ermenegildo
Zegna
Dress Shirts Hugo Boss, Canali,
Robert Talbott, Ermenegildo
Zegna
Neckwear Hugo Boss, Brioni,
Robert Talbott, Ermenegildo
Zegna
Shoes Cole Haan, Gravati,
Moreschi, Donald J. Pliner,
Prada, Terra Plana
Tailored Clothing Giorgio
Armani, Hugo Boss, Brioni, Canali,
Ermenegildo Zegna, Pal Zileri
Sales Semiannual, January and
July

Kenneth Cole
(949)219-0671
www.kennethcole.com

Lucky Brand Dungarees
(949)759-7800
www.luckyjeans.com

Neiman Marcus
(949)759-1900
www.neimanmarcus.com

Casual Wear Brioni, Loro Piana,
Ralph Lauren Purple Label,
Ermenegildo Zegna
Dress Shirts Giorgio Armani, Ike

Behar, Hugo Boss, Brioni, Lorenzini, Ermenegildo Zegna *Neckwear* Giorgio Armani, Ike Behar, Charvet, Salvatore Ferragamo, Ermenegildo Zegna *Tailored Clothing* Brioni, ETRO, Paul Smith, Ermenegildo Zegna

P.O.S.H.
Independent
John and Dick Braeger,
Owners
(949)640-8310
www.garysonline.com
Large store with appealing arrangement of merchandise. Part of Gary's Inc., and targeted toward more traditional tastes.

Accessories Some cuff links
Casual Wear Tommy Bahama, Ike Behar, Barry Bricken, Haupt, P.O.S.H., Robert Talbott
Dress Shirts Ike Behar, P.O.S.H., Robert Talbott
Neckwear Joseph Abboud, P.O.S.H., Ferrell Reed, Robert Talbott
Shoes Cole Haan, Mezlan
Tailored Clothing Joseph Abboud, Canali, Hickey Freeman, Oxxford, P.O.S.H., Zanella
Sales Semiannual, January and July

St. Croix
(949)760-8191
www.stcroixshop.com

ONTARIO MILLS
Location and Stores:
One Mills Circle, Ontario, CA 91764
www.ontariomills.com

Hugo Boss
Outlet Store
(909)484-3610 www.hugoboss.com

Nordstrom Rack
Outlet Store
(909)476-3160 www.nordstrom.com

Casual Wear Tricots St. Raphael
Dress Shirts Ike Behar, Robert Talbott
Neckwear XMI, Robert Talbott
Tailored Clothing Joseph Abboud, Ballin, Kenneth Cole, Tallia, Zanella, Bernard Zins

Off Rodeo Drive
Outlet Store
(909)484-1544 www.bernini.com

Casual Wear Ermenegildo Zegna
Dress Shirts Brioni, Lorenzini
Neckwear Canali, Ermenegildo Zegna
Tailored Clothing Canali, Versace

Saks Off Fifth
Outlet Store
(909)980-7558
www.saksfifthavenue.com

Casual Wear Giorgio Armani, Diesel, Theory, Versace
Dress Shirts Ike Behar, Hugo Boss, Ermenegildo Zegna
Neckwear Giorgio Armani, Hugo Boss, Gianfranco Ferré, Ermenegildo Zegna
Tailored Clothing Giorgio Armani, Hugo Boss, Caruso, Hickey Freeman, Zegna Soft

Saks Off Fifth
Outlet Store
The Block at Orange, 20 City Blvd.

West, Orange, CA 92868
(714)769-4200
www.saksfifthavenue.com

Dress Shirts Ermenegildo Zegna
Neckwear Versace, Ermenegildo Zegna

Threads for Men
Independent
Gene Muntean, Owner/
Joseph Cipolla, General Manager/
Michael Soriano, Manager/
Art Heller, Associate Manager
1907 S. Catalina Ave., Redondo Beach, CA 90274 (310)375-7575
Attractive store for the traditional shopper. Great customer service.

Accessories Brighton belts
Casual Wear Tommy Bahama, Michael Brandon, Massoti, Tori Richard, Riscatto Portofino, Reyn Spooner
Dress Shirts Marco Trani
Neckwear Azzizo
Tailored Clothing Pincus Bros., Corbin, Austin Reed

Winston International
Independent
Gene Muntean, Owner/
Bent Simonsen, Manager/
Joseph Cipolla, General Manager
The Avenue of the Peninsula, 550 Deep Valley Dr., Rolling Hills Estates, CA 90274 (310)541-2446
Spacious, attractive shopping environment for the traditional shopper. Excellent customer service. Great quality clothing at reasonable prices.

Accessories St. John and Royall aftershave, Brighton belts, Byford socks
Casual Wear Tommy Bahama,

Equilibrio, Forsyth, Riscatto Portofino, Reyn Spooner, Robert Talbott, Viyella
Dress Shirts Forsyth, Gitman Bros., Robert Talbott
Neckwear Robert Talbott
Tailored Clothing Hart, Schaffner, & Marx, Hickey Freeman

Island Sport
Independent
Gene Muntean, Owner/
Joseph Cipolla, General Manager/
Debbie Zerbe, Manager
2434 S. Western Ave., San Pedro, CA 90732 (310)548-5084
Good destination for casual or beach wear. Great customer service.

Casual Wear Tommy Bahama, Michael Brandon, Koko Island, Tori Richard, Riscatto Portofino, Paradise Found, Reyn Spooner

SANTA ANA MAINPLACE
Location and Stores:
2800 N. Main St., Santa Ana, CA 92705 www.westfield.com

Guccini
Independent
Abdullah Mojadidi, Proprietor
(714)835-1925
Tasteful store with some unusual and distinctive pieces.

Accessories Some cuff links; interesting selection of leather outerwear
Casual Wear Leonard, Versace
Dress Shirts Tino Cosma, Gianfranco Ferré, Gorena
Neckwear Leonard, Versace
Shoes Magnanni, Versace
Tailored Clothing d'Avenza, Versace

Nordstrom
(714)972-2020 www.nordstrom.com

Sy Devore
Independent
Danny Marsh, Vice President
12930 Ventura Blvd., Ste. 124, Studio
City, CA 91604 (818)783-2700 or
(310)420-4429 www.sydevore.com
Spacious store with lots of light.
Merchandise presented well in
attractive wood fixtures. Sy Devore
made his name dressing many
Hollywood stars, most notably the
members of the Rat Pack. His
niece now runs the business with
two partners, including Mr. Marsh,
who is great to shop with. Also a
nice women's section.

Casual Wear Tommy Bahama, Ted
Baker, Hugo Boss Red Label, Nat
Nast, Paul Smith, John Varvatos,
Ermenegildo Zegna, Zegna Soft,
Arnold Zimberg
Dress Shirts Eton, Sy Devore, Paul
Smith, Ermenegildo Zegna
Neckwear Canali, Robert Daskal,
Sy Devore, Ermenegildo Zegna
Shoes Borgioli, Canali, Certo
Tailored Clothing Hugo Boss Black
Label, Canali, Sy Devore, Paul
Smith, Zegna Soft

Gary's Rack
Outlet Store
John and Dick Braeger,
Owners
148 W. Main St., Tustin, CA 92680
(714)832-8466 www.garysonline.com
Outlet store for the Gary's group
of stores in southern CA. Outstand-
ing buys on quality merchandise.
Casual Wear Hugo Boss, Henry
Cotton's, Gran Sasso,

Ermenegildo Zegna, Zegna Sport
Dress Shirts Canali, Hugo Boss,
Giorgio Armani, Ermenegildo
Zegna, Brioni
Neckwear Breuer, Canali,
Ermenegildo Zegna
Shoes Cole Haan
Tailored Clothing Canali, Giorgio
Armani, Ermenegildo Zegna

John Varvatos
8800 Melrose Avenue, West
Hollywood, CA 90069 (310)859-2970
www.johnvarvatos.com

Nordstrom Rack
Outlet Store
21490 Victory Blvd., Woodland Hills,
CA 91367 (818)884-6771
www.nordstrom.com

Casual Wear Joseph Abboud,
Robert Barakett
Dress Shirts Ike Behar, Fratelli
Moda
Neckwear Daks, ETRO, Robert
Talbott, XMI
Tailored Clothing Joseph Abboud,
Jhane Barnes, Tallia, Bernard Zins

Metro Area: Memphis

James Davis
Independent
Joe Augustine, Buyer
400 Grove Park, Memphis, TN 38117
(901)767-4640
Great selection of high-quality
merchandise in large, aesthetically
appealing store. Hickey Freeman
store-in-store; one of only two in
the U.S. Mr. Augustine was very
helpful and generous with his time.

Accessories Carrot & Gibbs,
R. Hanauer, Robert Talbott bow

ties; Robert Talbott, Robert
Tateossian, Abba Accessories,
Alfred Dunhill, and Ferragamo
cuff links; formal bow ties, cum-
merbunds, and vests from Robert
Talbott, Carrot & Gibbs, and
Favourbrook of London; Alfred
Dunhill, Ferragamo, Ghurka, Art
of Shaving gentleman's accessories;
Robert Tateossian jewelry;
Burberry, Armani Collezioni, and
Hickey Freeman tuxedos; Cartier
writing instruments
Casual Wear Armani Collezioni,
Tommy Bahama, Jhane Barnes,
Ike Behar, Barry Bricken, Hugo
Boss, Burberry, Cortina, Salvatore
Ferragamo, Gran Sasso, Haupt,
Bobby Jones, Loro Piana, Polo
Ralph Lauren, Jeff Rose, Tricots
St. Raphael
Dress Shirts Armani Collezioni, Ike
Behar (also C.E.O Program),
Brioni (also M2M), Luigi Borrelli
(also M2M), Gitman Bros (also
M2M), Hickey Freeman, Robert
Talbott (also M2M), individual-
ized custom
Neckwear Armani Collezioni,
Burberry, Brioni, Boss, Cortina,
Salvatore Ferragamo, Hickey
Freeman, Robert Talbott
Shoes Bacco Bucci, Cole Haan,
Allen Edmonds, Johnston &
Murphy, Mezlan, Donald J. Pliner
Tailored Clothing Armani
Collezioni (also M2M), Barry
Bricken, Brioni (Also M2M),
Burberry (also M2M), Lauren by
Ralph Lauren, Hugo Boss, Hickey
Freeman (also M2M), Coppley
M2M (seven day turnaround!),
Majer, Oxxford (also M2M),
Linnea Trussini, Zanella
Sales Semiannual

Oak Hall
Independent
Bill and Bob Levy, Proprietors
6150 Poplar Ave., Ste. 150, Memphis,
TN 38119 (901)761-3580
Family business begun in 1859.
Helpful, friendly sales staff.
Ermenegildo Zegna store-in-store,
Hermès boutique, also a great
women's department.

Tailored Clothing Ermenegildo
Zegna (also M2M), Canali (also
M2M), Oxxford (also M2M),
Samuelsohn (also M2M), Hickey
Freeman (also M2M), Hart,
Schaffner & Marx (also M2M),
Jack Victor (also M2M), Bradford,
Zanella, Ballin
Dress Shirts Ermenegildo Zegna,
Luigi Borrelli, Robert Talbott,
Gitman Bros., Ike Behar, Canali,
Oak Hall
Neckwear Hermès, Ermenegildo
Zegna, Robert Talbott, Charvet,
Tino Cosma, Canali
Casual Wear Scott Barber, Bills
Khakis, Polo Ralph Lauren,
Lacoste, Tricots St. Raphael, Gran
Sasso, Zanella, Ermenegildo Zegna
Accessories Good selection of cuff
links, Trafalgar braces, and bow ties,
also Remy and Barbour outerwear
Shoes Alden, Allen Edmonds,
Lorenzo Banfi, Cole Haan,
Salvatore Ferragamo, Gucci,
Prada, Ecco, Peter Huber,
Johnston & Murphy, Gravati

Metro Area: Miami
AVENTURA MALL
Location and Stores:
19501 Biscayne Blvd., Aventura, FL
33180 www.shopaventuramall.com

A/X Armani Exchange
(305)682-3602
www.giorgioarmani.com

Coach
(305)935-7549 www.coach.com

Stuart Norman
Independent
(305)936-8006
Interesting concept store. Huge
selection of unique chinos, corduroys, and jeans of every color
and size imaginable stacked in
neat piles on the floor.

Casual Wear Ermenegildo Zegna
Neckwear Ermenegildo Zegna

Donald J. Pliner
(305)792-4774
www.donaldjpliner.com

Surreys
Independent
Pete Rosenberg, Store Manager
(305)932-7726
Spacious, well-appointed store.
Good selection of quality mer-
chandise, reasonably priced. Mr.
Rosenberg was great to work with.

Casual Wear Jhane Barnes,
Hugo Boss, Canali, Versace
Dress Shirts Fabio Inghirami,
Rodin, Ermenegildo Zegna
Neckwear Altea, Canali,
Pancaldi, Ermenegildo Zegna
Tailored Clothing Hugo Boss
Black Label, Canali
Sales Semiannual

Surrey's Sport
Independent
(305)931-4494
Sportswear only.

BAL HARBOUR SHOPS
Location and Stores:
9700 Collins Ave., Bal Harbour, FL 33154
www.balharbourshops.com

A/X Armani Exchange
(305)864-3661
www.giorgioarmani.com

Giorgio Armani
(305)861-1515
www.giorgioarmani.com

Brooks Brothers
(305)865-8686
www.brooksbrothers.com

Cole Haan
(305)866-7890 www.colehaan.com

Dolce & Gabbana
(305)866-0503
www.dolcegabbana.it

Alfred Dunhill
(305)861-0132 www.dunhill.com

Enrico
Independent
(305)866-4117
Shoes Lorenzo Banfi, Moreschi

Gianfranco Ferré
(305)866-1460
www.gianfrancoferre.com

Galtrucco
Independent
Daniel Demarin, Proprietor
(305)866-0477
Very appealing store. All items
of the highest quality; many
unique items of exquisite taste.

Casual Wear Avon Celli,
Galtrucco

Dress Shirts Brioni, Stefano Ricci
Neckwear Brioni, Stefano Ricci
Tailored Clothing Brioni,
d'Avenza, Stefano Ricci

Gucci
(305)868-6504 www.gucci.com

Hermès
(305)868-0118 www.hermes.com

Lacoste
(305)867-0530 www.lacoste.com

Bruno Magli
(305)868-1050
www.brunomagli.com

Malo
(305)861-0600

Neiman Marcus
(305)865-6161
www.neimanmarcus.com
Brioni store-in-store. Also the
largest selection of Leonard ties
at any Neiman's I've seen.

Dress Shirts Giorgio Armani, Ike
Behar, Luigi Borrelli, Brioni,
Lorenzini, Turnbull & Asser,
Ermenegildo Zegna
Neckwear Giorgio Armani,
Brioni, Salvatore Ferragamo,
Leonard, Ermenegildo Zegna
Tailored Clothing Giorgio
Armani, Brioni, Hickey
Freeman, Ermenegildo Zegna

Paul & Shark
(305)864-9212 www.paulshark.it

Prada
(305)864-9111 www.prada.com

Louis Vuitton
(305)866-4470
www.louisvuitton.com

Ermenegildo Zegna
(305)865-8652 www.zegna.com

Zegna Sport
(305)867-5955 www.zegna.com

Tommy Bahama
418 Plaza Real, Boca Raton, FL 33431
(561)394-9060
www.tommybahama.com

Guy La Ferrera
Independent
Guy La Ferrera, Proprietor
Boca Center, 5050 Town Center Cir.,
#223, Boca Raton, FL 33486
(561)620-0011
Extremely attractive establishment
with well-arranged merchandise in
handsome wooden fixtures. Customer service pleasant and helpful.

Accessories Some cuff links
Casual Wear Brioni Sport, Tino
Cosma, Gran Sasso, Paul & Shark,
Ermenegildo Zegna, Zegna Soft
Dress Shirts Brioni, Canali, Eton,
Ermenegildo Zegna
Neckwear Brioni, Canali,
Ermenegildo Zegna
Shoes Allen Edmonds, Mezlan
Tailored Clothing Brioni, Canali,
Marzotto Sartoriale, Ravazzolo,
Zanella, Ermenegildo Zegna
Sales Semiannual

Maus and Hoffman
Independent
Bill and John Maus, Owners
400 E. Palmetto Park Rd., Boca Raton,
FL 33432 (561)368-9983

www.mausandhoffman.com
(see chapter 9)
Great merchandise for customer
with both traditional and
European tastes.

Accessories Zimmerli undergarments
Casual Wear Brioni, Hickey
Freeman, Liberty of London,
Maus and Hoffman
Dress Shirts Brioni, Maus and
Hoffman
Neckwear Brioni, Maus and
Hoffman, Leonard
Shoes Allen Edmonds, Maus and
Hoffman
Tailored Clothing Brioni, Hickey
Freeman, Oxxford, Maus and
Hoffman
Sales Semiannual

TOWN CENTER AT BOCA RATON
Location and Stores:
6000 Glades Rd., Boca Raton, FL
33431 www.shopsimon.com

A/X Armani Exchange
(561)750-0046
www.giorgioarmani.com

Bernini
(561)368-6000 www.bernini.com

Casual Wear Hugo Boss,
Ermenegildo Zegna
Dress Shirts Hugo Boss,
Ermenegildo Zegna
Neckwear Hugo Boss, Canali,
Ermenegildo Zegna
Tailored Clothing Hugo Boss
Sales Semiannual

BOSS Hugo Boss
(561)368-6000 www.hugoboss.com

Coach
(561)392-7227 www.coach.com

Lacoste
(561)392-5660 www.lacoste.com

Ralph Lauren
(561)395-7656 www.polo.com

Lucky Brand Dungarees
(561)361-6429
www.luckybrandjeans.com

Nordstrom
(561)620-5555 www.nordstrom.com
Nice formal wear department.

Casual Wear Joseph Abboud,
Jhane Barnes, Zanella,
Ermenegildo Zegna
Dress Shirts Robert Talbott
Neckwear Robert Talbott, XMI,
Ermenegildo Zegna
Tailored Clothing Joseph
Abboud, Hickey Freeman, Pal
Zileri

Saks Fifth Avenue
(561)393-9100
www.saksfifthavenue.com

Casual Wear Joseph Abboud,
Giorgio Armani, Brioni, Polo
Ralph Lauren, Prada,
Ermenegildo Zegna
Dress Shirts Giorgio Armani,
Baldessarini, Hugo Boss, Brioni,
Ermenegildo Zegna
Neckwear Giorgio Armani,
Brioni, Burberry, Salvatore
Ferragamo, Ermenegildo Zegna
Tailored Clothing Giorgio
Armani, Brioni, Canali,
Corneliani, Prada, Ermenegildo
Zegna

Surreys

(561)368-6000
Also a Surrey's Sport in Town
Center Mall.

Casual Wear Tommy Bahama,
Gillio, Nat Nast, Tulliano
Dress Shirts Fabio Inghirami,
Rodin, Ermenegildo Zegna
Neckwear Canali, Pancaldi
Tailored Clothing Hugo Boss
Black Label, Canali, Gianfranco
Ferré Studio
Sales Semiannual

Pepe Bertini

Independent
Pepe Bertini, Owner
315 Miracle Mile, Coral Gables, FL
33134 (305)461-3374
Attractive store with handsome
wood fixtures. Unique, attractive
merchandise; helpful staff.

Accessories M2M and custom self-
labeled shirts
Casual Wear Canali, Zanella
Dress Shirts Bertini, Canali, Stefano
Ricci
Neckwear Canali, Stefano Ricci
Tailored Clothing Canali

J. Bolado Clothiers

Independent
Jose P. Bolado, Owner
336 Miracle Mile, Coral Gables, FL
33134 (305)448-5905
Appealing, good-sized store. More
traditional selection of clothing.

Accessories Breuer, Trafalgar braces
Casual Wear Tommy Bahama,
Haupt, Gran Sasso
Dress Shirts Ike Behar, Robert
Talbott
Neckwear Robert Talbott
Tailored Clothing Corneliani,

Hickey Freeman, Samuelsohn
Sales Semiannual

Canali

Adolfo Mendez, Sales
320 Avenue San Lorenzo, Coral
Gables, FL 33146 (305)446-1499
www.canali.it
Only Canali boutique in U.S.,
opened March 2003.

Façonnable

342 Avenue San Lorenzo, Ste. 1005,
Coral Gables, FL 33146 (305)774-5861
www.nordstrom.com

Giorgio's at Franco B.

Independent
Joey Milanes, Manager
350 Miracle Mile, Coral Gables, FL
33134 (305)448-4302
Lots of wood fixtures, clubby
atmosphere in this great Miami
establishment. Old World
dedication to personalized
service. Mr. Milanes is knowledgeable and congenial and will
take the time to assist you in
developing your personal sense
of style.

Accessories Good selection of cuff
links and pocket squares
Casual Wear Brioni, Canali
Dress Shirts Brioni, Canali, Franco
B. custom shirts made on premises
Neckwear Brioni, Canali,
Ermenegildo Zegna
Tailored Clothing Brioni, Canali,
Ravazzolo

Nordstrom

4310 Ponce de Leon Blvd., Coral
Gables, FL 33146 (786)999-1313
www.nordstrom.com

Neiman Marcus
390 Avenue San Lorenzo, Coral
Gables, FL 33146 (786)999-1000
www.neimanmarcus.com

Donald J. Pliner
320 Avenue San Lorenzo, Coral
Gables, FL 33146 (305)774-5880

**THE GALLERIA AT
FORT LAUDERDALE**
Location and Stores:
2456 E. Sunrise Blvd., Fort
Lauderdale, FL 33304
www.galleriamall-fl.com

Coach
(954)564-0710 www.coach.com

Johnston & Murphy
(954)630-0334
www.johnstonmurphy.com

Kiss and Makeup
Independent
Susan Behar, Owner
(954)537-3577
Some very stylish and unique
Hawaiian shirts you may not
even be able to find in the
islands. Also a nice selection of
merchandise for women. The
staff is very cordial, embodying
the more personalized service
you can expect from a small,
independent business.

Neiman Marcus
(954)566-6666
www.neimanmarcus.com
Casual Wear Giorgio Armani,
Polo Ralph Lauren,
Ermenegildo Zegna
Dress Shirts Giorgio Armani,
Ermenegildo Zegna

Neckwear Ermenegildo Zegna
Tailored Clothing Giorgio
Armani, Ermenegildo Zegna

Saks
(954)563-7600
www.saksfifthavenue.com
Staff extremely helpful.

Maus and Hoffman
Independent
Bill and John Maus, Owners
800 E. Las Olas Blvd., Fort
Lauderdale, FL 33301 (954)463-1472
www.mausandhoffman.com
(see chapter 9)
Large, elegant store. Great merchandise mix between European
and updated traditional tastes.

Accessories Zimmerli undergarments
Casual Wear Brioni, Hickey
Freeman, Liberty of London,
Maus and Hoffman
Dress Shirts Brioni, Maus and
Hoffman
Neckwear Brioni, Maus and
Hoffman, Leonard
Shoes Allen Edmonds, Maus and
Hoffman
Tailored Clothing Brioni, Hickey
Freeman, Oxxford, Maus and
Hoffman
Sales Semiannual

Moda Mario
Independent
822 E. Las Olas Blvd., Fort
Lauderdale, FL 33301 (954)467-3258
Spacious boutique with quality mer-
chandise that is presented well.

Casual Wear Moda Mario
Dress Shirts Moda Mario, Pal Zileri
Neckwear: Brioni, Italo Ferretti,
Moda Mario

Tailored Clothing Mabro, Pal Zileri
Shoes Moda Mario
Sales Semiannual

Stuart Norman
Independent
300 SW First Ave., Fort Lauderdale, FL
33301 (954)522-6590
Pleasant store with great customer
service and interesting collection
of tailored clothing.

Casual Wear Ermenegildo Zegna
Tailored Clothing Rene Lezard,
Vestimenta, Ermenegildo Zegna

Irving Berlin
Independent
*Ronni and Lewis Cohen, Owners/
Gustavo Goldman, Fashion
Consultant*
1919 Hollywood Blvd., Hollywood, FL
33020 (954)921-2561
2003 marks the fiftieth anniversary
of this establishment's location in
historic downtown Hollywood.
First-rate customer service; the
Cohens and Mr. Goldman are
great to work with.

Accessories Nice selection of cuff
links, tuxedos, and formal accessories
Casual Wear Ted Baker, Jhane
Barnes, Cortigiani, Dalmine,
Mirto, St. Croix, Ermenegildo
Zegna, Pal Zileri
Dress Shirts Brioni, Canali,
Ermenegildo Zegna
Neckwear Brioni, Canali, Pancaldi,
Ermenegildo Zegna
Shoes Bruno Magli, Mezlan,
Moreschi
Tailored Clothing Brioni, Canali,
Ravazzolo, Tallia, Jack Victor, Pal
Zileri
Sales Semiannual

DADELAND MALL
Location and Stores:
7525 N. Kendall Dr., Miami, FL 33156
www.shopsimon.com

Bernini
Julio Espinosa, Manager
(305)668-4786
Spacious store with ample selection. Mr. Espinosa was helpful
and informative.

Casual Wear Ermenegildo
Zegna
Neckwear Canali, Ermenegildo
Zegna
Tailored Clothing Belvest, Canali

Coach
(305)668-2946 www.coach.com

Kenneth Cole
(305)668-1789
www.kennethcole.com

Saks Fifth Avenue
(305)662-8655
www.saksfifthavenue.com

Casual Wear Giorgio Armani,
Ermenegildo Zegna
Dress Shirts Giorgio Armani,
Hugo Boss, Ermenegildo Zegna
Neckwear Giorgio Armani,
Hugo Boss, Stefano Ricci,
Ermenegildo Zegna
Tailored Clothing Giorgio
Armani, Ermenegildo Zegna

Surrey's
Independent
(305)665-6226
Spacious, well-appointed store.
Good selection of quality merchandise. Also a Surrey's Millen-
nium located in Dadeland Mall.

Accessories Some formal wear
Casual Wear Jhane Barnes,
Hugo Boss, Canali, Versace
Dress Shirts Ermenegildo Zegna
Neckwear Altea, Canali,
Pancaldi, Ermenegildo Zegna
Tailored Clothing Hugo Boss,
Canali
Sales Semiannual

Damiani
Independent
Jorge Gonzalez, Sales
8865 S. Dixie Hwy., Miami, FL 33156
(305)661-0002
Casual Wear Damiani, Kiton,
Optimum, Gran Sasso
Dress Shirts Damiani
Neckwear Damiani, Gianfranco
Ferré, Ermenegildo Zegna
Tailored Clothing Hugo Boss Back
Label, Lubiam 1911, Ermenegildo
Zegna

DOLPHIN MALL
Location and Stores:
11401 N.W. 12th St., Miami, FL 33172
www.dolphinmall.com

Brooks Brothers
Outlet Store
Cedric Brown, Store Manager
(786)845-0881
www.brooksbrothers.com

Giorgio's
Outlet Store
Marcos Bicciomello, Manager
(305)599-5230
www.dolphinmall.com
Outlet for Giorgios's at Franco
B. in Coral Gables. Some
GREAT buys here!

Casual Wear Canali, Dalmine,
Franco B.

Dress Shirts Franco B.
Tailored Clothing Brioni, Canali,
Corneliani, Ravazzolo,
Ermenegildo Zegna,
Ermenegildo Zegna Soft, Pal
Zileri
Sales Further semiannual mark-
downs

Saks Off Fifth
Outlet Store
(786)845-3867
www.saksfifthavenue.com

Casual Wear Giorgio Armani,
Hugo Boss, Diesel, Marc
Jacobs, Theory, Ermenegildo
Zegna
Dress Shirts Ike Behar, Burberry
Neckwear Gianfranco Ferré,
Gucci, Ermenegildo Zegna
Tailored Clothing Giorgio
Armani, Hugo Boss, Dolce &
Gabbana, Salvatore Ferragamo,
Pal Zileri

Giorgio Armani
242 Worth Ave., Palm Beach, FL
33480 (561)655-1641
www.giorgioarmani.com

Luigi Borrelli
313½ Worth Ave., Palm Beach, FL
33480 (561)833-3373
www.luigiborrelli.com
Store opened spring 2002. Only
other location is in Manhattan.

Salvatore Ferragamo
200 Worth Ave., Palm Beach, FL
33480 (561)659-0602
www.salvatoreferragamo.it

Giorgio's of Palm Beach
Independent
George Sharoubim, President

230 Worth Ave., Palm Beach, FL
33480 (561)655-2446
Beautiful, opulent store, filled with
menswear and other unique treas-
ures of the highest quality. Everything is self-labeled. This boutique
also has some magnificent, unique
pieces, particularly clothing and
other items in exotic skins.

Lacoste
206 Worth Ave., Palm Beach, FL
33480 (561)655-5666
www.lacoste.com

Ralph Lauren
300 Worth Ave., Palm Beach, FL
33480 (561)651-3900 www.polo.com
Great selection of seasonal linen
trousers.

Malo
228 Worth Ave., Palm Beach, FL
33480 (561)655-3312

Maus and Hoffman
Independent
Bill and John Maus, Owners
312 Worth Ave., Palm Beach, FL
33480 (561)655-1141 or (800)585-5123
www.mausandhoffman.com
(see chapter 9)
Large, elegant store. Great merchandise mix between European
and updated traditional tastes.

Accessories Zimmerli undergar-
ments
Casual Wear Brioni, Hickey
Freeman, Liberty of London,
Maus and Hoffman
Dress Shirts Brioni, Maus and
Hoffman
Neckwear Brioni, Maus and
Hoffman, Leonard

Shoes Allen Edmonds, Maus and
Hoffman
Tailored Clothing Brioni, Hickey
Freeman, Oxxford, Maus and
Hoffman
Sales Semiannual

Mr. Sid's
Independent
Barry Segel, Vice President
331 Worth Ave., Palm Beach, FL
33480 (561)832-5885 www.mrsid.com
Attractive storefront. Mr. Segel
was very informative and gracious.
Great shopping destination.

Accessories Good selection of belts,
very nice formal wear section
Casual Wear Giorgio Armani,
Tommy Bahama, Luigi Borrelli,
Brioni, Polo Ralph Lauren, Gran
Sasso, Robert Talbott, Zanella,
Ermenegildo Zegna and Zegna
Soft
Dress Shirts Giorgio Armani, Luigi
Borrelli, Brioni, Ermenegildo
Zegna
Neckwear Altea, Brioni, Robert
Talbott, Ermenegildo Zegna
Shoes Salvatore Ferragamo, Bruno
Magli, Moreschi, Santoni, J.M.
Weston
Tailored Clothing Giorgio Armani,
Brioni, Canali, Corneliani, Hickey
Freeman, Polo Ralph Lauren,
Ermenegildo Zegna, Zegna Napoli
Couture, Zegna Soft
Sales Semiannual

Napoleon
Independent
244 Worth Ave., Palm Beach, FL
33480 (561)655-5252
www.napoleonfashions.com
Store filled with many unique and

vibrantly colored resort-wear items.

Accessories Distinctive, elegant formal wear items
Casual Wear Napoleon
Dress Shirts Napoleon (made by Luigi Borrelli and Stefano Ricci)
Neckwear Brioni, Leonard, Stefano Ricci
Tailored Clothing Brioni, Napoleon
Sales Semiannual

Neiman Marcus

151 Worth Ave., Palm Beach, FL 33480 (561)805-6150
www.neimanmarcus.com

Casual Wear Giorgio Armani, Brioni, Bobby Jones, Ermenegildo Zegna
Dress Shirts Giorgio Armani, Luigi Borrelli, Brioni, Ermenegildo Zegna
Neckwear Giorgio Armani, Brioni, Ralph Lauren Purple Label, Ermenegildo Zegna
Tailored Clothing Giorgio Armani, Brioni, Ermenegildo Zegna

Saks Fifth Avenue

172 Worth Ave., Palm Beach, FL 33480 (561)833-2551
www.saksfifthavenue.com

Casual Wear Giorgio Armani, Brioni, Ermenegildo Zegna
Dress Shirts Luigi Borrelli, Lorenzini, Ermenegildo Zegna
Neckwear Brioni, Ermenegildo Zegna
Tailored Clothing Giorgio Armani, Brioni, Ermenegildo Zegna

Santoni

245 Worth Ave., Palm Beach, FL 33480 (561)655-2338

Trillion

Independent
315 Worth Ave., Palm Beach, FL 33480 (561)832-3525
Impressive establishment. Outstanding, colorful selection of casual slacks and fine cashmere sweaters. Also an outlet store located behind the main store.

Casual Wear Trillion
Dress Shirts Sartoria Attolini, Fray
Neckwear Kiton, Trillion
Tailored Clothing Sartoria Attolini, Kiton

Valentino

204 Worth Ave., Palm Beach, FL 33480 (561)659-7533
www.valentio.it

PALM BEACH GARDENS MALL
Location and Stores:
3101 PGA Blvd. East, Palm Beach Gardens, FL 33410
www.thegardensmall.com

Davinci

Independent
(561)625-6795
Pleasant storefront with great atmosphere. Many unique and attractive self-labeled items in both casual and business wear. Sales staff was most helpful and professional.

Accessories Brioni, Redaelli, Marco Zalli
Casual Wear Bertone, Brioni, DaVinci, Jack Lipson
Dress Shirts Brioni, DaVinci
Neckwear Brioni, Stefano Ricci
Shoes Belvedere
Tailored Clothing Brioni, Redaelli, Marco Zalli

Sales Semiannual, January and July

Saks Fifth Avenue
(561)694-9009
www.saksfifthavenue.com

Casual Wear Giorgio Armani, Ermenegildo Zegna
Dress Shirts Giorgio Armani, Hugo Boss, Ermenegildo Zegna
Neckwear Giorgio Armani, Hugo Boss, Stefano Ricci, Ermenegildo Zegna
Tailored Clothing Giorgio Armani, Hugo Boss, Brioni, Hickey Freeman, Ermenegildo Zegna

SAWGRASS MILLS
Location and Stores:
12801 Sunrise Blvd., Sunrise, FL 33323 www.sawgrassmillsmall.com

Joseph Abboud
Outlet Store
(954)846-9874

Ike Behar
Outlet Store
(954)846-9369 www.ikebehar.com
Only Ike Behar outlet store; always some great buys to be found here!

Hugo Boss
Outlet Store
(954)835-9120 www.hugoboss.com

Brooks Brothers
Outlet Store
(954)845-0404
www.brooksbrothers.com

Kenneth Cole
Outlet Store

(954)845-9777
www.kennethcole.com

Cole Haan
Outlet Store
(954)835-0020 www.colehaan.com

Damiani
Outlet Store
(954)838-7774
Outlet for Kendall store. You'll find some great values here.

Casual Wear Damiani, Gran Sasso
Dress Shirts Damiani
Neckwear Gianfranco Ferré, Ermenegildo Zegna
Tailored Clothing Belvest, Corneliani, Ermenegildo Zegna

Johnston & Murphy
(954)845-9725
www.johnstonmurphy.com

Calvin Klein
(954)835-1343

Neiman Marcus Last Call
(954)846-9777
www.neimanmarcus.com
One of the largest and best selections in any Last Call I visited.

Casual Wear Jhane Barnes, Ermenegildo Zegna
Dress Shirts Ike Behar, Luigi Borrelli, Bergdorf Goodman, Ermenegildo Zegna
Neckwear Ike Behar, Ermenegildo Zegna
Tailored Clothing Giorgio Armani, Brioni, Hickey Freeman, Oxxford, Ermenegildo Zegna

Polo Jeans Company
(954)835-1412 www.polo.com

Saks Off Fifth
Outlet Store
(954)846-7746
www.saksfifthavenue.com
One of the larger selections of menswear in any Off Fifth I visited, particularly in tailored clothing.

Casual Wear Lorenzini, Robert Talbott, Ermenegildo Zegna
Dress Shirts Ermenegildo Zegna
Neckwear Giorgio Armani, Hugo Boss, Versace, Ermenegildo Zegna
Tailored Clothing Giorgio Armani, Corneliani, Vestimenta, Ermenegildo Zegna

Surrey's
Outlet Store
(954)846-8085
Surrey's Menswear of Florida's Outlet Store

Casual Wear Jhane Barnes, Hugo Boss, Canali, Versace
Dress Shirts Ermenegildo Zegna
Neckwear Altea, Canali, Pancaldi, Ermenegildo Zegna
Tailored Clothing Hugo Boss, Canali

Metro Area: Nashville

Levy's
Independent
David Levy, Owner
3900 Hillsboro Rd., Ste. 36, Nashville, TN 37215 (615)383-2800
Five-generation family business that has sold men's clothing since 1855. Excellent customer service—many of the salespeople have more than 25 years of retail experience. Ermenegildo Zegna store-in-store. Fine women's department as well.

Accessories Colonel Littleton gen-tleman's accessories, Bruno Magli leather outerwear
Casual Wear Bills Khakis, Canali, Gran Sasso, Bobby Jones, Lacoste, St. Croix, Ermenegildo Zegna
Dress Shirts Brioni, Canali, Gitman Bros., Robert Talbott, Ermenegildo Zegna
Neckwear Brioni, Canali, Salvatore Ferragamo, Robert Talbott, Ermenegildo Zegna
Shoes Allen Edmonds, Lorenzo Banfi, Cole Haan, Peter Huber, Salvatore Ferragamo, Gucci, Mephisto, Prada, Terra Plana
Tailored Clothing Armani Collezioni, Ballin, Berle, Canali, Hickey Freeman, Jack Victor, Zanella, Ermenegildo Zegna
Sales Semiannual

J. Michaels Clothiers
Independent
Mike Mahaffey, Owner/Tom Repass, Owner/Jim Brandon, Owner
2525 West End Ave., Nashville, TN 37203 (615)321-0686
Primarily a custom clothier. However, there are also many interesting, high-quality items available ready-to-wear. Mr. Mahaffey was extremely congenial in showing me his establishment.

Accessories Good selection of bow ties and cuff links
Casual Wear Luciano Barbera, Barbour cashmere, Bills Khakis, Barry Bricken, Forté Cashmere, MacCluer, Normandy & Moore, Jeff Rose, John Smedley, Robert Talbott, Tricots St. Raphael, Victorinox
Dress Shirts Barba, Luigi Borrelli, Thomas Mason (M2M), Royal Label (M2M), Robert Talbott

Neckwear Robert Talbott, Venanzi
Shoes Alden, Allen Edmonds, Paraboot
Tailored Clothing Aquascutum,
Luciano Barbera, Barry Bricken,
Burberry, Nick Hilton (also M2M),
Incotex, J. Michaels (Loro Piana), NH
1888, Oxxford (also M2M), Polo
Ralph Lauren Ralph Lauren (also
M2M), Southwick (also M2M), Tallia

The Oxford Shop
Independent
J. Eric Viars and David Garris,
Proprietors
4001 Hillsboro Rd., Nashville, TN
37215 (615)383-4442
An updated traditional store with
many great items to choose from.
Mr. Viars and Mr. Garris are a
pleasure to shop with.

Accessories Great selection of bow
ties, interesting collection of striped
braces, cuff links
Casual Wear Scott Barber, Ike
Behar, Bills Khakis, Barry Bricken,
Henry Cotton's, Madeline Finn,
Gitman Bros., Oxford Shop, Jeff
Rose, Robert Talbott, Tricots
St. Raphael
Dress Shirts Ike Behar, Gitman
Bros., Venanzi
Neckwear Breuer, Robert Talbott
Shoes Alden, Cole Haan, H.S. Trask
Tailored Clothing Burberry,
Samuelsohn, Southwick

Metro Area: New York City

**CLINTON CROSSING
PREMIUM OUTLETS**
Location and Stores:
20-A Killingworth Turnpike, Clinton,
CT 06413
www.premiumoutlets.com

Barney's New York
Outlet Store
(860)664-0006 www.barneys.com

Casual Wear Hugo Boss,
Hickey Freeman
Neckwear Brioni
Tailored Clothing Hugo Boss,
Hickey Freeman

Brooks Brothers
Outlet Store
(860)664-0470
www.brooksbrothers.com

Kenneth Cole
Outlet Store
(860)669-3780
www.kennethcole.com

Donna Karan
Outlet Store
(860)669-3530
www.donnakaran.com

Calvin Klein
Outlet Store
(860)664-0500

Malo
Outlet Store
(860)664-8000
Only other outlet store for this
brand of luxurious cashmere is
in Woodbury Common, Central
Valley, NY. Big discounts on distinctive, first-quality items.

Polo Ralph Lauren Factory Store
Outlet Store
(860)664-0050 www.polo.com

Polo Jeans Company
Outlet Store
(860)669-2839 www.polo.com

Saks Off Fifth

Outlet Store
(860)669-8248
www.saksfifthavenue.com

Dress Shirts Ermenegildo Zegna
Neckwear Versace, Ermenegildo
Zegna
Tailored Clothing Joseph
Abboud, Giorgio Armani, Hugo
Boss, Hickey Freeman,
Ermenegildo Zegna

Versace

Outlet Store
Ronnie Taylor, Store Manager
(860)664-3667 www.versace.com
Great selection of Couture jeans.

Fairfield Clothiers

Independent
Naresh Mansukhani, Style
Consultant
1551 Post Rd., Fairfield, CT 06430
(203)255-8889
www.suityourself.com
(see chapter 9)
A truly delightful destination store.
Mr. Mansukhani is cheerful and
knowledgeable. I received perhaps
the best customer service at
Fairfield Clothiers during all of my
travels researching this book. Mr.
Mansukhani even pressed my shirt
and suit coat while giving me additional pointers on dressing. In
addition to an outstanding collection of designers in custom, ready-
to-wear, and made-to-measure,
this establishment has a great website set up for e-commerce. I highly recommend this store.

Accessories Alden Belts, Duchamp
cuff links, and most of the other
accessories are made exclusively for
Fairfield Clothier's under their
own label
Casual Wear Dalmine Uomo,
Nick Hilton, Tallia Uomo and pri-
vate label
Dress Shirts Eugenio B, Marol,
C. DeFranceschi, Gitman Bros.,
Kenneth Gordon, Ferrell Reed,
and private label
Shoes Alden of USA, Cheaney of
UK, Magnanni of Spain, Mezlan
of Spain
Tailored Clothing Belvest,
d'Avenza, Hilton, Tallia Uomo,
Oliver, Jack Victor, Coppley.
Custom Tailoring Fairfield
Clothiers is well known for their
expertise in making custom clothes
for men and women

Richards of Greenwich

Independent
Jack, Bill, Bob, Todd, Scott, Russ,
Linda, and Andrew Mitchell,
Proprietors
350 Greenwich Ave., Greenwich, CT
06830 (203)622-0551
Impressive winding staircase is
center of visual presentation of this
first-rate establishment. Women's
section is upstairs, menswear
downstairs. Named one of best
men's stores in U.S. by *Robb*
Report. Ermenegildo Zegna,
Giorgio Armani, and Hermès
store-in-stores.

Accessories Crookhorn belts, David
Yurman jewelry, Rainforest outer-
wear
Casual Wear Joseph Abboud,
Giorgio Armani, Avon Celli,
Tommy Bahama, Ted Baker, Scott
Barber, Luciano Barbera, Hugo
Boss, Canali, Henry Cotton's,
Brunello Cuccinelli, Hickey

Freeman, Bobby Jones, Loro
Piana, Marzotto Lab, Nat Nast,
Polo Ralph Lauren, Ralph Lauren
Purple Label, Richards, Jeff Rose,
John Varvatos, Zanella,
Ermenegildo Zegna, Zegna Sport
(separate boutique across the street)
Dress Shirts Joseph Abboud,
Giorgio Armani, Ike Behar, Luigi
Borrelli, Hugo Boss, Canali,
Hermès, Hickey Freeman, Robert
Talbott, Ermenegildo Zegna
Neckwear Joseph Abboud, Giorgio
Armani, Canali, Salvatore
Ferragamo, Hermès, Hickey
Freeman, Vineyard Vines, Robert
Talbott, Ermenegildo Zegna
Shoes Cole Haan, Salvatore
Ferragamo, Gravati, Edward
Green, To Boot New York, Tod's,
Donald J. Pliner
Tailored Clothing Giorgio Armani,
Baldessarini, Ballin, Brioni, Canali,
Hickey Freeman, Kiton, Polo
Ralph Lauren, Jack Victor,
Zanella, Ermenegildo Zegna

Family Britches
Independent
*Rick Buggee and Barry Mishkin,
Owners/Mark Gust, Manager*
39 Elm St., New Canaan, CT 06840
(203)966-0518
www.familybritches.com
(see chapter 9)
Outstanding store with many
unique items I didn't see anywhere
else. Mr. Gust was one of the most
gracious and knowledgeable hosts
I met in my travels.

Accessories Good selection of
Corneliani formal wear; large,
interesting collection of leather
outerwear

Casual Wear Tommy Bahama,
Burberry, Gran Sasso, Hickey
Freeman, Polo Ralph Lauren
Robert Talbott, Zanella,
Ermenegildo Zegna
Dress Shirts Hickey Freeman,
Robert Talbott (also M2M),
Ermenegildo Zegna
Neckwear Robert Talbott,
Vineyard Vines, Ermenegildo
Zegna
Shoes Allen Edmonds, Cole Haan
Tailored Clothing Corneliani (also
M2M), Hickey Freeman (also
M2M), Oxxford (M2M), Trussini,
Zanella (trousers), Ermenegildo
Zegna (also M2M)
Sales Semiannual

STAMFORD TOWN CENTER
Location and Stores:
100 Greyrock Place, Stamford, CT 06901
www.shopstamfordtowncenter.com

Brooks Brothers
(203)359-2300
www.brooksbrothers.com

Coach
(203)965-0666 www.coach.com

Johnston & Murphy
(203)964-1331
www.johnstonmurphy.com

Saks Fifth Avenue
(203)323-3100
www.saksfifthavenue.com

Casual Wear Joseph Abboud,
Henry Cotton's, Zanella, Zegna
Sport
Dress Shirts Giorgio Armani,
Hugo Boss, Hickey Freeman
Neckwear Salvatore Ferragamo,

Ermenegildo Zegna
Tailored Clothing Joseph
Abboud, Hugo Boss, Burberry

Victorinox
(203)325-1965
www.victorinoxstores.com

Mitchells of Westport
Independent
Jack, Bill, Bob, Todd, Scott, Russ,
Linda, and Andrew Mitchell,
Proprietors
670 Post Road East, Westport, CT
06880 (203)227-5165
First-rate establishment in process
of remodeling during summer
2003. Excellent merchandise and
customer service.

Accessories Crookhorn belts; David
Yurman jewelry; Rainforest outer-
wear
Casual Wear Joseph Abboud,
Giorgio Armani, Avon Celli,
Tommy Bahama, Ted Baker, Scott
Barber, Luciano Barbera, Hugo
Boss, Canali, Henry Cotton's,
Bruno Cuccinelli, Hickey
Freeman, Bobby Jones, Loro
Piana, Marzotto Lab, Nat Nast,
Polo Ralph Lauren, Ralph Lauren
Purple Label, Richards, Jeff Rose,
John Varvatos, Zanella,
Ermenegildo Zegna, Zegna Sport
Dress Shirts Joseph Abboud,
Giorgio Armani, Ike Behar, Luigi
Borrelli, Hugo Boss, Canali,
Hermès, Hickey Freeman, Robert
Talbott, Ermenegildo Zegna
Neckwear Joseph Abboud, Giorgio
Armani, Canali, Salvatore
Ferragamo, Hermès, Hickey
Freeman, Vineyard Vines, Robert
Talbott, Ermenegildo Zegna
Shoes Salvatore Ferragamo, Gravati,

Edward Green, Cole Haan, To
Boot New York, Tod's, Donald J.
Pliner
Tailored Clothing Giorgio Armani,
Baldessarini, Ballin, Brioni, Canali,
Hickey Freeman, Kiton, Polo
Ralph Lauren, Jack Victor,
Zanella, Ermenegildo Zegna

JERSEY GARDENS OUTLET MALL
Location and Stores:
651 Kapkowsi Rd., Elizabeth, NJ
07201 www.jerseygardens.com

Jhane Barnes Xtras
Outlet Store
(908)436-9090
www.jhanebarnes.com

Brooks Brothers
Outlet Store
(908)355-2845
www.brooksbrothers.com

Loutie's
Outlet Store
(908)355-8323
Some real values on tailored
clothing the day I visited.

Casual Wear Hugo Boss, Pal
Zileri
Dress Shirts Pal Zileri
Tailored Clothing Hugo Boss,
Pal Zileri

Bruno Magli
Outlet Store
(908)355-9389
www.brunomagli.com
Only Bruno Magli outlet store
in America.

Neiman Marcus Last Call
Outlet Store
(908)994-1911

www.neimanmarcus.com
No tailored clothing inventory
at this location.

Casual Wear Ralph Lauren
Purple Label, Ermenegildo
Zegna
Dress Shirts Ike Behar

Saks Off Fifth Outlet Store
Outlet Store
(908)353-7257

Dress Shirts Ike Behar
Tailored Clothing Giorgio
Armani, Jhane Barnes, Hugo
Boss, Hickey Freeman

Vero Uomo
Independent
*Mario Roselli, Owner/Sally Rezai
and Nabila Bouzar, Sales*
26 E. Palisade Ave., Englewood, NJ
07631 (201)894-1424
One of the few quality stand-alone
specialty stores in northern New
Jersey. Pleasant shopping ambience
and helpful, courteous sales staff.

Accessories Good selection of
Crookhorn belts and braces
Casual Wear Tommy Bahama,
Brioni, Brunello Cuccinelli, Pal
Zileri
Dress Shirts Eugenio B (also M2M)
Neckwear Brioni, Vero Uomo, Pal
Zileri, Zilli
Tailored Clothing Belvest, Brioni,
Pal Zileri (including Sartoriale line)
Sales Semiannual

RIVERSIDE SQUARE
Location and Stores:
One Riverside Square, Hackensack,
NJ 07601 www.shopriverside.com

Coach
(201)487-1772 www.coach.com

Johnston & Murphy
(201)489-0260
www.johnstonmurphy.com

Onore
Independent
(201)343-0110
Beautiful store with marble
columns in the doorway,
baroque print carpeting, and
ornate fixtures. Carries unusual
and distinctive clothing lines.

Casual Wear Raffi
Dress Shirts Fabio Inghirami,
Onore
Neckwear Italo Ferretti, Stefano
Ricci
Shoes Bruno Magli
Tailored Clothing Fabio
Inghirami, Nervesa, Tombolini,
Arnold Zimberg
Sales Semiannual

Papillon
Independent
*Harun Rashidzada, Public
Relations*
(201)489-2122
First-class retail emporium filled
with unique, quality items you
won't find anywhere else.
Customer service is prompt and
helpful.

Accessories Avon Celli, Canali,
Gallotti, Herno, Mabrum, and
Torras leather outerwear
Casual Wear Avon Celli, Brioni,
Canali, Dalmine, Andrea Fezzi,
Verri, Zanella
Dress Shirts Luigi Borrelli,
Canali, Fray, Stefano Ricci
Neckwear Villa Bolgheri, Brioni,
Canali, Tino Cosma, Hubert,
Italo Ferretti, Stefano Ricci, Zilli

Tailored Clothing Canali, d'Avenza, Ravazzolo (also M2M), Trussini, Verri, Zanella
Sales Semiannual

Saks Fifth Avenue
(201)646-1800
www.saksfifthavenue.com

Casual Wear Joseph Abboud, Giorgio Armani, Jhane Barnes, Hugo Boss, Ermenegildo Zegna
Dress Shirts Giorgio Armani, Hugo Boss, Ermenegildo Zegna
Neckwear Joseph Abboud, Giorgio Armani, Hugo Boss, Hickey Freeman, Ermenegildo Zegna

Louis Vuitton
(201)489-4409
www.louisvuitton.com

GARDEN STATE PLAZA
Location and Stores:
One Garden State Plaza, Paramus, NJ 07652 www.westfield.com

A/X Armani Exchange
(201)712-0136
www.giorgioarmani.com

Bernini
(201)587-0022 www.bernini.com

Casual Wear Versace, Ermenegildo Zegna
Neckwear Versace, Ermenegildo Zegna
Tailored Clothing Canali, Hugo Boss, Versace

BOSS Hugo Boss
(201)587-1733 www.hugoboss.com

Brooks Brothers
(201)845-6700
www.brooksbrothers.com

Coach
(201)587-1442 www.coach.com

Kenneth Cole
(201)587-0089
www.kennethcole.com

Johnston & Murphy
(201)843-5365
www.johnstonmurphy.com

Loutie
Independent
(201)291-7866
Pleasant store with some unusual inventory items, particularly by Pal Zileri.

Casual Wear Equilibrio, Versace, Pal Zileri
Dress Shirts Versace, Pal Zileri
Neckwear Loutie, Versace Pal Zileri
Shoes Mezlan
Tailored Clothing Giorgio Armani, Hugo Boss, Pal Zileri

Mephisto
(201)291-0761 www.mephisto.com

Neiman Marcus
(201)291-1920
www.neimanmarcus.com

Casual Wear Giorgio Armani, Hugo Boss, Loro Piana, Polo Ralph Lauren, Ralph Lauren Purple Label, Ermenegildo Zegna
Dress Shirts Giorgio Armani, Luigi Borrelli, Fray, Gucci, Kiton, Lorenzini, Turnbull & Asser Ermenegildo Zegna
Neckwear Giorgio Armani, Hugo Boss, Brioni, Fabergé, Ermenegildo Zegna

Tailored Clothing Giorgio
Armani, Hugo Boss, Brioni,
Burberry, Dolce & Gabbana,
Ermenegildo Zegna, Zegna Soft

Nordstrom
Louis Hios, Men's Clothing
(201)843-1122 www.nordstrom.com
Great tailored clothing selection.
Mr. Hios was a pleasure to shop
with.

Casual Wear Robert Talbott,
Ermenegildo Zegna
Dress Shirts Ike Behar, Robert
Talbott, Zanella
Neckwear Robert Talbott, XMI
Platinum, Ermenegildo Zegna
Tailored Clothing Giorgio
Armani, Hickey Freeman,
Vestimenta, Ermenegildo Zegna

Pelle Line Shoes
Independent
(201)845-3040 www.pelleline.com

Shoes Joseph Abboud, Alden,
Allen Edmonds, Bacco Bucci,
Mezlan, Moreschi, Pelle Line

Saks Off Fifth
Outlet Store
Bergen Mall, 221 South Mall, Ste.
536, Paramus, NJ 07652 (201)291-1949
www.saksfifthavenue.com
One of the larger and better Off
Fifths I visited. Men's department
occupies an entire floor.

Casual Wear Giorgio Armani,
Hugo Boss, Salvatore Ferragamo,
Ermenegildo Zegna
Dress Shirts Ike Behar, Hugo Boss,
Lorenzini, Vestimenta,
Ermenegildo Zegna
Neckwear Versace, Ermenegildo
Zegna

Tailored Clothing Joseph Abboud,
Giorgio Armani, Hugo Boss,
Canali, Ermenegildo Zegna

Garmany
Independent
105 Broad St., Red Bank, NJ 07701
(732)576-8500
www.garmany.com
Excellent store with top-notch,
knowledgeable salespeople. In-
store boutiques by Giorgio
Armani, Hugo Boss, Brioni,
Canali, Dolce & Gabbana, Prada,
Ermenegildo Zegna.

Accessories Ermenegildo Zegna
braces; nice formal wear section;
Bruno Magli leather outerwear
Casual Wear Giorgio Armani,
Tommy Bahama, Hugo Boss,
Brioni, Canali, Dolce & Gabbana,
Salvatore Ferragamo, Garmany,
Prada, Ermenegildo Zegna
Dress Shirts Giorgio Armani, Hugo
Boss, Brioni, Canali, Ermenegildo
Zegna
Neckwear Giorgio Armani, Hugo
Boss, Brioni, Canali, Ermenegildo
Zegna
Shoes Cole Haan, Dolce &
Gabbana, Salvatore Ferragamo,
Prada, a. testoni
Tailored Clothing Giorgio Armani,
Hugo Boss, Brioni, Dolce &
Gabbana, Prada, Ermenegildo
Zegna

THE MALL AT SHORT HILLS
Location and Stores:
1200 Morris Turnpike, Short Hills, NJ
07078 www.shopshorthills.com

A/X Armani Exchange
Marsha Amchir, Manager
(973)467-1318
www.giorgioarmani.com

Armani Collezioni
Kim Weiss, Manager
(973)376-7800
www.giorgioarmani.com

Bally
(973)379-4770 www.bally.com

Bernini
Tony Gancitano, Manager
(973)258-1786 www.bernini.com

Casual Wear Hugo Boss,
Versace, Ermenegildo Zegna
Neckwear Canali, Versace,
Ermenegildo Zegna
Tailored Clothing Canali, Zegna
Soft

**Brick Church Gentlemen's
Collection**
Independent
Brenden Lam
(973)379-6920

Accessories Cartier accessories;
Trafalgar braces (including
Limited Edition); huge cum-
merbund selection; Golden Bear
leather outerwear
Casual Wear Scott Barber,
Pringle, Viyella
Dress Shirts Kenneth Gordon,
MacCluer

BOSS Hugo Boss
Sherif Emera, Manager
(973)379-7779 www.hugoboss.com

Brooks Brothers
Amy Bertsch, Manager
(973)467-5400
www.brooksbrothers.com

Burberry
Brenda Bomysoad, Manager
(973)379-7100 www.burberry.com

Coach
Sue Dales, Manager
(973)376-2747 www.coach.com

Kenneth Cole
Jim Weth, Manager
(973)258-1601
www.kennethcole.com

Cole Haan
Rachael Benton, Manager
(973)218-1133 www.colehaan.com

DKNY
Patrick Perez, Manager
(973)921-1909 www.dkny.com

Gucci
Colleen Cusick, Manager
(973)564-7600 www.gucci.com

Johnston & Murphy
Marty Florez, Manager
(973)379-9055
www.johnstonmurphy.com

Ralph Lauren
Winston Miller, Manager
(973)467-4680 www.polo.com

Lucky Brand Dungarees
Shaifa Akhtar, Manager
(973)218-9013
www.luckyjeans.com

Bruno Magli
Janet Maisano, Manager
(973)564-9100
www.brunomagli.com

Neiman Marcus
Nancy Taylor, Manager
(973)912-0080
www.neimanmarcus.com

Casual Wear Giorgio Armani,

Tommy Bahama, Cifonelli, Loro Piana, Polo Ralph Lauren, Ermenegildo Zegna
Dress Shirts Giorgio Armani, Ike Behar, Luigi Borrelli, Brioni, Turnbull & Asser, Ermenegildo Zegna
Neckwear Giorgio Armani, Luigi Borrelli, Hugo Boss, Brioni, Burberry, Salvatore Ferragamo, Turnbull & Asser, Ermenegildo Zegna
Tailored Clothing Giorgio Armani, Hugo Boss, Brioni, Hickey Freeman, Ermenegildo Zegna

Nordstrom
Glenn Bellman, Store Manager
(973)467-1500 www.nordstrom.com

Casual Wear Corneliani, John Smedley, Ermenegildo Zegna
Dress Shirts Robert Talbott, Zanella
Neckwear Robert Talbott, XMI Platinum, Ermenegildo Zegna
Tailored Clothing Corneliani, Hickey Freeman, Zanella, Ermenegildo Zegna, Zegna Soft

Papillon
Independent
Harun Rashidzada, Public Relations
(973)467-4757
First-class retail emporium filled with unique, quality items you won't find anywhere else. Customer service is prompt and helpful.

Accessories Avon Celli, Canali, Gallotti, Herno, Mabrum, and Torras leather outerwear
Casual Wear Avon Celli, Brioni,

Canali, Dalmine, Andrea Fezzi, Verri, Zanella
Dress Shirts Luigi Borrelli, Canali, Fray, Stefano Ricci
Neckwear Villa Bolgheri, Brioni, Canali, Tino Cosma, Hubert, Italo Ferretti, Stefano Ricci, Zilli
Tailored Clothing Canali, d'Avenza, Ravazzolo (also M2M), Trussini, Verri, Zanella
Sales Semiannual

Pelle Line Shoes
Independent
Carlos Izqierdo, Manager
(973)564-8777 www.pelleline.com

Saks Fifth Avenue
Gary Blender, Manager
(973)376-7000
www.saksfifthavenue.com
Casual Wear Giorgio Armani, Hugo Boss, Hickey Freeman, Ermenegildo Zegna
Dress Shirts Giorgio Armani, Ike Behar, Hugo Boss, Hickey Freeman, Ermenegildo Zegna
Neckwear Giorgio Armani, Hugo Boss, Ermenegildo Zegna
Tailored Clothing Joseph Abboud, Giorgio Armani, Hugo Boss, Hickey Freeman, Vestimenta, Ermenegildo Zegna

Gianni Versace
Kim Klein, Store Manager
(973)379-9871 www.versace.com

Louis Vuitton
Jennifer Garippa, Manager
(973)564-9788
www.louisvuitton.com

Garmany
Independent
356 Springfield Ave., Summit, NJ

07901 (908)277-9600
www.garmany.com
Excellent store with top-notch, knowledgeable salespeople. Slightly smaller than Red Bank location.

Accessories Ermenegildo Zegna braces; nice formal wear section; Bruno Magli leather outerwear
Casual Wear Giorgio Armani, Tommy Bahama, Hugo Boss, Brioni, Canali, Dolce & Gabbana, Salvatore Ferragamo, Garmany, Prada, Ermenegildo Zegna
Dress Shirts Giorgio Armani, Hugo Boss, Brioni, Canali, Ermenegildo Zegna
Neckwear Giorgio Armani, Hugo Boss, Brioni, Canali, Ermenegildo Zegna
Shoes Cole Haan, Dolce & Gabbana, Salvatore Ferragamo, Prada, a. testoni
Tailored Clothing Giorgio Armani, Hugo Boss, Brioni, Dolce & Gabbana, Prada, Ermenegildo Zegna

Hollywood Collection
Independent
Tony Kaid, Owner
117 E. Fordham Rd., Bronx, NY 10468 (718)563-4317
Great selections of Zanetti, Mauri, and Mezlan.

Casual Wear Zanetti
Dress Shirts Zanetti
Neckwear Zanetti
Shoes Mauri, Mezlan
Tailored Clothing Zanetti, including Extrema line

Terlin's
Independent
Tony Kaid, Owner
116 E. Fordham Rd., Bronx, NY 10468 (718)295-0527

Great selections of Zanetti, Mauri, and Mezlan.

Casual Wear Zanetti
Dress Shirts Zanetti
Neckwear Zanetti
Shoes Mauri, Mezlan
Tailored Clothing Zanetti, including Extrema line

Garage Clothing
Outlet Store
1909 Stilwell Ave., Brooklyn, NY 11223 (718)996-2342
Large, garagelike atmosphere, hence the name. Great price and nice assortment of solid-color Brioni dress shirts, GREAT prices on sport coats the day I stopped by. Some terrific buys on high-quality pieces if you're willing to hunt for your bargains!

Casual Wear Raffi, Tulliano
Dress Shirts Brioni
Neckwear Giorgio Armani, Gucci, Ermenegildo Zegna
Shoes Mezlan (great selection)
Tailored Clothing Corneliani, DKNY, Ralph Lauren

Jimmy's
Independent
1226 Kings Highway, Brooklyn, NY 11229 (718)645-9685
Interesting destination with select inventory items you won't find elsewhere.

Casual Wear Agnona, Luciano Barbera, John Varvatos
Dress Shirts Luciano Barbera, Brioni, Lorenzini
Shoes Gucci
Tailored Clothing Agnona, John Varvatos

Jonathan, Ltd.
Independent
Jonathan Serafin, Proprietor
456 Central Ave., Cedarhurst, NY
11516 (516)569-2626
Family business with many distinctive clothing selections. Mr. Serafin was very gracious showing me around the store. Major brands carried include Giorgio Armani, Hugo Boss, Coppley, and Ermenegildo Zegna.

Accessories Some interesting selections in cuff links and formal wear; Gimo's leather outerwear
Sales Some merchandise usually offered at value pricing

WOODBURY COMMON PREMIUM OUTLETS
Location and Stores:
498 Red Apple Ct., Central Valley, NY
10917 www.premiumoutlets.com

Joseph Abboud
Outlet Store
(845)928-4682

A/X Armani Exchange
Outlet Store
(845)928-4547
www.giorgioarmani.com

Armani General Store
Outlet Store
(845)928-4000
www.giorgioarmani.com
Spacious store, interesting selections from both Collezioni and Black Label lines.

Bally
Outlet Store
(845)928-4522 www.bally.com

Barney's New York
Outlet Store
(845)928-4455 www.barneys.com

Hugo Boss
Outlet Store
(845)928-4333 www.hugoboss.com

Brooks Brothers
Outlet Store
(845)928-2664
www.brooksbrothers.com
One of largest Brooks Brothers outlets I've seen, with excellent selection.

Burberry
Outlet Store
(845)928-4500 www.burberry.com

Coach
Outlet Store
(845)928-4465 www.coach.com
Largest Coach discount outlet with best selection I saw.

Kenneth Cole
Outlet Store
(845)928-4434
www.kennethcole.com

Cole Haan
Outlet Store
(845)928-9425 www.colehaan.com

Dolce & Gabbana
Outlet Store
(845)928-5221
www.dolcegabbana.com
Interesting and unusual pieces at great discounts.

Alfred Dunhill
Outlet Store
Peter Katz, Manager

(845)928-7223 www.dunhill.com
Only Dunhill outlet store in U.S.

ETRO
Outlet Store
(845)928-9256 www.etro.it
Only ETRO outlet store in U.S.

Salvatore Ferragamo
Outlet Store
(845)928-7116
www.salvatoreferragamo.it
Some great buys on shoes and
ties. No dress shirts, sportswear,
or tailored clothing.

Ghurka
Outlet Store
(845)928-4943
www.ghurka.com
Only Ghurka outlet store in U.S.

Gucci
Outlet Store
(845)928-8034 www.gucci.com

Johnston & Murphy
Outlet Store
(845)928-4911
www.johnstonmurphy.com

Calvin Klein
Outlet Store
(845)928-4979

Malo
Outlet Store
(845)928-4324
Great prices on original, unusual
pieces of high-quality cashmere.

Andrew Marc
Outlet Store
(845)928-5108
www.andrewmarc.com

Neiman Marcus Last Call
Outlet Store
(845)928-4993
www.neimanmarcus.com

Tailored Clothing Brioni,
Corneliani, Zanella,
Ermenegildo Zegna

Donald J. Pliner
Outlet Store
(845)928-5187
www.donaldjpliner.com

Polo Ralph Lauren Factory Store
Outlet Store
(845)928-4637 www.polo.com

Saks Off Fifth
Outlet Store
(845)928-4351
www.saksfifthavenue.com
Excellent tailored clothing
inventory, with great discounts.

Casual Wear Ermenegildo
Zegna
Dress Shirts Ermenegildo Zegna
Neckwear Versace, Ermenegildo
Zegna
Tailored Clothing Joseph
Abboud, Giorgio Armani, Hugo
Boss, Canali, Corneliani,
Salvatore Ferragamo,
Ermenegildo Zegna

Tod's
Outlet Store
(845)928-3636 www.tods.com

Versace
Outlet Store
(845)928-3774 www.versace.com

Ermenegildo Zegna
Outlet Store
(845)928-2424 www.zegna.com
Huge inventory, great pricing.

Family Britches
Independent
Rick Buggee and Barry Mishkin,
Owners
70 King St., Chappaqua, NY 10514
(914)238-8017
www.familybritches.com
(see chapter 9)
Truly outstanding store with many
unique items I didn't see anywhere
else. Mr. Mishkin was a pleasure to
shop with.

Accessories Good selection of
Corneliani formal wear; large,
interesting collection of leather
outerwear
Casual Wear Tommy Bahama,
Burberry, Gran Sasso, Hickey
Freeman, Polo Ralph Lauren
Robert Talbott, Zanella,
Ermenegildo Zegna
Dress Shirts Hickey Freeman,
Robert Talbott (also M2M),
Ermenegildo Zegna
Neckwear Robert Talbott,
Vineyard Vines, Ermenegildo
Zegna
Shoes Allen Edmonds, Cole Haan
Tailored Clothing Corneliani (also
M2M), Hickey Freeman (also
M2M), Oxxford (M2M), Trussini,
Zanella (trousers), Ermenegildo
Zegna (also M2M)
Sales Semiannual

ROOSEVELT FIELD
Location and Stores:
630 Old Country Rd., Garden City, NY
11530 www.shopsimon.com

A/X Armani Exchange
(516)877-9026
www.giorgioarmani.com

Bernini
(516)739-0923 www.bernini.com

Casual Wear Versace,
Ermenegildo Zegna
Neckwear Giorgio Armani,
Canali, Versace, Ermenegildo
Zegna
Tailored Clothing Canali,
Versace

Brooks Brothers
(516)746-0212
www.brooksbrothers.com

Coach
(516)877-1772 www.coach.com

Kenneth Cole
(516)877-0197
www.kennethcole.com

Johnston & Murphy
(516)742-0802
www.johnstonmurphy.com

Nordstrom
(516)746-0011 www.nordstrom.com

Dress Shirts Ike Behar
Neckwear Ermenegildo Zegna
Tailored Clothing Ermenegildo
Zegna, Pal Zileri

Saks Fifth Avenue
1300 Franklin Ave., Garden City, NY
11530 (516)248-9000
www.saksfifthavenue.com
Casual wear only at this location.

Casual Wear Giorgio Armani
Jhane Barnes, Hugo Boss

Victor Talbot
Independent
Victor T. Scognamiglio, President
47 Glen Cove Rd., Greenvale, NY
11548 (516)625-1787
www.victortalbots.com
(see chapter 9)

Excellent formal wear department, largest and most varied selection I've seen. Comfortable, clubby shopping atmosphere. Mr. Scognamiglio was generous in sharing his time and knowledge. Forty minutes from Manhattan and New York City.

Accessories Hugo Boss, Brioni, Kiton, Oxxford, Polo Ralph Lauren, and Ralph Lauren Purple Label formal wear, also great selection of formal vests and unusual ties to pair with evening wear
Dress Shirts Victor Talbot M2M, Robert Talbot M2M, Luigi Borrelli M2M
Neckwear Victor Talbot seven-fold and five-fold ties and Robert Talbot seven-fold ties
Shoes Cole Haan, Bruno Magli, Moreschi, J.M. Weston
Tailored Clothing Victor Talbot (also M2M), d'Avenza (also M2M), Brioni (also M2M), Kiton (also M2M), Ralph Lauren Purple Label, H. Freeman, Corneliani

Marsh's
Independent
270 Main St., Huntington, NY 11743
(631)423-1660
Good-looking, spacious store with lots of dark rich wood. Helpful and informative customer service.

Accessories Trafalgar braces (including Limited Edition); some formal wear; Guy Laroche leather outerwear
Casual Wear Jhane Barnes, Riscatto Portofino, Tundra
Dress Shirts Canali, Eton, Robert

Talbott
Neckwear Giorgio Armani, Hugo Boss, Pancaldi, Robert Talbott
Shoes Allen Edmonds, Bally, Cole Haan, Salvatore Ferragamo, Bruno Magli
Tailored Clothing Giorgio Armani, Hugo Boss, Arnold Brant, Canali, Tallia, Pal Zileri
Sales Semiannual

WALT WHITMAN MALL
Location and Stores:
160 Walt Whitman Rd., Huntington Station, NY 11746
www.shopsimon.com

Brooks Brothers
(631)549-7089
www.brooksbrothers.com

DKNY
(631)385-7292 www.dkny.com

Johnston & Murphy
(631)427-0861
www.johnstonmurphy.com

Saks Fifth Avenue
(631)350-1100
www.saksfifthavenue.com

Casual Wear Joseph Abboud, Giorgio Armani, Jhane Barnes, Hugo Boss, Polo Ralph Lauren, Ermenegildo Zegna
Dress Shirts Joseph Abboud, Giorgio Armani, Hugo Boss, Ermenegildo Zegna
Neckwear Joseph Abboud, Giorgio Armani, Hugo Boss, Brioni, Ermenegildo Zegna
Tailored Clothing Joseph Abboud, Giorgio Armani, Hugo Boss, Ermenegildo Zegna

AMERICANA AT MANHASSET
Location and Stores:
2110 Northern Blvd., Manhasset, NY
11030 www.americanamanhasset.com

Giorgio Armani
(516)627-6001
www.giorgioarmani.com

Barney's New York
(516)627-5200 www.barneys.com
Casual Wear Giorgio Armani,
Barney's, Ermenegildo Zegna
Dress Shirts Giorgio Armani,
Barney's, Ermenegildo Zegna
Neckwear Giorgio Armani,
Barney's, ETRO, Ermenegildo
Zegna
Tailored Clothing Giorgio
Armani, John Varvatos,
Ermenegildo Zegna, Zegna Soft

Brooks Brothers
(516)365-3502
www.brooksbrothers.com

Burberry
(516)365-7900
www.burberry.com

Coach
(516)365-2777
www.coach.com

Hermès
(516)869-6660
www.hermes.com

Hirshleifer's
Independent
(516)627-3566
www.hirshleifers.com
Great-looking store with first-
rate customer service. Distinctive

selections for the more modern
dresser. Large women's section
as well.
Casual Wear Dolce & Gabbana,
Malo
Dress Shirts Sartoria Attolini,
Dolce & Gabbana, Helmut
Lang
Neckwear Dior, Dolce &
Gabbana
Shoes Gucci
Tailored Clothing Sartoria
Attolini, Dolce & Gabbana,
Helmut Lang, Yohji Yamamoto

Donna Karan
(516)869-0500
www.donnakaran.com

Ralph Lauren
(516)365-9595 www.polo.com
Huge, magnificent store.
Includes women's, home, and
children's section as well. Great
inventory of Purple Label items.
Visiting the Americana mall is
worthwhile for this store alone.

Loro Piana
(516)869-9469

Thomas Pink
(516)869-1540
www.thomaspink.com

Prada
(516)365-9700 www.prada.com

APC
131 Mercer St., New York, NY 10012
(212)966-9685
Attractive boutique for this excit-
ing new label. Watch your step
with the uneven, unfinished floor

planks! High-quality, reasonably priced French clothing line.

Addison on Madison

Independent

698 Madison Ave., New York, NY 10021 (212)308-2660

Self-labeled shirts and ties, both made in America. These items are of good quality; prices are very reasonable, and store inventories some unusual colors in both solids and stripes.

Allen Edmonds

24 E. 44th St., New York, NY 10017 (212)682-3144

www.allenedmonds.com

Allen Edmonds

551 Madison Ave., New York, NY 10022 (212)308-8305

www.allenedmonds.com

Ameri

Independent

Kass Ameri, Owner

1149A Second Ave., New York, NY 10021 (212)838-1301

Store filled with unique and colorful merchandise. These pieces are made of great fabrics, with vibrant colors and patterns and fabrics luxurious to the touch. Helpful sales staff.

Casual Wear Ameri, Damiani
Dress Shirts Ameri, Damiani
Neckwear Versace
Tailored Clothing Canali, Damiani, Redaelli, Versace
Sales Semiannual

Ameri

Independent

Kass Ameri, Owner

1010 Third Ave., New York, NY 10021 (212)935-2111

Store filled with unique and colorful merchandise. These pieces are made of great fabrics, with vibrant colors and patterns and luxurious fabrics. Helpful sales staff.

Casual Wear Ameri, Damiani
Dress Shirts Ameri, Damiani
Neckwear Versace
Tailored Clothing Canali, Damiani, Redaelli, Versace
Sales Semiannual

Giorgio Armani

760 Madison Ave., New York, NY 10021 (212)988-9191

www.giorgioarmani.com

Largest Giorgio Armani store with best selection in U.S.

Ascot Chang

7 W. 57th St., New York, NY 10019 (212)759-3333 www.ascotchang.com

Dress Shirts Custom
Neckwear Dormeuil
Tailored Clothing Made to measure

Ted Baker

107 Grand St., New York, NY 10013 (212)343-8989

www.tedbaker.co.uk

Very cool SoHo boutique for this British designer. Lots of interesting and unusual pieces.

Barney's

Madison Ave. at 61st St., New York, NY 10021 (212)826-8900

www.barneys.com

Huge store, with awesome selection and great service. From the lengthy list of brands, you can surmise Barney's is an interesting and desirable shopping destination.

Casual Wear Giorgio Armani, Barney's, Hugo Boss, CoSTUME NATIONAL, Christian Dior, Dolce & Gabbana, Marc Jacobs, Hickey Freeman, Donna Karan, Helmut Lang, Moreno Martini Da Firenze, Prada, John Smedley, Paul Smith, John Varvatos, Ermenegildo Zegna
Dress Shirts Giorgio Armani, Barney's, Battistoni, Hickey Freeman, Kilgour, French & Stanbury, Lorenzini, Ronaldus Shamansk, Ermenegildo Zegna
Neckwear Altea, Giorgio Armani, Barney's, ETRO, Ermenegildo Zegna
Shoes Giorgio Armani, Barney's, Cole Haan, Salvatore Ferragamo, Gucci, Bruno Magli, Prada
Tailored Clothing Giorgio Armani, Luciano Barbera, Barney's, Belvest, Hugo Boss, Brioni, Canali, Hickey Freeman, Gianluca Isaia, Kilgour, French & Stanbury, Oxxford, Polo Ralph Lauren, Ralph Lauren Purple Label, Vestimenta, Ermenegildo Zegna
Sales Semiannual

Bergdorf Goodman
Independent
Roger Rossi, Men's Furnishings
745 Fifth Ave., New York, NY 10019
(212)753-7300
Beautiful, ornate store. Exquisite fixtures and presentation of merchandise on all three floors. Filled with excellent selection of finest menswear in the world. Many store-in-stores. Consistently named as one of America's best specialty stores by *Robb Report*.
Accessories One of the best cuff link

selections I've seen, and many other distinctive items too numerous to mention
Casual Wear Giorgio Armani, Luciano Barbera, Bergdorf Goodman, Coast, Gucci, Jil Sander, Paul Smith, John Varvatos, Ermenegildo Zegna
Dress Shirts Sartoria Attolini, Bergdorf Goodman, Fray, Kiton, Lorenzini, Ermenegildo Zegna
Neckwear Bergdorf Goodman, ETRO, Richard James, Kiton, Marinella, Nicky's of Milan, Ermenegildo Zegna
Tailored Clothing Giorgio Armani, Sartoria Attolini, Luciano Barbera, Brioni, Dolce & Gabbana, Kiton, Many labels available M2M on third floor
Sales Semiannual

Bloomingdale's
1000 Third Ave., New York, NY 10022
(212)750-8139
www.bloomingdales.com
Famous name and location. Great store-in-store selections of Joseph Abboud, Giorgio Armani, Hugo Boss, and Canali.

Casual Wear Joseph Abboud, Hugo Boss
Dress Shirts Joseph Abboud, Hugo Boss
Neckwear Joseph Abboud, Giorgio Armani, Hugo Boss, Canali
Tailored Clothing Joseph Abboud, Giorgio Armani, Hugo Boss, Canali

Luigi Borrelli
16 E. 60th St., New York, NY 10022
(212)644-9610
www.luigiborrelli.com

Delightful boutique filled with quality Luigi Borrelli ready-to-wear items. Great selection of fabrics to order, made-to-measure shirts, shoes, and tailored clothing as well.

BOSS Hugo Boss
717 Fifth Ave., New York, NY 10022
(212)485-1800
www.hugoboss.com
Largest and most impressive U.S. Hugo Boss retail location.

Brioni
57 E. 57th St., New York, NY 10022
(212)376-5777 www.brioni.com

Brioni
55 E. 52nd St., New York, NY 10055
(212)355-1940 www.brioni.com

British American House
Independent
488 Madison Ave., New York, NY
10022 (212)752-5880
Attractive store with good selection of high-quality merchandise.

Casual Wear Hugo Boss, Canali, Dolce & Gabbana, Ermenegildo Zegna
Dress Shirts Canali, Ermenegildo Zegna
Neckwear Brioni, Canali, Lanvin, Versace, Ermenegildo Zegna
Shoes Lorenzo Banfi, Kenneth Cole
Tailored Clothing Belvest, Hugo Boss, Brioni, Burberry, Canali, Corneliani, d'Avenza, Valentino, Versace, Vestimenta, Ermenegildo Zegna
Sales Semiannual

Burberry
10 W. 57th St., New York, NY 10022
(212)371-5010 www.burberry.com

Camouflage
Independent
Norman Usiak, Proprietor
139–141 Eighth Ave., New York, NY
10011 (212)691-1750
These side-by-side Chelsea boutiques are a New York institution. Very appealing aesthetically—lots of windows and light wood. Great selection—unusual items from designers you won't find elsewhere. Mr. Usiak is a pleasure to deal with.

Casual Wear ETRO, Marc Jacobs, Helmut Lang, Moreno Martini Da Firenze, John Smedley, Paul Smith
Dress Shirts Helmut Lang, ETRO, Paul Smith
Neckwear ETRO, Gianfranco Ferré, Helmut Lang

Roberto Cavalli
711 Madison Ave., New York, NY
10021 (212)755-7722
www.robertocavalli.com
This boutique is large, visually appealing, and filled with interesting, fashion-forward items.

Davide Cenci
801 Madison Ave., New York, NY
10021, (212)628-5910
Merchandise is all self-labeled, made of exceptional fabrics, and displayed attractively in spacious, four-story building furnished with lots of great-looking wood.

Century 21
Outlet Store
22 Cortlandt St., New York, NY 10007
(212)227-9092
The definitive outlet store. More interesting, eclectic selection of designers and clothing than anywhere else I visited in America.

Prices can also be very reasonable, depending on what you're seeking.

Accessories Canali and Ermenegildo Zegna belts; good selection of solid-colored braces; bow ties
Casual Wear Joseph Abboud, Giorgio Armani, Hugo Boss, Jean Paul Gaultier, Romeo Gigli, John Varvatos, Ermenegildo Zegna
Dress Shirts Giorgio Armani, Brioni, Gucci, Ralph Lauren Purple Label, Ermenegildo Zegna
Neckwear Canali, Ralph Lauren Purple Label, Leonard, Versace, Ermenegildo Zegna
Tailored Clothing Joseph Abboud, Armani Collezioni, Canali, Mani, Valentino, Jack Victor, Zanella

Mark Christopher Custom Clothier
Independent
Mark Lingley, Proprietor
55 W. 26th St., Ste. 18H, New York, NY 10010 (212)686-9190
www.markchristophercustom shirts.com
First-quality self-labeled clothing line. Shirts made of soft luxurious material, primarily Swiss cotton. Ties made 3 inches longer from fine British silk for those who enjoy spread collars and full Windsor knots. Suits made of great fabric— Italian high-twist wool with a great hand. All custom pieces are hand-made from scratch, using a paper pattern, and are surprisingly afford-able for the quality. Mr. Lingley is one of the nicer and more knowl-edgeable people I've met in retail, and I recommend him and his clothing highly.

Kenneth Cole
130 E. 57th St., New York, NY 10022
(212)688-1670
www.kennethcole.com

Kenneth Cole
42nd St. and Vanderbilt, New York, NY 10017 (212)949-8079
www.kennethcole.com

Kenneth Cole
353 Columbus Ave., New York, NY 10024 (212)873-2061
www.kennethcole.com

Kenneth Cole
610 Fifth Ave., New York, NY 10020 (212)373-5800 www.kennethcole.com

Kenneth Cole
95 Fifth Ave., New York, NY 10003 (212)675-2550
www.kennethcole.com

Kenneth Cole
597 Broadway, New York, NY 10012 (212)965-0283
www.kennethcole.com

Cole Haan
Rockefeller Center, 620 Fifth Ave., New York, NY 10020 (212)765-9747
www.colehaan.com

DeLisi
Independent
St. Regis Hotel, 14 E. 55th St., New York, NY 10022 (212)753-3344
Attractive store with distinctive selection, particularly of Brioni tai-lored items.

Dress Shirts Burini, Zilli
Neckwear Brioni, Stefano Ricci
Tailored Clothing Brioni

Diesel
1 Union Square West, New York, NY 10003 (646)336-8552 www.diesel.com

Diesel
770 Lexington Ave., New York, NY
10021 (212)308-0055 www.diesel.com

DKNY
655 Madison Ave., New York, NY
10022 (212)223-DKNY www.dkny.com

DKNY
420 W. Broadway, New York, NY
10012 (646)613-1100 www.dkny.com

Dolce & Gabbana
434 W. Broadway, New York, NY
10012 (212)965-8000
www.dolcegabbana.com

Dolce & Gabbana
816 Madison Ave., New York, NY
10021 (212)249-4100
www.dolcegabbana.com

Alfred Dunhill
Peter Katz, Manager
711 Fifth Ave., New York, NY 10022
(212)753-9292
www.dunhill.com
Dunhill's flagship store does a
brisk business in Savile Row–style
made-to-measure suits.

Peter Elliot
Independent
Peter Elliot Rabin, Owner
1070 Madison Ave., New York, NY
10028 (212)570-2300
Cozy boutique filled with excellent
collections from first-quality
designers. Excellent customer service. Women's store across the
street as well. One of my favorite
New York destinations.

Accessories Good selection of belts,
braces, bow ties, and cuff links,
Barbour outerwear, fun socks

Casual Wear Barbour, Luigi Borrelli,
Peter Elliot, Kiton, Paul Smith
Dress Shirts Luigi Borrelli, Peter
Elliot, Kiton
Neckwear Drake, Peter Elliot, Kiton
Tailored Clothing Peter Elliot,
Hickey Freeman, Kiton

Emporio Armani
601 Madison Ave., New York, NY
10022 (212)317-0800
www.giorgioarmani.com

ETRO
720 Madison Ave., New York, NY
10021 (212)317-9096 www.etro.it
Large boutique filled with interesting, colorful ETRO takes on classic European designs.

Façonnable
689 Fifth Ave., New York, NY 10022
(212)319-0111 www.nordstrom.com

Salvatore Ferragamo
663 Fifth Ave., New York, NY 10022
(212)759-3822
www.salvatoreferragamo.it

Salvatore Ferragamo
725 Fifth Ave., New York, NY 10022
(212)759-7990
www.salvatoreferragamo.it

Gianfranco Ferré
845 Madison Ave., New York, NY
10021 (212)717-5430
www.gianfrancoferre.com

William Fioravanti Inc.
Independent
Bill Fioravanti, Proprietor
45 W. 57th St., 4th Floor, New York,
NY 10019 (212)355-1540
Everything here is made with

utmost precision and attention to detail. Tailored clothing is selected from the finest fabrics in the world. Mr. Fioravanti was most gracious with his time and in sharing expertise gained over 40 years in the tailoring profession. Marvelous place to have a one-of-a-kind, classic suit made that will last a lifetime. See article about this business in March 2001 *Esquire* and August 2002 *Robb Report* magazines.

Alan Flusser Custom Shop
Alan Flusser, Principal/Mark Rykken, Principal and Managing Partner, George Broderick, Principal and Merchandise Manager
3 E. 48th St., New York, NY 10017 (212) 888-4500
Brand-new establishment opened in April 2003. Great atmosphere, comfortable clubby surroundings showing film clips of famous Hollywood actors dressed in the classic style of the '30s and '40s. Most clothing is self-labeled and of the utmost quality. You'll find items here you can't find anywhere else in the world. Mr. Rykken and Mr. Broderick were very gracious with their time. Great shopping destination!

Fratelli Rossetti
625 Madison Ave., New York, NY 10022 (212)980-9448
www.rossetti.it

Ghurka
41 E. 57th St., New York, NY 10022 (212)826-8300
www.ghurka.com

Gucci
685 Fifth Ave., New York, NY 10022 (212)826-2600 www.gucci.com

H. Herzfeld Haberdasher
Independent
Jonathon D. Cline, Manager
507 Madison Ave., New York, NY 10022 (212)753-6756
www.herzfeldonline.com *(see chapter 9)*
Fine selection of unique, quality items you won't find elsewhere in New York. Sales staff is eager to help. Merchandise targeted toward more traditional tastes.

Accessories Great selection of Trafalgar braces (including Limited Edition), Duchamp cuff links
Casual Wear Cugat, Herzfeld, Jeff Rose
Dress Shirts Cugat, Herzfeld, custom
Neckwear Herzfeld, Hunter
Tailored Clothing Hickey Freeman, custom

Hickey Freeman
666 Fifth Ave., New York, NY 10103 (212)586-6481 www.hickeyfreeman.com
Recently opened boutique features the best of the Hickey Freeman line, including Bobby Jones sportswear.

Holland & Holland
50 E. 57th St., New York, NY 10022 (212)752-7755
Large, luxurious three-floor store. Does brisk made-to-measure tailored clothing business. Excellent customer service.

Matt Hunter & Company
Independent
Matt Hunter, Owner/ David Shreve, Manager
56 Grand Central Terminal, New York, NY 10017 (212)681-7480
Choice location, features some great items from Hickey Freeman

and Ermenegildo Zegna.

Casual Wear Ermenegildo Zegna, Hickey Freeman
Dress Shirts Eton, Ermenegildo Zegna, Hickey Freeman
Neckwear Ermenegildo Zegna, Hickey Freeman

Matt Hunter & Company
Independent
Matt Hunter, Owner/
David Shreve, Manager
693 Third Ave., New York, NY 10017
(212)697-9411
Convenient location, features some great items from Hickey Freeman and Ermenegildo Zegna.

Casual Wear Ermenegildo Zegna, Hickey Freeman
Dress Shirts Eton, Ermenegildo Zegna, Hickey Freeman
Neckwear Ermenegildo Zegna, Hickey Freeman
Tailored Clothing Ermenegildo Zegna, Hickey Freeman

JJ Hat Center
Independent
310 Fifth Ave., New York, NY 10001
(800)622-1911
An excellent place to select stylish headwear. Visit in person, online, or call for a catalog to view JJ's great selection of hats.

Jeffrey
Independent
Jeffrey Kalinsky, Owner
449 W. 14th St., New York, NY 10014
(212)206-1272
New York's premier destination for the man interested in modern, trendy clothing. Many interesting and unique items you won't find elsewhere.

Casual Wear Jean Paul Gaultier, Gucci, Helmut Lang, Jil Sander
Tailored Clothing Gucci, Helmut Lang

Jodamo International Ltd.
Independent
Aby Jodamo, Owner
321 Grand St., New York, NY 10002
(212)219-1039
Family business, sells clothing wholesale and retail. Outstanding customer service. Great buys on reputable brand names.

Casual Wear Hugo Boss, Brioni, Gianfranco Ferré, Versace, Valentino, Zanetti
Dress Shirts Eton, Gianfranco Ferré, Valentino
Shoes Bruno Magli, Versace
Tailored Clothing Hugo Boss, Brioni, Gianfranco Ferré Valentino, Versace, Zanetti

Johnston & Murphy
345 Madison Ave., New York, NY 10017 (212)697-9375
www.johnstonmurphy.com

Johnston & Murphy
520 Madison Ave., New York, NY 10022 (212)527-2342
www.johnstonmurphy.com

Donna Karan
819 Madison Ave., New York, NY 10021 (212)861-1001
www.donnakaran.com

Calvin Klein
654 Madison Ave., New York, NY 10022 (212)292-9000
Striking contrast between walls and fixtures in pure white and dark-colored clothing (fall/winter

at the time) arranged monochro-
matically.

Jay Kos
Independent
Rod Springer, Erik Vaughn Walker
988 Lexington Ave., New York, NY
10021 (212)327-2382
Featured in *GQ*'s January 2003
Local Heroes list as one of the best
local stores in the world. Great-
looking boutique filled with Kos's
self-labeled merchandise. Clothes
are excellent quality first-rate construction.

Accessories Great selection of
Albert Thurston braces
Shoes Edward Green, J.M. Weston

Krizia
769 Madison Ave., New York, NY
10021 (212)879-1211
An interesting selection of well-
made pieces at surprisingly affordable prices.

Lacoste
543 Madison Ave., New York, NY
10022 (212)750-8115
www.lacoste.com

Helmut Lang
80 Greene St., New York, NY 10012
(212)925-7214
www.helmutlang.com
Extremely cool boutique filled
with Lang's famous minimalist
designs. Exquisite visual atmosphere, marvelous presentation of
merchandise.

Ralph Lauren
867–888 Madison Ave., New York, NY
10021 (212)606-2100 or (212)434-8000

www.polo.com
Flagship U.S. store for this iconic
American brand.

Ralph Lauren
379 W. Broadway, New York, NY
10012 (212)625-1660 www.polo.com

Leopold
Independent
530 7th Ave., New York, NY 10018
(212)302-6060
Attractive store with good selection of Italian collections, particularly Canali.

Casual Wear Bertone, Hugo Boss,
Canali, Versace
Dress Shirts Hugo Boss, Canali,
Corneliani, Leopold, Versace
Neckwear Canali, Leopold, Richel
Shoes Mezlan
Tailored Clothing Canali,
Corneliani, Leopold
Sales Semiannual

John Lobb
680 Madison Ave., New York, NY
10020 (212)888-9797
www.johnlobb.com
Largest American Lobb boutique,
great selection of this world-
famous footwear.

Loro Piana
821 Madison Ave., New York, NY
10021 (212)980-7961
www.loropiana.com
Large, attractive Loro Piana store.
Sales staff courteous and professional.

Bruno Magli
677 Fifth Ave., New York, NY 10022
(212)752-7900 www.brunomagli.com

Malo
814 Madison Ave., New York, NY
10021 (212)396-4721

Maurizio Custom Tailors
Independent
Anthony Maurizio, Proprietor
18 E. 53rd St., 5th Floor, New York, NY
10022 (212)759-3230
A myriad of choices in exclusive
fabrics like Dormeuil, Holland &
Sherry, Scabal, and Ermenegildo
Zegna. Old-world craftsmanship
with precise attention to detail. All
garments are handmade on the
premises. Mr. Maurizio is very
knowledgeable about the tailoring
industry and is delightful to deal
with. If you're in the market for an
exquisite, hand-tailored garment, I
highly recommend a visit to
Maurizio Custom Tailors!

Moschino
803 Madison Ave., New York, NY
10021 (212)639-9600
Large boutique filled with whimsical, interesting designs.

Napoleon
Independent
The Plaza Hotel, 769 Fifth Ave., New
York, NY 10019 (212)759-8000
www.napoleonfashions.com
Intimate boutique designed prima-
rily to serve Plaza Hotel guests.

Napoleon
Independent
Trump Plaza, 1048 Third Ave., New
York, NY 10021 (212)308-3000
www.napoleonfashions.com

Accessories Good selection of cuff
links
Casual Wear Napoleon

Dress Shirts Brioni, Napoleon,
Stefano Ricci
Neckwear Brioni, Leonard,
Pancaldi
Tailored Clothing Brioni,
Napoleon
Sales Semiannual, January and July

Oxxford Clothes
36 E. 57th St., New York, NY 10022
(212)593-0204
www.theoxxfordstore.com
Largest and most unique selection
of Oxxford clothing in the U.S.
Great customer service; sales staff
is very knowledgeable about tailored clothing in general and
Oxxford in particular. Store also
has a great selection of Trafalgar
Limited Edition braces and first-
quality shoes made for Oxxford by
Edward Green of England.

Paul & Shark
772 Madison Ave., New York, NY
10021 (212)452-9868
www.paulshark.it

Thomas Pink
520 Madison Ave., New York, NY
10022 (212)838-1928
www.thomaspink.com

Thomas Pink
1155 Avenue of the Americas, New
York, NY 10036 (212)840-9663
www.thomaspink.com

Prada
724 Fifth Ave., New York, NY 10019
(212)664-0010 www.prada.com

Prada
841 Madison Ave., New York, NY
10021 (212)327-4200 www.prada.com

Prada Sportswear
116 Wooster St., New York, NY 10012
(212)925-2221 www.prada.com

RRL
271 Mulberry St., New York, NY 10021
(212)343-0841 www.polo.com

Refinery
Independent
Mark Rykken, Principal/
George Broderick, Principal
3 E. 48th St., 4th Floor, New York, NY
10017 (212)888-4500
Brand-new establishment opened
in April 2003 by these two former
senior employees of Britches of
Georgetown. High-quality self-
labeled merchandise value priced
and intended to introduce the
younger man to the finer art of
dressing. Emphasis on custom
clothing, but many fine ready-to-
wear items as well.

Riflessi
Independent
James Lee, Sales
47 W. 57th St., New York, NY 10019
(212)935-4747
GREAT prices, particularly on
Bruno Magli and Loro Piana outerwear and Ermenegildo Zegna
and Canali suits.

Accessories Magli leather and shear-
ling coats, Loro Piana cashmere
overcoats
Dress Shirts Giorgio Armani,
Balmain, Donna Karan
Neckwear Canali, Salvatore
Ferragamo, Gucci, Ermenegildo
Zegna
Tailored Clothing Canali, Cerruti
1881, Gianfranco Ferré,
Ermenegildo Zegna

Rothman's
Independent
Union Square, 200 Park Ave. South,
New York, NY 10003 (212)777-7400
Large, well-appointed store.
Quality inventory of brands, great
customer service.

Casual Wear Axis, Tommy
Bahama, Ted Baker, Rothman's,
Robert Talbott
Dress Shirts Canali, Gitman Bros.,
Hickey Freeman, Jack Victor
Neckwear Jhane Barnes, Canali,
Rothman's
Shoes Kenneth Cole, Cole Haan,
Johnston & Murphy, Donald J.
Pliner
Tailored Clothing Joseph Abboud,
Hugo Boss, DKNY, Tallia
Sales Semiannual

Saks Fifth Avenue
Besharam Nehme, Armani
Specialist
611 Fifth Ave., New York, NY 10022
(212)753-4000
www.saksfifthavenue.com
Largest floor space and selection of
any Saks in the U.S., in majestic and
historic building. The forestlike
motif on the first floor, antique ele-
vators, and marble and mahogany in
the men's lounge are highlights.
Has great complement of designers.
Recently added Domenico Spano's
custom tailoring business as an in-
house department. Mr. Nehme is
one of my all-time favorite clothing
consultants; he really knows the
business and will go the extra mile
to give you excellent service.

Casual Wear Giorgio Armani,
Baldessarini, Brioni, Canali, Dolce
& Gabbana, Gucci, Gianluca Isaia,

Michael Kors, Helmut Lang, Moreno Martini Da Firenze, Polo Ralph Lauren, Ralph Lauren Purple Label, Paul Smith, Yohji Yamamoto, Ermenegildo Zegna
Dress Shirts Giorgio Armani, Ike Behar, Luigi Borrelli, Hugo Boss, Brioni, Donna Karan, Lorenzini, Ermenegildo Zegna
Neckwear Giorgio Armani, Brioni, Charvet, Salvatore Ferragamo, Ralph Lauren Purple Label, Ermenegildo Zegna
Tailored Clothing Giorgio Armani, Baldessarini, Hugo Boss, Brioni, Canali, Hickey Freeman, Gianluca Isaia (only U.S. store-in-store), Donna Karan Signature, Ralph Lauren Purple Label, Ermenegildo Zegna

Jil Sander
121 Fifth Ave., New York, NY 10010 (212)447-9200
www.jilsander.com

Sanitate Tailors and Shirtmakers
Independent
Vincenze and Cosimo Sanitate, Owners
27 W. 55th St., New York, NY 10019 (212)755-0937
www.sanitatetailors.com
Many luxurious fabrics to choose from. Clothing is handmade from paper patterns on the premises. The elder Mr. Sanitate designs women's couture as well and can arrange for private showings. The stylish, unique pieces in the younger Mr. Sanitate's ready-to-wear line help to make this a superb shopping destination.

Santoni
864 Madison Ave., New York, NY 10021 (212)794-3820

Paul Smith
108 Fifth Ave., New York, NY 10011 (212)627-9770
Flagship American boutique for this hot designer. Many interesting and unique items; the cuff link selection alone makes the store worth a visit.

Paul Stuart
Independent
Madison Ave. at 45th St., New York, NY 10017 (212)682-0320
www.paulstuart.com
Very large and appealing store. Most merchandise is privately labeled. Good selection of bow ties, braces, and cuff links. For the more traditional dresser. First-rate customer service.

Robert Talbott
680 Madison Ave., New York, NY 10021 (212)751-1200

a. testoni
665 Fifth Ave., New York, NY 10022 (212)223-0909 www.testoni.com

The Art of Shaving
141 E. 62nd St., New York, NY 10021 (212)317-8436
www.theartofshaving.com

The Art of Shaving
373 Madison Ave., New York, NY 10017 (212)986-2905
www.theartofshaving.com

Turnbull & Asser
Robert Gillotte, Bespoke Manager/Simon Hobbs, Store Manager
42 E. 57th St., New York, NY 10022 (212)752-5700
www.turnbullandasser.com
Mr. Hobbs is one of the best sales-people I've ever had the pleasure

of dealing with. No one does the classic British ensemble better, and no one can better advise you on how to achieve it. Turnbull's American flagship has a great selection of ready-to-wear items, including unique leather accessories, sized socks, and braces that can't be found anywhere else. Also has a huge assortment of fabrics available to order Turnbull's world-famous shirts and high-end British suits made to measure.

Valentino
747 Madison Ave., New York, NY
10021 (212)772-6969

John Varvatos
149 Mercer Street, New York, NY
10012 (212)965-0700
www.johnvarvatos.com

J. M. Weston
812 Madison Ave., New York, NY
10021 (212)535-2100

Yohji Yamamoto
103 Grand St., New York, NY 10013
(212)966-9066
www.yohjiyamamoto.com
Unique, elegant designer boutique. Very unusual pieces, marvelous presentation of merchandise amid sumptuous cherry wood fixtures and flooring. Even the distinctive, ethereal music added to the overall experience.

Ermenegildo Zegna
743 Fifth Ave., New York, NY 10022
(212)421-4488 www.zegna.com
Largest and most appealing
U.S. Zegna location. Being
remodeled.

Ziani
Independent
1400 Broadway, New York, NY 10018
(212)302-3661
Very nice boutique with interesting and unique items. More modern clothing selections.

Casual Wear Pal Zileri
Dress Shirts Romeo Gigli, Fabio Inghirami, Xacus, Pal Zileri
Neckwear Romeo Gigli
Tailored Clothing Pal Zileri
Sales Semiannual

Tyrone
Independent
Richard and Norman Buksbam, Owners
1432 Old Northern Blvd., Roslyn, NY
11576 (516)484-3330
Large, beautiful store. Quality merchandise mix between modern and traditional brands. Arranged in handsome wooden fixtures. Great atmosphere and sales staff.

Accessories Good selection of cuff links
Casual Wear Avon Celli, Coast, Prada, Jil Sander
Dress Shirts Giorgio Armani, Luigi Borrelli, Dolce & Gabbana, Fray, Ermenegildo Zegna
Neckwear Nicky's of Milan, Ermenegildo Zegna
Tailored Clothing Canali, Gianluca Isaia, Prada, Ermenegildo Zegna

THE MALL AT THE SOURCE
Location and Stores:
1504 Old Country Rd., Westbury, NY
11590 www.shopsimon.com

Nordstrom Rack
Outlet Store
(516)222-5544 www.nordstrom.com

Casual Wear Tricots St. Raphael, Zanella
Dress Shirts Ike Behar, Façonnable, Robert Talbott
Neckwear Ermenegildo Zegna
Tailored Clothing Jhane Barnes, Zanella

Saks Off Fifth
Outlet Store
(516)228-2165
www.saksfifthavenue.com
One of better sections of tailored clothing at any Off Fifth I visited in the U.S.

Casual Wear Vestimenta, Ermenegildo Zegna
Dress Shirts Ike Behar, Ermenegildo Zegna
Neckwear Versace, Ermenegildo Zegna
Tailored Clothing Giorgio Armani, Jhane Barnes, Burberry, Hickey Freeman, Ermenegildo Zegna

THE WESTCHESTER MALL
Location and Stores:
125 Westchester Ave., White Plains, NY 10601 www.shopsimon.com

A/X Armani Exchange
(914)683-6188
www.giorgioarmani.com

Bernini
(914)686-1786 www.bernini.com

Casual Wear Ermenegildo Zegna
Neckwear Canali
Tailored Clothing Belvest, Hugo Boss, Canali, Zanella

BOSS Hugo Boss
(914)681-1955 www.hugoboss.com

Brooks Brothers
(914)644-8616
www.brooksbrothers.com

Burberry
(914)997-7770 www.burberry.com

Coach
(914)644-8244 www.coach.com

Kenneth Cole
(914)684-2653
www.kennethcole.com

Cole Haan
(914)997-7480 www.colehaan.com

Johnston & Murphy
(914)328-3503
www.johnstonmurphy.com

Lacoste
(914)948-0971 www.lacoste.com

Loutie
Independent
(914)328-2840
Pleasant store, great selection of Pal Zileri merchandise.

Casual Wear Equilibrio, Versace, Pal Zileri
Dress Shirts Versace, Pal Zileri
Neckwear Loutie, Versace, Pal Zileri
Shoes Mezlan
Tailored Clothing Giorgio Armani, Hugo Boss, Pal Zileri

Neiman Marcus
Lou Dellis, Men's Clothing
(914)428-2000
www.neimanmarcus.com
Large, attractive Neiman's store. Mr. Dellis was a pleasure to work with.

Casual Wear Loro Piana, Ralph Lauren Purple Label, Ermenegildo Zegna
Dress Shirts Giorgio Armani, Ike Behar, Luigi Borrelli, Brioni, Charvet, Fray, Lorenzini, Turnbull & Asser, Ermenegildo Zegna
Neckwear Charvet, Brioni, Salvatore Ferragamo, Turnbull & Asser, Ermenegildo Zegna, Giorgio Armani
Tailored Clothing Giorgio Armani, Ermenegildo Zegna, Hickey Freeman, Brioni

Nordstrom
(914)946-1122 www.nordstrom.com
Appealing, spacious store with great selection of quality merchandise.

Casual Wear Robert Talbott, Zanella, Ermenegildo Zegna
Dress Shirts Ike Behar, Robert Talbott
Neckwear Robert Talbott, XMI, Ermenegildo Zegna
Tailored Clothing Joseph Abboud, Hickey Freeman, Pal Zileri

St. Croix
Suzanne Meyer, Manager
(914)328-3000
www.stcroixshop.com
Largest and most attractive St. Croix location I saw.

Versace Jeans Couture
(914)684-1394 www.versace.com

Louis Vuitton
(914)289-1809
www.louisvuitton.com

Thomas Miller
Independent
Thomas Miller, Owner/Gerry Henry, Manager/Marco DeStefano, Sales
Woodbury Common, 8285 Jericho Turnpike, Woodbury, NY 01797
(516)367-3590
Spacious, two-story establishment. Lots of attractive wood fixtures, great selection of first-quality merchandise. One of more genial, informed sales staffs I encountered.

Accessories Good selection of braces
Casual Wear Luciano Barbera, Brioni, Gran Sasso, Ermenegildo Zegna
Dress Shirts Brioni, Luigi Borrelli, Kiton, Ermenegildo Zegna
Neckwear Luciano Barbera, Brioni, Kiton, Ermenegildo Zegna
Shoes Cole Haan, Salvatore Ferragamo, Gucci, Donald J. Pliner
Tailored Clothing Brioni, Coppley, Kiton, Ermenegildo Zegna, all also M2M

Metro Area: Orlando
BELZ FACTORY OUTLET CENTRE
Location and Stores:
5269 International Dr., Orlando, FL 32819 www.belz.com

Coach
Outlet Store
(407)352-6772 www.coach.com

Kenneth Cole
Outlet Store
(407)903-1191
www.kennethcole.com

Cole Haan
Outlet Store

(407)351-2272 www.colehaan.com

Polo Ralph Lauren Factory Store
Outlet Store
(407)352-3632 www.polo.com

Saks Off Fifth
Outlet Store
(407)354-5757
www.saksfifthavenue.com

Dress Shirts Ermenegildo Zegna
Neckwear Ermenegildo Zegna

ORLANDO PREMIUM OUTLETS
Location and Stores:
8200 Vineland Ave., Orlando, FL 32821
www.premiumoutlets.com

Armani General Store
Outlet Store
(407)465-2121
www.giorgioarmani.com

Hugo Boss
Outlet Store
(407)465 0660 www.hugoboss.com

Burberry
Outlet Store
(407)238-7777 www.burberry.com

Coach
Outlet Store
(407)465-0555 www.coach.com

Kenneth Cole
Outlet Store
(407)239-1116
www.kennethcole.com

Cole Haan
Outlet Store
(407)239-4900 www.colehaan.com

Salvatore Ferragamo
Outlet Store
(407)477-0091
www.salvatoreferragamo.it

Johnston & Murphy
Outlet Store
(407)239-8099
www.johnstonmurphy.com

Calvin Klein
Outlet Store
(407)465-0234

Donald J. Pliner
Outlet Store
(407)239-6844
www.donaldjpliner.com

Tod's
Outlet Store
(407)465-1820 www.tods.com
www.premiumoutlets.com

Versace
Outlet Store
(407)239-8800 www.versace.com

Ermenegildo Zegna
Outlet Store
(407)239-6300 www.zegna.com

THE FLORIDA MALL
Location and Stores:
8001 S. Orange Blossom Trail,
Orlando, FL 32809
www.shopsimon.com

Brooks Brothers
(407)251-0701
www.brooksbrothers.com

Johnston & Murphy
(407)857-7133
www.johnstonmurphy.com

Saks Fifth Avenue
(407)812-4500
www.saksfifthavenue.com

Casual Wear Joseph Abboud,
Giorgio Armani, Hugo Boss,

Hickey Freeman, Ermenegildo
Zegna
Dress Shirts Giorgio Armani,
Hugo Boss, Canali, Hickey
Freeman, Ermenegildo Zegna
Neckwear Giorgio Armani, Hugo
Boss, Canali, Ermenegildo Zegna
Tailored Clothing Giorgio Armani,
Hugo Boss, Canali, Hickey
Freeman, Ermenegildo Zegna

John Craig
Independent
H. Craig DeLongy, Owner
132 Park Ave. South, Winter Park, FL
32789 (407)629-7944
Very attractive store using only
antique and custom-made fixtures.
Aimed more at the casual and
business casual dresser. Great
shopping destination.

Accessories Martin Dingman belts;
Colonel Littleton gentleman's
accessories; Remy leather outerwear
Casual Wear Jhane Barnes, Bills
Khakis, Cifonelli, Como Sport,
Henry Cotton's, Gran Sasso,
Haupt, Bobby Jones, Lucky
Brand, Tricots St. Raphael,
Ermenegildo Zegna
Dress Shirts Ike Behar, Canali,
Ermenegildo Zegna
Neckwear Altea, Ermenegildo
Zegna
Shoes Cole Haan, Bruno Magli,
Mezlan, Santoni
Tailored Clothing Arnold Brant,
Canali, Coppley, Samuelsohn,
Bernard Zins, Ermenegildo Zegna
(M2M also)

Milano's Clothier
Independent
*Auke Hempenius, Sean Azarian,
Owners*

316 N. Park Ave., Winter Park, FL
32789 (407)645-5506
www.milanosclothier.com
Impressive new store with everything custom designed for the store
by its owner. Mr. Hempenius also
does color analysis and will travel
anywhere in the U.S. to deliver an
order. Milano's Clothier has a mas-
sage chair as well, and food and wine
on the rear terrace to enhance the
discerning man's shopping experience.

Accessories Martin Dingman belts;
Trafalgar Limited Edition braces;
Nancy and Risé cuff links
Casual Wear Avon Celli, Como
Sport, Luciano Moresco, Georg
Roth, John Smedley, Versace
Dress Shirts Ike Behar, Brioni,
Versace
Neckwear Brioni, Tino Cosma,
Pancaldi, Versace, XMI
Shoes Johnston & Murphy, Dieter
Kuckenhorn, Marron
Tailored Clothing Coppley, Hiltl,
Lubiam, Ravazzolo (also M2M),
Versace V2, Pal Zileri, Arnold
Zimberg

Siegel's Clothing Co.
Independent
*John Siegel, Owner/John Dickson,
Sales*
330 Park Ave. South, Winter Park, FL
32789 (407)645-3100
Spacious, well-lighted store. Great
selection of merchandise presented
appealingly, primarily in wood fixtures. Caters primarily to the traditional dresser. Mr. Siegel and Mr.
Dickson were both helpful and a
pleasure to speak with.

Accessories Good selection of bow
ties, Trafalgar braces (including

Limited Edition), cuff links, and
Golden Bear leather outerwear
Casual Wear Tommy Bahama,
Jhane Barnes, Barry Bricken,
Henry Cotton's, Gitman Bros.,
Gran Sasso, Haupt, Nat Nast, Tori
Richards, Jeff Rose, Tricots
St. Raphael, Zanella
Dress Shirts Eton, Siegel's (Gitman
Bros.), Robert Talbott
Neckwear Altea, Villa Bolgheri,
Robert Talbott
Shoes Cole Haan, Mezlan,
Donald J. Pliner, H.S. Trask
Tailored Clothing Coppley, Corbin
(also M2M), Dormeuil M2M,
Hart, Hickey Freeman (also
M2M), Marx, Oxxford M2M,
Marzotto Sartoriale, Schaffner,
Jack Victor, Zanella
Sales Semiannual

Metro Area: Philadelphia

Centofanti Tailors
Independent
Joseph Centofanti, Owner
7 Station Rd., Ardmore, PA 19003
(610)642-1926
Many choices in exclusive fabrics
like Dormeuil, Holland & Sherry,
Scabal, and Ermenegildo Zegna.
Superb old-world service with
handcrafted attention to detail. All
garments are handmade from
paper patterns on the premises.
Mr. Centofanti does a particularly
brisk business in cashmere sport
coats and has a notable client list.
He is very knowledgeable about
the industry and a real pleasure to
deal with. I highly recommend his
establishment!

Saks Fifth Avenue
Bala Cynwyd Plaza, 2 Bala Cynwyd
Plaza, Bala Cynwyd, PA 19004
(610)667-1550
www.saksfifthavenue.com

Casual Wear Joseph Abboud,
Giorgio Armani, Hugo Boss,
Ermenegildo Zegna
Dress Shirts Joseph Abboud, Hugo
Boss
Neckwear Joseph Abboud, Giorgio
Armani, Hugo Boss, Ermenegildo
Zegna
Tailored Clothing Joseph Abboud,
Giorgio Armani, Hugo Boss

Ventresca Ltd.
Independent
Frank Ventresca, Owner
315 Old York Rd., Jenkintown, PA
19046 (215)576-1178
www.ventresca.com
Fantastic store with top-notch,
come-to-you service. In existence
since 1981. Mr. Ventresca is one of
the most truly engaging and
knowledgeable people I encountered while researching this book.

Casual Wear Tommy Bahama,
Bills Khakis, Brioni, Corneliani,
Haupt, Ermenegildo Zegna
Dress Shirts Brioni, Corneliani,
Fabio Inghirami, Xacus,
Ermenegildo Zegna
Neckwear Brioni, Corneliani,
Gianluca Napoli, Versace,
Ermenegildo Zegna
Shoes Cole Haan, Bruno Magli,
Moreschi
Tailored Clothing Brioni,
Corneliani, Gianluca Napoli,
Studio Milan, Versace Classic
Ermenegildo Zegna, Zegna Soft

KING OF PRUSSIA MALL
Location and Stores:
Rt. 202 at Mall Blvd., King of Prussia, PA 19406
www.kingofprussiamall.com

A/X Armani Exchange
(610)354-9810
www.giorgioarmani.com

Bernini
(610)354-9111 www.bernini.com
Casual Wear Giorgio Armani, Ermenegildo Zegna
Neckwear Versace, Ermenegildo Zegna
Tailored Clothing Versace, Hugo Boss

BOSS Hugo Boss
(610)992-1400 www.hugoboss.com

Brooks Brothers
(610)337-9888
www.brooksbrothers.com

Coach
(610)265-1772 www.coach.com

Kenneth Cole
(610)337-2650
www.kennethcole.com

DKNY
(610)337-4020 www.dkny.com

Hermès
(610)992-9730 www.hermes.com

Johnston & Murphy
(610)265-0165
www.johnstonmurphy.com

Neiman Marcus
(610)354-0500
www.neimanmarcus.com

Casual Wear Giorgio Armani, Jhane Barnes, Hugo Boss, Loro Piana, Polo Ralph Lauren, Ralph Lauren Purple Label, Ermenegildo Zegna
Dress Shirts Giorgio Armani, Luigi Borrelli, Brioni, Lorenzini, Turnbull & Asser, Ermenegildo Zegna
Neckwear Giorgio Armani, Brioni, Charvet, Salvatore Ferragamo, Turnbull & Asser, Ermenegildo Zegna
Tailored Clothing Giorgio Armani, Hugo Boss, Brioni, Hickey Freeman, Oxxford, Incotex, Ermenegildo Zegna

Nordstrom
(610)265-6111 www.nordstrom.com
Casual Wear Robert Talbott, Ermenegildo Zegna
Dress Shirts Ike Behar, Robert Talbott, Ermenegildo Zegna
Neckwear Robert Talbott, XMI, Ermenegildo Zegna

Versace Jeans Couture
(610)337-4774 www.versace.com

Louis Vuitton
(610)992-0392
www.louisvuitton.com

Allure
Independent
Bob Palidora, Owner
4255 Main St., Manayunk, PA 19127
(215)482-5299
www.allureonline.com
Appealing destination store in historic, cobblestoned Philadelphia suburb.

Accessories Good selection of Tateossian cuff links

Casual Wear ABS, Tommy
Bahama, Bugatchi, ETRO, G Star,
Gimos, Robert Graham, Pringle
Dress Shirts Allure Private Label,
Luigi Borrelli, Lorenzini
Neckwear Giorgio Armani, Kolte,
Pendleton
Tailored Clothing Giorgio Armani,
Belvest, Jack Victor

Boyd's
Independent
*Jeff Glass, Vice President/Kent
Guschner, Buyer/Ralph Yaffe, Vice
President*
1818 Chestnut St., Philadelphia, PA
19103 (215)564-9000
www.boydsphila.com
Large, elegant store with lots of
burnished wood and marble in
central downtown location. Lunch
café; free parking across the street.
Excellent customer service. Free
alterations by 50 European tailors.
Great women's boutique as well.

Accessories Good selection of
braces and cuff links, great selec-
tion of pocket squares,
Philadelphia's largest collection of
outerwear
Casual Wear Luciano Barbera,
Hugo Boss, Gran Sasso, Linnea
Trussini, Ermenegildo Zegna,
Zegna Sport, Franco Ziche
Dress Shirts Giorgio Armani, Ike
Behar, Luigi Borrelli, Canali,
Dolce & Gabbana, Kiton, Linnea
Trussini, Ermenegildo Zegna
Neckwear Giorgio Armani, Jhane
Barnes, Villa Bolgheri, Brioni,
Canali, Ermenegildo Zegna
Shoes Cole Haan, Salvatore
Ferragamo, Mezlan, Santoni,
a. testoni

Tailored Clothing Giorgio Armani,
Hugo Boss, Burberry, Canali,
Hickey Freeman, Kiton, Linnea
Trussini, Ermenegildo Zegna

Burberry
1705 Walnut St., Philadelphia, PA
19103 (215)557-7400
www.burberry.com

Kenneth Cole
1420 Walnut St., Philadelphia, PA
19103 (215)790-1690
www.kennethcole.com

Distante
Independent
1506 Walnut St., Philadelphia, PA
19102 (215)545-2850
Interesting boutique located in
downtown Philadelphia. Geared
primarily toward elegant casual
dresser. Many unique, one-of-a-
kind sweaters the day I visited, and
other stylish casual items.

Wayne Edwards
Independent
Wayne Glassman, Proprietor
1521 Walnut St., Philadelphia, PA
19102 (215)563-6801
Great selection of high-quality
clothing collections unique to the
Philadelphia area. Mr. Glassman
and his staff are fantastic to deal
with.

Casual Wear Avon Celli, Luciano
Barbera, Brunello Cuccinelli, Malo
Dress Shirts Luigi Borrelli,
Gianluca Isaia
Neckwear Luciano Barbera,
Massimo Bizzocchi, Gianluca Isaia,
Kiton
Shoes Barrett, Gravati, Silvano

Lattanzi, Sutor Mantellassi
Tailored Clothing Gianluca Isaia,
Kiton, Vestimenta

Ernesto's
Independent
Edward DeSumma, President
612 S. Fifth St., Philadelphia, PA 19147
(215)627-7887
Reasonably priced, high-quality
custom-made clothing from
sources around the world. Second-
generation family-owned business.

FRANKLIN MILLS
Location and Stores:
1455 Franklin Mills Circle,
Philadelphia, PA 19154
www.franklinmills.com

Brooks Brothers
Outlet Store
(215)632-9004
www.brooksbrothers.com

Kenneth Cole
Outlet Store
(215)281-9330
www.kennethcole.com

Neiman Marcus Last Call
Outlet Store
(215)637-5900
www.neimanmarcus.com

Casual Wear Hugo Boss
Dress Shirts Ike Behar, Hugo
Boss
Neckwear Ike Behar
Tailored Clothing Brioni,
Oxxford

Nordstrom Rack
Outlet Store
(215)281-3800 www.nordstrom.com

Casual Wear Ike Behar, Tricots
St. Raphael
Dress Shirts Façonnable, Hickey
Freeman, Zanella
Neckwear Ermenegildo Zegna

Polo Ralph Lauren Factory Store
Outlet Store
(215)632-2060
www.polo.com

Saks Off Fifth
Outlet Store
(215)632-5600
www.saksfifthavenue.com

Casual Wear Lorenzini, Robert
Talbott
Dress Shirts Ermenegildo Zegna
Neckwear Ermenegildo Zegna
Tailored Clothing Hugo Boss,
Corneliani

Ralph Lauren
The Bellvue, 200 S. Broad St.,
Philadelphia, PA 19102 (215)985-2800
www.polo.com

MBC Clothing Company
Independent
Ray Massimiano, President
Passyunk Ave. at 12th and Morris
Sts., Philadelphia, PA 19148 (215)468-
2116
Philadelphia tradition for 75 years.
True custom garments are pattern
made for each customer, and each
garment is bench made by hand.
Highest quality fabrics such as
Loro Piana and Ermenegildo
Zegna. Mr. Massimiano is very
informed about the tailoring
industry and produces first-class
clothing the old-fashioned way.

Metro Area: Phoenix

CHANDLER FASHION CENTER
Location and Stores:
3199 W. Chandler Blvd., Chandler, AZ
85226 www.westcor.com

Coach
(480)792-9464 www.coach.com

Lucky Brand Dungarees
(480)722-0760
www.luckybrandjeans.com

Nordstrom
(480)855-2500 www.nordstrom.com

Dress Shirts Ike Behar
Neckwear Ike Behar, Robert
Talbott, Ermenegildo Zegna
Tailored Clothing Joseph
Abboud, Hart, Schaffner &
Marx, Tallia

Nordstrom Rack
Outlet Store
(480)722-2000 www.nordstrom.com

Dress Shirts Façonnable
Neckwear Robert Talbott
Tailored Clothing Hart,
Schaffner, & Marx

BILTMORE FASHION PARK
Location and Stores:
2400 E. Camelback Rd., Phoenix, AZ
85016 www.shopbiltmore.com

Allen Edmonds
Becky May, Store Manager
(602)267-1410
www.allenedmonds.com

Cole Haan
Linda Duncan, Store Manager
(602)955-8686
www.colehaan.com

Gucci
Laurel Charnas, Store Manager
(602)957-8710 www.gucci.com

Ralph Lauren
*Carolyn Westerman, General
Manager*
(602)952-0155 www.polo.com

Moda Georgio Custom Clothing
Independent
*Nicholas Sr., Nicholas Jr., and
Jeff Esposito, Owners*
(800)5-SHIRTS or (602)955-2003
www.modageorgio.com
Excellent store, top-notch fabrics
and first-class, old-world service.
The Espositos are a pleasure to
work with.

Accessories Gentlemen's Closet,
Zimmerli undergarments
Casual Wear Avon Celli, In
Fiamme, Moda Georgio Casual
Line and golf shirts
Dress Shirts Burini, Fray, Marol,
Moda Georgio Custom
Neckwear Altea, Tino Cosma,
Hubert, Pancaldi, Stefano Ricci
Shoes Cole Haan, Zelli, Moda
Georgio Custom
Tailored Clothing Ready to Wear
Ravazzolo, M2M fabrics from
Dormeuil, Holland & Sherry,
Loro Piana, Scabal,
Ermenegildo Zegna

Rangoni Firenze
Drew Walsh, Store Manager
(602)667-6303
www.rangonishoes.com
Shoes Bally, Cole Haan, Johnston
& Murphy, Moreschi, Donald J.
Pliner

Saks Fifth Avenue
Cheryl Fordham, General Manager

(602)955-8000
www.saksfifthavenue.com
Casual Wear Giorgio Armani,
Prada, Ermenegildo Zegna
Dress Shirts Giorgio Armani,
Hugo Boss, Ermenegildo Zegna
Neckwear Giorgio Armani,
Hugo Boss, Ermenegildo Zegna
Tailored Clothing Giorgio
Armani, Hugo Boss, Prada,
Ermenegildo Zegna

The Clotherie
Independent
Jackson LaBaer and Greg Eveloff,
Owners
(602)956-8600
www.theclotherie.com
Founded in 1969 by practicing
attorney Jackson LaBaer, this
establishment offers a fine inventory of clothes directed primarily
toward customers interested in
European-style clothing. Over
the years it has evolved into a
total wardrobe specialty shop for
men who want a level of quality
and international sophistication
that would allow them to feel well
dressed anyplace in the world. Also
fundamental at The Clotherie is
expert tailoring and attention to
detail offered with sincere caring.

Accessories Belts, cuff links,
hosiery, and silk pocket squares
Casual Wear Alberto jeans, Axis,
Ted Baker, Barry Bricken, Canali,
Cousin Johnny, Madeline Finn,
Nat Nast, John Smedley, The
Clotherie, Zanella, Ermenegildo
Zegna
Dress Shirts Eton, Canali,
Ermenegildo Zegna (also
M2M), Individualized M2M

Neckwear Canali, The Clotherie,
Ermenegildo Zegna
Shoes Bacco Bucci, Ecco, Hush
Puppies, Mezlan, Donald J.
Pliner, Michael Toschi
Tailored Clothing Barry Bricken,
Canali, Tallia Sartoria, The
Clotherie, Zanella, Ermenegildo
Zegna (also M2M), Bernard Zins
Sales Semiannual, January and
June

Carter's Men's Wear
Independent
Mike Carter, Owner/
Dale Anthony, Sales
5045 N. 44th St., Phoenix, AZ 85018
(602)952-8646
Large store with quality inventory
of updated traditional clothing.
Amicable, responsive sales staff;
Mr. Carter and Mr. Anthony are
great to shop with.

Accessories Bow ties, some
Trafalgar braces, cuff links
Casual Wear Tommy Bahama,
Scott Barber, Bills Khakis, Hugo
Boss, Madeline Finn, Hickey
Freeman, Bobby Jones, Lacoste,
Lucky Brand, Reyn Spooner,
Robert Talbott
Dress Shirts Gitman Bros., Kenneth
Gordon
Neckwear Breuer, Ferrell Reed,
Robert Talbott
Shoes Alden, Cole Haan, Johnston
& Murphy
Tailored Clothing Corbin, Hickey
Freeman (also M2M), Samuelsohn
(also M2M), Southwick, Zanella
Sales Semiannual

Last Chance (Nordstrom Rack)
Outlet Store
1919 E. Camelback Rd., Phoenix, AZ

85016 (602)248-2843
www.nordstrom.com
Extra-low prices, but no returns.

Barry Bricken
8787 N. Scottsdale Rd., A-108,
Scottsdale, AZ 85253 (480)951-9232
www.barrybricken.com

Patrick James
Independent
Patrick Mon Pere Sr., CEO
6137 N. Scottsdale Rd., Ste. B110,
Scottsdale, AZ 85250 (480)998-8765
www.patrickjames.com
Helpful staff, excellent destination
for traditionally oriented men's
clothing.

Accessories Some Trafalgar Braces
Casual Wear Tommy Bahama,
Scott Barber, Jhane Barnes,
Haupt, Patrick James, Nat Nast,
Reyn Spooner, Tricots St. Raphael
Dress Shirts Joseph Abboud,
Kenneth Gordon, Hickey
Freeman, Robert Talbott
Neckwear Joseph Abboud, Ike
Behar, Robert Talbott, XMI,
Ermenegildo Zegna
Shoes Allen Edmonds, Cole Haan,
H.S. Trask
Tailored Clothing Joseph Abboud,
Aquascutum, Ballin, Jhane Barnes,
Barry Bricken, Corbin,
Hickey Freeman, Lords of
London, Tallia, Jack Victor,
Zanella
Sales Semiannual

KIERLAND COMMONS
Location and Stores:
15044 N. Scottsdale Rd., Scottsdale,
AZ 85254
www.kierlandcommons.com

Tommy Bahama
(480)607-3388
www.tommybahama.com

Lucky Brand Dungarees
(480)348-1208
www.luckybrandjeans.com

The Clotherie
Independent
Jackson LaBaer and Greg Eveloff,
Owners
(480)778-1775
www.theclotherie.com
Founded in 1969 by practicing
attorney Jackson LaBaer, this
establishment offers a fine inventory of clothes directed primarily
toward customers interested in
European-style clothing. Over
the years it has evolved into a
total wardrobe specialty shop for
men who want a level of quality
and international sophistication
that would allow them to feel
well dressed anyplace in the
world. Also fundamental at The
Clotherie is expert tailoring and
attention to detail offered with
sincere caring.

Accessories Belts, cuff links,
hosiery, and silk pocket squares
Casual Wear Alberto jeans, Axis,
Ted Baker, Barry Bricken,
Canali, Cousin Johnny,
Madeline Finn, Nat Nast, John
Smedley, The Clotherie, Zanella,
Ermenegildo Zegna
Dress Shirts Eton, Canali,
Ermenegildo Zegna (also
M2M), Individualized M2M
Neckwear Canali, The Clotherie,
Ermenegildo Zegna
Shoes Bacco Bucci, Ecco, Hush

Puppies, Mezlan, Donald J.
Pliner, Michael Toschi
Tailored Clothing Barry Bricken,
Canali, Tallia Sartoria, The
Clotherie, Zanella, Ermenegildo
Zegna (also M2M), Bernard
Zins
Sales Semiannual, January and
June

Nordstrom Rack
Outlet Store
16245 Scottsdale Rd., Scottsdale, AZ
85254 (480)624-2200
www.nordstrom.com

Casual Wear Joseph Abboud,
Façonnable, Hart, Schaffner &
Marx, Lucky Brand, Tricots St.
Raphael, XMI, Ermenegildo
Zegna
Dress Shirts Ike Behar, Daks,
Robert Talbott
Neckwear Jhane Barnes, Robert
Talbott, XMI
Tailored Clothing Joseph Abboud,
Joseph Abboud Black Label,
Giorgio Armani, Kenneth Cole,
Corneliani, Hickey Freeman, Pal
Zileri, Zanella, Zegna Soft,
Bernard Zins

SCOTTSDALE FASHION SQUARE
Location and Stores:
7014 E. Camelback Rd., Scottsdale,
AZ 85251 www.westcor.com

At Ease
Independent
(480)947-3800
Spacious, comfortable store,
filed with dark wood and over-
sized leather chairs.

Accessories Robert Comstock
leather outerwear; walking sticks

Casual Wear Axis, Ike Behar,
Barry Bricken, Brioni, Cutter &
Buck, Bobby Jones, Riscatto
Portofino, Reyn Spooner,
Tricots St. Raphael, Zanella
Dress Shirts Ike Behar (also
M2M)
Neckwear Tino Cosma, XMI
Tailored Clothing Aquascutum,
Tallia, Zanella
Sales January and July

BOSS Hugo Boss
(480)970-3393 www.hugoboss.com

Brooks Brothers
(480)425-1115
www.brooksbrothers.com

Coach
(480)949-1772 www.coach.com

Kenneth Cole
(480)941-1305
www.kennethcole.com

Johnston & Murphy
(480)425-7748
www.johnstonmurphy.com

Lucky Brand Dungarees
(480)425-0562
www.luckybrandjeans.com

Neiman Marcus
(480)990-2100
www.neimanmarcus.com

Casual Wear Giorgio Armani,
Jhane Barnes, Loro Piana, Polo
Ralph Lauren, Ermenegildo
Zegna
Dress Shirts Brioni, Lorenzini,
Paul Smith, Ermenegildo Zegna
Neckwear Giorgio Armani,

Hugo Boss, Salvatore Ferragamo, Hermès, Ermenegildo Zegna
Tailored Clothing Giorgio Armani, Hugo Boss, Brioni, Hickey Freeman, Oxxford, Ermenegildo Zegna

Nordstrom

(480)946-4111 www.nordstrom.com
Great men's department!

Casual Wear Joseph Abboud, Zanella, Ermenegildo Zegna
Dress Shirts Barba, Ike Behar, Façonnable, Robert Talbott, Ermenegildo Zegna
Neckwear Duchamp, ETRO, Robert Talbott, XMI Platinum, Ermenegildo Zegna
Tailored Clothing Joseph Abboud, Giorgio Armani, Hart, Schaffner & Marx, Hickey Freeman, Zanella, Ermenegildo Zegna, Pal Zileri, Bernard Zins

St. Croix Shop

(480)423-0600
www.stcroixshop.com

Louis Vuitton

(480)946-1700
www.louisvuitton.com

THE BORGATA OF SCOTTSDALE
Location and Stores:

6166 N. Scottsdale Rd., Scottsdale, AZ 85253 www.westcor.com

Jhane Barnes

Ken Hanover, Managing Partner/ Angie Kruger, Sales Manager
(480)425-7780
www.jhanebarnes.com
Good-sized store, with ample selection evenly divided between casual wear and tailored clothing.

Da Vinci Mens Wear

Independent
William Nasralla, Buyer
(480)922-3685
Impressive store with distinctive inventory of quality merchandise. Tasteful women's department also on premises.

Casual Wear Bertone, Brioni, Carlo Colucci, DaVinci, Jack Lipson
Dress Shirts Brioni, DaVinci
Neckwear Brioni, Carnival De Venise
Shoes Belvedere
Tailored Clothing Brioni, Redaelli
Sales Semiannual, January and July

ARIZONA MILLS
Location and Stores:

5000 Arizona Mills Circle, Tempe, AZ 85282 www.arizonamills.com

Kenneth Cole

Outlet Store
(480)456-8650
www.kennethcole.com

Neiman Marcus Last Call

Outlet Store
(480)831-7979
www.neimanmarcus.com

Casual Wear Barry Bricken, Brioni, Jhane Barnes, Coogi, Polo Ralph Lauren, Ralph Lauren Purple Label, Versace, Ermenegildo Zegna
Dress Shirts Giorgio Armani, Ike Behar, Hugo Boss, Brioni, Kiton, Lorenzini, Turnbull & Asser, Ermenegildo Zegna, Zegna Soft

Neckwear Luigi Borrelli, Brioni,
Ralph Lauren Purple Label,
Turnbull & Asser
Tailored Clothing Giorgio
Armani, Hugo Boss, Brioni,
Kiton, Oxxford, Jil Sander
Ermenegildo Zegna, Zegna Soft

Off Rodeo Drive
Outlet Store
(480)839-1786 www.bernini.com

Dress Shirts Brioni, Lorenzini
Tailored Clothing Hugo Boss,
Canali

Polo Jeans Company
Outlet Store
(480)755-0885 www.polo.com

Saks Off Fifth
Outlet Store
(480)838-5708
www.saksfifthavenue.com

Casual Wear Como Sport,
Iceberg, Versace
Dress Shirts Ike Behar, Hugo
Boss, Burberry, Hickey
Freeman, Hilditch & Key
Neckwear Hugo Boss, Burberry,
Salvatore Ferragamo, Gianfranco
Ferré, Hugo Boss, Ermenegildo
Zegna
Tailored Clothing Giorgio
Armani, Hugo Boss, Caruso,
Salvatore Ferragamo, Hickey
Freeman, Mani, Pal Zileri,
Vestimenta

Metro Area: Pittsburgh

Frank Cicco Custom Tailor
Independent
Frank Cicco, Owner
133 W. North St., Butler, PA 16001
(724)287-5814

Mr. Cicco has been in business 47
years in a family of tailors. He cre-
ates each garment from scratch
using paper patterns, using only
the finest fabrics; examples are
Holland & Sherry, Dormeuil,
Loro Piana, and Ermenegildo
Zegna. Mr. Cicco's trademark is a
unique silk lining for each coat he
tailors, complete with matching
tie—a true one-of-a-kind expression of personal style.

GROVE CITY PRIME OUTLETS
Location and Stores:
1911 Leesburg Rd., Grove City, PA
16127 www.primeoutlets.com

Brooks Brothers
Outlet Store
(724)748-4163
www.brooksbrothers.com

Johnston & Murphy
Outlet Store
(724)748-4002
www.johnstonmurphy.com

Polo Ralph Lauren Factory Store
Outlet Store
(724)748-5444 www.polo.com

Polo Jeans Company
Outlet Store
(724)748-3010 www.polo.com

Saks Off Fifth
Outlet Store
(724)748-5626
www.saksfifthavenue.com

Dress Shirts Ike Behar
Neckwear Giorgio Armani,
Ermenegildo Zegna
Tailored Clothing Joseph
Abboud, Hugo Boss, Mani

GALLERIA
Location and Stores:
1500 Washington Rd., Mt. Lebanon, PA 15228

Larrimor's
Independent
Tom Michael, Owner
(412)344-5727
Large, appealing spaces with great selection and helpful sales staffs. Ermenegildo Zegna store-in-store.

Accessories Robert Talbott cuff links
Casual Wear Luciano Barbera, Canali, Dolce & Gabbana, Gran Sasso, Bobby Jones, Larrimor's, Loro Piana, Ermenegildo Zegna
Dress Shirts Ike Behar, Canali, Eton, Ermenegildo Zegna
Neckwear Canali, Tino Cosma, Robert Talbott, Ermenegildo Zegna
Shoes Allen Edmonds, Salvatore Ferragamo, Moreschi, Santoni
Tailored Clothing Giorgio Armani, Canali, Hickey Freeman, Larrimor's, Oxxford, Jack Victor, Zanella, Ermenegildo Zegna
Sales Semiannual

LS Altman Haberdashery
Independent
Larry Altman, Owner
(412)344-9610
Mr. Altman was very friendly and helpful. I enjoyed visiting with him and highly recommend this store. Also an outlet store in the same mall complex.

Accessories Nancy and Risé cuff links; great selection of leather outerwear

Casual Wear Joseph Abboud, Hugo Boss, Burberry, Coogi, Henry Cotton's, Kenneth Gordon, Marzotto Lab, Missoni, Tricots St. Raphael
Dress Shirts Joseph Abboud, Hugo Boss, Kenneth Gordon, Robert Talbott (also collar and cuff selection program)
Shoes Cole Haan
Tailored Clothing Joseph Abboud, Jhane Barnes, Hugo Boss

Kountz & Rider
Independent
Frank Zimmerman, Proprietor
One Oxford Centre, Pittsburgh, PA 15219 (412)642-6600
Mr. Zimmerman was one of the more colorful and enjoyable people I encountered during my travels. I found many unique and interesting items here I didn't see anywhere else in the U.S. Kountz & Rider caters primarily to the traditional dresser.

Accessories Good selection of Carrot & Gibbs bow ties; Trafalgar Limited Edition braces; Robert Talbott leather outerwear
Casual Wear Murray Allen cashmere, Tommy Bahama, Gitman Bros., Tricots St. Raphael, Viyella shirts
Dress Shirts Gitman Bros., Kenneth Gordon, Robert Talbott (also M2M)
Neckwear Fabergé, Robert Talbott, XMI
Shoes Alden
Tailored Clothing Corbin, H. Freeman & Son (also M2M), Oliver, Tallia
Sales Semiannual

Larrimor's
Independent
Tom Michael, Owner
Location: Union Trust Building, 501
Grant St., Pittsburgh, PA 15219
(412)471-5727
Recently remodeled location.
Large, appealing space with great
selection and helpful sales staff.
Ermenegildo Zegna store-in-store.

Accessories Robert Talbott cuff
links; nice formal wear department
Casual Wear Luciano Barbera,
Canali, Dolce & Gabbana, Gran
Sasso, Bobby Jones, Larrimor's,
Loro Piana, Ermenegildo Zegna
Dress Shirts Ike Behar, Canali,
Eton, Ermenegildo Zegna
Neckwear Canali, Tino Cosma,
Robert Talbott, Ermenegildo
Zegna
Shoes Allen Edmonds, Salvatore
Ferragamo, Moreschi, Santoni
Tailored Clothing Giorgio Armani,
Canali, Hickey Freeman,
Larrimor's, Oxxford, Jack Victor,
Zanella, Ermenegildo Zegna
Sales Semiannual

London Dock
Independent
Sheldon Wolk, Owner
5842 Forbes Ave., Pittsburgh, PA
15217 (412)421-5710
Quality store with interesting inte-
rior design motif. Mr. Wolk was
great to visit with. Also a women's
section.

Casual Wear Axis, Tommy
Bahama, Robert Barakett, Bills
Khakis, Kenneth Cole, Henry
Cotton's, DKNY, Tricots
St. Raphael
Dress Shirts Joseph Abboud

Neckwear Joseph Abboud, Robert
Talbott
Tailored Clothing Joseph Abboud,
Tommy Bahama, Corbin, Mani

Joseph Orlando
Independent
Joseph Orlando, Owner
606 Liberty Ave., Pittsburgh, PA 15222
(412)765-1726
Handsome establishment, lots of
glass with polished steel fixtures.
Great customer service.

Accessories Interesting braces and
cuff links
Casual Wear Axis, Ballin, Joseph
Orlando, Raffi, Tricots St. Raphael,
Pal Zileri
Dress Shirts Klauss Bohler, Joseph
Orlando (Gitman Bros.), Robert
Talbott, Pal Zileri
Neckwear Joseph Orlando, Robert
Talbott, Pal Zileri
Shoes Cole Haan, Moreschi
Tailored Clothing Joseph Orlando
(Tallia, also M2M), Jack Victor,
Samuelsohn, Pal Zileri
Sales Semiannual, after Christmas
and Father's Day

Saks Fifth Avenue
513 Smithfield St., Pittsburgh, PA
15222 (412)263-4800
www.saksfifthavenue.com

Casual Wear Joseph Abboud,
Giorgio Armani, Jhane Barnes,
Hugo Boss, Polo Ralph Lauren
Ermenegildo Zegna
Dress Shirts Giorgio Armani, Ike
Behar, Hugo Boss, Ermenegildo
Zegna
Neckwear Giorgio Armani, Hugo
Boss, Brioni (limited),
Ermenegildo Zegna

Tailored Clothing Joseph Abboud, Giorgio Armani, Hugo Boss, Canali, Ermenegildo Zegna

Charles Spiegel for Men
Independent
Charles Spiegel, Owner
5841 Forbes Ave., Pittsburgh, PA 15217 (412)421-9311
Vestimenta store-in-store. You'll also find the latest in 7 for All Mankind, AG, Diesel, and G-Star jeans and vintage sports apparel in the Garage section, managed by Spiegel's son, Josh. Mr. Spiegel was congenial and gracious; I highly recommend this establishment.

Accessories Michael Kors and John Varvatos outerwear, La Matta leather outerwear
Casual Wear Cifonelli, Coast, Brunello Cuccinelli, Gran Sasso, Masons, Vestimenta, John Varvatos
Dress Shirts Barba, Eton, ETRO, Vestimenta
Neck Wear Villa Bolgheri, ETRO, Kolte, Vestimenta
Tailored Clothing Vestimenta, John Varvatos, Coppley Custom

Metro Area: Portland
Michael Allen's
Independent
Mike Fredrickson, Owner/
Jared Heiden, Sales
915 S.W. Ninth Ave., Portland, OR 97205 (503)221-9963
Pleasant, open downstairs location close to Pioneer Square. Black steel and medium-blond wood fixtures combine to present merchandise handsomely. Includes thoughtfully built-in steel coat

hangers in fitting rooms. Lots of colorful, unique pieces.
Accessories Trafalgar Limited Edition braces; tasteful selection of cuff links
Casual Wear Barry Bricken, Carlo Colucci, Corneliani, Tori Richards, Georg Roth, Signum, Zanella
Dress Shirts Custom
Neckwear Joseph Abboud, Tino Cosma, Kolte, Georg Roth, Santo Stefano
Shoes Allen Edmonds, Bruno Magli, Michael Toschi
Tailored Clothing Custom

Barcelino
Independent
340 S.W. Morrison St., Portland, OR 97204 (503)796-9999
www.barcelino.com
Large, tastefully decorated store. Great sales staff.

Casual Wear Barcelino
Dress Shirts Barcelino
Neckwear Barcelino, Pancaldi, Serica Elite, Versace
Tailored Clothing Barcelino, Belvest, Canali
Sales Semiannual

Estes
Independent
Tony Spear, Owner
Uptown Shopping Center, 2328 W. Burnside St., Portland, OR 97210 (503)227-0275
In business since 1952. Lots of colorful clothes; best selection of sweaters in Portland.

Accessories Remy leather outerwear
Casual Wear Ike Behar, Burma Bibas, Estes, St. Croix
Dress Shirts Ike Behar, Estes M2M

Neckwear Robert Daskal, Estes
Private Label
Tailored Clothing Burberry, Estes
M2M, Hickey Freeman

Mario's
Independent
*Mario Bisio, Proprietor/Gordon
Schwartz, Men's Store Manager/
Summer Jameson, Women's Store
Manager*
833 S.W. Broadway, Portland, OR
97205 (503)227-3477
www.marios.com
Fine Northwest family sartorial
tradition begun in 1938. Elegant,
attractive stores filled with first-quality merchandise. Excellent customer
service. Portland store brand-new
in November 2002. Also a fine
women's store at both locations.

Casual Wear Agnona, Giorgio
Armani, Tommy Bahama, Dolce &
Gabbana, Mario's Private Label,
Kiton, Loro Piana, Prada, Jil
Sander, John Smedley,
Ermenegildo Zegna
Dress Shirts Giorgio Armani, Luigi
Borrelli, Hugo Boss, Brioni,
Hamilton Shirtmakers M2M,
Kiton, Lorenzini, Mario's,
Ermenegildo Zegna
Neckwear Giorgio Armani,
Massimo Bizzocchi, Hugo Boss,
Kiton, Ermenegildo Zegna
Shoes Gravati, Prada, Tod's, To
Boot New York, Michael Toschi
Tailored Clothing Giorgio Armani,
Hugo Boss, Canali, Dolce &
Gabbana, Mario's, Kiton,
Vestimenta, Ermenegildo Zegna
Sales Semiannual

Nordstrom
701 S.W. Broadway, Portland, OR

97205 (503)224-6666
www.nordstrom.com

Dress Shirts Ike Behar
Neckwear Robert Talbott, XMI,
Ermenegildo Zegna (limited)
Tailored Clothing Hickey Freeman

Nordstrom Rack
Outlet Store
Clackamas Town Center, 11900 S.E.
82nd Ave., Portland, OR 97266
(503)652-1810 www.nordstrom.com

Philip Stewart Men's Clothing
Independent
James Maer, Owner
1202 S.W. 19th, Portland, OR 97205
(503)226-3589
A great place to find quality traditional clothing. Specializes in repeat,
made-to-measure business. Mr.
Maer was tremendous to talk with;
he'll willingly share his consider-
able knowledge of men's fashion.

Accessories Trafalgar Limited
Edition braces
Casual Wear Aquascutum,
H. Freeman & Son, Gitman Bros.,
Reyn Spooner, Philip Stewart
Dress Shirts Kenneth Gordon,
Phillip Stewart M2M
Neckwear Aquascutum, Phillip
Stewart
Tailored Clothing Aquascutum,
H. Freeman (also M2M), Oxxford
Sales Semiannual

Metro Area: Raleigh
O'Neills Fine Clothing
Independent
John O'Neill, Owner
Carr Mill Shops, 299 N. Greensboro
St., Carrboro, NC 27510 (919)967-3100

Tasteful boutique in convenient, upscale mall location. Mr. O'Neill was fun to shop with and is very informed about the retail industry. O'Neill's clothing is directed primarily toward the updated traditional dresser.

Accessories Good selection of Trafalgar belts, some bow ties and braces
Casual Wear Axis, Ike Behar, Charleston Khaki's, Majer, Nat Nast, Tricots St. Raphael
Dress Shirts Ike Behar, Kenneth Gordon, Ferrell Reed
Neckwear Robert Talbott, XMI
Shoes H.S. Trask, Zelli
Tailored Clothing Burberry, Majer, Oliver/Hartz, H. Oritsky
Sales Semiannual

Norman Stockton
Independent
Meadowmont Village, 107 Meadowmont Village Circle, Chapel Hill, NC 27517 (919)945-0800
www.normanstockton.com
In business since 1909. Great selection of first-quality lines. Pleasant atmosphere. Cordial, helpful sales staff.

Casual Wear Bills Khakis, Canali, Gitman Bros., Bobby Jones, Alexander Julian Estate, McKenzie Tribe, St. Croix, Bob Timberlake, Tricots St. Raphael, Ermenegildo Zegna
Dress Shirts Canali, Gitman Bros., Robert Talbott, Ermenegildo Zegna
Neckwear Breuer, Canali, Robert Talbott, Ermenegildo Zegna
Shoes Cole Haan, Santoni, H.S. Trask
Tailored Clothing Aquascutum, Canali, Hickey Freeman, Jack

Victor, Ermenegildo Zegna, Zegna Soft
Sales Semiannual

THE STREETS AT SOUTHPOINT
Location and Stores:
6910 Fayetteville Rd., Durham, NC 27713
www.thestreetsatsouthpoint.com

Coach
(919)572-5555 www.coach.com

Cole Haan
(919)361-3600 www.colehaan.com

Lucky Brand Dungarees
(919)806-5900
www.luckybrandjeans.com

Nordstrom
(919)806-3700 www.nordstrom.com

Casual Wear Robert Barakett, Zanella, Ermenegildo Zegna
Dress Shirts Ike Behar, Hugo Boss
Neckwear Robert Talbott, XMI, Ermenegildo Zegna
Tailored Clothing Abboud, Hart, Schaffner & Marx, Hickey Freeman

Rangoni Firenze
(919)544-4333
www.rangonifirenze.com

Shoes Cole Haan, Johnston & Murphy, Moreschi, Donald J. Pliner

Ashworth's
Independent
Steve Ashworth, Proprietor
210 S. Main St., Fuquay-Varina, NC 27526 (919)552-5501
Spacious, family-owned business established in 1937. Mr. Ashworth

was very cordial and helpful. Merchandise caters toward the updated traditional dresser.

Accessories Some bow ties and braces; Polo Ralph Lauren leather outerwear and wallets
Casual Wear Axis, Barbour, Bills Khakis, Bobby Jones, Lacoste, Polo Ralph Lauren, Robert Talbott
Dress Shirts Burberry, Gitman Bros., MacCluer, Robert Talbott (also M2M)
Neckwear Ashworth's, Burberry, Robert Talbott
Shoes Cole Haan, Florsheim, Johnston & Murphy, H.S. Trask
Tailored Clothing Berle, Brannoch, Burberry, Lauren by Ralph Lauren, Hart, Schaffner & Marx, Tallia
Sales Semiannual

Saks Off Fifth
Outlet Store
Triangle Factory Stores, 1001 Airport Blvd., Morrisville, NC 27560 (919)467-5054 www.saksfifthavenue.com

Casual Wear Joseph Abboud, Giorgio Armani, Burberry, Diesel, Bobby Jones, Versace, Ermenegildo Zegna
Dress Shirts Ike Behar, Hugo Boss
Neckwear Versace, Ermenegildo Zegna
Tailored Clothing Joseph Abboud, Giorgio Armani, Jhane Barnes, Hickey Freeman, Missoni, Polo Ralph Lauren

Chockey's
Independent
Chockey Kassem, Owner/ Chris Petersen, Sales

1641 N. Market Dr., Raleigh, NC 27609 (919)872-3166
Attractive establishment with quality items in a pleasant shopping environment. Convenient, stand-alone location. Cordial, informative customer service as well.

Casual Wear Tommy Bahama, Jhane Barnes, Canali, Giorgio Danieli, Equilbrio, Gran Sasso, Marzotto Lab, Tulliano, Pal Zileri
Dress Shirts Canali, Eton, Fabio Inghirami
Neckwear Jhane Barnes, Brioni, Pancaldi
Shoes Cole Haan, Magnanni, Mezlan
Tailored Clothing Canali, Tallia, Trussini, Zanella, Pal Zileri
Sales Semiannual

CRABTREE VALLEY MALL
Location and Stores:
4325 Glenwood Ave., Raleigh, NC 27612 www.crabtree-valley-mall.com

Brooks Brothers
(919)783-9050
www.brooksbrothers.com

Coach
(919)786-9117 www.coach.com

Johnston & Murphy
(919)781-2240
www.johnstonmurphy.com

Varsity Men's Wear
Independent
Colon Wood, Outside Sales
(919)782-2570
www.varsitymenswear. citysearch.com
Great selection of quality clothing catering to the updated

traditional dresser. Mr. Wood was very responsive and informative. Convenient location.

Accessories Some belts, braces, bow ties, leather outerwear
Casual Wear Tommy Bahama, Casa Moda, Gitman Bros., Haupt, Hickey Freeman, Bobby Jones, Alexander Julian Private Reserve, Raffi, Riscatto Portofino, St. Croix, Robert Talbott, Tricots St. Raphael, Tundra
Dress Shirts Ike Behar, Gitman Bros., Hickey Freeman, Robert Talbott collar and cuff M2M, Exclusive Custom
Neckwear Breuer, Tino Cosma, Robert Talbott, Varsity
Shoes Alden, Allen Edmonds, Cole Haan, Magnanni, H.S. Trask
Tailored Clothing Ballin, Berle, Corbin, Hickey Freeman (also M2M), Alexander Julian Estate, Samuelsohn (also M2M), Southwick, Tallia, Jack Victor
Sales Semiannual

Richard B. Hardy Custom Clothier
Independent
Richard B. Hardy, Owner
Raleigh, NC 27608, (919)836-9903
www.rbhardy.citysearch.com
Mr. Hardy is strictly a come-to-you custom clothier, resulting in highly personalized and responsive customer service. He was very informed about the retail industry and easy to talk with. Call or e-mail for an appointment.

Accessories Trafalgar belts
Dress Shirts Robert Talbott (stock size), Gambert Custom
Neckwear Dormeuil, Robert Talbott

Tailored Clothing Haas and Adrian Jules custom

Liles Clothing Studio
Independent
Bruce Liles, Owner/
Hamayoun Naimee, Tailor
7422 Creedmoor Rd., Raleigh, NC 27613 (919)870-5402
Excellent store filled with first-quality merchandise, most of which is attractively presented on wood rolling racks. Mr. Naimee spent quite a bit of time with me and was most informative about the industry and Liles's clothing lines and philosophy. I highly recommend this store.

Accessories Some formal wear, including ties by Massimo Bizzocchi, which can also be used as ascots
Casual Wear Acorn, Luciano Barbera, Robert Comstock, Kiton, Nat Nast
Dress Shirts Ike Behar, Lorenzini, Kiton
Neckwear Luciano Barbera, Massimo Bizzocchi, Kiton
Shoes Cole Haan, Martin Dingman, JB Hill western-style boots, Mezlan, Zelli
Tailored Clothing Gianluca Isaia, Kiton, Lile's, Vestimenta, Zanella
Sales Semiannual

Nowell's
Independent
435 Daniels St., Raleigh, NC 27605 (919)828-7285
Huge store with large inventory of quality items. Cheerful, informed sales staff. Equally nice women's section next door.

Accessories Good selection of braces and cuff links; formal wear section
Casual Wear Burberry, Henry Cotton's, Gitman Bros., Gran Sasso, Bobby Jones, Lacoste, Ermenegildo Zegna
Dress Shirts Hugo Boss, Brioni, Gitman Bros., Mani, Robert Talbott, Ermenegildo Zegna
Neckwear Hugo Boss, Brioni, Burberry, Polo Ralph Lauren, Robert Talbott, Ermenegildo Zegna
Shoes Allen Edmonds, Cole Haan, Johnston & Murphy
Tailored Clothing Brioni, Hickey Freeman, Marzotto, Zanella, Ermenegildo Zegna
Sales Semiannual

Kannon's
Independent
George Knuckley, Owner
10 Main St., Wendell, NC 27591
(919)365-7074
www.kannons.citysearch.com
Family-owned business begun in 1916. Pleasant store, attractive wood fixtures, lots of light. Mr. Knuckley provided excellent customer service. Women's section immediately adjacent to men's department. Well worth the short drive east from Raleigh to visit.

Accessories Trafalgar belts and braces, Colonel Littleton gentleman's accessories, Swiss Army knives
Casual Wear Axis, Tommy Bahama, Bills Khakis, Barry Bricken, Burberry, Henry Cotton's, Cypress Grove, Gitman Bros., Bobby Jones, Lacoste,

Robert Talbott, Tricots St. Raphael
Dress Shirts Gitman Bros., Robert Talbott
Neckwear Audrey Bruckner, Tino Cosma, R. Hanauer, Ferrell Reed, Kannon's, J.Z. Richards, Robert Talbott
Shoes Allen Edmonds, Cole Haan, H.S. Trask, Zelli
Tailored Clothing Ballin, Berle, Burberry, Hart Schaffner & Marx (also M2M), Majer, Samuelsohn (also M2M), Tallia, Jack Victor, Zanella
Sales Semiannual

Metro Area: Richmond

beecroft & bull
Independent
Craig and Bryan Beecroft, Proprietors
Barracks Road Shopping Center, 1037 Emmet St., Charlottesville, VA 22903
(434)979-9010
www.beecroftandbull.com
Excellent family-owned small chain of stores specializing in providing men with clothing that works over a lifetime of dressing. Great starter wardrobe packages for the young man beginning his business career.

Accessories Good selection of bow ties, braces, and cuff links
Casual Wear Tommy Bahama, Scott Barber, Luciano Barbera, beecroft & bull, Ike Behar, Bills Khakis, Gran Sasso, Lacoste, Lucky Brand, Robert Talbott, Tricots St. Raphael, Ermenegildo Zegna, Zegna Sport, Bernard Zins
Dress Shirts beecroft & bull, Canali, Robert Talbott (also

M2M), Ermenegildo Zegna
Neckwear beecroft & bull, Breuer, Tino Cosma, NH 1888, Robert Talbott, Ermenegildo Zegna
Shoes Alden, Cole Haan
Tailored Clothing Ballin, Arnold Brant, Burberry (also M2M), Canali, Corbin, Samuelsohn (also M2M), Southwick (also M2M), Jack Victor, Zanella, Zegna

Franco's
Independent
Mark Ambrogi, Manager
The Shoppes at Belgrade, 11400 West Huguenot Rd., Midlothian, VA 23113 (804)378-5220
www.francos.com *(see chapter 9)*
A truly extraordinary family-owned business that prides itself on inventory and tailoring. Attentive, extremely responsive customer service.

Accessories Good selection of braces and bow ties; great selection of cuff links
Casual Wear Joseph Abboud, Axis, Tommy Bahama, Barbour, Bills Khakis, Hugo Boss, Brioni, Burberry, Gitman Bros., Bobby Jones, Lacoste, St. Croix Knits, Tricots St. Raphael, Tundra, Victorinox, Windsor Lake, Ermenegildo Zegna
Dress Shirts Ike Behar, Brioni, Burberry, Canali, Hickey Freeman, Robert Talbott, Ermenegildo Zegna (some custom orders available on some brands)
Neckwear Villa Bolgheri, Breuer, Brioni, Carrot & Gibbs, Tino Cosma, Fabergé, Vitaliano Pancaldi, Stefano Ricci, Robert Talbott, Ermenegildo Zegna
Shoes Allen Edmonds, Tommy

Bahama, Borgioli, Cole Haan, Gravati, Moreschi, Santoni (some custom orders available on some brands)
Tailored Clothing Joseph Abboud, Brioni (also M2M), Arnold Brant, Hugo Boss, Burberry, Canali, Hart, Shaffner & Marx, Hickey Freeman (also M2M), Oxxford (also M2M), Zanella

J. Altis Ltd.
Independent
James Altis, Owner
Stony Point Shopping Center, 3072 Stony Point Rd., Richmond, VA 23235 (804)272-7731
Very nice store. Quality lines of updated traditional merchandise. Mr. Altis was great to shop with.

Accessories Good selection of bow ties, Trafalgar braces, and Newport Harbor outerwear
Casual Wear Ike Behar, Berle, Forte Cashmere, Gitman Bros., Bobby Jones, Raffi, Jeff Rose, St. Croix, Tricots St. Raphael, Tundra
Dress Shirts Ike Behar (also custom stock program), Gambert (M2M), Gitman Bros (also M2M)
Neckwear Robert Talbott, XMI
Shoes Cole Haan
Tailored Clothing Ballin, Corbin, Jack Victor

beecroft & bull
Independent
Craig and Bryan Beecroft, Proprietors
Shockoe Slip, 1213 E. Cary St., Richmond, VA 23219 (804)783-0633
www.beecroftandbull.com
Excellent family-owned small chain of stores specializing in providing

men with clothing that works over a lifetime of dressing. Great starter wardrobe packages for the young man beginning his business career. This particular store is located in a historic downtown section of Richmond in an attractive wood-lined space filled with quality merchandise you don't want to miss.

Accessories Good selection of bow ties, braces, and cuff links.
Casual Wear Tommy Bahama, Scott Barber, Luciano Barbera, beecroft & bull, Ike Behar, Bills Khakis, Gran Sasso, Lacoste, Lucky Brand, Robert Talbott, Tricots St. Raphael, Ermenegildo Zegna, Zegna Sport, Bernard Zins
Dress Shirts beecroft & bull, Canali, Robert Talbott (also M2M), Ermenegildo Zegna
Neckwear beecroft & bull, Breuer, Tino Cosma, NH 1888, Robert Talbott, Ermenegildo Zegna
Shoes Alden, Cole Haan
Tailored Clothing Ballin, Arnold Brant, Burberry (also M2M), Canali, Corbin, Samuelsohn (also M2M), Southwick (also M2M), Jack Victor, Zanella, Zegna

Franco's
Independent
Paul Thomas, Sales/Ron Rider, Shoes/Franco Ambrogi, Owner
5321 Lakeside Ave., Richmond, VA 23228 (804)264-2994
www.francos.com *(see chapter 9)*
A truly extraordinary family-owned business that prides itself on inventory and tailoring. Franco's inventory is as large as many men's department stores I've seen. Attentive, extremely responsive customer service. Also a large

women's store directly across the hall in the same complex.

Accessories Good selection of braces and bow ties, great selection of cuff links, nice formal wear section, and excellent selection of colorful pocket squares; Borsalino hats, Robert Comstock and Remy leather outerwear, excellent selection of extra-long ties
Casual Wear Joseph Abboud, Axis, Tommy Bahama, Barbour, Bills Khakis, Hugo Boss, Brioni, Burberry, Gitman Bros., Bobby Jones, Lacoste, St. Croix Knits, Tricots St. Raphael, Tundra, Victorinox, Windsor Lake, Ermenegildo Zegna
Dress Shirts Ike Behar, Brioni, Burberry, Canali, Hickey Freeman, Robert Talbott, Ermenegildo Zegna (some custom orders available on some brands)
Neckwear Villa Bolgheri, Breuer, Brioni, Carrot & Gibbs, Tino Cosma, Fabergé, Vitaliano Pancaldi, Stefano Ricci, Robert Talbott, Ermenegildo Zegna
Shoes Allen Edmonds, Tommy Bahama, Borgioli, Cole Haan, Gravati, Moreschi, Santoni (some custom orders available on some brands)
Tailored Clothing Joseph Abboud, Brioni (also M2M), Arnold Brant, Hugo Boss, Burberry, Canali, Hart, Shaffner & Marx, Hickey Freeman (also M2M), Oxxford (also M2M), Zanella

Franco's
Independent
Mark Ambrogi, Manager
Short Pump Crossings, 11527 West Broad St., Richmond, VA 23233

(804)360-9260 www.francos.com *(see chapter 9)*
A truly extraordinary family-owned business that prides itself on inventory and tailoring. Attentive, extremely responsive customer service.

Accessories Good selection of braces and bow ties; great selection of cuff links
Casual Wear Joseph Abboud, Axis, Tommy Bahama, Barbour, Bills Khakis, Hugo Boss, Brioni, Burberry, Gitman Bros., Bobby Jones, Lacoste, St. Croix Knits, Tricots St. Raphael, Tundra, Victorinox, Windsor Lake, Ermenegildo Zegna
Dress Shirts Ike Behar, Brioni, Burberry, Canali, Hickey Freeman, Robert Talbott, Ermenegildo Zegna (some custom orders available on some brands)
Neckwear Villa Bolgheri, Breuer, Brioni, Carrot & Gibbs, Tino Cosma, Fabergé, Vitaliano Pancaldi, Stefano Ricci, Robert Talbott, Ermenegildo Zegna
Shoes Allen Edmonds, Tommy Bahama, Borgioli, Cole Haan, Gravati, Moreschi, Santoni (some custom orders available on some brands)
Tailored Clothing Joseph Abboud, Brioni (also M2M), Arnold Brant, Hugo Boss, Burberry, Canali, Hart, Shaffner & Marx, Hickey Freeman (also M2M), Oxxford (also M2M), Zanella

D. M. Williams
Independent
1211 E. Cary St., Richmond, VA 23219 (804)783-9211

In historic section of downtown Richmond. Sales staff attentive and cordial. Women's department also.

Accessories Trafalgar Limited Edition braces; Ghurka leather goods; good selection of ISDA & Co. and DS Williams leather outerwear
Casual Wear Axis, Jhane Barnes, Barry Bricken, Ferrell Reed, Bob Timberlake, Tundra
Dress Shirts Joseph Abboud, Ferrell Reed, Kenneth Gordon, MacCluer
Neckwear Joseph Abboud, Ferrell Reed, XMI
Shoes Cole Haan, H.S. Trask
Tailored Clothing Joseph Abboud, Jhane Barnes, Tallia

Metro Area: Salt Lake City

Nordstrom
Fashion Place, 6191 South State, Murray, UT 84107 (801)261-4402
www.nordstrom.com

Nordstrom
University Mall, 693 East University Pkwy., Orem, UT 84097 (801)426-2800
www.nordstrom.com

Nordstrom
50 South Main Street, Salt Lake City, UT 84144 (801)322-4200
www.nordstrom.com

Nordstrom Rack
Outlet Store
Sugarhouse, 2236 South 1300 East, Ste. D-1, Salt Lake City, UT 84106 (801)484-8880 www.nordstrom.com

Utah Woolen Mills
Independent
Briant, Bart, and B. J. Stringham,
Proprietors
59 W. South Temple, Salt Lake City,
UT 84101 (801)364-1851
Utah Woolen Mills is now in its
fifth generation of a distinctive
family tradition. Featuring the
finest the world has to offer in
clothing and accessories, Utah
Woolen Mills boasts over 97 years
of outstanding knowledge and
service to ensure the most appropriate look for any occasion. They
are large enough to serve your every
need and small enough to care.

Accessories Allen Edmonds, Byford,
Crookhorn; Trafalgar braces (includ-
ing Limited Edition); cuff links
Casual Wear Scott Barber, Geiger,
Nat Nast, Pendleton, St. Croix,
Robert Talbott, Tundra, Viyella
Dress Shirts Hickey Freeman,
Robert Talbott, Utah Woolen
Mills custom shirts
Neckwear Huge selection of
Brioni, Italo Ferretti, Robert
Talbott
Tailored Clothing Baumler, Brioni,
Hickey Freeman, Oxxford,
Ravazzolo, Samuelsohn, Vila di
Roma
Sales By customer invitation only

Metro Area: San Antonio

Satel's
Independent
James Satel, Owner/Bob Vielock,
General Manager
5100 Broadway, San Antonio, TX
78209 (210)822-3376

Both Satel's are fun to visit, with
great selections of quality items.
First-rate customer service.
Accessories Trafalgar braces; some
cuff links; formal wear dept.;
Colonel Littleton gentleman's
accessories; walking sticks
Casual Wear Axis, Tommy
Bahama, Ike Behar, Hugo Boss,
Casa Moda, Kenneth Gordon,
Gillio, Lacoste, Polo Ralph
Lauren, Jeff Rose, Tricots
St. Raphael, Viyella, Zanella
Dress Shirts Ike Behar, Gitman
Bros., Kenneth Gordon, Hickey
Freeman, custom
Neckwear Ike Behar, Breuer, Tino
Cosma, Salvatore Ferragamo,
Hickey Freeman, Ferrell Reed,
Robert Talbott
Shoes Alden, Cole Haan, H.S.
Trask
Tailored Clothing Hugo Boss,
Barry Bricken, Coppley (also
M2M), Corneliani, Hickey
Freeman (also M2M), Oxxford
(also M2M), Tallia (also M2M),
Zanella

NORTH STAR MALL
Location and Stores:
7400 San Pedro, San Antonio, TX
78216 www.northstarmall.com

Coach
(210)348-7010 www.coach.com

Johnston & Murphy
(210)349-3504
www.johnstonmurphy.com

Joseph's
Independent
Ralph Nelson, Assistant
Manager

(210)344-9285
Large, well-stocked store. Mr.
Nelson was courteous and helpful.

Accessories Bow ties, cuff links
Casual Wear Axis, Tommy
Bahama, Jhane Barnes, Hugo
Boss, Burberry
Dress Shirts Hugo Boss,
Burberry, Kenneth Cole, custom
private label
Neckwear Jhane Barnes, Hugo
Boss, Burberry, yAprè
Shoes Kenneth Cole, Johnston &
Murphy, Mezlan, H.S. Trask
Tailored Clothing Jhane Barnes,
Hugo Boss, Burberry, Jack
Victor

Saks Fifth Avenue
D. Scott Looney, Men's Clothing
(210)341-4111
www.saksfifthavenue.com
Separate men's store is one of the
better Saks men's departments I've
seen. In-store boutiques include
Armani, Jhane Barnes, Brioni,
Canali, Corneliani, Versace, and
Zegna. Mr. Looney was very pleasant and a pleasure to shop with.

Casual Wear Giorgio Armani,
Brioni, Henry Cotton's,
Versace, Ermenegildo Zegna
Dress Shirts Giorgio Armani,
Brioni, Lorenzini, Ermenegildo
Zegna
Neckwear Giorgio Armani,
Brioni, Canali, Versace,
Ermenegildo Zegna
Tailored Clothing Giorgio
Armani, Brioni, Canali,
Corneliani, Versace,
Ermenegildo Zegna

Todd's Haute Couture
Independent

*Frederique Calluaud, Marketing
Manager*
(210)349-6464
Excellent establishment in prime
location. Hermès in-store boutique—rare for an independent
store. Excellent customer service.

Casual Wear Giorgio Armani,
Luciano Barbera, Hugo Boss,
Salvatore Ferragamo, Hermès,
Loro Piana, Tassio, Versace
Dress Shirts Giorgio Armani
(also M2M), Canali, Charvet,
Hermès (also M2M), Tassio
(also M2M), Ermenegildo
Zegna (also M2M)
Neckwear Altea, Charvet,
Hermès, Ermenegildo Zegna
Tailored Clothing Giorgio Armani,
Brioni, Canali, Kiton, Tassio,
Versace, Ermenegildo Zegna

Satel's
Independent
*James Satel, Owner/Bob Vielock,
General Manager*
The Colonnade, 9801 IH 10 West, San
Antonio, TX 78230 (210)694-0944
Both Satel's are fun to visit, with
great selections of quality items.
First-rate customer service. Large
big and tall men's section at this
location

Accessories Trafalgar braces; some
cuff links; formal wear dept.;
Colonel Littleton gentleman's
accessories; walking sticks
Casual Wear Axis, Tommy
Bahama, Ike Behar, Hugo Boss,
Casa Moda, Kenneth Gordon,
Gillio, Lacoste, Polo Ralph Lauren,
Jeff Rose, Tricots St. Raphael,
Viyella, Zanella
Dress Shirts Ike Behar, Gitman

Bros., Kenneth Gordon, Hickey
Freeman, custom
Neckwear Ike Behar, Breuer, Tino
Cosma, Salvatore Ferragamo,
Hickey Freeman, Ferrell Reed,
Robert Talbott
Shoes Alden, Cole Haan, H.S. Trask
Tailored Clothing Hugo Boss,
Barry Bricken, Coppley (also
M2M), Corneliani, Hickey
Freeman (also M2M), Oxxford
(also M2M), Tallia (also M2M),
Zanella

Metro Area: San Diego

Patrick James
Independent
Patrick Mon Pere Sr., CEO
2650 Via De La Valle, Suite C240, Del
Mar, CA 92014 (858)794-0806
www.patrickjames.com
Helpful staff, excellent destination
for traditionally oriented men's
clothing.

Accessories Some Trafalgar braces
Casual Wear Tommy Bahama,
Scott Barber, Jhane Barnes,
Haupt, Patrick James, Nat Nast,
Reyn Spooner, Tricots St. Raphael
Dress Shirts Joseph Abboud,
Kenneth Gordon, Hickey
Freeman, Robert Talbott
Neckwear Joseph Abboud, Ike
Behar, Robert Talbott, XMI,
Ermenegildo Zegna
Shoes Allen Edmonds, Cole Haan,
H.S. Trask
Tailored Clothing Joseph Abboud,
Aquascutum, Ballin, Jhane Barnes,
Barry Bricken, Corbin, Hickey
Freeman, Lords of London, Tallia,
Jack Victor, Zanella
Sales Semiannual

A/X Armani Exchange
7802 Girard Ave., La Jolla, CA 92037
(858)551-8193
www.giorgioarmani.com

Gentlemen's Quarter
Independent
Romy Eichler, General Manager
1200 Prospect St., La Jolla, CA 92037
(858)459-3351
Aesthetically appealing store with
extremely well presented first-quality merchandise. Great customer
service. Also a fine women's section.

Accessories Ermenegildo Zegna,
Armani Collezioni, Canali, Rizal,
and Robert Comstock outerwear;
Tateossian cuff links
Casual Wear Ermenegildo Zegna,
Zegna Sport, Armani Collezioni,
Canali, Brunello Cuccinelli, Gran
Sasso, Ted Baker, Arnold Zimberg,
Zanella, Per Lui Per Lei, Elements,
Incotex
Dress Shirts Luigi Borrelli,
Lorenzini, Ermenegildo Zegna,
Giorgio Armani
Neckwear Ermenegildo Zegna,
Armani Collezioni, Michele Sartori
Shoes Cole Haan, Zegna Sport
Tailored Clothing Armani
Collezioni, Ermenegildo Zegna,
Canali, Incotex

Ralph Lauren
7830 Girard Ave., La Jolla, CA 92037
(858)459-0554 www.polo.com

Saks Fifth Avenue
1055 Wall St., La Jolla, CA 92037
(858)551-6100
www.saksfifthavenue.com

Casual Wear Joseph Abboud,
Giorgio Armani, Jhane Barnes,

Ermenegildo Zegna
Dress Shirts Joseph Abboud,
Giorgio Armani, Hugo Boss
Neckwear Giorgio Armani,
Ermenegildo Zegna
Tailored Clothing Joseph Abboud,
Giorgio Armani, Hugo Boss,
Ermenegildo Zegna

FASHION VALLEY MALL
Location and Stores:
7007 Friars Rd., San Diego, CA 92108
www.shopfashionvalley.com

Brady's
Independent
(619)296-8898
Brady's largest store with best
selection. Great assortment of
both dress and casual pieces.

Casual Wear Jhane Barnes, Gran
Sasso, Haupt, Nat Nast, Georg
Roth, Ermenegildo Zegna
Dress Shirts Brady's, Canali,
Eton, Ermenegildo Zegna
Neckwear Canali, Tino Cosma,
Pancaldi, Ermenegildo Zegna
Tailored Clothing Jhane Barnes,
Hugo Boss, Canali,
Ermenegildo Zegna
Sales Semiannual, January and
July

Brooks Brothers
(619)692-9607
www.brooksbrothers.com

Neiman Marcus
(619)692-9100
www.neiman.marcus.com
Casual Wear Giorgio Armani,
Burberry, Hugo Boss, Polo
Ralph Lauren, Ermenegildo
Zegna, Zegna Sport

Dress Shirts Ike Behar, Hugo
Boss, Brioni, Kiton,
Ermenegildo Zegna, Zegna Soft
Neckwear Giorgio Armani,
Brioni, Charvet, Salvatore
Ferragamo, Hermès,
Ermenegildo Zegna
Tailored Clothing Giorgio
Armani, Hugo Boss, Brioni,
Incotex, Oxxford, Polo Ralph
Lauren, Ermenegildo Zegna,
Zegna Soft

Nordstrom
(619)295-4441 www.nordstrom.com

Casual Wear Jhane Barnes,
Riscatto Portofino, Tricots St.
Raphael, Ermenegildo Zegna
Dress Shirts Ike Behar, Robert
Talbott
Neckwear Robert Talbott, XMI,
Ermenegildo Zegna
Tailored Clothing Joseph Abboud,
Hugo Boss, Hickey Freeman

Saks Fifth Avenue
(619)260-0030
www.saksfifthavenue.com
Great sportswear section.
Giorgio Armani, Hugo Boss,
Canali, and Ermenegildo Zegna
in-store boutiques.

Casual Wear Giorgio Armani,
Hugo Boss, Theory, Versace,
Ermenegildo Zegna, Zegna
Sport
Dress Shirts Giorgio Armani,
Hugo Boss, Ermenegildo Zegna
Neckwear Giorgio Armani,
Brioni, Hugo Boss,
Ermenegildo Zegna
Tailored Clothing Giorgio
Armani, Hugo Boss, Canali,
Corneliani, Ermenegildo Zegna

HORTON PLAZA
Location and Stores:
324 Horton Plaza, San Diego, CA
92101 www.westfield.com

Johnston & Murphy
(619)236-1714
www.johnstonmurphy.com

Nordstrom
(619)239-1700 www.nordstrom.com

Louis Vuitton
(619)237-1882
www.louisvuitton.com

Nordstrom Rack
Outlet Store
1640 Camino Del Rio North, Ste. 1310,
San Diego, CA 92108 (619)296-0143
www.nordstrom.com
Excellent tailored clothing selection the day I visited.

Casual Wear Jhane Barnes, Tricots St. Raphael
Dress Shirts Ike Behar, Robert Talbott
Neckwear ETRO, Duchamp, Ermenegildo Zegna
Tailored Clothing Joseph Abboud, Jhane Barnes, Kenneth Cole, Façonnable, Zanella, Ermenegildo Zegna, Pal Zileri

Saks Off Fifth
Outlet Store
Park in the Valley, 1750 Camino De La Reina, San Diego, CA 92108
(619)296-4896
www.saksfifthavenue.com
Excellent selection the day I visited. Many items I didn't see at any other Off Fifth stores.

Casual Wear Joseph Abboud,

Agnona, Giorgio Armani, Hugo Boss, Roberto Cavalli, Como Sport, Ralph Lauren Purple Label, Vestimenta, Ermenegildo Zegna
Dress Shirts Ermenegildo Zegna
Neckwear Hugo Boss, Salvatore Ferragamo, Gucci, Ermenegildo Zegna
Tailored Clothing Giorgio Armani, Hugo Boss, Burberry, Hickey Freeman, Versace, Ermenegildo Zegna, Pal Zileri

UNIVERSITY TOWN CENTRE
Location and Stores:
4321 La Jolla Village Dr., San Diego, CA 92122 www.westfield.com

Nordstrom
(858)457-4575 www.nordstrom.com

Casual Wear Riscatto Portofino
Dress Shirts Hugo Boss
Neckwear Robert Talbott, XMI, Ermenegildo Zegna
Tailored Clothing Joseph Abboud, Hickey Freeman, Pal Zileri

Steeplechase
Independent
(858)909-0905
Pleasant store with good inventory of traditional merchandise. Nice selection of Hawaiian shirts.

Casual Wear Burberry, Gitman Bros, Polo Ralph Lauren, Toscano, Tricots St. Raphael
Dress Shirts Hugo Boss, Burberry, Gitman Bros., Kenneth Gordon
Neckwear Burberry, Ferrell Reed City of London, Polo Ralph Lauren

Shoes Allen Edmonds
Tailored Clothing Aquascutum,
Jhane Barnes, Hugo Boss,
Hickey Freeman, Polo Ralph
Lauren
Sales Semiannual, January and
July

Metro Area: San Francisco

Malouf's
Independent
1426 Burlingame Ave., Burlingame,
CA 94010 (650)347-2191
www.maloufs.com
Attractive storefront in choice
location. Great customer service.

Accessories David Yurman jewelry,
Zimmerli undergarments
Casual Wear Tommy Bahama,
Bills Khakis, Bobby Jones, Lacoste,
Loro Piana, Polo Ralph Lauren,
Zanella, Ermenegildo Zegna,
Zegna Sport
Dress Shirts Ike Behar, Luigi
Borrelli, Brioni, Canali, Robert
Talbott, Ermenegildo Zegna
Neckwear Brioni, Charvet, Charles
Hill, Robert Talbott, Ermenegildo
Zegna
Shoes Allen Edmonds, Star Artioli,
Cole Haan, Salvatore Ferragamo,
Gravati, Edward Green, Mephisto,
Michael Toschi, Zegna Sport
Tailored Clothing Brioni, Hickey
Freeman, Incotex, Oxxford,
Ermenegildo Zegna, Zanella

Nordstrom Rack
Outlet Store
81 Colma Blvd., Colma, CA 94014
(650)755-1444
www.nordstrom.com

Casual Wear Jhane Barnes, Tricots
St. Raphael
Dress Shirts Ike Behar, Robert
Talbott
Neckwear Robert Talbott, XMI
Platinum, Ermenegildo Zegna
Tailored Clothing Joseph Abboud,
Jhane Barnes, Hugo Boss,
Corneliani, Bernard Zins

THE VILLAGE AT CORTE MADERA
Location and Stores:
1618 Redwood Dr., Corte Madera, CA
94925
www.villageatcortemadera.com

Coach
(415)924-5046 www.coach.com

Lucky Brand Dungarees
(415)927-4102
www.luckyjeans.com

Nordstrom
(415)927-1690 www.nordstrom.com
Casual Wear Tommy Bahama,
Ermenegildo Zegna
Dress Shirts Ike Behar, Robert
Talbott, Ermenegildo Zegna
Neckwear Robert Talbott, XMI,
Ermenegildo Zegna
Tailored Clothing Tallia,
Ermenegildo Zegna (also
M2M), Pal Zileri

Patrick James
Independent
Patrick Mon Pere Sr., CEO
3494 Blackhawk Plaza Circle,
Danville, CA 94506 (925)736-0787
www.patrickjames.com
Helpful staff, excellent destination
for traditionally oriented men's
clothing.

Accessories Some Trafalgar braces
Casual Wear Tommy Bahama,
Scott Barber, Jhane Barnes,
Haupt, Patrick James, Nat Nast,
Reyn Spooner, Tricots St. Raphael
Dress Shirts Joseph Abboud,
Kenneth Gordon, Hickey Freeman,
Robert Talbott
Neckwear Joseph Abboud, Ike
Behar, Talbott, XMI, Ermenegildo
Zegna
Shoes Allen Edmonds, Cole Haan,
H.S. Trask
Tailored Clothing Joseph Abboud,
Aquascutum, Ballin, Jhane Barnes,
Barry Bricken, Corbin, Hickey
Freeman, Lords of London, Tallia,
Jack Victor, Zanella
Sales Semiannual

Foley and Bonny
Independent
Dan Turley, Manager
El Cerrito Plaza, 400 El Cerrito Plaza,
El Cerrito, CA 94530 (800)510-7848 or
(510)524-5215
Brand-new store filled with quality
merchandise, mixed nicely between
the updated traditional and European-style dresser. Prompt personable customer service.

Accessories Torino belts, Newport
Harbor outerwear, Remy leather
outerwear
Casual Wear Tommy Bahama,
Gran Sasso, Haupt, St. Croix
Dress Shirts Klauss Bohler, Robert
Talbott
Neckwear Kolte, Robert Talbott
Tailored Clothing Baumler, Hickey
Freeman, Jack Victor
Sales Annual

Patrick James
Independent

Patrick Mon Pere Sr., CEO
306 Strawberry Village, Mill Valley,
CA 94961 (415)383-2174
www.patrickjames.com
Helpful staff, excellent destination
for traditionally oriented men's
clothing.

Accessories Some Trafalgar Braces
Casual Wear Tommy Bahama,
Scott Barber, Jhane Barnes,
Haupt, Patrick James, Nat Nast,
Reyn Spooner, Tricots St. Raphael
Dress Shirts Joseph Abboud,
Kenneth Gordon, Hickey
Freeman, Robert Talbott
Neckwear Joseph Abboud, Ike
Behar, Talbott, XMI, Ermenegildo
Zegna
Shoes Allen Edmonds, Cole Haan,
H.S. Trask
Tailored Clothing Joseph Abboud,
Aquascutum, Ballin, Jhane Barnes,
Barry Bricken, Corbin,
Hickey Freeman, Lords of
London, Tallia, Jack Victor,
Zanella
Sales Semiannual

GREAT MALL OF THE BAY AREA
Location and Stores:
447 Great Mall Dr., Milpitas, CA 92821
www.greatmallbayarea.com

Bossini
Outlet Store
Abdullah Mojadidi, Proprietor
(408)263-9260
Tasteful store with some unusual
and distinctive pieces.

Accessories Some cuff links, interesting selection of leather outerwear
Casual Wear Tino Cosma,
Gianfranco Ferré, Gorena

Neckwear Leonard, Versace
Shoes Magnanni, Versace
Tailored Clothing d'Avenza,
Versace

Donna Karan
Outlet Store
(408)935-8036
www.donnakaran.com

Polo Jeans Company
Outlet Store
(408)945-9772 www.polo.com

Saks Off Fifth
Outlet Store
(408)945-9650
www.saksfifthavenue.com
Largest men's department wtih
great selection.

Casual Wear Giorgio Armani,
Caruso, Polo Ralph Lauren,
Missoni, Moreno Martini Da
Firenze
Dress Shirts Hugo Boss,
Burberry, Ermenegildo Zegna
Neckwear Giorgio Armani,
Burberry, Gucci, Salvatore
Ferragamo, Ermenegildo Zegna
Tailored Clothing Giorgio
Armani, Canali, Corneliani,
Ermenegildo Zegna

Bossini
Independent
Abdullah Mojadidi, Proprietor
NewPark Mall, 2086 NewPark Mall,
Newark, CA 94560 (510)791-0999
Tasteful store with some unusual
and distinctive pieces.

Accessories Some cuff links; interest-
ing selection of leather outerwear
Casual Wear Tino Cosma,
Gianfranco Ferré, Gorena

Neckwear Leonard, Versace
Shoes Magnanni, Versace
Tailored Clothing d'Avenza,
Versace

Patrick James
Independent
Patrick Mon Pere Sr., CEO
20 Town & Country Village, Palo Alto,
CA 94301 (650)328-3701
www.patrickjames.com
Helpful staff, excellent destination
for traditionally oriented men's
clothing.

Accessories Some Trafalgar braces
Casual Wear Tommy Bahama,
Scott Barber, Jhane Barnes,
Haupt, Patrick James, Nat Nast,
Reyn Spooner, Tricots St. Raphael
Dress Shirts Joseph Abboud,
Kenneth Gordon, Hickey
Freeman, Robert Talbott
Neckwear Joseph Abboud, Ike
Behar, Talbott, XMI, Ermenegildo
Zegna
Shoes Allen Edmonds, Cole Haan,
H.S. Trask
Tailored Clothing Joseph Abboud,
Aquascutum, Ballin, Jhane Barnes,
Barry Bricken, Corbin,
Hickey Freeman, Lords of
London, Tallia, Jack Victor,
Zanella
Sales Semiannual

STANFORD SHOPPING CENTER
Location and Stores:
680 Stanford Shopping Center, Palo
Alto, CA 94304
www.stanfordshop.com

A/X Armani Exchange
(650)325-7583
www.giorgioarmani.com

Arthur Beren Shoes
Independent
(800)487-0078 or (650)325-5833
www.berenshoes.com
Carries a GREAT assortment of top-quality shoes.

Shoes Joseph Abboud, Hugo Boss Black Label, Cole Haan, Salvatore Ferragamo, Johnston & Murphy, Bruno Magli, Mephisto, Moreschi, Paraboot, Terra Plana, Prada, Michael Toschi, John Varvatos
Sales June/December—previous season, 30% markdown; July/August—warehouse-type sale, 50% markdown

Barcelino
Independent
(650)326-9170 www.barcelino.com
One of Barcelino's largest in square footage. Great selection of quality merchandise.

Casual Wear Barcelino, Haupt
Dress Shirts Barcelino (Cellini/Belvest), Canali
Neckwear Barcelino (Sattori), Brioni, Pancaldi, Sazzari
Shoes Barcelino
Tailored Clothing Barcelino, Belvest, Canali, Ravazzolo
Sales Semiannual

Wilkes Bashford
Independent
Wilkes Bashford, Owner
(650)322-7080
www.wilkesbashford.com
Bashford's newest store. Sleek, with burnished steel fixtures and blond wood. Lots of full-length windows to let in light and visually expand the space.

Casual Wear Luciano Barbera, Loro Piana, Ermenegildo Zegna
Dress Shirts Luigi Borrelli, Brioni, Kiton
Neckwear Wilkes Bashford, Luigi Borrelli, Kiton, Ermenegildo Zegna
Shoes Santoni, a. testoni, Heschung
Tailored Clothing Brioni, Kiton, Oxxford
Sales Semiannual

Brooks Brothers
(650)462-0936
www.brooksbrothers.com

Kenneth Cole
(650)853-8365 www.kennethcole.com

Johnston & Murphy
(650)328-5787
www.johnstonmurphy.com

L'Uomo
Independent
Sandeep Jaiswal, Proprietor
(650)321-2593
Excellent establishment with great sales help. I've picked up many great values here over the years. The buyer for this chain of independent stores is very good at selecting tasteful and distinctive items each season to add to one's wardrobe.

Casual Wear Avon Celli, Luciano Barbera, Brioni, Salvatore Ferragamo, Gran Sasso, Verri, Ermenegildo Zegna, Pal Zileri
Dress Shirts Luigi Borrelli, Brioni, Ermenegildo Zegna,
Neckwear Brioni, Tino Cosma, L'Uomo, Ermenegildo Zegna, Pal Zileri Sartoriale

Shoes Gravati
Tailored Clothing Brioni,
Thierry Mugler, Pal Zileri
(including Sartoriale line)

Neiman Marcus
(650)329-3300
www.neimanmarcus.com

Casual Wear Brioni, Ralph
Lauren Purple Label, Loro
Piana, Ermenegildo Zegna
Dress Shirts Ike Behar, Brioni,
Lorenzini, Ermenegildo Zegna
Neckwear Brioni, Charvet,
Salvatore Ferragamo, Kiton,
Versace, Ermenegildo Zegna
Tailored Clothing Giorgio
Armani, Brioni, Incotex,
Ermenegildo Zegna

Nordstrom
(650)323-5111 www.nordstrom.com

Casual Wear Ermenegildo
Zegna
Dress Shirts Ike Behar,
Ermenegildo Zegna
Neckwear Robert Talbott, XMI,
Ermenegildo Zegna
Tailored Clothing Hickey
Freeman, Boss

Ralph Lauren
(650)326-1710 www.polo.com
One of Polo's largest and most
impressive retail spaces.

St. Croix
(650)473-1229
www.stcroixshop.com

**PETALUMA VILLAGE
PREMIUM OUTLETS
Location and Stores:**
2200 Petaluma Blvd. North, Petaluma,
CA 94952 www.premiumoutlets.com

Brooks Brothers
Outlet Store
(707)766-8144
www.brooksbrothers.com

Coach
Outlet Store
(707)763-7201 www.coach.com

Saks Off Fifth
Outlet Store
(707)778-6011
www.saksfifthavenue.com

Casual Wear Burberry, Robert
Talbott, Zanella, Ermenegildo
Zegna
Dress Shirts Hugo Boss,
Burberry, Lorenzini,
Ermenegildo Zegna
Neck Wear Giorgio Armani,
Hugo Boss, Gianfranco Ferré
Tailored Clothing Giorgio
Armani, Baldessarini, Hugo
Boss, Hickey Freeman, Mani,
Zanella Ermenegildo Zegna

A/X Armani Exchange
2090 Union St., San Francisco, CA
94123 (415)749-0891
www.giorgioarmani.com

Emporio Armani
1 Grant Ave., San Francisco, CA
94108 (415)677-9400
www.giorgioarmani.com

Giorgio Armani
278 Post St., San Francisco, CA 94108
(415)434-2500
www.giorgioarmani.com

Arthur Beren Shoes
Independent
222 Stockton St., San Francisco, CA
94108 (800)899-2626 or (415)397-8900
www.berenshoes.com
Carries a GREAT assortment of

top-quality shoes.

Shoes Joseph Abboud, Hugo Boss Black Label, Cole Haan, Salvatore Ferragamo, Johnston & Murphy, Bruno Magli, Mephisto, Moreschi, Paraboot, Prada, Terra Plana, Michael Toschi, John Varvatos
Sales June/December—previous season, 30% markdown; July/August—warehouse-type sale, 50% markdown

Barcelino
Independent
Reggie Myrick, Store Manager
498 Post St., San Francisco, CA 94102
(415)781-5777 www.barcelino.com
Casual Wear Barcelino, Haupt
Dress Shirts Barcelino (Cellini/ Belvest), Canali
Neckwear Barcelino (Sattori), Brioni, Pancaldi, Sazzari
Shoes Barcelino
Tailored Clothing Barcelino, Belvest, Canali, Ravazzolo
Sales Semiannual

Wilkes Bashford
Independent
Wilkes Bashford, Owner/Ross Hunter, Buyer/Franc Calvo, Manager
375 Sutter St., San Francisco, CA 94108 (415)986-4380
www.wilkesbashford.com
Honored by *Robb Report* as one of the finest men's stores in the U.S. Five-star emporium, established in 1966. Well-trained, attentive sales staff makes Wilkes Bashford one of the more pleasurable shopping experiences anywhere.
Casual Wear Luciano Barbera, Brioni, Kiton, Lorenzini, Loro Piana, Ermenegildo Zegna

Dress Shirts Luigi Borrelli, Kiton, Ermenegildo Zegna
Neckwear Altea, Luciano Barbera, Wilkes Bashford, Oxxford, Gianluca Isaia, Kiton, Ermenegildo Zegna
Shoes Stefano Bi, Barretti, Gravati
Tailored Clothing Luciano Barbera, Brioni, Kiton, Oxxford, Ermenegildo Zegna
Sales Semiannual, annual ware-house sale; tremendous pricing on extremely high quality merchandise

Billyblue
Independent
Billy Bragman, Owner/Jim Bickert, Manager
54 Geary St., San Francisco, CA 94104 (415)781-2111
www.billyblue.com
Featured in GQ's January 2003 Local Heroes as one of the best local stores in the world. Prices here are reasonable, and the inventory always offers something unique and tasteful. Billyblue's salespeople are also great to work with.

Accessories Distinctive outerwear selections each season
Casual Wear Acorn, Billyblue, Luciano Moresco
Dress Shirts Eton, Luciano Moresco
Neckwear Altea, Billyblue
Tailored Clothing Billyblue, Vestimenta
Sales Semiannual, early December and early June

Brooks Brothers
150 Post St., San Francisco, CA 94108 (415)397-4500
www.brooksbrothers.com

Burberry
225 Post St., San Francisco, CA 94108
(415)392-2200 www.burberry.com

Button Down
Independent
Michael Sabino, Owner/
John DiQuattro, Manager
3415 Sacramento St., San Francisco,
CA 94118 (415)563-1311
A most tantalizing establishment.
Uses antique steamer trunks, old
luggage, and bookcases to display
merchandise in a very appealing
manner. A great destination store
for anyone who appreciates dressing down with style. Attractive
women's section as well, sportswear and accessories.

Accessories Good selection of bow
ties, cuff links, and shaving acces-
sories
Casual Wear Luciano Barbera,
Baretta, Luigi Borrelli, Bruli,
Button Down (developed private
label), Coast, Brunello Cuccinelli,
ETRO, Gran Sasso, La Zetagi,
Longhi, Guy Rover, Zanella
Neckwear Luciano Barbera,
Cifonelli

Cole Haan
324 Stockton St., San Francisco, CA
94108 (415)391-1760
www.colehaan.com

Henry Cotton's
105 Grant Ave., San Francisco, CA
94108 (415)391-5557
www.henrycottons.com
Only Cotton's boutique in the U.S.

Courtoué
Independent
Walter Fong, Owner/William,
Maria, Ken, and Doreen Fong, Sales
459–465 Geary St., San Francisco,
CA 94102 (415)775-2900
Family-owned, excellent merchandise and selection store. I always
receive first-rate, personalized service when I visit. Custom tailoring
is also done on the premises.

Accessories Ermenegildo Zegna
braces
Casual Wear Brioni, Canali, Gran
Sasso, Versace, Zanella,
Ermenegildo Zegna
Dress Shirts Brioni, Canali,
Ermenegildo Zegna
Neckwear Brioni, Pancaldi, Stefano
Ricci, Versace, Ermenegildo Zegna
Shoes Star Artioli, Moreschi
Tailored Clothing Brioni, Canali,
Versace, Ermenegildo Zegna,
Zanella
Sales Quarterly

CROCKER GALLERIA
Location and Stores:
50 Post St., San Francisco, CA 94104
www.shopatgalleria.com

Barcelino
Independent
Al Hessabi, Store Manager
(415)273-2800 www.barcelino.com
One of Barcelino's largest in
square footage. Great selection
of quality merchandise.

Accessories Torras leather outer-
wear
Casual Wear Barcelino, Haupt,
Torras
Dress Shirts Barcelino (Cellini/
Belvest), Canali, Pancaldi
Neckwear Barcelino (Sattori),
Brioni, Pancaldi, Sazzari
Shoes Barcelino

Tailored Clothing Marco Azzali,
Barcelino, Belvest, Canali,
Ravazzolo
Sales Semiannual

Fil à Fil
Independent
(415)392-1150
Great quality items designed and
made in France.
Dress Shirts Fil à Fil
Neckwear Fil à Fil

Ralph Lauren
(415)788-7656 www.polo.com
Luxurious two-story establishment. One of Polo's larger and
nicer stores.

Gianni Versace
(415)616-0604 www.versace.com

Versace Jeans Couture
(415)616-0600 www.versace.com

The Custom Shop
Independent
Bruce Zuckerman, Sales
2 New Montgomery St., San
Francisco, CA 94105 (415)536-9306
www.customshop.com
(see chapter 9)
First-rate customer service. Great
quality fabrics and exceptional tailoring at reasonable prices. An excellent place to build one's wardrobe
and develop individualized style.

Accessories Custom Shop
Casual Wear Custom Shop
Dress Shirts Custom Shop
Neckwear Custom Shop, Kolte,
Genesis, Richel, Pancaldi, Pavone
Shoes Allen Edmonds
Tailored Clothing Custom Shop

Diesel
101 Post. St., San Francisco, CA
94108 (415)982-7077 www.diesel.com
Four floors of Diesel merchandise
for the entire family. Great shopping ambience and selection.

Alfred Dunhill
Rebecca Weinstein, Manager
250 Post St., San Francisco, CA 94108
(415)781-3368 www.dunhill.com

Allen Edmonds
171 Post St., San Francisco, CA 94108
(415)391-4545
www.allenedmonds.com

Salvatore Ferragamo
233 Geary St., San Francisco, CA
94102 (415)391-6565
www.salvatoreferragamo.it

Ghurka
170 Post St., San Francisco, CA 94108
(415)392-7267 www.ghurka.com
One of only two Ghurka boutiques
in the U.S. Interesting supply of
Ghurka leather goods, accessories,
and Trafalgar braces.

Gucci
One Union Square Building, 200
Stockton St., San Francisco, CA
94108 (415)392-2808 www.gucci.com

Hermès
125 Grant St., San Francisco, CA
94108 (415)391-7200
www.hermes.com
Newly remodeled location.

The Hound
Independent
*Walt Schorno, Owner/Kay Puffer,
Sales*

140 Sutter St., San Francisco, CA
94104 (415)989-0429
www.thehound.com
Traditional and European styles.
Friendly and helpful sales staff.
Great Hawaiian shirt selection.

Accessories Zimmerli undergarments
Casual Wear Hickey Freeman,
Reyn Spooner, Robert Talbott,
Tricots St. Raphael, Zanella
Dress Shirts Ike Behar, Gitman
Bros., Robert Talbott
Neckwear Ike Behar, Tino Cosma,
Polo Ralph Lauren, Robert
Talbott
Tailored Clothing Corneliani (also
M2M), Hickey Freeman,
Samuelsohn (also M2M), Sartori,
Zanella
Sales Semiannual, January and July

Patrick James
Independent
Patrick Mon Pere Sr., CEO
216 Montgomery St., San Francisco,
CA 94104 (415)986-1043
www.patrickjames.com
Newly remodeled location. Helpful staff, excellent destination for
traditionally oriented men's clothing.

Accessories Some Trafalgar braces
Casual Wear Tommy Bahama,
Scott Barber, Jhane Barnes,
Haupt, Patrick James, Nat Nast,
Reyn Spooner, Tricots St. Raphael
Dress Shirts Joseph Abboud,
Kenneth Gordon, Hickey
Freeman, Robert Talbott
Neckwear Joseph Abboud, Ike
Behar, Talbott, XMI, Ermenegildo
Zegna
Shoes Allen Edmonds, Cole Haan,
H.S. Trask
Tailored Clothing Joseph Abboud,

Aquascutum, Ballin, Jhane Barnes,
Barry Bricken, Corbin,
Hickey Freeman, Lords of
London, Tallia, Jack Victor,
Zanella
Sales Semiannual

Johnston & Murphy
299 Post St., San Francisco, CA 94108
(415)392-0199
www.johnstonmurphy.com

L'Uomo International
Independent
Sandeep Jaiswal, Proprietor
2121 Fillmore St., San Francisco, CA
94115 (415)776-0669
Excellent establishment with great
sales help. I've picked up many
great bargains here over the years.
The buyer for this chain of independent stores is very good at
selecting tasteful and distinctive
items each season to add to one's
wardrobe. This particular store is
more sportswear oriented.

Casual Wear Avon Celli, Hugo
Boss, Gran Sasso, Verri,
Ermenegildo Zegna, Pal Zileri
Neckwear Brioni, Tino Cosma,
L'Uomo, Ermenegildo Zegna
Shoes Hugo Boss, Cole Haan
Sales Semiannual

Macy's
170 O'Farrell St., San Francisco, CA
94102 (415)397-3333 www.macys.com
Hugo Boss and Armani Collezioni
store-in-stores, as well as selections
from some other brands like Diesel
and Donna Karan.

Casual Wear Giorgio Armani,
Hugo Boss, Diesel, Versace
Dress Shirts Giorgio Armani, Hugo

Boss
Neckwear Giorgio Armani, Hugo
Boss, Polo Ralph Lauren, Versace,
Ermenegildo Zegna
Tailored Clothing Giorgio Armani,
Hugo Boss

Neiman Marcus
*Fritz Boneberg, Men's Clothing
Manager*
150 Stockton St., San Francisco, CA
94108 (415)362-3900
www.neimanmarcus.com
My favorite Neiman's men's
department in the U.S. Occupies
entire lower floor. Huge Zegna
store-in-store with excellent selection, Armani store-in-store as well.
Mr. Boneberg and all his staff are
great to work with. In the unlikely
event they don't have an item,
they will find it for you, whether at
full or sale price.

Casual Wear Giorgio Armani,
Tommy Bahama, Jhane Barnes,
Cifonelli, Kiton, Loro Piana, Polo
Ralph Lauren, Ralph Lauren
Purple Label, Ermenegildo Zegna
Dress Shirts GREAT selection—
Giorgio Armani, Ike Behar, Luigi
Borrelli, Charvet, Dolce &
Gabbana, Kiton, Lorenzini, Paul
Smith, Turnbull & Asser (also
M2M), Ermenegildo Zegna
Neckwear Giorgio Armani,
Massimo Bizzocchi, Luigi Borrelli,
Charvet, Salvatore Ferragamo,
Kiton, Robert Talbott, Turnbull &
Asser, Ermenegildo Zegna
Tailored Clothing Giorgio Armani
(also M2M), Brioni, Dolce &
Gabbana (also M2M), Incotex,
Enrico Isaia (Also M2M), Kiton
(also M2M), Oxxford (also M2M),

Prada, Ermenegildo Zegna (also
M2M)

SAN FRANCISCO CENTRE
Location and Stores:
865 Market St., San Francisco, CA
94103 www.westfield.com

Coach
(415)543-7152 www.coach.com

Kenneth Cole
(415)227-4536 www.kennethcole.com

Lucky Brand Dungarees
(415)281-9020
www.luckyjeans.com

Nordstrom
*Lisa Marelich Manager, Men's
Sportswear*
(415)243-8500 www.nordstrom.com
Magnificent two-tiered men's
department, one of my favorite
Nordstrom locations in America.
Accessories LARGE selection of
Trafalgar Limited Edition braces
and cuff links
Casual Wear Giorgio Armani,
Ike Behar, Hugo Boss, Robert
Talbott, Ermenegildo Zegna
Dress Shirts Barba, Ike Behar
(also M2M), Enrico Isaia,
Robert Talbott (also M2M),
Ermenegildo Zegna
Neckwear ETRO, Duchamp,
Enrico Isaia, Robert Talbott,
great selection of XMI Platinum,
Ermenegildo Zegna
Tailored Clothing Joseph
Abboud, Giorgio Armani, Hugo
Boss, Hickey Freeman (also
M2M), Enrico Isaia (also M2M),
Ermenegildo Zegna (also M2M)

Nordstrom Rack
Outlet Store

555 9th St., San Francisco, CA 94107
(415)934-1211 www.nordstrom.com
Dress Shirts Ike Behar, Robert
Talbott
Neckwear Robert Talbott, XMI

Thomas Pink
255 Post St., San Francisco, CA 94108
(415)421-2022 www.thomaspink.com

Saks Fifth Avenue
*John McGreevy, Dennis Lee, Ric
Baluot, Men's Clothing/
Dan Gatmaitan, Men's Clothing*
220 Post St., San Francisco, CA 94108
(415)986-4300
www.saksfifthavenue.com
Spacious, luxurious men's-only
store occupies five floors. Large
Giorgio Armani store-in-store and
a nice evening and outerwear section. All of the salespeople are
great to work with; I've received
great customer service dealing
with them over the years.

Casual Wear Joseph Abboud,
Giorgio Armani, Jhane Barnes,
Brioni, Como Sport, Corneliani,
Dolce & Gabbana, Gucci, Bobby
Jones, Michael Kors, Helmut
Lang, Moreno Martini Da Firenze,
Paul Smith, Yohji Yamamoto,
Ermenegildo Zegna
Dress Shirts Baldessarini, Ike Behar,
Luigi Borrelli, Hugo Boss, Brioni,
Dolce & Gabbana, Donna Karan,
Lorenzini, Vestimenta,
Ermenegildo Zegna
Neckwear Giorgio Armani, Brioni,
Charvet, Salvatore Ferragamo,
Ermenegildo Zegna
Tailored Clothing Giorgio Armani,
Baldessarini, Boss, Corneliani,
Dolce & Gabbana, Donna Karan
Signature, Hickey Freeman (also

M2M), Prada, Ralph Lauren Purple
Label, Vestimenta, Ermenegildo
Zegna (also M2M), Pal Zileri

David Stephen
*Independent
David Gronowski, Owner/
Jack Ried, Sales*
50 Maiden Lane, San Francisco, CA
94108 (415)982-1611
www.davidstephen.com
Tasteful store with informative,
congenial customer service. Lots
of sophisticated looks for dressing
down with style.

Accessories Anthony, Art of Shaving
toiletries
Casual Wear Allegri, La Matta,
Theory, Vestimenta, Ermenegildo
Zegna
Dress Shirts Canali, Ermenegildo
Zegna
Tailored Clothing Canali, Incotex,
Vestimenta, Ermenegildo Zegna

Louis Vuitton
233 Geary St., San Francisco, CA
94102 (415)391-6200

Nordstrom Rack
Outlet Store
Westgate Mall, 1600 Saratoga Ave.,
San Jose, CA 95129 (408)374-4144
www.nordstrom.com

Casual Wear Robert Talbott, XMI
Platinum
Dress Shirts Joseph Abboud, Ike
Behar, Hickey Freeman, Robert
Talbott
Neckwear Robert Talbott, XMI
Tailored Clothing Jhane Barnes,
Daks-Simpson, Hickey Freeman

Nordstrom Rack
Outlet Store

1285 Marina Blvd., San Leandro, CA
94577 (510)614-1742
www.nordstrom.com

Casual Wear Jhane Barnes, Tricots
St. Raphael
Dress Shirts Ike Behar, Robert Talbott
Neckwear Robert Talbott, XMI
Platinum, Ermenegildo Zegna
Tailored Clothing Joseph Abboud,
Jhane Barnes, Hugo Boss,
Corneliani

Trend
Independent
Sandeep Jaiswal, Proprietor
334 Santana Row, #1070, San Jose,
CA 95128 (408)244-6338
European cutting-edge sportswear
and accessories for men and
women by Dolce & Gabbana, D
Squared, Dirk Bikkembergs,
Gianni Versace, Marithe & Francois
Girbaud, Roberto Cavalli, Gianfran-
co Ferré, Hugo, Giorgio Armani,
Sixty, Energie, Chloe, Voyage

HILLSDALE SHOPPING CENTER
Location and Stores:
177 Hillsdale Shopping Center, San
Mateo, CA 94403 www.hillsdale.com

Barcelino
Independent
(650)345-4200 www.barcelino.com

Casual Wear Barcelino, Haupt
Dress Shirts Barcelino (Cellini/
Belvest), Canali
Neckwear Barcelino (Sattori),
Brioni, Pancaldi, Sazzari
Shoes Barcelino
Tailored Clothing Barcelino,
Belvest, Canali, Ravazzolo
Sales Semiannual

Nordstrom
(650)570-5111 www.nordstrom.com

Dress Shirts Ike Behar
Neckwear Robert Talbott, XMI,
Ermenegildo Zegna
Tailored Clothing Joseph
Abboud, Hart, Scaffner &
Marx, Tallia

Patrick James
Independent
Patrick Mon Pere Sr., CEO
14527 Big Basin Way, Saratoga, CA
95070 (408)741-3150
www.patrickjames.com
Helpful staff, excellent destination
for traditionally oriented men's
clothing.

Accessories Some Trafalgar Braces
Casual Wear Tommy Bahama,
Scott Barber, Jhane Barnes,
Haupt, Patrick James, Nat Nast,
Reyn Spooner, Tricots St. Raphael
Dress Shirts Joseph Abboud,
Kenneth Gordon, Hickey Freeman,
Robert Talbott
Neckwear Joseph Abboud, Ike
Behar, Talbott, XMI, Ermenegildo
Zegna
Tailored Clothing Joseph Abboud,
Aquascutum, Ballin, Jhane Barnes,
Barry Bricken, Corbin, Hickey
Freeman, Lords of London, Tallia,
Jack Victor, Zanella
Shoes Allen Edmonds, Cole Haan,
H.S. Trask
Sales Semiannual

VALLEY FAIR SHOPPING CENTER
Location and Stores:
2855 Stevens Creek Blvd., Santa
Clara, CA 95050 www.westfield.com

5 Pocket
Independent
Sandeep Jaiswal, Proprietor
(408)248-5758

Best denim and accessories destination store in Bay Area. Men's and women's styles.

Casual Wear Giorgio Armani, Diesel, Dolce & Gabbana, E-play, Evisu, Adriano Goldschmeid, Miss 60, Paper, Denim & Cloth, 7 for All Mankind, Versace, and 30 other brands

A/X Armani Exchange
(408)423-9260
www.giorgioarmani.com

Barcelino
Independent
(408)556-6666 www.barcelino.com
Newly remodeled location.

Casual Wear Barcelino, Haupt
Dress Shirts Barcelino (Cellini/Belvest), Canali
Neckwear Barcelino (Sattori), Brioni, Pancaldi, Sazzari
Shoes Barcelino
Tailored Clothing Barcelino, Belvest, Canali, Ravazzolo
Sales Semiannual

BOSS Hugo Boss
(408)984-0100 www.hugoboss.com

Coach
(408)249-1772 www.coach.com

Kenneth Cole
(408)246-2001
www.kennethcole.com

Lucky Brand Dungarees
(408)261-9410
www.luckybrandjeans.com

L'Uomo International
Independent
Sandeep Jaiswal, Proprietor
(408)247-6100

Casual Wear Giorgio Armani, Gran Sasso, Thierry Mugler, Verri, Gianni Versace, Ermenegildo Zegna, Pal Zileri
Dress Shirts Giorgio Armani, Luigi Borrelli, Brioni, Ermenegildo Zegna
Neckwear Giorgio Armani, Brioni, Tino Cosma, L'Uomo, Ermenegildo Zegna, Pal Zileri Sartoriale
Shoes Giorgio Armani, Salvatore Ferragamo, Gravati
Tailored Clothing Giorgio Armani, Verri, Gianni Versace, Ermenegildo Zegna, Pal Zileri (including Sartoriale line)

Nordstrom
(408)248-2180 www.nordstrom.com
Brand-new, very attractive store.

Casual Wear Ermenegildo Zegna
Dress Shirts Barba, Ike Behar, Robert Talbott, Ermenegildo Zegna
Neckwear Robert Talbott, XMI, Ermenegildo Zegna
Tailored Clothing Joseph Abboud, Hugo Boss, Tallia

St. Croix
(408)984-7675
www.stcroixshop.com

Louis Vuitton
(408)247-0020
www.louisvuitton.com

Gene Hiller
Independent
Gene Hiller, Owner/Tom Gangitano, Partner andBuyer/Wayne Kaleck, General Manager
729 Bridgeway, Sausalito, CA 94965
(415)332-3636 www.genehiller.com

Elegant and aesthetically appealing store. One of the more agreeable and responsive sales staffs you'll find anywhere.

Accessories Some cuff links and unique, classic formal wear
Casual Wear Jhane Barnes, Gene Hiller, Nicole Miller, Luciano Moresco, Pancaldi, Georg Roth, St. Croix, Versace, Ermenegildo Zegna
Dress Shirts Canali, Gene Hiller (also custom), Marol, Rodin, Ermenegildo Zegna
Neckwear Brioni, Canali, Gene Hiller, Pancaldi, Ermenegildo Zegna
Shoes Bragitani, Mezlan
Tailored Clothing Brioni (also M2M), Canali, d'Avenza (also M2M), Scabal (M2M), Versace, Zanella, Ermenegildo Zegna, Pal Zileri
Sales Semiannual

BROADWAY PLAZA
Location and Stores:
1275 Broadway Plaza, Walnut Creek, CA 94596
www.broadwayplaza.com

Jhane Barnes
(925)943-1550
www.jhanebarnes.com
One of larger Barnes stores. Great selection in all facets of the Jhane Barnes line.

Coach
(925)938-2775 www.coach.com

Daskalos European Fashions
Independent
Tom Daskalos and Christina

Daskalos Kouros, Owners
(925)937-1808
Great-looking store with first-rate merchandise and excellent customer service.

Accessories Bresciani socks, good selection of pocket squares; formal wear, leather outerwear
Casual Wear Luigi Borrelli, Brioni, Canali, Brunello Cuccinelli, Haupt, Georg Roth, Zanella
Dress Shirts Luigi Borrelli, Canali, Lorenzini
Neckwear Brioni, Canali, Tino Cosma, Vestimenta
Shoes Canali, Michael Toschi, Moreschi
Tailored Clothing Brioni, Canali, Vestimenta, Zanella
Sales Semiannual

Johnston & Murphy
(925)933-3562
www.johnstonmurphy.com

Nordstrom
(925)930-7959 www.nordstrom.com
Casual Wear Ermenegildo Zegna
Dress Shirts Ike Behar, Robert Talbott, Ermenegildo Zegna
Neckwear Giorgio Armani, Robert Talbott, XMI, Ermenegildo Zegna
Tailored Clothing Joseph Abboud, Hickey Freeman, Ermenegildo Zegna

Patrick James
Independent
Patrick Mon Pere Sr., CEO
1389 N. Broadway, Walnut Creek, CA 94596 (925)933-5544
www.patrickjames.com

Helpful staff, excellent destination for traditionally oriented men's clothing.

Accessories Some Trafalgar Braces
Casual Wear Tommy Bahama, Scott Barber, Jhane Barnes, Haupt, Patrick James, Nat Nast, Reyn Spooner, Tricots St. Raphael
Dress Shirts Joseph Abboud, Kenneth Gordon, Hickey Freeman, Robert Talbott
Neckwear Joseph Abboud, Ike Behar, Talbott, XMI, Ermenegildo Zegna
Shoes Allen Edmonds, Cole Haan, H.S. Trask
Tailored Clothing Joseph Abboud, Aquascutum, Ballin, Jhane Barnes, Barry Bricken, Corbin, Hickey Freeman, Lords of London, Tallia, Jack Victor, Zanella
Sales Semiannual

Metro Area: Seattle

Nordstrom Rack
Outlet Store
SuperMall of the Northwest, 1101 Supermall Dr., Auburn, WA 98001
(253)833-8824
www.nordstrom.com

BELLEVUE SQUARE
Location and Stores:
575 Bellevue Square, Bellevue, WA 98004 www.bellevuesquare.com

Albert Ltd.
Independent
(425)455-2970
Pleasant store with select inventory of clothing primarily for the traditional dresser.

Casual Wear Tommy Bahama, Reyn Spooner, Robert Talbott
Neckwear Ferrell Reed, Robert Talbott
Tailored Clothing Corbin, Gitman Bros., Hickey Freeman, Polo Ralph Lauren
Sales Semiannual, usually after Christmas and early June

Barcelino
Independent
(425)462-2000 www.barcelino.com
Pleasant store with great atmosphere and nice selection of quality, well-presented merchandise.

Casual Wear Barcelino, Haupt, Georg Roth
Dress Shirts Barcelino
Neckwear Barcelino, Pancaldi, Serica Elite
Shoes Barcelino
Tailored Clothing Barcelino, Belvest, Canali, Vestimenta
Sales Semiannual, January and July

Brooks Brothers
(425)646-9688
www.brooksbrothers.com

Coach
(425)453-0141 www.coach.com

Johnston & Murphy
(425)451-8570
www.johnstonmurphy.com

David Lawrence
Independent
(425)688-1669
www.david-lawrence.com
This location carries more colorful clothes and a larger selection of fashion-forward brands.

Casual Wear Roberto Cavalli,
Dolce & Gabbana, Gran Sasso,
Versace
Neckwear Hugo Boss, Tino Cosma
Tailored Clothing Hugo Boss,
Donna Karan, Calvin Klein,
Tallia, John Varvatos
Sales Semiannual, January and
July

Nordstrom
(425)455-5800 www.nordstrom.com

Casual Wear Jhane Barnes,
Ermenegildo Zegna
Dress Shirts Ike Behar
Neckwear Robert Talbott, XMI,
Ermenegildo Zegna
Tailored Clothing Hickey
Freeman, Zanella, Ermenegildo
Zegna

Nordstrom Rack
Outlet Store
Golde Creek Plaza, 19500 Alderwood
Mall Pkwy., Lynnwood, WA 98036
(425)774-6569 www.nordstrom.com

Barcelino
Independent
Rainier Square, 411 Union St.,
Seattle, WA 98101 (206)262-9111
www.barcelino.com
Pleasant store with great atmosphere and quality inventory of
well-presented merchandise.

Casual Wear Barcelino, Haupt,
Georg Roth
Dress Shirts Barcelino
Neckwear Barcelino, Pancaldi,
Serica Elite
Shoes Barcelino
Tailored Clothing Barcelino,
Belvest, Canali, Vestimenta
Sales Semiannual, January and July

Barney's New York
1420 Fifth Ave., Seattle, WA 98101
(206)622-6300 www.barneys.com

Accessories Excellent selection of
cuff links
Casual Wear Barney's, Lorenzini,
Ermenegildo Zegna
Dress Shirts Giorgio Armani,
Barney's, Hugo Boss, Lorenzini,
John Varvatos, Ermenegildo
Zegna
Neckwear Giorgio Armani,
Barney's, Hugo Boss, Dolce &
Gabbana, ETRO, Prada
Tailored Clothing Giorgio Armani,
Barney's, Donna Karan, Calvin
Klein, John Varvatos, Zegna Soft

Butch Blum
Independent
*Butch Blum and Kay Smith-Blum,
Proprietors*
1408 Fifth Ave., Seattle, WA 98101
(206)622-5760
www.butchblumworld.com
Sleek, urban look to both this
store and the great clothes to be
found here. Great customer service, a fine women's store as well.
One of my favorite Seattle destinations.

Casual Wear Giorgio Armani
Black Label, Luciano Barbera,
Butch Blum, Hugo Boss, Carpe
Diem, DKNY, Romeo Gigli,
Helmut Lang, Marzotto Lab,
Yohji Yamamoto, Ermenegildo
Zegna
Dress Shirts Giorgio Armani Black
Label, Bagutta, Brioni, Romeo
Gigli, Calvin Klein, Vestimenta,
Ermenegildo Zegna
Neckwear Giorgio Armani Black
Label, Butch Blum, Brioni, Romeo

Gigli, Donna Karan, Vestimenta,
Ermenegildo Zegna
Shoes Salvatore Ferragamo, Bruno
Magli, Donald J. Pliner, To Boot
New York, Via Spiga, Yohji
Yamamoto
Tailored Clothing Giorgio Armani
Black Label, Brioni, Romeo Gigli,
Helmut Lang, Marzotto Lab,
Vestimenta, Ermenegildo Zegna

Butch Blum
Independent
*Butch Blum and Kay Smith-Blum,
Proprietors*
4512 University Village Court, Seattle,
WA 98105 (206)524-5860
www.butchblumworld.com
Sleek, urban look to both this
store and the great clothes to be
found here. Excellent customer
service, a fine women's store as well.

Casual Wear Giorgio Armani
Black Label, Luciano Barbera,
Butch Blum, Hugo Boss, Carpe
Diem, DKNY, Romeo Gigli,
Helmut Lang, Marzotto Lab,
Yohji Yamamoto, Ermenegildo
Zegna
Dress Shirts Giorgio Armani Black
Label, Bagutta, Brioni, Romeo
Gigli, Calvin Klein, Vestimenta,
Ermenegildo Zegna
Neckwear Giorgio Armani Black
Label, Butch Blum, Brioni, Romeo
Gigli, Donna Karan, Vestimenta,
Ermenegildo Zegna
Shoes Salvatore Ferragamo, Bruno
Magli, Donald J. Pliner, To Boot
New York, Via Spiga, Yohji
Yamamoto
Tailored Clothing Giorgio Armani
Black Label, Brioni, Romeo Gigli,
Helmut Lang, Marzotto Lab,
Vestimenta, Ermenegildo Zegna

Kenneth Cole
520 Pike St., Seattle, WA 98101,
(206)382-1680 www.kennethcole.com

Gian DeCaro Sartoria
Independent
Gian DeCaro, Proprietor
2025 First Ave., Ste. D, Seattle, WA
98121 (206)448-2812
www.giandecaro.com
Rated one of America's Top
Tailors by *Town & Country* magazine, and featured in many international publications such as *GQ*,
Forbes, and *Wired* magazines. Gian
DeCaro sells only the finest fabrics,
purchased directly from the best
mills in Italy. All clothes are custom-made; great place to start
buying custom clothes and truly
personalizing your style. Exclusive
neckwear made of the finest silks,
super luxurious knitwear, elegant
outerwear, and gentleman's accessories, from soft Italian cotton T-
shirts (one of the best selections in
larger sizes I've seen) to elegant
extra-fine Merino wool polo shirts,
all on hand for immediate purchase. Mr. DeCaro was very generous with his time, discussing his
family's business and philosophy
about dressing. He has an extensive, notable client list, specializing
in the technology sector.

Europa
Independent
City Centre, 1420 5th Ave., Ste. 203,
Seattle, WA 98101 (206)621-0350
Great place to shop for colorful
casual shirts and sweaters.

Casual Wear Jhane Barnes,
Riscatto Portofino, St. Croix,
Tricots St. Raphael

Neckwear Robert Daskal, Stefano Milano
Sales Semiannual, January and July

David Lawrence
Independent
1318 Fourth Ave., Seattle, WA 98101
(206)622-2544
www.david-lawrence.com
Downtown store is larger but carries more conservative selections.

Casual Wear Roberto Cavalli, Dolce & Gabbana, Gran Sasso, Versace Classic, Versace V2, Versace Jeans Couture
Neckwear Hugo Boss, Tino Cosma
Tailored Clothing Hugo Boss, Donna Karan, Calvin Klein, Tallia, John Varvatos
Sales Semiannual, January and July

Mario's
Independent
Mario Bisio, Proprietor/ Jennifer Serna, Store Manager
1513 Sixth Ave., Seattle, WA 98101
(206)223-1461
www.marios.com
Fine Northwest family sartorial tradition begun in 1938. Elegant, attractive stores filled with first-quality merchandise. Excellent customer service. Also a fine women's store.

Casual Wear Agnona, Giorgio Armani, Tommy Bahama, Dolce & Gabbana, Mario's Private Label, Kiton, Loro Piana, Prada, Jil Sander, John Smedley, Ermenegildo Zegna
Dress Shirts Giorgio Armani, Luigi Borrelli, Hugo Boss, Brioni, Hamilton Shirtmakers M2M, Kiton, Lorenzini, Mario's, Ermenegildo Zegna

Neckwear Giorgio Armani, Massimo Bizzocchi, Hugo Boss, Kiton, Ermenegildo Zegna
Shoes Gravati, Prada, Tod's, To Boot New York, Michael Toschi
Tailored Clothing Giorgio Armani, Hugo Boss, Canali, Dolce & Gabbana, Mario's, Kiton, Vestimenta, Ermenegildo Zegna
Sales Semiannual

Nordstrom
500 Pine St., Seattle, WA 98101
(206)628-2111 www.nordstrom.com
Original Nordstrom store.

Casual Wear Jhane Barnes, Ermenegildo Zegna
Dress Shirts Ike Behar, Ermenegildo Zegna
Neckwear Robert Talbott, XMI, Ermenegildo Zegna
Tailored Clothing Hickey Freeman, Zanella, Ermenegildo Zegna

Nordstrom Rack
Outlet Store
1601 Second Ave., Seattle, WA 98101
(206)448-8522 www.nordstrom.com

Dress Shirts Ike Behar, Robert Talbott
Neckwear Robert Talbott, XMI

Metro Area: Tampa
Maus and Hoffman
Independent
Bill and John Maus, Owners
3rd Street S. at 14th Ave., Naples, FL 34102 (941)262-7611
www.mausandhoffman.com
(see chapter 9)
Great merchandise for customer with both traditional and European tastes.

Accessories Zimmerli undergarments
Casual Wear Brioni, Hickey
Freeman, Liberty of London,
Maus and Hoffman
Dress Shirts Brioni, Maus and
Hoffman
Neckwear Brioni, Maus and
Hoffman, Leonard
Shoes Allen Edmonds, Maus and
Hoffman
Tailored Clothing Brioni, Hickey
Freeman, Oxxford, Maus and
Hoffman
Sales Semiannual

Maus and Hoffman
Independent
Bill and John Maus, Owners
40 S. Blvd. of Presidents, St. Armands
Circle, Sarasota, FL 34236 (941)388-
2551 www.mausandhoffman.com
(see chapter 9)
Great merchandise for customer
with both traditional and European
tastes.

Accessories Zimmerli undergarments
Casual Wear Brioni, Hickey
Freeman, Liberty of London,
Maus and Hoffman
Dress Shirts Brioni, Maus and
Hoffman
Neckwear Brioni, Maus and
Hoffman, Leonard
Shoes Allen Edmonds, Maus and
Hoffman
Tailored Clothing Brioni, Hickey
Freeman, Oxxford, Maus and
Hoffman
Sales Semiannual

Tommy Bahama
1623 Snow Ave., Tampa, FL 33606
(813)258-8688
www.tommybahama.com

Greiner's
Independent
Doug Tozier and Chris Blowers,
Owners/Juan Sanchez, Sales
117 Whiting St., Tampa, FL 33602
(813)226-3207
www.greinersclothing.com
Attractive retail outlet featuring
updated traditional and European
clothing. All merchandise of very
high quality and presented well
with dark wood fixtures that create
an intimate, clubby setting. Mr.
Tozier and Mr. Sanchez were very
helpful and thorough in explaining
the store's philosophy and showing me its inventory.

Accessories Bow ties; good selection
of Trafalgar braces (including
Limited Edition); cuff links
Casual Wear Tommy Bahama, Ted
Baker, Ballin, Robert Barakett,
Scott Barber, Bills Khakis, Coast,
Henry Cotton's, Madeline Finn,
Haupt, Hickey Freeman, Gillio,
Gran Sasso, Julio, Lucky Brand,
Nat Nast, Riscatto Portofino, Tori
Richards, Jeff Rose, Pal Zileri
Dress Shirts Ike Behar, Luigi
Borrelli, Gitman Brothers,
Robert Talbott, Custom SGA
shirts
Neckwear Altea, Breuer, Luigi
Borrelli, Hickey Freeman, Robert
Talbott
Shoes Alden, Allen Edmonds, Cole
Haan
Tailored Clothing Ballin, Coppley
(also M2M), Hickey Freeman (also
M2M), Incotex, Oxxford (also
M2M), Ravazzolo (also M2M),
Samuelsohn (also M2M), Jack
Victor, Pal Zileri (also M2M),
Bernard Zins

INTERNATIONAL PLAZA
Location and Stores:
West Shore and Boy Scout Blvd.,
Tampa, FL 33607
www.shopinternationalplaza.com

BOSS Hugo Boss
David Khan, Store Manager
(813)354-7744 www.hugoboss.com

Coach
Gloria Rosario, Store Manager
(813)348-4770 www.coach.com

Cole Haan
Dana Burke, Store Manager
(813)353-1010 www.colehaan.com

Diesel
Angela Coffey, Store Manager
(813)353-0755 www.diesel.com

Lucky Brand Dungarees
*Shannon Rusmisel, Store
Manager*
(813)353-1102
www.luckybrandjeans.com

Neiman Marcus
Wendy Krimins, Store Manager
(813)877-5700
www.neimanmarcus.com
Newer Neiman's store, very
attractive aesthetically. DKNY,
Polo Ralph Lauren, and
Ermenegildo Zegna in-store
boutiques.

Casual Wear Joseph Abboud,
Giorgio Armani, DKNY, Polo
Ralph Lauren, Ermenegildo
Zegna
Dress Shirts Giorgio Armani,
Brioni, Lorenzini, Ermenegildo
Zegna

Neckwear Giorgio Armani,
Brioni, Ermenegildo Zegna
Tailored Clothing Joseph
Abboud, Giorgio Armani, Polo
Ralph Lauren, Ermenegildo
Zegna

Nordstrom
Joe Greco, Store Manager
(813)875-4400 www.nordstrom.com

Dress Shirts Ike Behar
Neckwear Robert Talbott, XMI,
Ermenegildo Zegna
Tailored Clothing Zanella

Surrey's
Independent
(813)871-6966

Casual Wear Jhane Barnes,
Hugo Boss, Canali, Versace
Dress Shirts Ermenegildo Zegna
Neckwear Altea, Canali,
Pancaldi, Ermenegildo Zegna
Sales Semiannual

Louis Vuitton
Tony Butera, Store Manager
(813)353-3713
www.louisvuitton.com

Kirby's Mens Wear
Independent
*Martin L. Shine, Owner/
Dan Shreeve, Sales*
1707 S. Dale Mabry, Tampa, FL 33629
(813)253-2681
Second-generation men's specialty
retailer. Great store with impressive selection of high-quality, well-
presented inventory. Both Mr.
Shreeve and Mr. Shine were generous with their time and expertise.

Accessories Good selection of
braces and pocket squares

Casual Wear Jhane Barnes, Casa
Moda, Dalmine, Equilibrio, Haupt,
Raffi, Tori Richard, Riscatto
Portofino, Tricots St. Raphael
Dress Shirts Ike Behar, Canali,
Tino Cosma, Enro, Eton, Kenneth
Gordon, Jack Lipson, Pancaldi
Neckwear Tino Cosma, Gianfranco
Ferré, Pancaldi, Ermenegildo Zegna
Shoes Allen Edmonds, Cole Haan,
Mezlan, Michael Toschi
Tailored Clothing Arnold Brant,
Canali, Marzotto Sartoriale,
Zanella, Ermenegildo Zegna

Metro Area: Toledo

The Custom Shop
Independent
Mike Smith, CEO
8110 W. Central Ave., Toledo, OH
43617 (419)841-6112
www.customshop.com
(see chapter 9)
First-rate, come-to-you customer
service. Great quality fabrics and
exceptional tailoring at reasonable
prices. An excellent place to build
one's wardrobe and develop individualized style.

Accessories Custom Shop
Casual Wear Custom Shop
Dress Shirts Custom Shop
Neckwear Custom Shop, Kolte,
Genesis, Richel, Pancaldi, Pavone
Shoes Allen Edmonds
Tailored Clothing Custom Shop

Metro Area: Tucson

Firenzi Boutique
Independent
2951 North Swan Rd., Tucson, AZ
85712 (520)299-2992
Well-presented upscale merchandise

in elegant boutique with great
atmosphere. Collections directed
toward European tastes. Also an
elegant women's department.

Accessories Versace belts
Casual Wear Equilibrio, Riscatto
Portofino, Versace Classic
Dress Shirts Tino Cosma, Versace
Classic, Zanelli
Neckwear Tino Cosma, Gianni
Versace
Shoes Bruno Magli, Versace
Tailored Clothing Cavalli, Zanella

Little Outlet Men's Shoes
Independent
Phil Touché, Store Manager
Crossroads Festival, 4811 E. Grant,
Ste. 123, Tucson, AZ 85712
(520)327-5342
Part of Mills Touché group.
Excellent customer service and
great shoes at great prices.

Shoes Alden, Cole Haan, Allen
Edmonds, Foot Joy, Johnston &
Murphy, Sebago

Mills Touché
Independent
Ben Allen, Store Manager
Crossroads Festival, 4811 E. Grant,
Ste 119, Tucson, AZ 85712
(520)795-5573
Family business begun in 1956.
Great-looking store in convenient
location. Helpful, polite sales staff.
Clothing primarily for updated tra-
ditional tastes. Great women's sec-
tion as well.

Accessories Royall fragrances; good
selection of cuff links, Martin
Dingman leather goods,
Pantherella socks
Casual Wear Scott Barber, Bills

Khakis, Barry Bricken, Gran Sasso, Haupt, Bobby Jones
Dress Shirts Ike Behar, Breuer, Mills Touché, Robert Talbott
Neckwear Breuer, JZ Richards, Robert Talbott
Shoes Alden, Martin Dingman, Allen Edmonds, H. S. Trask
Tailored Clothing Hickey Freeman, Samuelsohn, Jack Victor

Metro Area: Washington, DC

Nordstrom
Westfield Shoppingtown Annapolis, 2002 Annapolis Mall, Annapolis, MD 21401 (410)573-1121
www.nordstrom.com
Dress Shirts Robert Talbott
Neckwear Robert Talbott, XMI, Ermenegildo Zegna
Tailored Clothing Joseph Abboud, Pal Zileri (some)

George Howard
Independent
Alan Pressman, Proprietor
Village of Cross Keys, 94 Village Square, Baltimore, MD 21210 (410)532-3535
Extremely pleasant shopping environment in great retail location. First-rate inventory; one of better selections of Luciano Barbera you'll find anywhere. Mr. Shapiro and Mr. Pressman are a pleasure to converse and shop with.

Accessories Great selection of belts; good selection of bow ties and cuff links; some formal wear; Luciano Barbera and Golden Bear leather outerwear
Casual Wear Avon Celli, Luciano

Barbera, Scott Barber, Luigi Borrelli, Barry Bricken, Dalmine, Jeff Rose, Paul & Shark, Viyella, Ermenegildo Zegna, Zegna Soft
Dress Shirts Luciano Barbera, Luigi Borrelli, Ermenegildo Zegna
Neckwear Luciano Barbera, Ermenegildo Zegna
Shoes Salvatore Ferragamo, Santoni
Tailored Clothing Luciano Barbera, Zanella, Ermenegildo Zegna (also M2M)

MONTGOMERY MALL
Location and Stores:
7101 Democracy Blvd., Bethesda, MD 20817 www.westfield.com

A/X Armani Exchange
(301)365-9095
www.giorgioarmani.com

Nordstrom
(301)365-4111 www.nordstrom.com
Casual Wear Robert Talbott, Ermenegildo Zegna
Dress Shirts Robert Talbott
Neckwear Robert Talbott, XMI, Ermenegildo Zegna
Tailored Clothing Joseph Abboud, Façonnable, Hickey Freeman, Pal Zileri

Winn Brothers
Independent
Steve Winnick, Todd Winnick, and Dana Winnick, Owners
(301)365-9466
Highly specialized men's store featuring soft European clothing. The Winnicks are a pleasure to work with.

Accessories Comstock, Remy leather outerwear

Casual Wear Barry Bricken,
Equilibrio, St. Croix, Zanella
Dress Shirts Luciano Moresco,
Xacus
Neckwear Winn Bros., imported
direct from Italy
Tailored Clothing Borghesi,
Marzotto Sartoriale, Zanella,
Bernard Zins

Gianni Versace
5454 Wisconsin Ave., Chevy Chase,
MD 20815 (301)907-9400
www.versace.com

ARUNDEL MILLS
Location and Stores:
7000 Arundel Mills Circle, Hanover,
MD 21076 www.arundelmills.com

Cole Haan
Outlet Store
(443)755-1430 www.colehaan.com

Hugo Boss
Outlet Store
(443)755-1570 www.hugoboss.com

Kenneth Cole
Outlet Store
(410)799-2027
www.kennethcole.com

Saks Off Fifth
Outlet Store
(410)799-4541
www.saksfifthavenue.com

Dress Shirts Ermenegildo Zegna
Neckwear Ermenegildo Zegna
Tailored Clothing Joseph
Abboud, Giorgio Armani, Hugo
Boss, Canali, Salvatore Ferragamo

WHITE FLINT MALL
Location and Stores:
11301 Rockville Pike, North Bethesda,
MD 20895 www.shopwhiteflint.com

Boardroom Clothiers
Independent
Jim Jones, President.
(301)468-5777
www.boardroomclothiers.com
Nice selection of quality brands
for the traditional dresser.

Casual Wear Tulliano, Tundra
Dress Shirts Ike Behar
Neckwear Ferrell Reed, Robert
Talbott
Tailored Clothing Aquascutum,
Hickey Freeman, Tallia

Bruno Cipriani
Independent
Alex Abbaszadeh, Manager/
Eduardo DePandi, Owner
(301)468-0484
Great store with attractively presented merchandise. Unique,
first-quality pieces you won't
find anywhere else. Both Mr.
Abbaszadeh and Mr. DePandi are
most cordial and accommodating.

Accessories Great selection of
Tateossian cuff links; Gimo and
Versace leather outerwear
Casual Wear Coogi, Verri, Versace
Dress Shirts Luigi Borrelli,
Bruno Cipriani, Xacus
Neckwear Tino Cosma, Hubert,
Pancaldi, Pavone, Versace
Shoes Versace
Tailored Clothing Luigi Borrelli,
d'Avenza, Nervesa, Redaelli,
Tombolini, Versace
Sales Four per year—July,
August, December, January

Gentlemen's Jodhpur
Independent
(301)770-5880

Shoes Bacco Bucci, Lorenzo
Banfi, Belvedere, Borgioli,

Mephisto, Bruno Magli,
Mezlan, Moreschi

Nordstrom Rack
Outlet Store
City Place, 8661 Colesville Rd., Silver
Spring, MD 20910 (301)608-8118
www.nordstrom.com

Casual Wear Tricots St. Raphael
Dress Shirts Robert Talbott
Tailored Clothing Joseph Abboud,
Jhane Barnes, Corneliani,
Ermenegildo Zegna

TOWSON TOWN CENTER
Location and Stores:
825 Dulaney Valley Rd., Towson, MD
21286

Coach
(410)494-1772 www.coach.com

Nordstrom
(410)296-2111 www.nordstrom.com
Casual Wear Robert Talbott,
Ermenegildo Zegna
Dress Shirts Ike Behar, Burberry,
Robert Talbott, Zanella
Neckwear Burberry, XMI,
Ermenegildo Zegna
Tailored Clothing Joseph
Abboud, Pal Zileri (some)

Nordstrom Rack
Outlet Store
(410)494-9111 www.nordstrom.com
Located on ground floor of
Nordstrom.

**THE FASHION CENTRE AT
PENTAGON CITY**
Location and Stores:
1100 S. Hayes St., Arlington, VA 22202
www.shopsimon.com

Bernini
(703)415-5786 www.bernini.com
Casual Wear Ermenegildo
Zegna
Tailored Clothing Versace

Coach
(703)418-6787 www.coach.com

Kenneth Cole
(703)415-3522
www.kennethcole.com

Cole Haan
(703)415-0006 www.colehaan.com

Johnston & Murphy
(703)418-6181
www.johnstonmurphy.com

Nordstrom
(703)415-1121 www.nordstrom.com
Casual Wear Robert Talbott,
Ermenegildo Zegna
Dress Shirts Ike Behar, Robert
Talbott, Ermenegildo Zegna
Neckwear Robert Talbott, XMI,
Ermenegildo Zegna
Tailored Clothing Joseph
Abboud, Hickey Freeman,
Zanella, Ermenegildo Zegna,
Zegna Soft, Pal Zileri

Refinery
Independent
*Mark Rykken, Principal/
George Broderick, Principal*
1600 Tysons Blvd., Ste. 800, McLean,
VA 22102 (703)245-3017
Brand-new establishment opened
in April 2003 by these two former
senior employees of Britches of
Georgetown. High-quality self-
labeled merchandise value priced
and intended to introduce the

younger man to the finer art of dressing. Emphasis on custom clothing, but many fine ready-to-wear items as well.

TYSONS CORNER CENTER
Location and Stores:
1961 Chain Bridge Rd., McLean, VA 22102 www.shoptysons.com

A/X Armani Exchange
(703)761-1406
www.giorgioarmani.com

Brooks Brothers
(703)556-6566
www.brooksbrothers.com

Coach
(703)883-1772 www.coach.com

Kenneth Cole
(703)821-7606
www.kennethcole.com

Johnston & Murphy
(703)556-9833
www.johnstonmurphy.com

Nordstrom
(703)761-1121 www.nordstrom.com

Casual Wear Robert Talbott, Zanella, Ermenegildo Zegna
Dress Shirts Robert Talbott, Zanella, Ermenegildo Zegna
Neckwear Robert Talbott, XMI, Ermenegildo Zegna
Tailored Clothing Corneliani, Hickey Freeman, Zegna Soft, Pal Zileri

TYSONS GALLERIA
Location and Stores:
2001 International Dr., McLean, VA 22102 www.shoptysonsgalleria.com

Bally
(703)760-8924 www.bally.com

BOSS Hugo Boss
(703)848-2197 www.hugoboss.com

Cole Haan
(703)506-2115 www.colehaan.com

James Clothiers
Independent
(703)883-1444
Great-looking store with high-quality merchandise and helpful staff.

Accessories Good selection of cuff links; Brioni, Canali, Gimo, Kiton, and Pal Zileri leather outerwear
Casual Wear Luciano Barbera, Luigi Borrelli, Brioni, Dalmine, Gran Sasso, Pal Zileri, Ermenegildo Zegna
Dress Shirts Sartoria Attolini, Luigi Borrelli, Brioni, Canali, Fray, Kiton, Lorenzini, Ermenegildo Zegna
Neckwear Brioni, Tino Cosma, Pancaldi, Stefano Ricci, Ermenegildo Zegna, Zilli
Shoes Salvatore Ferragamo, Bruno Magli, Santoni, Michael Toschi
Tailored Clothing Sartoria Attolini, Brioni (also M2M), Canali, d'Avenza (also M2M), Kiton, Ermenegildo Zegna (also M2M), Pal Zileri (also M2M)

Lacoste
(571)633-0241 www.lacoste.com

Lucky Brand Dungarees
(703)917-1630
www.luckyjeans.com

Neiman Marcus
(703)761-1600
www.neimanmarcus.com
Casual Wear Giorgio Armani,
Jhane Barnes, Hugo Boss, Loro
Piana, Polo Ralph Lauren,
Ermenegildo Zegna
Dress Shirts Giorgio Armani, Ike
Behar, Luigi Borrelli, Kiton,
Lorenzini, Turnbull & Asser
Neckwear Giorgio Armani,
Charvet, Luigi Borrelli,
Salvatore Ferragamo, Kiton,
Turnbull & Asser, Ermenegildo
Zegna
Tailored Clothing Giorgio
Armani, Brioni, Incotex, Kiton,
Oxxford, Ermenegildo Zegna

Thomas Pink
(703)891-1176
www.thomaspink.com

Saks Fifth Avenue
(703)761-0700
www.saksfifthavenue.com
Casual Wear Giorgio Armani,
Polo Ralph Lauren,
Ermenegildo Zegna
Dress Shirts Ike Behar, Hugo
Boss, Hickey Freeman,
Ermenegildo Zegna
Neckwear Giorgio Armani,
Hugo Boss, Ermenegildo Zegna
Tailored Clothing Giorgio
Armani, Ermenegildo Zegna,
Zegna Soft

Versace Jeans Couture
(703)448-5554 www.versace.com

POTOMAC MILLS
Location and Stores:
2700 Potomac Mills Circle, Prince

William, VA 22192
www.potomacmills.com

Brooks Brothers
Outlet Store
(703)491-2950
www.brooksbrothers.com

Calvin Klein
Outlet Store
(703)494-6292

Nordstrom Rack
Outlet Store
(703)490-1440 www.nordstrom.com
Casual Wear Ike Behar, Tricots
St. Raphael, Zanella, Pal Zileri
Dress Shirts Ike Behar, Hickey
Freeman, Robert Talbott
Neckwear Robert Talbott, XMI,
Ermenegildo Zegna
Tailored Clothing Joseph
Abboud, Hugo Boss,
Corneliani, Pal Zileri

Polo Ralph Lauren Factory Store
Outlet Store
(703)492-4566 www.polo.com

Rangoni Firenze
Outlet Store
(703)491-5818
www.rangonishoes.com

Saks Off Fifth
Outlet Store
(703)497-2100
www.saksfifthavenue.com
Dress Shirts Giorgio Armani,
Lorenzini, Vestimenta,
Ermenegildo Zegna
Neckwear Gianfranco Ferré,
Versace, Ermenegildo Zegna
Tailored Clothing Giorgio
Armani, Hugo Boss, Corneliani,
Ermenegildo Zegna, Zegna Soft

BOSS Hugo Boss
1517 Wisconsin Ave., N.W.,
Washington, DC 20007 (202)625-2677
www.hugoboss.com

Church's English Shoes
1820 L St., N.W., Washington, DC
20036 (202)296-3366
www.churchsshoes.com

Kenneth Cole
1259 Wisconsin Ave., N.W.,
Washington, DC 20007 (202)298-0007
www.kennethcole.com

The Custom Shop
Independent
Neal Dreskin, Sales
1033 Connecticut Ave., N.W.,
Washington, DC 20036 (202)659-8250
www.customshop.com
(see chapter 9)
First-rate customer service. Great
quality fabrics and exceptional tailoring at reasonable prices. An
excellent place to build one's
wardrobe and develop individualized style.

Accessories Custom Shop
Casual Wear Custom Shop
Dress Shirts Custom Shop
Neckwear Custom Shop, Kolte,
Genesis, Richel, Pancaldi, Pavone
Shoes Allen Edmonds
Tailored Clothing Custom Shop

Wm. Fox & Co.
Independent
Craig Fox, President
1427 G St., N.W., Washington, DC
20005 (202)783-2530 www.wmfox.com
Attractive store with lots of wood
fixtures lending a clubby, comfortable atmosphere. Located two

blocks from the White House;
founded in 1965. Caters to the
updated traditional shopper. Mr.
Fox is great to work with.

Accessories Trafalgar Limited
Edition braces, Kenneth Gordon
formal shirts and cummerbunds,
Barbour outerwear
Casual Wear Scott Barber, Bills
Khakis, Gran Sasso, Bobby Jones,
Jeff Rose, Robert Talbott, Viyella
Dress Shirts Gitman Bros., Kenneth
Gordon, Robert Talbott,
Individualized shirts (custom)
Neckwear Altea, Breuer, Drake,
Robert Talbott
Tailored Clothing Corbin, Nick
Hilton, and Keithmoor trousers,
Samuelsohn (also M2M)

Everett Hall Designs
Chevy Chase Pavilion, 5345
Wisconsin Ave, N.W., Washington,
DC 20015 (202)362-0191
www.everetthalldesigns.com
This store features three brothers
who design and market their own
line of clothing throughout the
United States. Their clothes are
great-looking, original takes on
classic designs and made of quality
Italian fabrics with soft hands.

Everett Hall Designs
1230 Connecticut Ave., Washington,
DC 20036 (202)467-0003
www.everetthalldesigns.com
This store features three brothers
who design and market their own
line of clothing throughout the
United States. Their clothes are
great-looking, original takes on
classic designs and made of quality
Italian fabrics with soft hands.

The Men's Clothing Guide

GEORGETOWN PARK MALL
Location and Stores:
3222 M St., N.W., Washington, DC 20007
www.shopsatgeorgetownpark.com

Ralph Lauren
(202)965-0904 www.polo.com

Niccolo
Independent
(202)338-3638
Pleasant store with quality assortment of distinctive items.

Accessories Torras Leather outerwear
Casual Wear Gran Sasso
Dress Shirts Gianfranco Ferré, Stefano Ricci
Neckwear Gianfranco Ferré, Verri
Tailored Clothing Belvest, Redaelli

Papillon Ties and Accessories
Independent
(202)625-7446

Neckwear Hermès, Leonard, Pancaldi, Versace, Ermenegildo Zegna

MAZZA GALLERIE
Location and Stores:
5300 Wisconsin Ave., N.W., Washington, DC 20015
www.mazzagallerie.net

Neiman Marcus
(202)966-9700
www.neimanmarcus.com
First-rate Neiman Marcus location.

Casual Wear Luigi Borrelli, Brioni, Kiton, Lorenzini, Prada, Ralph Lauren Purple Label, Ermenegildo Zegna
Dress Shirts Luigi Borrelli, Brioni, Kiton, Lorenzini, Prada, Ermenegildo Zegna
Neckwear Luigi Borrelli, Brioni, Kiton, Ermenegildo Zegna
Tailored Clothing Brioni, Everett Hall, Kiton, Oxxford, Ermenegildo Zegna

Saks Fifth Avenue
(202)363-2059
www.saksfifthavenue.com
Men's store only at this location. Great in-store boutiques for Giorgio Armani, Vestimenta, and Ermenegildo Zegna.

Casual Wear Giorgio Armani, Brioni, Vestimenta, Ermenegildo Zegna
Dress Shirts Ike Behar, Hugo Boss, Canali, Hickey Freeman, Lorenzini, Ermenegildo Zegna
Neckwear Giorgio Armani, Hugo Boss, Brioni, Charvet, Ermenegildo Zegna
Tailored Clothing Giorgio Armani, Hugo Boss, Vestimenta, Ermenegildo Zegna

Thomas Pink
1127 Connecticut Ave., N.W., Washington, DC 20036 (202)223-5390
www.thomaspink.com

11

Afterword: Pardon My Soapbox

I try to buy clothing that has been made in a socially responsible manner, and I avoid purchasing any items that have even the remotest chance of being made by exploited labor. Exploited labor means children, it means forced labor, and it means those making slave labor wages. I don't believe an exploited garment worker in Malaysia is better off today than when she or he was a starving farmer. I think Americans should promote responsible economic growth. We should spend our hard-earned clothing dollars in a way that preserves the positive energy that great clothing is created with. Buy only clothes you know have been made in places open for inspection that pay reasonable wages. If you buy garments made in Italy, the U.K., Canada, or here in the United States, you can be reasonably assured of this. If a garment has been made else-where, don't buy it, unless its producer can prove it was made under working conditions you approve of. Clothing is made "off-shore" to minimize labor costs and maximize the bottom line for some faceless, nameless corporation. Apparel made under these conditions wears out faster. I know, I've bought it, worn it, and learned the hard way. Apparel made cheaply adversely affects your price per wearing. I know you can't always buy responsibly made clothing. But at least try. After all, no one will make clothing off-shore if no one buys it, right?

A New Business Is Born!

I've started a new business called Men's Specialty Retail Services that will support all of the skills you've learned in this book. For a low monthly fee you'll be able to complete a profile that will enable our company to keep you current on men's clothing and dressing properly for any occasion. We'll inform you of sales and promotional events in your area in advance of the general public. We'll also keep you abreast of what's happening nationally with your favorite brands and stores. If you've told us you like a certain label's clothing and are looking for it in a given price range, we'll let you know when it's discounted, even if you live in L.A. and it's in Boston. We'll inform you when your favorite store is having a promotion, regardless of where you live. You'll be able to access and download newer versions of the book and the directory as they become available. We currently plan to expand and improve the printed version of *The Men's Clothing Guide* at least every two years. We will also update the Online and Brick-and-Mortar Shopping Guides at least quarterly online. We have a great online community to refer you to, www.StyleForum.net, to discuss fashion, shopping, and issues affecting men. But best of all, we plan to negotiate discounts on clothing at selected stores for members of Men's Specialty Retail Services. If you qualify, we'll even issue you a fancy credit card to shop with. Just make sure to pay it off monthly, OK?

Notes

1. Bureau of Labor Statistics, Consumer Expenditure Survey, 1901.

2. Bureau of Labor Statistics, Consumer Expenditure Survey, 1998.

3. My thanks to Gian DeCaro, proprietor of DeCaro Sartoria in Seattle, for this insight. (See chapter 10 for contact information.)

4. My thanks to Stan Blunck at Glenn Laiken A L A N D A L E S in Los Angeles for advice on this matter. (See chapter 10 for contact information.)

5. Bernhard Roetzel, *Gentleman's Guide to Grooming and Style* (New York: Barnes and Noble, 2000), 46.

6. My thanks again to Stan at A L A N D A L E S for this tip.

7. My thanks to Johnny Mykoff, manager of the shoe department at Harolds in the Heights in Houston, for this practical, well-expressed concept. (See chapter 10 for contact information.)

8. Sherry Maysonave, *Casual Power* (Austin, TX: Bright Books, 1999), 56, 57, 172.

9. My thanks to Chuck Haidet, managing partner of Keeper's, Austin, TX, and his staff for this handy, easy-to-remember axiom. (See chapter 10 for contact information.)

10. Bob Mitchell, *Principles of Casual Dress* (promotional pamphlet), Fall 2000. (See chapter 10 for contact information for

Mitchells in Westport and Richards in Greenwich, CT.)

11. My thanks to Martin Shine, owner of Kirby's, Tampa, FL, for this utilitarian principle. (See chapter 10 for contact information.)

12. My thanks to Mark Christopher, Mark Christopher Custom Shirts, New York, NY, for his insight on this matter of formal dress. (See chapter 10 for contact information.)

13. Roetzel, *Gentleman's Guide,* 323–25.

Acknowledgments

To Mom, for teaching me how to match colors, and for always pushing me to be better than I was.

To Dad, for showing me what was right, whether I chose to follow it or not.

My brother Carl—for inspiration, help with writing, and unconditional love and support.

John Martens—for his friendship, encouragement, and the passion he brings to everything he does.

Luis Rodriguez, for believing in me more than I ever could myself.

Bob McNeice, for the idea to write a book in the first place.

Steve Lillo, web developer par excellence.

Kim Markison, who designed one hell of a book without a lot to work with.

Priscilla Stuckey, editor, for making me clear, concise, and better, always better.

Bert Pulitzer, for a HUGE amount of encouragement and assistance on vital parts of the manuscript.

Rory Earnshaw and Anthony Nex, expert photographers!

Julie Stokes, stylist.

Glenn Laiken A L A N D A L E S, for their support of this project and dedication to helping men look their best always. For their kindness in allowing me to take some more pictures at the eleventh hour. Doesn't Glenn make a great model?

The Fongs at Courtoué, for always having a kind word, for their concern for me and my family, and for letting me borrow their mannequin for my photo shoot.

Julie Lauer, fact checker, production editor and indexer.

Thomas Fok-Yuen, for *a lot* of help on L.A. stores and information on modern designers.

Naresh Mansukhani, my first customer.

Steve Davis, for giving me belief in myself and this project when I needed it.

Giacamo Trabalza, for encouragement to pursue my dreams no matter what others thought.

Robert D. Skach, for giving me a meaningful job when I needed one.

To Donald J. Townley, wherever you are, for teaching me the value of my time, and how to see the big picture.

Readers Fritz Boneberg, Butch Blum, Fred Derring, Randy and Christina Walker, David Moorman, Carla Ruff, Bob Cecca, Bjorn Sedleniek, for giving me much-needed and appreciated feedback.

Fact checkers Mike Clerico, Dave Ip, Tim Sepp, Michael Jay.

Grcevich family at Sherman Cleaners, Oakland, CA, for their help with the section on dry cleaning, and for keeping my clothes looking great.

Bonnie Carpenter, my tailoress (is that a word?), for her many words of encouragement and her meticulous attention to detail that also keeps me looking great.

Marilyn Gordon, for help and inspiration early in the creative process. Check out her book *Extraordinary Healing.*

Seo family at Berkland Cleaners in Berkeley, CA. Maybe Mike and I will finally have time for golf now.

Joel, Marilyn, and David Marks, for providing a wonderful home away from home while I was in the New York area.

Dan Poynter, the godfather of so many self-published books— great seminar, couldn't have done this without your help.

Joel Roberts, excellent media preparation course, and for introducing me to A L A N D A L E S.

Bill Hilton, for early help with editing.

Cara Witte, great job on research.

Glossary

Traditionally book glossaries have covered only terms used in that particular book. However, for *The Men's Clothing Guide* I've expanded this section to include some additional terms I feel may be of use to you. For still more explanation of unfamiliar terms you may encounter in your new sartorial journey, pick up a copy of Bernhard Roetzel's *Gentleman's Guide* or Alan Flusser's *Dressing the Man*.

Argyle A large, usually multicolor, interlocking diamond pattern used primarily on socks and sweater vests.

Banded bottom A garment that has a woven border at the bottom. Most often found on a pullover sweater.

Barrel cuff A single-button cuff used to fasten the sleeves of a long-sleeved shirt. Most popular form of shirt cuff.

Bench-made shoes Shoes made by hand.

Bespoke Custom-made.

Blazer Solid colored sport coat used for business casual and casual wear. Most often made of wool; many have patch or flap pockets.

Boxer briefs Tighter-fitting style of underclothing covering groin area. Leg fabric length extends to midthigh. Elastic waistband and leg closure results in tighter fit. Most support for one's most personal items. Usually made of machine-combed cotton fabric.

Boxer shorts Looser-fitting style of underclothing covering groin area. Can be made of cotton or silk. Elastic at waist, hemmed, but not gathered and usually more and longer fabric at legs. Less support for one's most personal items. Named for attire worn by prize fighters.

Break The appearance of the bottom of a pair of trousers. The front of the trouser should rest on the front of the shoe, causing a vertical wrinkle, or break, in the drape of the pant fabric. The larger the wrinkle, the "bigger" the break.

Briefs Tighter-fitting style of underclothing covering groin area. Elastic waistband and leg closure. Fabric ends at top of thigh.

Broadcloth Thick, flat-finish cotton used primarily for dress shirts.

Business casual Situations that require professional dress but not necessarily a dress shirt and tie.

Button-up A shirt that fastens with buttons up the torso.

Calf-length hosiery Unfortunately, the best-selling length of hosiery. Made to fit slightly over the ankle and partially up the calf.

Cap toe Lace-up dress shoe with a strip of leather where the toes begin, forming a cap.

Car coat Outerwear with hem that ends at the hip.

Cardigan A button-up, V-neck sweater; may or may not have sleeves.

Cashmere Soft, luxurious wool made from the fleece of a Kashmir goat. Used primarily in sweaters and sport coats and occasionally blended with wool in suits.

Casual wear Any dressing situation not requiring professional attire.

Center vent A jacket style with a single opening in the rear center of the coat, allowing for ease of movement and accessibility to rear trouser pockets.

Chinos Casual slacks constructed of cotton. Unfortunately, the most common form of business casual pants. Also called khakis because that is the most common color.

Collar, button-down A shirt collar held in place by buttons fastening through the collar at the point the collar attaches to the body of the shirt.

Collar, contrasting A collar that is a different color—most often white—from the body of a shirt.

Collar, hidden button-down A button-down collar where buttons attach to loops or holes on the underside of the collar, hiding them from view.

Collar, point A buttonless shirt collar with points aiming straight down at the ground and coming together in a point.

Collar, spread A dress shirt collar with points spreading out from the neck at 45-degree angles and leaving a wide area for a tie.

Collar, tab A dress shirt collar with a small strip of fabric that passes underneath a necktie. Fastens in the middle with a snap or button.

Collar, wing A formal raised shirt collar with tips that bend outward to resemble wings.

Contrasting cuff A cuff that is a different color—most often white—from the body of a shirt.

Cordovan Originally a term for high-quality Spanish leather. Now a color synonymous with oxblood, or a deep burgundy color of leather.

Corduroy Heavier-weight cotton with sunken lines, called wales, running vertically through the fabric. Found mostly in trousers; the wider the wale, the more casual the pant. Usually worn in fall and winter.

Cotton A soft natural fiber derived from the cotton plant. Cotton fibers are graded in terms of staple length, or the degree to which they can be pulled to achieve a spinnable quantity of fiber. Generally the higher the thread count number, the softer the hand, and the better the fabric.

Crepe Medium-weight wool fabric with rough, crinkly finish. Highly twisted yarns produce cloth that drapes well, resists wrinkles, and is excellent for year-round wear.

Crew neck A neckline flush with the top of the shoulders and bottom of the neck. Typically found in T-shirts and sweaters.

Cuffs Fabric at bottom of pants doubled over and hemmed. Weight of the cuff on the bottom of the trousers helps garment drape smoothly without wrinkles from the waist and break over the top of the shoe. Pleated pants look best with cuffs.

Cummerbund Pleated horizontal sash worn around waist in a formal ensemble. Often made of silk; always should be worn with pleats facing upward.

Double vent See Side Vent.

Double-barrel cuff Two-button cuff used to fasten the sleeves of a long-sleeved shirt. Buttons may be aligned horizontally or vertically (most common style).

Drape How clothing flows vertically, according to gravitational forces. The more natural and unwrinkled the clothing looks from head to toe, the better the drape.

European Store that specializes in clothing made in Europe, usually Italy, with updated styles, cuts, fabric weaves, and colors.

Evening wear Semiformal dress appropriate for the evening. Usually black or dark shades of color that complement it.

Flat-front slacks Slacks without pleats; look best uncuffed.

Formal wear Tailored clothing usually black or midnight blue in color. The trousers should match the jacket in color, with a plain silk stripe (called a braid) running down the outside of each pant leg. Most often matched with white, French-cuffed shirt and black bow tie. Cummerbunds and vests as an option fade in and out of fashion. Black patent leather shoes have traditionally completed the formal ensemble.

Four-button suit A single-breasted suit style with four buttons fastening up the torso. A style rarely seen in sport coats; bottom button best left unfastened.

French/Double cuff Sleeve cuff that folds over onto itself and fastens with cuff links to hold the sleeves together.

Full-length Style of outerwear in which fabric terminates between the knee and ankle.

Geek chic The act of dressing in a slovenly or amateurish manner. The mistaken belief that such a practice will attract people to what you say and to your brain power, not how you look. Leads to a "but" career, as in, "He's done great work and should get promoted, *but* he looks completely unprofessional."

Grosgrain Matte-finish lapel style worn with formal wear.

Hand How a particular fabric feels to the touch. The softer and more natural the feel of a fabric, the better its hand.

Hat, fedora Pinched-front hat with soft, relatively narrow brim that may be turned up or down.

Hat, porkpie Circular-shaped hat with matching circular indentation in the top of its crown. Usually narrow-brimmed.

Herringbone A fabric pattern that places diagonal rows of lines side by side to create a striped look to the fabric.

Houndstooth A fabric pattern with small checks that run together in a diagonal pattern. Most often seen with sport coats and slacks.

Inseam Measurement from crotch to bottom of trousers.

Jacket, double breasted A sport coat or suit jacket that has two columns of buttons, one for ornamentation down the front of the jacket, the second row fastening the jacket. The bottom fastening button is always left fashionably undone.

Jacket, one-button A single-breasted style of sport coat or suit that has only one button and corresponding buttonhole. May be left buttoned or unbuttoned, depending on the occasion or one's mood.

Jacket, single breasted A sport coat or suit jacket that has one row of buttons.

Jacket, three-button A single-breasted style of suit or sport coat with three buttons and corresponding buttonholes. The middle button only is buttoned when on a sport coat; the top two buttons are fastened on a suit.

Jacket, two-button A single-breasted style of jacket with two buttons. The bottom button is never fastened; both buttons may be left undone in casual situations.

Knee length Garment ending at the knee.

Lace-up A shoe that fastens with laces up the instep.

Lapel Folded-over portion of jacket fabric extending from the top button around the curve of the shoulder.

Lapel, notched Lapel with a symmetric, diagonal opening, or notch, approximately three-quarters of the way up the lapel. Most popular form of lapel.

Lapel, peaked Lapel with narrow-spaced notch in which the upper point is long and points upward toward the shoulder. Most often found in double-breasted suits and tuxedos.

Last Wooden model of a human foot, used to construct finer shoes either wholly or partially by hand.

Linen Natural fiber made from the flax plant. Easily wrinkled; wrinkles considered proper and part of the fabric's charm. Fiber breathes extraordinarily well, and clothing composed of linen is a staple of warm-weather dressing.

Loafer Slip-on style of shoe without laces and open around the instep of the foot.

Monk strap Shoes with straps fastened by buckles on the side.

Necktie, printed Tie with the pattern screened or rolled onto the fabric after it's woven. Usually silk.

Necktie, seven-fold A tie composed of two pieces of fabric sewn together and folded inward seven times.

Necktie, woven Tie with pattern woven into the cloth rather than applied afterward by external means. Most often silk, but may also be composed of other fabrics.

Nylon A fiber made of thermoplastic fibers melted together. Used primarily in combination with other fabrics for suit linings, outer-wear linings, and hosiery.

Over-the-calf hosiery A casual or dress style extending to just below the knee.

Paisley Comma-shaped patterns of a contrasting color on a solid background. Used most often in ties and sport shirts.

Pants, double-pleat Two pleats on the front of any pant.

Pants, single-pleat One pleat on the front of any pant.

Pants, triple-pleat Three pleats on the front of any pant.

Pinstripe A solid background with contrasting stripes generally spaced ½ inch to 1 inch apart.

Piqué knit Cotton with a pebble- or waffle-like finish. Used most often in short-sleeved, polo-collared summer shirts.

Placket The front portion of a shirt that attaches with buttons to fasten up the torso. Normally formed by doubling the shirt fabric on itself, then sewing both sides of the placket vertically up the shirt where the buttons fasten through.

Placket, European A shirtfront with a simple fold-under-and-hem placket where the buttons fasten, creating a seamless look to the front of the shirt.

Placket, hidden/covered A placket that is covered or hidden by fabric, giving the shirt the look of not having any buttons.

Plaid Multicolored, wider stripes on different color backgrounds to create patterns.

Pleat The gathering of fabric on the front of trousers creating a darted look to the pant front. Pleats normally face the center of the garment.

Pleat, reverse Pleats that face away from the center of the garment.

Pocket, flap A pocket with a piece of matching fabric that folds over it. Well-made shirts usually fasten with a button. Also frequently seen on blazers and sport coats.

Pocket, patch Pocket on a suit or sport coat made of matching fabric and attached to jacket without a flap. Worn in more casual situations.

Pocket square Handkerchief used for aesthetic rather than utilitarian purposes. Usually made of silk or linen.

Polka dot A fabric pattern in which dots are spaced randomly or at regular intervals on a solid background.

Polo A pullover shirt that has two to four buttons in a shortened placket with a soft collar.

Polyester A synthetic fiber blended most often with cotton in dress, casual, and sport shirts.

Pullover A shirt you must pull over your head to put on.

Rayon A fiber made by forcing cellulose through fine holes then solidifying it into thread in either a chemical bath or warm air. This fiber is primarily used in sport shirts and occasionally in suits to provide superior drape and to fight wrinkles.

Rise Measurement from crotch to top of trouser waistband.

Saddle shoes Lace-up shoes with a leather overlay resembling a saddle sewn over the arch of the foot.

Savile Row Term used to describe classic British tailoring style; street on which many of the more famous custom tailors are located.

Shawl collar A rounded lapel without notches or peaks.

Side vent A jacket style that has two openings on the sides, most often lining up with the trouser seams.

Silk A fine, soft fiber spun by the silkworm as part of its cocoon. Used primarily in ties and shirts, sometimes in underclothing.

Soft collar A collar without stays or buttons. Designed to be worn unbuttoned, and therefore more appropriate for casual dressing.

Soft shoulder Also called natural shoulder. Tailored clothing with less padding in the shoulders, designed to fit the shoulder's natural shape.

Split toe Shoe with a vertical seam dividing, or splitting, the toe.

Sportswear Term interchangeable with casual wear; any attire not worn in a business formal situation. Rarely refers to dress required for physical activity.

Stay A small, rectangular, pointed piece of plastic or metal that fits inside a shirt's collar point to help keep its shape.

Tassels Cylinder-shaped ornaments, usually made of fringed leather and attached to the front of a shoe.

Tattersall A fabric pattern using overlying, different-color window-panes to make small squares on a solid background.

Tencel A synthetic fiber made from tree bark. Wrinkle-free fabric used in casual shirts and pullovers.

Thread count Term used usually to describe the level of fabric quality in a cotton shirt. The higher the thread count, the finer the weave and more desirable the fabric.

Three button A single-breasted style of suit or sport coat with three buttons and corresponding buttonholes. The middle button only is buttoned when on a sport coat; the top two buttons are fastened on a suit.

Traditional A store that specializes in conservative clothing, usually American-made labels in muted styles, cuts, fabric weaves, and colors.

Turtleneck A sweater with two to four inches of fabric at the neck folding over onto itself and gathering closely about the neck.

Turtleneck, mock A shorter version of a turtleneck, with protruding neckline that does not fold over.

Twill A fabric style characterized by a subtle diagonal texture, or twill, found throughout the fabric. Found most often in slacks and in cotton, wool, or blended fabric.

Two button A single-breasted style of jacket with two buttons. The bottom button is never fastened; both buttons may be left undone in casual situations.

Two-ply fabric Made of two pieces of fabric woven together into a bolt of cloth, from which the garment is constructed.

Updated traditional See Traditional. A store that carries traditional clothing with more flair—more modern construction and weaves, also some brighter color accents.

V-neck A shirt or sweater collar that forms a point, or V, at the front of the neck.

Valet Wooden frame (usually on wheels) designed specifically for setting out and coordinating an ensemble for the next day or airing out an outfit before returning it to the closet.

Ventless A style of suit coat or sport jacket that does not have an opening, or vent, in the back.

Vested Also called three piece. Suit with an additional, sleeveless garment fitting underneath the suit coat and buttoning up the torso. In well-made suits, the front of the vest is composed of the same fabric as the suit, and the back is made of the same material as the suit's lining and has an adjustable band to fit the vest around the torso.

Watch fob An ornament that is affixed to a pocket-watch chain. Can hang either from a point along the chain or from its end.

Windowpane A fabric pattern using thin stripes of a single color to form squares about an inch wide on a solid ground. The color of the lines forming the squares is typically different from that of the ground.

Wing tip Classic style of shoe with an overlay of decorative punched perforations over the toe and front of the shoe resembling the spread wings of a bird.

Wool A natural fiber made from the growth of hair from sheep. Used for shirts, sweaters, suits, sport coats, and dress pants.

Wool, Super 100s Term used to denote a grade of raw wool used to manufacture the best fabrics in a tailored garment. Based upon thickness of the wool shorn from select sheep, usually from Australia and New Zealand. This thickness measurement is derived from microscopic evaluation of fibers as compared to other such fibers and is in keeping with internationally agreed-upon standards. As with cotton, the higher the number, the softer the hand, and the better and more desirable the fabric.

Wool, Super 120s Fabric superior to super 100s.

Wool, Super 150s Fabric superior to super 100s and super 120s.

Index

Socks, 26, 27, 43
Specialty stores, 2, 8, 63–64
Sport coat, see Tailored Clothing
Style guidelines, body types, 17–19
Suits
  business casual, 42
  business formal, 29–32
  color coordinating, 35–37
  construction, 69, 70
  first suit, 29
Sunglasses, 32
Suspenders, 50, 51
Sweaters, 41

T
Tailored clothing
  business casual, 44–47
  business formal, 28–32
  made-to-measure, 53–57
  shopping for, 68
Ties
  essential, 25, 26
  bow ties, 26, 53
  shopping for, 66
Travel and wardrobe maintenance, 75–80
Travel tips, 76
Trousers
  business casual, 46
  business formal, 31
  shopping for, 66, 67
T-shirts, 39, 40
Turtlenecks, 41
Tuxedo, 52, 53

U
Umbrellas
  accessorizing an outfit, 34
  shopping for, 73
Undershirts, 22
Underwear, 21, 22, 39

V
Value, basic principle of, 59, 60

W
Wallets
  shopping for, 71
  styles, 33
Wardrobe
  business casual, 39–48
  essentials, business formal, 21–37
  maintenance and storage, 77–80
Watches
  pocket, 51
  shopping for, 71
  sport, 48
  styles, 33
Weekend casual, 39
Weight, style considerations, 18, 19
When and where to shop, 60–74
Wool slacks, 46

Notes

Notes

Notes

Notes

Notes

ORDER FORM

Dapper Press
1722 Liberty Street, Suite A
El Cerrito, CA 94530
phone (510)235-7249
fax (510)235-2760
web: www.MensSpecialtyRetail.com

Name _____ Date _____

Street _____

_____

City _____ State _____

Zip Code _____ Country _____

The Men's Clothing Guide

Quantity   x $19.95   _____

Sales Tax for California Residents (8.25%)   _____

Shipping & Handling*   _____

TOTAL   _____

Check

Check # _____ (Make checks payable to Dapper Press)

Credit Card   ☐ Visa   ☐ Mastercard

Card Number   _____

Name on Card   _____

Expiration Date   _____

Signature   _____

*Shipping & Handling: within US $5, within Canada $10 US.